Outposts of Monopoly Capitalism: Southern Africa in the Changing Global Economy

Outposts of Monopoly Capitalism: Southern Africa in the Changing Global Economy

by

Neva Makgetla and
Ann Seidman

Lawrence Hill & Company
WESTPORT CONNECTICUT

Zed Press
LONDON ENGLAND

Library of Congress Cataloging in Publication Data

Seidman, Ann Wilcox, 1926–
   Outposts of monopoly capitalism.

   1. Investments, American—South Africa. 2. Corpo-
rations, American—South Africa. 3. South Africa—
Economic conditions—1961–   I. Makgetla, Neva,
joint author. II. Title.
HG5831.A3S43 1980   338.8'8'0968
ISBN 0-88208-114-4
ISBN 0-88208-115-2 (pbk.)

Library of Congress Catalogue Card Number: 80-80525

10 9 8 7 6 5 4 3 2 1

Lawrence Hill & Company, Publisher, Inc.
Westport, Connecticut 06880

Published in the U.K. by Zed Press, London
ISBN: cloth: 0 86232-020-8
ISBN: paper: 0 86232-015-1

Manufactured in the United States of America
Designed by Rainstone Designs
South Salem, NY 10590

Contents

Prologue

Throughout the 1960s and '70s—the very years during which almost 50 African states north of the Zambezi achieved political independence—transnational corporations poured billions of dollars into strategic sectors of the South African political economy. They helped build South Africa up as a dominant regional sub-center, a headquarters for their African business, a starting base for their deeper penetration throughout the southern third of the continent.

Despite the world's growing horror at the brutal oppression of *apartheid*, some two thousand corporations expanded their profitable business in South Africa in the years dubbed by the United Nations the "Development Decade." Talk of 'liberalization' of racist laws and company codes merely provided window-dressing: transnational corporations from all the leading capitalist nations continued to produce or ship in the technologies and finance to prop up the system which condemned the vast majority of the population to growing impoverishment, unemployment, malnutrition, disease—the daily unseen violence of perpetual hunger and early death.

This book seeks to place the theoretical issues in our earlier work, *South Africa and U.S. Multinational Corporations,** in a global context. It is not just the transnationals of the United States, but those of the United Kingdom, the Federal Republic of Germany, France and Japan that must be investigated. For the corporate behavior of transnationals based in three major industrial capitalist countries in building up South Africa is an integral, inevitably contradictory feature of a prolonged process of fundamental transformation taking place in the world social system. Since their recovery from World War II, the transnational corporations have engaged in a competitive struggle which has altered the international division of labor and profoundly affected the lives of working peoples throughout the world. Seeking to reduce costs to offset

*First published by Tanzania Publishing House and Lawrence Hill in 1977, and reprinted in 1978 and 1980.

falling profit rates, the corporations shifted investments and credit away from mature industrial areas where, over the years, workers had organized to win better wages, working conditions, and even a significant degree of state responsibility for social welfare. The transnationals sold advanced technologies and transferred entire manufacturing plants, not to third world countries seeking to meet their people's needs, but to regional sub-centers like South Africa, characterized by low wages and minimal taxes for social services. These states' growing military expenditures created a (temporarily) profitable market. As the worst economic crisis since before World War II spread throughout the capitalist world in the 1970s, transnational banks refused credits to core nation cities plagued by growing unemployment and falling tax revenues. They loaned vast sums, instead, to new sub-centers like South Africa, reaping greater profits from their expansion of strategic industries and military might. In a very real sense, transnational finance capital pitted the welfare of working people in the core industrial nations against the semi-slave labor conditions of the oppressive regional sub-centers.

In southern Africa, the liberation movements of Namibia, Zimbabwe and South Africa, backed by the Organization of African Unity and the Front Line States, sought by armed struggle—the only means left open to them—to capture state power and restructure the regional political economy. They proclaimed their desire to create increasingly productive employment opportunities and raise the living standards of all their peoples. If they succeed, over time their plans will also contribute to the spread of mutually beneficial trade and growing employment opportunities for workers in mature industrial areas; the populations of industrialized nations buy far more goods produced by factory workers than do the impoverished peasants of underdeveloped third world countries. If the 75 million inhabitants of southern Africa fulfill their plans for balanced, integrated industrial growth, they could become far more advantageous trading partners for the core industrial states. The ongoing struggle of the peoples of southern Africa to uproot, once and for all, the exploitative regional system had emerged, by the beginning of the 1980s, as a crucial phase of the worldwide process of social transformation.

In this historical context, the transnational corporations pressed their governments to collaborate with the South African regime in negotiating "moderate" solutions: the installation in public office of a few wealthy blacks, creating a supportive black "middle class," while leaving the exploitative *status quo* intact. The minority regime itself, preparing if necessary to block the wheels of history by sheer military might, continued to produce and buy the most sophisticated technologies of modern warfare: computerized systems of population control, guns, tanks, planes, missiles, even nuclear weapons. It jailed, tortured, and murdered opponents at home. Its troops, armed with automatic weapons, repeatedly invaded neighboring countries. They bombed villages and industrial installations. They aimed to cow the liberation movements into submission.

The regime sought, simultaneously, to forge a nuclear alliance with other militaristic regional sub-centers and even with core industrialized countries of the capitalist world. The nuclear blast, reported off the South African coast at the end of the 1970s, indicated that the minority, in its desperate effort to retain its regional supremacy, was prepared to threaten the future of humankind.

These far reaching implications of the on-going southern African struggle urge self-interested, united action by peoples of the core industrial nations, together with those of Africa and the rest of the world, to impose a total, mandatory United Nations boycott on the South African regime, before it is too late. A book like this is not the place to recommend specific tactics, but the possibilities are legion. In the years since our *South Africa and U.S. Multinational Corporations* first appeared, various approaches have been initiated. Nigeria's government has intervened in or taken over the local subsidiaries of some transnational firms which have invested in or loaned funds to bolster strategic sectors of the South African military-industrial complex. Working people, intellectuals, and students in core nations have pressed for divestiture from corporations and withdrawal of pension and other funds from banks that do business with South Africa. They have urged their governments to end firms' credit for taxes paid to South Africa, and to halt insurance or guarantees of loans used to finance exports to the minority regime. Simultaneously, they have begun to mobilize support for the liberation movements and the Front Line States.

It is our hope that the explanations embodied in this book will help to illuminate the way the struggle for liberation in southern Africa fits into the larger process of social transformation taking place throughout the world today. The book examines this process in three parts:

Part 1 explores, on the one hand, the nature and impact of the revolutionary technological changes which multiplied corporate size and productivity in core industrial capitalist economies; and, on the other, how the collapse of colonial empires and the spread of liberation struggles forced the transnationals to discover new ways to secure raw materials sources and markets for their rapidly accumulating surpluses of manufactured goods. Thus it exposes the emerging, frequently contradictory pressures pushing the transnational corporations to compete in reinvesting their accumulated capital and selling advanced technologies to oppressive militaristic regional sub-centers throughout the third world, not only in South Africa, but also in countries like Brazil and, formerly, Iran.

Part II analyzes the contradictory impact of sophisticated technologies in creating and strengthening the capacity of a minority regime like South Africa's, drawing on its particular historically-shaped institutions, to exploit the mass of its population and dominate an entire region; and simultaneously narrowing its domestic market, fostering growing unemployment, and aggravating the tendencies that, in South Africa, culminated in the political economic crisis of the '70s. Far from stimulating social advance, as claimed by their apologists, transnationals provided the minority regime with the industrial infrastructure and increasingly modernized military equipment to block the people's mounting struggles for change.

Part III examines the spread of the struggle for basic social transformation throughout the southern African region. It examines the political economic options open to the liberation movements in neighboring countries, seeking to break their dependence on the South African-transnational corporate alliance that continues to distort their national development. It exposes the way the so-called "Rhodesian-Zimbabwe" pattern of growth—urged by transnational spokesmen as a solution—would only condemn the peoples of the region to deepening poverty. It examines the problems and possibilities of the long-term development strategies adopted by the leading Front Line States—Tanzania, Mozambique and Angola—for achieving the more effective social transformation required to meet the needs of their peoples. It outlines the vast potential for development of the newly liberated states, in line with the initiatives taken by the Front Line States at Arusha in 1979, if they unite to shape new institutions and implement new patterns of resource allocation to break with South Africa and achieve industrial transformation of the entire region.

Events are changing so fast in southern Africa that we have written this book in the past tense. We are convinced that, in the long run, the liberation forces will ultimately free the peoples of the region. In so doing, they will contribute to the larger process of social change taking place throughout the world today. We have tried to identify, here, the contradictory tendencies and forces, suggesting how, at the time we wrote the manuscript, they fit into the larger regional and international transformation. We leave it to the readers to evaluate the subsequent extent and consequences of the continuing pattern of change. To aid the reader, this prologue is followed by a table of exchange rates of South Africa, its major trading partners and the neighboring countries.

We would like to express our appreciation to the many friends and colleagues—in Africa, the United States, England, Holland, and Germany—with whom we have discussed various aspects of the issues discussed in this book. Unfortunately, they number too many to mention by name. We would like also to thank the students who researched specific aspects; Professor Phil O'Keefe for his critical reading of the manuscript; and Professors Luchterhand and Stier for their valuable comments. And we would like, once again, to express our loving gratitude to our respective husbands, Zeph and Bob, without whose moral support and deep insights we could not have completed this book.

Neva Makgetla
Ann Seidman
Boston, November, 1979

Table of Exchange Rates of South Africa, its major trading partners and the Neighboring Countries, 1950, 1960, and 1970-79 in U.S. dollars[1]

A. South Africa and its major trading partners: (in U.S. dollars per currency unit)

Country (and Currency unit)	1950	1960	1970	1971	1972	1973	1974	1975	1976	1977	1978	1979
South Africa (rand (2))	2.79[2]	2.79[2]	1.40	1.39	1.30	1.44	1.47	1.36	1.15	1.15	1.15	1.15
United Kingdom (pound)	2.79	2.79	2.40	2.43	2.50	2.45	2.23	2.22	1.80	1.74	1.91	2.00
Federal Republic of Germany (DM)	4.20	4.17	3.66	3.49	3.18	2.67	2.59	2.46	2.51	2.32	2.00	1.85
France (franc)	349.70[3]	4.90	5.55	5.54	5.04	4.45	4.80	4.28	4.77	4.91	4.51	4.27
Japan (yen)	—	0.0027	0.0027	0.0028	0.0033	0.0035	0.0033	0.0032	0.0033	0.0041	0.0051	0.0046

B. Exchange rates of the neighboring countries, 1979[4]

Country (and currency unit)	Value Maintained Against[4]	Rate of Exchange	Country (and currency unit)	Value Maintained Against[4]	Rate of Exchange
Angola (Kwanza)	?	—	Namibia (Rand)	U.S.$	U.S.$1=0.87R
Botswana (Pula)	Rand	P1=R1.05	Rhodesia (Rhodesian Dollar)	U.S.$	U.S.$1=0.63R$
Lesotho (Rand)	U.S.$	U.S.$1=0.87R	Swaziland (Lilangeni)	Rand	1 R=1E
Malawi (Kwacha)	SDR[5]	SDR1=1.05K	Tanzania (shilling)	SDR[5]	1SDR=10.63Sh
Mozambique (Escudo)	Portuguese escudo	[6]	Zambia (kwacha)	SDR[5]	1SDR=0.98K

Notes: [1]Until the 1970s, the U.S. dollar was the international standard of currency which, together with gold (1 oz = $35) the International Monetary Fund upheld. After the U.S. devalued in 1971, all major currencies floated, but the IMF quoted them in terms of U.S. dollars and SDRs (a weighted average of 16 currencies). South Africa maintained its currency against the U.S. dollar.

[2]Until the 1960s, South Africa used the pound and maintained its value against the British pound.

[3]France devalued its currency and issued new notes at a rate of 1 new franc = 100 old.

[4]The other southern African states, by 1978, pursued different monetary policies, some pegging their currencies against the South African rand, others against the U.S. dollar, and still others against the SDRs. Mozambique maintained its currency's value against the Portuguese escudo, and Angola's floated.

[5]The SDR was a new international monetary standard created by the IMF, its value determined by the weighted average of 16 leading currencies (one of which was the South African rand from 1974 to 1978 when it was replaced).

[6]The escudo was valued at 1 US$ = 33 escudos in Feb., 1979.

Sources: The International Monetary Fund, International Financial Statistics, Oct., 1979; and the report of the Arusha Conference for Coordinated Southern African Regional Development, July 1979.

PART I
Intensified Transnational Corporate Competition

Introduction   1

Uneven development and regional sub-centers:

Uneven development increasingly characterized the Third World during the quarter of a century after World War II. A large number of countries remained impoverished. Their narrow so-called "modern" sectors remained geared to the export of a handful of crude materials to uncertain world markets. Their domestic handicraft industries had been undermined by the massive import of goods manufactured in the factories of the industrialized core nations of Europe and North America. The overwhelming majority of their populations seemed to vegetate on the verge of starvation.

Yet, contrary to the predictions of dependency theorists[1], a small number of Third World nations achieved what was proclaimed as a "growth miracle": rates of growth up to and even exceeding 10 percent a year, while they retained and strengthened their ties with transnational corporations. Less than 20 countries appeared sufficiently differentiated in economic structure (although not adopting a socialist perspective) from the remaining 120 or so countries of the periphery to be characterized as "semiperipheral." Only a few had, by the 1970s, achieved significant industrial growth. South Africa, along with Brazil, had emerged as an outstanding example of this type of "dependent development."

One might argue about which of the almost 50 independent African states should be included on a list of nations capable of attaining a similar industrial 'takeoff' in the coming decades. Nigeria had been identified as one possibility. [2]

The interesting question, though, was *why* some countries—only a very few in Africa by the 1970s—had or appeared likely to achieve this seemingly enviable status. Sheer size appeared to be one obvious requirement. Brazil, with a land area roughly equivalent to that of the continental United States, and well over 100 million inhabitants, clearly qualified on this ground. Nigeria, with a population of 70 to 80 million possessed obvious advantages compared to its much smaller African neighbors.

But size alone, although necessary, could not explain the phenomenon. Other large African states, like Sudan, showed no signs of breaking out of their peripheral status. On the other hand, South Africa, with only 25 million inhabitants, became far more industrially advanced than Nigeria, so much so that Western statistical compilations included it among the "developed" nations.[3] In Brazil, Evans identified the critical motivating force as the emergence of a "triple alliance"[4] between the elite among local firms, the national militarized state, and transnational corporations.* But the South African case introduces new puzzles. The vast continent of Africa spreads over a land area three times that of the United States. Its population totals more than 400 million. By the 1970s, as colonial rule disappeared, almost 50 African-ruled states had won political independence. Why did South Africa, ruled by a racist minority regime representing barely four million whites, alone experience industrial "takeoff?" What probable consequences did its dependent development hold for the more than 60 million Africans still struggling for full political as well as economic liberation in the southern third of the continent?

The On-going Struggle for Change:

To explain the seeming mystery, one must explore in depth the changing and complex post World War II interrelationships between the transnational corporations, the central feature of the core capitalist nations, and the emerging African states. These relationships were shaped by two interacting, sometimes contradictory, sometimes coincident sets of forces. In the developed capitalist nations, economic and political factors, while limiting the transnationals' growth at home, pushed them to expand in search of safe investment havens abroad. In independent Africa, the self-interest of government bureaucracies and

---

*Many authors use the term "multinational corporations," as we did in earlier book.[5] It seems preferable, however, to use the now internationally accepted term, "transnational corporations" (embodied in the title of the United Nations Center concerned with these globe-encircling conglomerates) as this points up the fact that, though they reach across international boundaries, their headquarters are located in one home state.

politicians, pressured by national liberation movements, contributed to uncertain responses to the transnationals' advances. South Africa's long-established white ruling class, in contrast, seemed to offer a profitable, stable base for penetration throughout the continent.

To understand these forces, one must examine them in their historical context, the on-going process of struggle between two fundamentally different political-economic systems. On the one hand, the growing corporate conglomerates sought, in time honored fashion, to maximize their global profits by retaining and expanding their sphere of domination. On the other hand, working people in both the core and the periphery nations struggled to gain greater control over the institutions shaping their lives, to plan rationally for full employment and higher living standards.

Some have termed this on-going contradictory struggle "the general crisis of capitalism."*

The Great Depression of the 1930s, which brought unemployment to upwards of one out of five workers in leading capitalist nations, seemed to many the ultimate expression of corporate capitalism's inability to meet the needs of the people. Then the fascist regimes of Germany, Italy and Japan, backed by powerful cartels, sought to escape the depression's impact by building up their military might. Cloaked as an anti-communist crusade their aim was to conquer and redivide the world.

World War II fundamentally altered the political economic situation confronting transnational corporations, not only in their home countries, but throughout the so-called "Third World." The war finally enabled the United States to escape the consequences of the Great Depression. Its industrial base remained intact, untouched by the bombing raids that destroyed so many European and Japanese factories. Its sales of the weapons of war to its allies left it the leading international creditor nation, with a major share of the world's gold supplies stored away in Fort Knox. Its wealth and industrial might endowed it with the dominant role in the newly created World Bank and International Monetary Fund, the twin institutions purportedly designed to finance the reconstruction of the postwar world, and to ensure

---

*Amin[6] objects that this concept is oversimplified, that after the war the "rate of growth of Western capitalism became faster, and, furthermore, growth lost its cyclical character." As indicated below, it is our thesis that, on the contrary, the underlying contradictions creating that crisis persisted and intensified.

permanent international monetary stablization.* The boundaries of the United States' invisible, but nevertheless real, postwar empire seemed to stretch endlessly into the horizons of time.

The war reduced the other major capitalist nations to poor cousins. The British Empire on which, it used to be said, the "sun never set," crumbled precipitously. Ten years of guerilla warfare in Kenya convinced the British government that it must grant political independence to its African colonies. It viewed the institutionalized ties of big British mining, trading and banking firms, built over the years of outright colonial rule, as the best remaining hope for continuing the profitable business of acquiring African raw materials and selling manufactured goods.

The French government, although defeated by the Nazis in Europe, retained its African colonial empire during its years in exile. But it, too, gave way before the postwar African struggle for national liberation, spearheaded by the guerilla war that ousted the Algerian settler regime. The French government still sought to perpetuate the corporate links forged during the colonial era through continued centralized control over the new African states' monetary systems**, preferential trade agreements and military ties.

Germany and Japan had lost their bid for world rule through war. Their home industries were smashed by saturation bombing. Their state-supported, cartelized industrial structures were dismantled by the victorious allies.

At the same time, however, World War II further narrowed the boundaries of future corporate expansion. A third of the world's populations opted for one or another variety of socialism. The nations of Eastern Europe established "people's democracies" in cooperation with the U.S.' former war ally, the Soviet Union. The Chinese ousted Chiang Kai Shek and declared for socialism—although they soon in-

---

*The International Bank for Reconstruction and Development (the World Bank) and the International Monetary Fund were established by the capitalist allies after the War. The first initially aimed to help reconstruct western Europe and then to finance development in member countries as long as it did not compete wth private enterprise. The second sought, in accord with orthodox western theory, to assist member states to balance their pay ıents with the (never achieved) goal of eliminating all blocks to the "free flow" of trade in the context of a stable monetary system. The voting strength of members of both organizations was determined by their capital contribution, and the U.S. always held the largest share of votes. Both were headquartered in Washington, D.C., in the United States.

**The French central bank held the foreign reserves of its former colonies in Paris, and their currencies remained linked to the French franc.

itiated a series of major disagreements with the Soviet Union and its European allies. By the end of the 1950s, Cuba, a mere 90 miles from U.S. shores, had nationalized foreign corporate assets and declared its right to build a socialist state.

The peoples of Vietnam in Southeast Asia began to intensify their guerrilla war which finally defeated the puppet regime implanted and backed by 500,000 U.S. troops. Increasing numbers of peoples in the rest of the Third World viewed socialism, not only as a viable, but as a preferable alternative to free-wheeling corporate domination of their lives.

In Africa, many new governments answered the growing demand for an end to neo-colonial[7] corporate rule with resounding socialist rhetoric. But most shied away from essential institutional changes.[8]

The transnational corporations based in the core nations continued their profitable business of accumulating and reinvesting capital. Over the years they revolutionized technology, multiplying industrial productivity. As the costs of new projects spiraled, they joined together in alliances, consortia, joint ventures, to penetrate new markets and new fields of production. But they never united monolithically. Their alliances broke down when one conglomerate sought to expand at its erstwhile partners' expense. They formed new alliances on the ruins of the old, only to break these up in turn as circumstances changed.

Competition between transnational giants was aggravated by and contributed to the increasingly uneven pattern of development within and between the core capitalist countries.

The bigger corporations in some nations accumulated greater amounts of capital and spent far greater amounts on research and development, taking the lead in innovative technological growth. They incorporated the most sophisticated technological advances into key sectors of their home base industries—with increasingly contradictory consequences.

These innovations pressured the competing national oligopolies to produce constantly greater output which they then had to sell to recover their increasingly heavy investments and reap their profits. They sought to expand their markets in Europe and abroad, entering into intensified competitive struggles. The growth of military production, spurred by the cold war and "brushfire" skirmishes[9] against liberation struggles, provided a partial but inadequate outlet. But, as the corporations poured more capital into new, even more technologically advanced machinery and equipment, they augmented economies of scale, increasing the amounts of capital which must be invested in each new industrial project. In effect, they raised what Marx termed the "organic composition of capital," reducing the relative amount of labor necessary for each unit of output. As a result, the overall profit rates in the core industrial centers tended to decline in real terms.[10]*

At the same time, workers in the core industrial nations organized to demand higher wages and greater social welfare—a larger share of the fruits of the multiplying output of goods and services they produced with the new technologies. Corporate managers, seeking to hold down costs in view of their relatively declining returns, concluded that labor's wages were one element they could control. The workers' demands provided an added reason to seek new areas of investment, where wages and taxes for welfare could be minimized.

The largest firms, the transnational corporations, took the lead in expanding their global operations into more profitable areas. They competed to discover new sources of raw material, to pry open new markets for their growing surplus manufactured goods in the Third World. They sought outlets, not only for light manufactures, as earlier in the century, but also for heavy machinery and equipment. They searched for nations in which to reinvest their accumulated capital in non-union areas where wages and social welfare taxes were lowest.

All these factors combined to intensify the contradictory pressures impelling the transnational corporations to invest in key sectors of selected semi-periphery countries like South Africa and Brazil. There, they found authoritarian regimes, backed by powerful military machines capable of holding in check the aspirations of the masses of their peoples. These welcomed their capital and, above all, the sophisticated new technologies needed to build their military-industrial might. The transnationals poured roughly half of all the capital they invested in Africa in the 1960s and 1970s into South Africa. Likewise, almost half of all Federal Republic of Germany[11] (F.R.G.) and British[12] investment, and almost a third of U.S.[13] investment in Latin America was located in Brazil. Behind glowing official rhetoric calling for the expansion of human rights, the transnational corporate managers kept their eye on the bottom line.

The transnational corporations concentrated on building more integrated manufacturing investments primarily in two types of Third World countries. They built entire factories, mainly taking advantage of lower wages in some countries, like Singapore, South Korea and Taiwan. There they imported intermediate products and materials for assembly

---

*The larger firms might squeeze the smaller ones to augment their share of surpluses; the impact of inflation might make their profits appear higher in dollar terms; but in real terms, across the board, the overall returns in relation to capital investment tended to decline.

and/or processing by low-cost (often female) labor to be re-exported, primarily to the large markets of the capitalist developed countries. The local markets of these countries remained marginal.

In countries like Brazil and South Africa, on the other hand, the transnationals invested in more integrated, basic manufacturing industries, seeking to gain access to the low-cost labor, valuable mineral resources and broadened markets of entire regions.[14] The managing director of Siemens South Africa, a subsidiary of the F.R.G. firm, explained[15]:

After defeat in the Second World War, the [F.R.G.] internal market was reduced to half its earlier size. It no longer suffices for the successful marketing of Siemens technology, systems, plant and manufactures, which anyway, by their very nature had been developed for national and international goals. After a hundred years experience, and especially after the Second World War, it was completely clear that, in future, the traditional exports had to be supported by technological planning, assembly, servicing and repairs transferred outside the country. This must in turn be followed by regionalized manufacturing, and in the end by regionalized research and development . . .,

The managements of transnational corporations established such integrated industries in the countries they perceived as "stable." In the late '60s and early '70s, they frequently applied this characterization to both Brazil and South Africa.[16] By contrast, they viewed most other developing countries as "unstable." A publication of Newmont Mining, a U.S. firm with substantial interests in southern Africa, declared[17]:

Even as late as the 1930's, an international mining company could still regard the world as its oyster. . . . Few men ever thought in terms of "political risk." The colonial powers had their possessions well in hand . . . .

This happy freedom really was lost in the explosion of World War II, although the fact of its loss did not become fully apparent for some years. In Africa, one does not deal with the French, the Belgians or the British any more. One deals with the governments of newly named countries, unknown previously, such as Zaire, Botswana, Zambia, Tanzania and Lesotho. In Latin America, and in much of the rest of the world, one faces a new breed of socialistically and nationalistically inclined military governments or dedicated Communists.

The corporate managers' view that countries like South Africa and Brazil were "stable" apparently rested on their belief that these nations' governments would continue to create an hospitable investment climate, protecting the market for foreign investors, refraining from expropriation and—of utmost importance—keeping wages low. Their low-cost, "disciplined" labor forces ensured profits high enough to leave part to local partners and the local state in the form of profits and/or taxes and still send home a share large enough to offset declining rates of profit at home.

Although the governments of these countries excluded foreign investors from particular key sectors of their economies, they guaranteed them freedom of activity in those sectors where they were permitted to invest. Those sectors preserved for local capital were frequently dominated by parastatals (that is, state corporations in which the government held a large minority or majority of the shares.) The state subsidized the parastatals' production of basic inputs like steel and chemicals. The parastatals sold these to the private sector, including transnational corporate subsidiaries, at prices competitive with those on the world market. The transnationals, in turn, found that the parastatals formed a major market for their surplus machinery and equipment embodying the most advanced technologies.

Even in countries like Brazil and South Africa, transnationals showed initial reluctance to invest in integrated production. The governments of these countries employed a variety of typical state-capitalist incentives, such as lower taxes for particular kinds of investments; and constraints, including legal requirements to produce locally a minimum percent of certain items, and tariffs to restrict competitive imports. They took advantage of the growing competition between transnational firms, threatening to give major contracts only to those companies willing to cooperate with their aims.

Increasingly, the transnationals sought to expand their profitable business through the sale and control of technology, sometimes facilitated by their purchase of minority shares in local plants. Expansion through establishment of wholly-owned subsidiaries lessened in importance. The transnationals almost never encouraged research or development outside their home factories:

...there is very little if any R&D activity in the subsidiaries of foreign corporations in Africa...technology which is "trickled down" to a periphery-based subsidiary primarily takes the form of a finished product to be sold directly on the market or assembled on the spot from its pre-fabricated parts. [19]

This pattern was not changed by the increased tendency for transnationals to export entire plants to regional sub-centers, as F.R.G. and Japanese firms began to compete vigorously with U.S. based transnationals for these markets in the 1970s. [20] The almost meteoric growth of transnational engineering firms like Lurgi (F.R.G.) and Fluor (U.S.) (see below, p. 189) reflected the growing importance transnationals placed on this form of sale. They found this an effective way to sell their expanding supluses of technologically advanced equipment and machinery without risking their capital in outright investments. Engineering firms, together with associated banks and trading companies, became the "nerve centers" of transnational corporate expansion. [21]

By building entire factories in regional sub-centers, the transnationals frequently squeezed out of the market not only rivals based in other developed core nations, but even those of the same nationality which continued to export directly from the home country. A number of transnational firms, for example, helped build huge projects to supply regional centers with the most up-to-date technology for steel production, undermining the exports of smaller national firms:

Europe's steelmakers have watched their traditional export markets being taken away from them by new exporting industries in countries as diverse as Brazil, South Africa and Taiwan. Over the last decade, Europe's customary 70 percent share of the Middle East, African and Asian market had been slashed by these newcomers to under 30 percent. [22]

The Deepening Crisis:

World War II appeared to have pulled capitalism out of the Great Depression, and the post-war boom, stimulated by reconstruction, fostered an intensified pace of transnational corporate growth and expansion. Yet this very growth heightened the contradictions that culminated in renewed manifestations of the general crisis which wracked the core nations and spread into the periphery of the capitalist world. By the beginning of the 1970s, unemployment accompanied by inflation characterized the economies of Western Europe and the United States. The traditional Keynsian remedies of state intervention appeared incapable of resolving these interlinked evils. Fiscal and monetary policies, designed to curb inflation in accord with by then conventional prescriptions, incurred higher rates of unemployment. Measures to stimulate industry and reduce unemployment spurred inflation.

The international monetary crisis emerged as a further visible expression of the underlying contradictory features of the deepening crisis. Its first signs appeared as developing countries, one after another, confronted balance of payments deficits arising from the low prices of their raw materials exports, the higher costs of imported manufactured goods, and the continued outflow of profits. International Monetary Fund orthodoxy forced them to devalue and adopt "austerity" measures, throwing the burden of the crisis on lower-income groups and narrowing markets for manufactured goods sold by core nation firms. Unable to market its surplus output, its profit inflow sharply reduced by the collapse of its empire, England was the first among the core countries to suffer payments deficits, despite repeated devaluations of the pound. The gold and foreign exchange reserves of the United States gradually diminished, eroded by continual overseas investments and mounting military expenditures. Over a decade of heavy spending on expensive modern weapons for a losing war against the Vietnamese struggle for freedom accelerated the drain. The U.S. currency devaluation shook the entire capitalist world monetary system, hinged to an assumed stability of the dollar, to its very foundations.

Several contradictory phenomena emerged in the growing chaos of the so-called "free" international market. United States interests pressed for greater protection against manufactured goods imported from countries catching up and even overtaking U.S. factories' technological leadership. The regional sub-centers argued for ending trade restrictions in order to broaden the markets for their growing manufactured goods. Third World countries demanded some stability for the prices of their raw materials and support for building their industries to reduce their dependence on the unstable world markets.

The International Monetary Fund, unable to win sufficient agreement among the core nations to replace the dollar with any other form of stable international currency, acquiesced to floating exchange rates. The currencies of the major capitalist nations fluctuated daily, aggravating speculation and the instability of international money marts arising from the intensified underlying structural contradictions of the whole system.

The U.S. government and press publicly blamed the crisis on OPEC. But closer examination showed the dramatic rise in oil prices to be yet another reflection of the inherent contradictions in the political-economic evolution of the core capitalist countries. Accelerating technological innovation multiplied oil consumption, not only for energy production, but also to manufacture plastics and petrochemicals. The OPEC nations simply united to exert national control over their deposits of this ever more necessary raw material. They raised its world price to levels more commensurate with the high prices they were forced to pay for the transnational corporations' products. The Western press typically ignored the fact that the major oil firms matched the price increases determined by the OPEC countries for crude oil with even higher increases for their refined products, reaping record profits. Reinvestments of these vast accumulations of capital enabled the oil majors and their associated financial institutions to expand their concentration and domination, not only of the periphery, but also the core nations' economies. The oil-producing nations, lacking the skills and labor resources required to absorb in full the windfall profits they reaped, reinvested them in transnational corporate banks and associated financial institutions. Thus they provided core nation conglomerates with still greater volumes of capital for reinvestment and control—still further aggravating the contradictory impact of the general crisis.

The transnational corporations and their associated home governments sought to escape the full impact of the crisis by adopting policies designed to throw the burden on smaller businesses and lower-income groups in the core nations as well as in the periphery.*

At home, they backed government plans to hold the line on money wages, cutting workers' real incomes as inflation pushed prices up even faster. They pressured local and state governments to reduce expenditures for education, health and housing. They supported cuts in welfare spending and unemployment compensation for the growing numbers of men and women unable to find work. Banks refused to lend money except at extortionate (10 percent or more) interest to cities confronting financial crises as tax revenues plummeted and debt service charges rose. Urban blight spread throughout inner cities, transforming them into ghettoes housing impoverished families of blacks and other poor workers.

Faced with spreading "stagflation" at home, the transnational corporations stepped up their competition in the 1970s for the profitable business of regional sub-centers like South Africa and Brazil. These states became central to the emergent reality of the "North-South

---

*Aghiri Emmanuel severely overstated the case when he suggested[23] that the working classes in core nations, as a result of their successful struggles to better their wages and social welfare, were thereby participating in the exploitation of third world countries; only a limited "aristocracy" of workers, even at the center, ever attained benefits high enough to be justifiably accused of participating in profits reaped from abroad. Only 25 percent of U.S. workers for example, were organized in unions—and not all of them received high wages. By the 1960s in England, and the '70s in the U.S., transnationals had introduced a systematic onslaught against the real wages and social welfare the workers had managed to improve through decades of struggle.

partnership" urged by the Trilateral Commission.[24]* The Commission had declared the need for forging new relations between the industrialized nations of Europe, North America and Asia, and the impoverished Third World countries of the southern hemisphere. The characteristics which apparently rendered sub-regional centers like South Africa eligible as the leading candidates for this partnership were: their "disciplined" low cost labor force; valuable mineral resources; a strong parastatal sector, providing infrastructure and cheap inputs and a market; powerful local firms to act as private-sector partners to a growing number of transnationals; and a state capable of maintaining these conditions, whatever the aspirations of their inhabitants.

These countries provided markets for technologies that were becoming increasingly difficult to sell in the developed capitalist countries. In the latter, extensive plant and equipment were already in place; a considerable portion lay idle. The developing countries had no choice but to import capital equipment for their essential infrastructure and new industries. A business analyst disclosed[25]:

Probably the most undiscussed issue regarding LDC (Less Developed Country) debt is the embarassing fact that, had the LDCs not maintained a steady level of imports, the 1974-5 recession in the North . . . would have become more severe.

The transnationals could count on their home governments to support their efforts to expand exports to reduce pressures on their home markets and balance of payments. Government guarantees in the mid 1970s covered the financing of 40 percent of British and Japanese exports; 30 percent of French exports; 15 percent of U.S. and 9 percent of F.R.G. exports.[26] Between the end of 1975 and 1976, F.R.G. export guarantees rose by 41 percent. Most of this rise went to finance exports to the developing countries.[27]

Although the U.S. export support agency, the Export-Import Bank, reduced its loans in 1976-77 for internal financial reasons, there was considerable pressure within the Administration to intensify the bank's efforts to meet foreign competition.

---

*The Trilateral Commission, established by David Rockefeller in the early 1970s and composed of participants from the United States, Europe and Japan, sought to devise new policies to escape the growing crisis. The signficance of its role was illustrated by the election of one of its U.S. participants, Jimmy Carter, as U.S. President, with Zbigniev Brezhinski, formerly the Commission's chief executive, and almost 20 other former Commission members on his staff.

On the other hand, the governments of the regional sub-centers, themselves, often guaranteed loans to finance continued import of sophisticated machinery and equipment for their industrial buildup. Between 1967 and 1973, the total debt of 86 developing countries surveyed by the International Monetary Fund tripled from about $50 billion to about $151 billion.[28] High and middle income countries— basically the regional sub-centers like Brazil and South Africa—accounted for a disproportionate share of this rising debt. In all cases, the growth of foreign debt was a fundamental feature of Third World countries' growing dependency. Private lenders financed a growing portion, 36 percent in 1974 compared to 27 percent in 1967, as core governments, affected by the mounting international economic crisis, cut back official aid.[29] Transnational corporate banks gladly expanded their loans, backed by government guarantees, to sub-centers willing to pay higher interest rates than they could obtain in their stagnant economies at home.

But the same underlying contradictory phenomena which fostered the competitive involvement of transnational corporations in regional sub-centers simultaneously spurred the emergence of struggles of the peoples in the surrounding regions for fundamental changes to create new political economic institutions capable of meeting their basic needs. By the end of the 1970s, southern Africa had emerged as a focal point of international conflict as liberation movements sought to end the domination of the region by the racist white-minority regimes and their transnational corporate allies. The liberation movements announced as their goal the control of their own national resources and the establishment of industries and agriculture capable of providing productive employment opportunities and raising the living standards of the region's inhabitants to levels made possible by 20th century technology.

To attain this goal, they inevitably came into head-on conflict with the transnational corporate interests whose investments had built up the military-industrial capacity of the South African minority regime that dominated the region.

References

1. For discussion, see P. Evans, *Dependent Development—The Alliance of Multinational, State and Local Capital in Brazil* (Princeton, New Jersey: Princeton University Press, 1979) pp. 25-35.

2. Eg. Paul Lubeck, in paper presented at 1979 annual meeting of the American Sociology Association.

3. Eg. See U.S. Department of Commerce, *Survey of Current Business*, "U.S. Direct Investment Position Abroad, Yearend 1977" (Washington: U.S. Government Printing Office, August, 1978) p. 28.

4. Evans, *Dependent Development, op. cit.* This book is a penetrating analysis of the way the triple alliance shaped the Brazilian "miracle."

5. A. and N. Seidman, *South Africa and U.S. Multinational Corporations* (Westport: Lawrence Hill, 1976; and Dar es Salaam: Tanzania Publishing House, 1976).

6. S. Amin, *Unequal Development: An Essay on the Social Formations of Peripheral Capitalism* (New York: Monthly Review Press, 1976) p. 102.

7. This phrase was first widely introduced by Kwame Nkrumah in his book, *Neo-Colonialism in Africa* (New York: International Publishers, 1966).

8. Ghana, itself, was an example; see, eg, A. Seidman, *Ghana's Development Experience, 1951-1966* (Nairobi: East African Publishing House, 1978).

9. John F. Kennedy coined this phrase back in the early 1960s as the Vietnam war was just heating up.

10. Eg. compare data for profits and capital investment in manufacturing for U.S. corporations throughout the 1950s, '60s, and '70s, using data from the U.S. Statistical Abstract (annual).

11. K. Funke, "Profitkäfer Multinational; V. W. in Brasilien," in *Drittewelt Magazine* No. 5, May 1977 (Bonn).

12. Board of Trade, United Kingdom, Trade and Industry, February 21, 1977.

13. U.S. Department of Commerce, *Survey of Current Business, op. cit.* August, 1978.

14. See *ibid.* for figures on exports by U.S. subsidiaries in developing countries exhibiting these trends.

15. W. E. Wentges, "Deutsches Investment in Sudafrika: Ein 'Case Study'—Siemens," paper presented to business seminar on South Africa in the Federal Republic of Germany, Nov. 4, 1976; translated by Neva Makgetla.

16. *Der Spiegel* (Bonn), No. 1-2, 1977.

17. *Business Week*, Dec. 5, 1977.

18. D. Metzger, *Das Beispiel Kupfer* (Bremen: Bremer Afrika Archiv. 1977); see also *Business Week*, Dec. 5, 1977.

19. H. Hveem, "The Extent and Type of Direct Foreign Investment in Africa" *Multinational Firms in Africa* (Uppsala: Nordiska Afrikaninstitutet, 1975).

20. *The Oriental Economist*, May, 1975, p. 32; see also *The New York Times*, May 16, 1977.

21. C. Palloix, *Les firmes multinationales*, p. 98; quoted in Mezger, *op. cit.*

22. *The New York Times*, May 23, 1977.

23. A. Emmanuel, *Unequal Exchange: a study of the imperialism of trade* (New York: Monthly Review Press, 1972).

24. Cf. R. N. Gardner, S. Okito and B. J. Udink, *A Turning Point in North-South Economic Relations*, Trilateral Commission Report No. 3, 1974; and R. J. Crozier, S. P. Huntington and J. Watanuki, *The Crisis of Democracy*, Report on the Governability of Democracy to the Trilateral Commission (New York University Press, 1975).

25. *Far Eastern Economic Review*, (Hong Kong), "Banking '77", April 8, 1977.

26. *The New York Times*, Feb. 12, 1978.

27. Bundesminister fur Wirtschaft LP, "Ausfuhrgartantien und Ausfuhrbürgschaften der BRD," 1976 BMWI Dokumentation (Bonn, 1977).

28. M. Odjagev, *United States Transnational Banking*, Report to the OECD, mimeo draft, Jan. 1977 (Paris) Appendix X, Table V.

29. *Ibid.*

The Technological Revolution and Growing Competition   2

The accumulation and reinvestment of capital in the leading capitalist nations after World War II intensified the contradictions which culminated in the re-emergence of the general crisis of the 1970s. An underlying factor aggravating the contradictory features of this process was the technological revolution. This chapter will look, first, at how technology on the one hand multiplied productivity, and facilitated the changing international division of labor; and, on the other, generated pressures contributing to a growing competitive struggle between transnational corporations to penetrate the crumbling British, French and Portuguese empires that, for over half a century, had spanned the African continent.

Technological Revolution:

World War II gave rise to new sciences and technologies, like computers and aeronautics, which formed the basis for advanced sophisticated industries in the core developed countries. After recovering from the war, European and Japanese firms began to compete with U.S. firms in the area of technological progress, endeavoring to cut costs and develop new products. This contributed to rapidly rising economies of scale. Between 1948 and 1966, U.S. expenditures on research and development in industries multiplied over five times, in constant dollars. [1] Although still smaller in absolute terms, the rate of growth of spending in the 1960s and '70s in other countries was even higher. [2] Heavy government outlays, a feature of growing state intervention in all developed capitalist countries, frequently for military projects, spurred technological innovation. Despite its official "free enterprise" stance, the U.S. government spent more on research in aircraft and electronics through its military and space programs, alone, than did the F.R.G., U.K., and French governments combined. [3] Its spending in these "expensive, fast-moving sectors" gave "U.S. industry a commanding lead."[4]

Table 2-1.

Government Spending in Selected Countries on Research and Development, 1960 and 1970: The United Kingdom, Federal Republic of Germany, France and Japan compared to the United States (Index: U.S. = 100)

	Military		Space		Civilian Nuclear		Other*	
	'60	'70	'60	'70	'60	'70	'60	'70
U.S.	100	100	100	100	100	100	100	100
U.K.	16	12	1	2	26	29	167	93
France	6	11	1	8	28	67	40	67
F.R.G.	3	6	0	4	17	54	0	42
Japan	2	4**	0	0.4**	3	10	60	21**

Notes: *Including aerospace and electronics.
        **1969

Source: K. Pavitt, " 'International' Technology and the U.S. Economy: Is There a Problem?" *National Science Foundation, the Effects of International Technology Transfers on the U.S. Economy* (Washington, D.C.: July, 1974) p. 66.

The resulting technological revolution led to rapid increases in productivity. From 1960 to 1970, output per work hour rose 34 percent in the U.S., 43 percent in the U.K., 74 percent in the Federal Republic of Germany (F.R.G.) and 289 percent in Japan.[5] A few examples may illustrate the impact of technological innovation in reducing labor requirements and increasing economies of scale. Mitsubishi developed a new technique for smelting copper, which eliminated 30 percent of the labor traditionally employed by introducing continuous processing and automation.[6] In the United States, about half of all new machine tools introduced by the mid-'70s were computerized and "numerically controlled." Steel plants, in an industry always characterized by large economies of scale, required production of at least six million tons a year to achieve optimum scale.

The average contract for transnational engineering and construction firms rose from $13 million in the mid-'60s to about $100 million in 1974.[7]

The technological revolution facilitated a fundamental shift in the international division of labor. Dramatic advances in distribution and communication technologies made possible the transfer of entire manufacturing plants to remote, low wage regions. Airplanes, air freight and improved telecommunications systems greatly increased the flexibility of world trade. By the 1970s, the widespread use of container-shipping reduced the cost and facilitated the expansion of bulk international trade, sharply cutting the amount of labor involved in shipping produce from one region of the world to another.

The huge size and capital expense of new projects designed to take advantage of these new technologies necessitated increased cooperation between transnational corporations in the form of consortia and joint ventures to remain competitive in the world market. Increasingly, the competitive pattern that emerged involved, not individual firms, but huge corporate alliances.[8] These alliances were built on and fostered corporate mergers, creating vast conglomerates which dominated whole sectors of national industries and spilled over into unrelated fields in the core developed countries.

The heavy costs of the technological revolution stimulated the continuous expansion of finance capital. The largest industrial conglomerates became increasingly interlocked with the dominant banks and financial institutions of their home countries. The vast amounts of capital required to finance the technological revolution spurred the growth of the largest banks. By the mid-'70s some 30 or 40 dominated the international banking market.[9] [In 1975, 16.5 percent of the total assets of the largest 300 banks was held by the top 10 banks . . .the size of the top five banks was greater than the size of the bottom 100 banks altogether.[10]]

The growing capital requirements of the largest transnationals in each core industrialized nation led to their close alliance with at least one or two of the largest banks which dominated their home economies. The particular mechanism facilitating these linkages varied in each country in conformance with their national legal structures.

In the U.S. and Britain, industrial and banking ties were typically embodied in shared directorships. In the F.R.G., banks could legally own stocks of industrial firms. In Japan, many of the largest banks joined as integral members of massive industrial groups. Through these relations, the banks played a major role in organizing the consortia necessary to finance the costs of huge new projects.

The banks' activities both reflected and contributed to the expansion of Euromoney markets. The " 'shrinkage' of time and space brought about by the technological advances in transportation and global communications systems"[11] facilitated the shift of bank capital from the U.S. to Japan and Europe, and from Europe and Japan to Africa, to finance expanding transnational corporate activities there.

The competitive efforts of transnational corporations to expand their output contributed to overproduction which, by the late '60s and '70s, especially characterized heavy industries. This overproduction became a prominent feature of the economic crisis that spread through the capitalist world, especially in auto,[12] steel,[13] and chemicals.[14] The transnational corporations entered into ever more vigorous competition to sell their surplus manufactured goods.

The technological revolution, in short, aggravated the pressures for transnational corporate expansion in a competitive search for new sources of raw materials and markets. But historical circumstances shaped differing responses to these pressures on the part of groups of transnationals based in different core countries.

The Crumbling of Colonial Rule:

The giant companies based in Britain and France, at the heart of their colonial empires, steadily lost ground after World War II. They had long profited from production of low-cost raw materials in the colonies, where imperial rule also granted them a near-monopoly on the sale of manufactured goods. The biggest British and French banks had facilitated their profitable activities by establishing supportive colonial branch networks. Thirty years after World War II, British and French firms retained the most extensive branch networks of all transnational corporations operating on the African continent.

In the colonial era, British and French corporations and banks relied on non-economic ties to retain their African markets. Both nations had industrialized early and relatively smoothly; they had already installed extensive industrial plants in the home country by the time they participated in the "scramble for Africa" in the late 19th century. Secure markets at home and in the colonies made development and installation of new technologies in home factories seem unnecessary. Instead of renovating domestic productive capacity, the giant firms invested in their expanding colonial empire, securing ever-greater control over cheap sources of agricultural and mineral raw materials, plus markets for their manufactured goods. By World War II, they had already begun to fall behind the U.S. and Germany in terms of technological innovation.[15] The lag was clearest in Britain's outdated steel industry.[16]

As their colonial empires collapsed after World War II, British and French companies at first remained dominant in Africa by virtue of their earlier investments and institutionalized relationships with the newly independent countries. As their home markets became saturated, profits from these low-wage, high-return areas became increasingly important. Rio Tino Zinc, one of the largest British mining firms, for example, reported in 1974[17] that while only 6.7 percent of its turnover was in Africa, it reaped 14.4 percent of its distributed profits there. In contrast, the 23.2 percent of its turnover in England and 8.1 percent in continental Europe produced only 6.7 and 5.6 percent, respectively, of its profits. To this day, two of the largest U.K. banks, Barclays and Standard, remain the leading commercial banks in most of the former British African colonies, especially in southern Africa. They accumulated well over a fourth of their international profits from South Africa, alone, in the mid-'70s. Over time, however, transnationals from other nations, primarily in the United States, the F.R.G. and Japan, began to challenge British and French hegemony.

U.S. Transnationals' Penetration:

U.S. companies had a long history of investment and domination in the economies of Canada and the politically independent countries of Latin America.[18] A few U.S. mining concerns participated in joint ventures with European partners long established in Africa. But many U.S. transnational corporations initially entered the African scene only when they purchased shares in British and French firms in the course of their expansion into Europe after World War II.

A few U.S. firms had acquired subsidiaries in Europe in the 1920s or even earlier, particularly in the auto industry. Following World War II, however, U.S. investment in Europe multiplied from about $2 billion in 1950, to $14 billion in 1965.[19] The "big three" auto firms, General Motors, Ford and Chrysler, penetrated the West European market by buying plants and equipment there. U.S. companies in other industries followed suit, primarily by acquiring controlling shares in existing European firms.[20] To withstand this invasion and strengthen their own capability to take advantage of the most modern technological innovations, the largest European firms further combined the financial and industrial capacity within each nation. In the auto industry, for example, Fiat took over Bianci and Lancia to become the largest auto firm, not only in Italy, but on the continent. F.R.G.'s Volkswagen took over Audi and NSU to become the second largest. British Leyland absorbed all the U.K.'s auto producing facilities except the subsidiaries of U.S. firms. The Swedish firms, Saab and Volvo, merged,[21] followed shortly after by the French firms, Citroen and Peugeot. Renault took over Citroen's Berliot truck division.[22] By the mid-'70s it was estimated that, to survive in the European auto market, a company must produce at least 1.25 million cars a year.[23]

The largest U.S. banks had forged close ties to the U.S. transnational industrial firms engaged in penetrating Europe. Chase Manhattan, for example, the third largest bank in the world and closely knit into the Rockefeller network, shared directors with some of the biggest U.S. industrial firms, including Firestone, General Motors, Chrysler, Exxon, General Electric, AT&T, U.S. Steel and other domestic companies, as well as the giant Royal Dutch petroleum. [24] Representatives of the Japanese Mitsubishi group, the Italian firm Fiat, the Swiss-owned Nestles, the British Dunlop, and the Swedish company, Volvo, also sit on Chase's International advisory board. The bank retain former U.S. Secretary of State, Henry Kissinger, as advisor. These ties enabled Chase to mobilize capital and organize consortia to expand production in a wide range of industries outside the U.S.

The U.S. transnational banks serviced their industrial clients' expansion abroad by opening overseas branches. In the 1960s, the U.S. Federal Reserve Bank imposed regulations in an effort to prevent capital from leaving the U.S. and further augmenting the nation's balance of payments deficits. Since the regulations prohibited banks from re-exporting funds returned to the United States from their overseas operations, they simply left their accumulated capital in their European branches. This movement of U.S. finance capital overseas was reflected in and contributed to the growth of the Eurodollar market. It enabled U.S. banks to mobilize increasing amounts of credit for further overseas investments outside of U.S. government controls.

U.S. transnational banks were highly concentrated. By 1975, the 20 largest controlled 92 percent of the total foreign branch assets of all U.S. banks. These banks controlled about 30 percent of all banking assets within the U.S. as well. [25]

In addition to the 137 lending banks domiciled in the United States there are 51 banks in the OECD countries and 29 banks elsewhere that are subjected to majority control of U.S. banks. Thus 210, or more than one-third of the 605 financial entities are American or American-controlled. [26]

In the 1970s, especially as the international crisis deepened, U.S. bank capital began to expand abroad more rapidly, although industrial investment there lagged. Between 1970 and 1975, foreign assets of U.S. banks rose from 8 to 18 percent of their domestic assets. In the same period, U.S. banks' international credit expanded by about 30 percent, more than three times the rate of expansion of domestic credit in the U.S. itself. [27]

By the mid-'70s, the overseas activities of some of the largest U.S. banks had become more important than their domestic business. In 1977, Citibank, the second largest U.S. bank, held over half of its assets and earned over 80 percent of its profits outside the United States.[28]

Increasingly, U.S. banks shifted their financial headquarters abroad from Europe to "financial centers" in places like the Caribbean, where they faced neither severe regulations nor high taxes. By 1975, their European branches' share of overseas business had dropped to 26 percent, reflecting the rapid growth of the Caribbean financial centers.

The lion's share of U.S. investment in Europe was in England. Between 1962 and 1969, U.S.-owned fixed assets there grew 80 percent, compared to a 45 percent growth in those of British companies. By 1966 U.S. controlled firms accounted for 10 percent of the manufactured goods output in the U.K., and 17.5 percent of British exports.[29] By 1970, U.S. investment in England totalled $8 billion, approximately 10 percent of all U.S. overseas investments.[30]

In a number of basic industries, a single British giant confronted the subsidiaries of U.S. firms on equal terms. The U.S. company, IBM, and the British owned ICL, for example, together dominated the British computer industry. Leyland and U.S. subsidiaries split the auto industry.[31] In several sectors, the British companies remained independent of U.S. control only with the help of the British government. In auto, Leyland was ultimately taken over entirely by the state.[32]

U.S. firms similarly penetrated basic French industries, but the French government protected the integrity of its domestic firms more aggressively. In several cases, it forced reduction of U.S. companies' shares in major French companies.[33]

A number of U.S. transnationals indirectly expanded their interests in Africa through their British and French affiliates. British ties were especially important in providing U.S. companies with entree into South Africa. The U.S. banks, in particular, maintained few branches in Africa: only 1.6 percent of all their foreign branches in 1966, dropping to 0.6 percent in 1975.[34] Almost all these branches were located in South Africa, with a scattering in the largest independent countries: Egypt, Nigeria, Zaire. Instead of opening their own branches in independent African countries, the largest U.S. banks operated there primarily through British and French affiliates. The second biggest bank in the U.S., Citicorp, acquired 49 percent of the French Banque d'Afrique de l'Ouest, which had branches in nearly every Francophonic African country. Citicorp had also purchased 49 percent of the British bank, Grindlays, which had long been active in East and Central Africa.[35] The largest bank in the world, the Bank of America, joined Barclays in a consortium bank, the Societe Financiere Europeene, and established direct ties to the British bank, Kleinwort Benson Lonsdale, which had two South African affiliates. The Kleinwort Benson connection also linked the Bank of America to the British consortium bank, Midland and International Banks, of which the Standard Bank had become a member. Standard remained one of the most important transnational banks in Anglophonic Africa, with over a third of its business in South Africa. Chase Manhattan, the third largest U.S. bank, had formed ties with the large French bank, the Societe Generale de Banque,[36] as well as extensive contacts with Standard.

These links enabled the U.S. banks to provide additional channels [see below pp. 208-9] into the former British and French colonial preserves for their clients, the largest U.S. transnational industrial companies.

New Rivals:

The largest companies based in the Federal Republic of Germany and Japan grew strong enough to seek entry into African markets and raw material sources only in the late '60s and early '70s. Unlike British and French firms, they had managed, with extensive state support, to withstand the invasion of U.S. transnational finance capital. At the same time, they managed to take advantage of U.S. companies' technological contributions.

U.S. investment in the F.R.G., second only to that in Britain, reached $2 billion by 1965.[37] U.S. firms took over many smaller local companies. Even well into the '60s, in fact, U.S. companies' expansion in the F.R.G. market seemed irresistable. By the late '60s, however, F.R.G. transnationals began to compete increasingly successfully. The largest corporate conglomerates and banks emerged as major European rivals of the United States, both in export markets and foreign investment. By the 1970s, they had mounted a counter-offensive that threatened the U.S. hegemony in the capitalist world, and led to their own entry into Africa.

After the Second World War, industry in the F.R.G. lay in ruins. Where the actual industrial plant had not been destroyed, the leading companies had been broken up because of their assistance to Nazi aggression. In several cases, their top managers were tried as war criminals. The largest bank, the Deutsche Bank, was split into three companies, and only reunited in 1956. I.G. Farben, the chemicals combine, which produced Zykon-B for the Nazi gas chambers, was divided into Bayer, BASF, and Hoechst. German overseas investments were confiscated in all but seven countries, one of which was South Africa.

U.S. firms backed by the Marshall Plan, stepped into this situation. A number of major American companies—among them Singer, IBM and Standard Oil—had invested in Germany before World War I. They were joined by others—including ITT, General Motors, Ford and Woolworths—in the '20s. But by far the largest wave of U.S. investment in the F.R.G. followed World War II.[38]

By the mid-'60s, G.M.'s Opel subsidiary and Ford, together, controlled 40 percent of the West German auto market; U.S. oil companies accounted for 35 percent of the petroleum industry; Owens supplied 40 percent of the glass market; and U.S. rubber companies had captured 20 percent of the market for rubber goods. IBM supplied four fifths of the market for electronic data equipment. Over a third of all foreign investments in the F.R.G. was from the United States. Half was accounted for by 28 major concerns, each of which held assets worth over DM 100 million.[39]

Yet the penetration of U.S. capital affected the huge indigenous F.R.G. companies—the chemical, auto, engineering and steel companies, and the banks—relatively little. Foreign interests acquired shares in a few, but the largest consistently acted independently. Minority shareholdings in some instances may have led some into alliances with U.S. firms, but they rarely permitted their own interests to become subordinate.[40] U.S. investment further stimulated increased concentration in F.R.G. industry, as U.S. firms or the largest F.R.G. firms took over smaller companies.

By the early '70s, the rate of expanding U.S. investment in the F.R.G. had slowed. From 1965 to 1970, the capital of F.R.G. enterprises in which foreign firms held at least a fourth of the equity rose from 17 to 31 percent of the captial of all F.R.G. companies. In the following three years, the rate of growth slowed so that their share rose only three percent more to 34 percent, although the absolute growth in money terms remained about the same.

In contrast to the situation in Britain, wholly locally owned F.R.G. firms grew faster than foreign firms' holdings in the heavy industrial sectors, notably chemicals and steel. The share of partially-held foreign enterprises began to decline in these sectors in the early '70s. The strength of indigenous firms was sufficient to ensure that the declining trend would continue.

In several industries, the share of capital owned by foreign-controlled firms grew. The share of firms with minority foreign participation, on the other hand, dropped.[41] This pattern reflected the increasing polarization in many important markets between huge foreign controlled and domestic firms. This parallelled the continued tendency towards increased concentration, as more and more capital was required to purchase machinery and equipment embodying the most advanced technologies.

Despite the continued high level of foreign holdings, F.R.G. based transnational corporations had emerged as a dynamic independent force by the 1970s. Their rejuvenation was partly a result of their close ties to the largest banks, and partly due to vigorous state capitalist intervention. The banks played a crucial role. As one authority explained:[42]

The rise of high finance (in the F.R.G.) is not the result of the "economic miracle" alone. It has a system. Although the allies broke up the German banking concerns after the War, the parts soon rejoined each other.

Today these institutions are centralized and universal, financially strong and aggressively managed, equalled by only a few banking giants around the world. The freedom of action of the German Grossbankiers is much larger than that of their colleagues in most other countries.

The biggest banks, the Grossbanken, functioned as the kingpins in the rapid recovery of the Federal Republic's economy:

A vast number of large German companies are closely controlled today by a relatively small number of financial institutions and organizations. These groups . . . enjoy great influence over every aspect of the development of West German Industry.[42a]

In the F.R.G., national legislation permits banks to become directly involved in ownership of industrial firms. In the 1970s they owned about 10 percent of the stock of all firms.[43] As one authority observed.[44]

In the F.R.G. . . . .ties between the credit establishments, in particular the three "Grossbanken" and industry are many and traditional . . . . The consequence is that the banks are represented almost in entirety in the administrative organs of major enterprises. Thus, they are assured of essential sources of information. In fact, the board of directors is charged with controlling the management of business.

The banks own outright major interests in such huge industrial companies as Daimler Benz, Metalgesellschaft and Deutsche Babcock.[45] Most of the shares are held by the three Grossbanken, Deutsche Bank, Dresdner Bank, and Commerzbank. The Deutsche Bank, with the largest holdings in industry of any F.R.G. bank, had especially close ties to the big electrical corporation, Siemens. Both companies were founded by the same man in the 19th century, and a Siemen's representative still sat on the bank's board in the 1970s.

The F.R.G. government, as well as the Grossbanken, played a key role in strengthening domestic industrial units' ability to withstand the penetration of U.S. firms. The F.R.G. government's close relationship to industrial capital stretched back into the early days of German industrialization at the turn of the century. It was reinforced during Nazi rule and, despite the allies' initial efforts to break up the largest industrial cartels, persisted in the postwar period. In 1963, the total value of industries controlled by the F.R.G. government, excluding banks and construction companies but including the railroads and post, accounted for approximately 21 percent of all corporate capital. This represented 13 percent of all corporate turnover, 7 percent of total employment, and 9 percent of non-agricultural employment.[46]

The F.R.G. government participated directly in some of the largest manufacturing firms. The State of Basse Saxe and the Federal government each held 20 percent of Volkswagen's capital. The Federal goverment nominated VW's chair and four of its 11 directors. The Federal government became involved in VEBA, which primarily produced steel, coal and electricity.[47] The Federal government also owned a majority of shares of Salzgitter, founded under the Nazis to develop iron and manganese production. F.R.G. state governments controlled several major banks, including the Westdeutsche Landesbank Girozentrale, one of the largest in the country.

The F.R.G. government used its parastatals to bolster private industry. Producing basic inputs for manufacturing industries, parastatals hold down prices to private firms to ensure the latters' profitability. The government strengthened its ties to the private sector by its "habit of electing to the board of directors members of the private sector as well as government functionaries."[48]

In short, the banks, government, and private industry in the Federal Republic of Germany formed a closely integrated network covering all major industries. Their coordination was facilitated by and contributed to the growing concentration of West German industry under the impact of advanced technology. A "considerable number of the leading industries here (in the F.R.G.) are now dominated by just a handful of companies."[49] The auto industry, displaying the full flowering of the state-corporation-bank complex, was dominated by Volkswagen, with its state connections; Daimler Benz, in which the Deutsche Bank (28.5 percent) and the Commerzbank and Friedrick Flick holding company were major shareholders; BMW; and the subsidiaries of American companies. The three companies formed from I. G. Farben—Hoechst, Bayer, and BASF—together with the chemical division of the state-owned VEBA and Henkel, dominated the chemicals industry. Dresdner Bank shared the ownership of Henkel's largest subsidiaries, Degussa.

Three of the largest machinery manufacturers, Metalgesellschaft (controlled by the Dresdner Bank and Siemens), Gutehoffnungshute and DEMAG, a subsidiary of Mannesman AG, shared directors.[50] This sort of extreme concentration, linked together by the banks and supported by direct government participation characterized all basic industry in the Federal Republic.

In one sense, the destruction of World War II had been an advantage: it enabled F.R.G. firms to install a totally new industrial plant. Concentration and state intervention enabled F.R.G. companies to mobilize the necessary knowhow and financial backing to adapt and utilize the advanced technologies initially transferred into the country by U.S. penetration. In contrast, U.S. transnationals permitted their equipment to lag in several home industries, notably steel.[51] The F.R.G. machinery and equipment, chemicals and steel sectors grew especially quickly in the 1960s. Only in the most technologically advanced sectors, like petroleum and computers, did U.S. firms remain dominant.

As F.R.G. firms grew in the 1960s and '70s, they rapidly expanded their exports, and then their overseas investments. By the 1970s, only Japan exported as high a percentage of its output.[52] The F.R.G. companies by then were investing more capital outside their home country than foreign firms were investing in it.

Table 2-2.
Foreign Investment in the F.R.G. compared to investment abroad by F.R.G. companies, 1956-'76 (in millions of Deutsche Marks)[1]

| | Average annual capital flow for investment | | |
	1965-'68	*1969-'72*	*1973-'76*
Into the F.R.G.	3311	3526	4715
From the F.R.G.	1498	3657	5087
Ration of captial inflow to capital outflow	2.2:1	1.0:1	0.9:1

Source: Deutsches Bundesbank, *Monatsberichte*, relevant years.

Furthermore, F.R.G. investments abroad expanded more rapidly than exports:

The export orientation has been greatly strengthened since 1961. While at that time 15.1 percent of industrial production went for export, in 1972 this share reached 20.0 percent. . . .The overseas involvement of [West] German enterprises through direct investment has developed still faster than through exports.[53]

F.R.G. firms' foreign investment totalled DM570 million ($135 million) in 1956. By 1965, this annual rate had doubled and began to climb more rapidly the following year.[54] Between 1967 and 1977, F.R.G. foreign holdings multiplied almost seven times, from $3 billion to $20.5 billion.[55] It is important to note that F.R.G. investment data, unlike those for the U.S. and Britain, do not include funds reinvested by overseas subsidiaries. They simply sum capital outflows. To provide comparable data, the F.R.G. figures should probably be raised by a minimum of 30 percent.[56]

This rapidly growing capital outflow reflected the determination of the largest F.R.G. firms to take advantage of cheaper overseas labor and to acquire new markets for their expanded manufactured goods output, markets which could in many cases be penetrated only through investment.[57]

F.R.G. based companies, many still somewhat smaller than their U.S. competitors, used their advanced technology to win contracts in the more wealthy developing countries. A director of Metalgesellschaft claimed that F.R.G. companies provided "less capital, but more know-how, technology, advances in construction, corporate initiative and experts" than other countries.[58] The branches of industries which predominated in F.R.G. exports and foreign investment were precisely those most technologically sophisticated. In order of importance, they were: machinery, chemicals, auto, iron and steel, and textiles. These branches exported an average of 29 percent of their output in 1972, compared to 11 percent for the rest of West German industry. In all, foreign production accounted for a higher share of total overseas sales and grew more rapidly than the average for the economy.[59]

The six industries which exported and invested most abroad were those in which the importance of foreign investment had grown most slowly or declined in the recent past. They were also characterized by the highest degree of concentration in the F.R.G. itself. Many of the dominant companies in these branches, like Siemens, AEG-Telefunken, Bosch and the successors of I. G. Farben, had established major production facilities outside Germany before World War II. Foreign investment was even more concentrated than was domestic F.R.G. production. VW and Daimler Benz, for instance, accounted for 90 percent of all foreign production by F.R.G. auto firms in 1969. The three largest chemicals firms, Hoechst, Bayer and BASF, held about 60 percent of F.R.G. foreign investment in chemicals production in 1971.[60] The high cost of sophisticated technologies and the risks involved in investing in them overseas may explain this pattern.

F.R.G. banks began to expand their foreign activities rapidly in the late '60s and early '70s, alongside the increased foreign investment of the major industrial firms. The Grossbanken, with their close ties to F.R.G.-based transnational corporations, organized bank consortia to finance the massive expansion of F.R.G. exports. Frequently the F.R.G. government underwrote the banks' financing packages for overseas sales.

As the international monetary crisis matured, the strength of the Deutsche Mark helped the F.R.G. banks move into international markets. The banks' new international strength was reflected in the growth of the DM-Eurobond market, monopolized by the Grossbanken.[61]

Even more than their American counterparts, F.R.G. banks conducted wholesale operations outside the Federal Republic. They operated primarily through their own or associated consortia's representative offices, and to a lesser extent through local affiliates, especially in peripheral countries.

In 1978, one authority observed[62]:

> Foreign involvement has developed six times as strongly as internal business. In the last five years, turnover with foreign customers has multiplied more than three times; with domestic customers, in contrast, only one and a half times. The three Grossbanken today earn about a third of their total profits outside the country.

The largest banks increased their capacity to operate by forming international consortia. Most of them belong to one of more groups of affiliated banks designed to facilitate the mobilization of major international credits. They provided member banks with contacts in a larger number of nations than each could maintain alone.

All the Grossbanken joined international consortia—the Deutsche Bank joined EBIC (European Banks International); Dresdner Bank, the Societe Financiere Europeene (SFE); and Commerzbank, Credit Lyonnaise and the Banco di Roma.[63] Through these consortia, the banks could draw on greater resources and contacts outside the F.R.G. to finance new investments. In addition to their use of representative offices and their participation in consortia, the Grossbanken operated through affiliates in developing countries. Unlike the U.S. banks, they generally did not acquire major shareholdings in British or French banks. Rather, they forged links to locally based banks. In Africa, the Grossbanken became affiliated with or represented by banks in ten countries, mostly in west and north Africa. Their shareholdings in these banks ranged from 0.4 to 18 percent. In South Africa, they opened their own offices or joined consortia to represent them. They appeared to rely on their superior international contacts to expand their influence.

Japanese post-war reconstruction followed a pattern remarkably similar to that of the Federal Republic of Germany. Some observers maintain that, after World War II, "Japan was transformed into a huge captive market for United States exports."[64] In the late '40s, the U.S. supplied two thirds of Japanese imports, but bought only a quarter of Japanese exports.[65]

U.S. companies nevertheless failed for several reasons to penetrate Japanese industry even to the extent that they did on the F.R.G. in the two decades after World War II. First, the successful revolution in China convinced the U.S. government of the need to help Japanese industrialists rebuild their own industry and "develop markets . . .in South East Asia in order to counteract Communist trade efforts."[66]

U.S. military ventures in Korea and Vietnam contributed to Japanese industrial growth by stimulating regional demand for both military and civilian goods. In the 1950s, U.S. military procurements in Japan averaged $600 million a year. As late as 1958-59, the foreign exchange Japan earned in this way covered 14 percent of Japanese imports. The escalation of the Vietnam war provided an even larger market for expanding Japanese productive capacity. In 1966-67, U.S. military contracts with Japanese firms totalled $505 million, and "war-related contracts" accounted for an even larger $1.2 billion.[67]

The Japanese government had initially introduced rigorous mechanisms to protect Japanese industry against foreign penetration. After the Second World War, all foreign capital investment was subject to prior authorization by the Foreign Investment Council. Among the main criteria for this authorization were considerations as to "whether the applied case would contribute to increasing Japan's foreign exchange holding and whether it would expedite industrial development and the economic self-reliance of Japan."[68] The Japanese government primarily aimed at "introducing foreign technology and drawing foreign investments as development funds into Japanese industry.[69] This protective policy severely restricted U.S. investment in Japan. After 1967, under considerable U.S. pressure the Japanese government gradually eliminated restrictions on the entry of foreign capital. By 1975, all the remaining limits had been removed.[70] By then, however, Japanese industrialists, their domestic holdings greatly strengthened and highly concentrated, did not have to worry about U.S. domination except in a few sectors. U.S. transnational corporate holdings in Japan in 1975 totalled only $3.3 billion, 2.5 percent of total U.S. foreign investment, compared to nearly $50 billion in Europe.

Companies with important foreign participation (over 20 percent)—mainly from the U.S.—provided less than 6 percent of the total Japanese market sales in all except four industries: pharmaceuticals (where the market share was 8.2 percent); petroleum products (56.1 percent); rubber products (16.8 percent); and general and transport machinery (6.4 percent). Only one foreign-owned company, the Japanese affiliate of the U.S. computer firm IBM, dominated the domestic market.[72] Even more than in the F.R.G., U.S. firms dominated what foreign investment there was in Japan. In the 1970s, U.S. companies held about four-fifths of it directly or indirectly. Foreign investment was also highly concentrated. In 1973, the 15 largest affiliates of foreign companies accounted for over half the turnover and profits of all companies in Japan in which there was any foreign participation.[73]

By the end of the 1960s, the Japanese economy once again had become essentially divided among a handful of huge Japanese owned industrial financial groups:

> Each industrial group constitutes a colossal pyramid whose apex consists of a handful of leading companies. The foundation consists of thousands of small subcontracting firms. The influence of such pyramids reaches every corner of Japan.[74]

These oligopolistic groups had been outlawed under U.S. pressure immediately after World War II, largely because of their role in Japan's imperialist ventures. The laws were soon changed, however, and by the early '60s the groups had re-emerged.[75]

Mitsubishi, one of the three largest, was typical. Its member companies engaged in finance, brewing, rayon, paper, chemicals, petrochemicals and plastics, glass, mining and cement, aluminum and steel, electrical equipment, transport equipment, and real estate, among other endeavors.[76] In 1970, Mitsubishi member companies accounted for almost 6 percent of the nominal capital of all Japanese companies.[77]

Each group was associated with key financial institutions which played an important role in assisting them to accumulate and reinvest capital:

The 'catalyst' in the formation of industrial groups was loans from financial institutions, specifically city banks, to their affiliated companies from the 1950s to the first half of the 1960s.[78]

Thirty-one percent of the outstanding 1974 debt of the Sumitomo Group member companies, for instance, had been borrowed from associated financial institutions. The figures for Mitsubishi and Mitsui were 29 and 21 percent, respectively.[79] A Japanese financial journal declared, "most industrial companies are actually run by the banks from which they borrow."[80]

The auto industry exemplified Japanese industrial concentration. Two companies controlled about four-fifths of its output. The largest single company, Toyota, had been associated with the Sumitomo Group since 1970.[81] Each of the two companies had taken over several smaller firms in the 1960s. As in the F.R.G., the Japanese auto industry apparently became more and more polarized between entirely domestically-based oligopolies and only slightly smaller firms associated with foreign transnationals. The smaller auto companies sold shares to the big U.S. auto firms in order to compete with the larger Japanese firms. Chrysler bought 10 percent of Mitsubishi Motors, the relatively small auto affiliate of one of Japan's largest industrial groups. General Motors purchased 34 percent of Isuzu.

In the basic iron and steel industry, five big companies produced over nine-tenths of the pig iron, three-quarters of crude and rolled steel, and half of special steels. Only ten integrated companies produced steel "from pig iron to final products."[82] The sector was "often referred to as the citadel of monopoly capitalism" in Japan.[83]

The reasons advanced for Japanese industrial concentration included: (1) the Japanese companies' desire to avoid takeover by foreign capital; and (2) the need for "systematic organization of technology."[84] This last was particularly significant in view of the leading groups' deep involvement in the development of new industries like nuclear power and data services. Concentration enabled the domestic companies to take advantage of foreign participation to gain control over foreign technologies:

. . .Japanese enterprises generally sought joint-venture partnerships with foreign enterprises in an attempt to explore new industrial fields by capitalizing on superior foreign technology. This explains why direct foreign investment concentrated in the machinery, chemicals and petroleum fields.[85]

The Japanese government helped private domestic companies to adapt and control foreign technologies. Because of destruction during World War II, Japanese firms like those in the F.R.G., had to install the newest technologies. The Japanese government's licensing system prevented imports of technology which would not, in its view, contribute to Japan's industrial strength. The effect of this policy was reflected in the changing geographical distribution of the technological exports of Japan. In the first half of the 1950s, 89 percent of Japanese technological exports went to less developed Asian countries while only 7 percent was sold to North America. By 1961, the Asian share had dropped to 40 percent, while the North American share reached 21 percent.[86] Furthermore, between 1960 and 1974, the value of licensed exports of technology, as a proportion of the value of licensed technological imports, grew from 2 to 16 percent.[87]

Dependence on the United States as a source of technology was overwhelmingly important until the 1970s. About 70 percent of technological imports from 1949 to 1970 originated in the U.S.[88] By 1975, however, the U.S. share had dropped to 50 percent and was still falling, while the F.R.G. had risen to second place as a supplier of technology.[89]

The Japanese government provided essential support for the post-World War II recovery and expansion of the shipbuilding, steel, power, coal and chemicals industries. The government gave these industries, now among the top Japanese exporters, long-term, low interest loans and export financing.[90]

Close coordination of business, government and banks helped Japan to become one of the major industrial powers of the world. Its modern technology gave it an edge over its rivals on the international scene in several sectors. Japan's "big six" steel companies, for example, produced 80 percent of their output by the modern oxygen-blast system, compared to about 60 percent of the output of U.S. firms. Japanese industry boasted 10 of the 15 largest blast furnaces in the world.[91] Japan's steel companies moved further than any others in introducing computerized controls.[92] As a result, Japanese steel output per workhour rose 166 percent between 1964 and '75, while in the U.S. it rose only 17.5 percent. In the latter year, Japanese steel workers produced about 9.35 metric tons of finished steel per hundred workhours, compared to 8.13 metric tons in the U.S.[93]

By the 1970s, however, continued Japanese domestic economic expansion confronted several difficulties. Two were most important:

first, Japan's industry expanded and became increasingly dependent on imported raw materials. By the 1960s, it was importing wool, natural rubber, bauxite, phosphate rock and nickel; and over nine-tenths of its demand for crude petroleum, tin ore, sugar, and iron ore.[94] Between 1956 and 1975, the share of imports in total coal supply rose from 8 to 86 percent.[95] The share of imports in iron ore consumption rose from 73 percent in 1968 to 86 percent in 1975. Second, as its domestic market became relatively saturated, Japanese industry, like that of the F.R.G., became increasingly dependent on exports. This became particularly evident in the economic crisis of the 1970s. The growing dependence of Japanese manufacturing industries on expanding exports was typified by the steel and auto industries. The auto branch, especially, began to export rapidly when high oil prices cut domestic auto demand. In 1976, the Japanese auto companies exported about half of their production. In that year, while production rose 13 percent over 1975, exports rose 39 percent and domestic consumption dropped by 5 percent.[96] It was argued that "for Japan...steel exports are widely considered as a matter of corporate survival." The country exported 44 percent of its crude steel production in 1976.[97]

Low Japanese wages permitted Japanese firms to penetrate and compete effectively in overseas markets. Resulting high profits contributed to rapid accumulation and reinvestment in new technologies in expanding domestic industries. In 1964, labor costs in manufacturing averaged eighty five cents an hour in Japan, compared to $4.61 in the U.S. In 1976, the average U.S. wage had risen to $12.22 an hour, while the Japanese wage, although rising at a faster rate, had only reached $6.31 an hour.[98] Only after the prolonged devaluation of U.S. and Western European currencies, in the context of floating exchange rates in the late '70s, did the Japanese industrialists finally lose this comparative advantage.

Japanese transnationals began to expand their foreign investment in the 1970s to secure their hold on vitally needed sources of raw materials, as well as markets for their expanding domestic manufactured goods. Their overseas investments more than doubled from less than seven billion dollars in 1971[99] to almost sixteen billion in 1976. The annual licensed capital outflow for investment averaged $45 million in 1951-61; rose to $904 million in 1970; doubled the following year; and continued to rise at a rate of over $2 billion per year through the mid '70s.[100] In 1975, it reached $30 billion.[101]

Not only did Japanese foreign investment multiply in the 1970s, its direction and characteristics changed significantly in comparison with the earlier postwar period. Until the end of the '50s, the largest share of

Japanese foreign investments was in Southeast Asia (where U.S. investments were minimal).[102] By the early '70s, Japanese investments in Europe and the U.S. were growing more rapidly, although developing countries still accounted for well over half. Japanese investment in Africa grew to 2.5 percent of the total. Japanese firms were not allowed by their government to invest in South Africa, which probably limited the amount of Japanese direct investment on that continent, but they found other means of participating in the profitable South African economy. (see below, p. 84).

The structure of Japanese foreign investments in the early '70s reflects the basic reasons for Japanese expansion overseas. Like transnationals from other major capitalist countries, the Japanese invested primarily in mining, especially in developing countries, to ensure raw materials supplies; and in last stage manufacturing to secure markets. The two largest categories were fishing and mining (35 percent of all foreign investments) and manufacturing (26 percent). The concentration on mining is far more evident in developing countries like those in Africa. Over half of Japanese investment there was in mining alone. Only a little over a fifth was in manufacturing, mostly last stage assembly.[103]

Japanese transnationals, like their U.S. and F.R.G. counterparts, concentrated their manufacturing investments, for the most part, in the western developed countries and in a few regional centers in developing countries, notably in Taiwan, South Korea, Brazil and, indirectly, South Africa. Investment in manufacturing, in developing countries, aimed primarily to penetrate otherwise closed markets and to take advantage of cheap labor.

A survey by the Japanese Export Import Bank reported as the primary reasons for Japanese investment in foreign manufacturing: good prospects for local markets (32 percent); abundant labor (28 percent); and domestic industry promotion policy (16 percent).

Japan explicitly aimed to develop raw materials sources overseas. This was achieved by contracts and participation in equity, usually through minority shareholdings.[104] In 1951-69, 36 percent of all Japanese foreign investment was directed to such "resource development projects."[105] At first located primarily in Asia, since the late '60s these investments had spread throughout the developing world. Much of Japanese companies' resource development was carried on through joint projects with transnationals based in other countries, notably the United States, Britain and South Africa.

Table 2-3.
Japan's Overseas Dependency and Resources Development,* 1968 and 1975, for Iron Ore, Coal and Uranium.

	Iron Ore (000t)		Coal (000t)		Uranium (short tonnes)	
	1968	*1975*	*1968*	*1975*	*1968*	*1975*
Demand	77,000	164,000	45,000	87,000	—	4,000
Overseas Dependency	85%	90%	72%	86%	100%	100%
Developed imports as % total imports	10%	52%	11%	52%	—	—

Note: *In contrast to simple imports, which are carried on through pure foreign transactions, development imports are importation of resources developed abroad through Japan's direct or indirect participation in development.

Source: M. Saito, "Japan's Overseas Resource Development Policy," in *Japanese Economic Studies*, Summer, 1975.

The growing involvement of Japanese firms in overseas mining projects was reflected by their increased representation on the London Metal Exchange. Until 1973, brokers on the Exchange were all controlled by North American, European and South African companies. By the late '70s, Sumitomo had obtained representation through buying a 50 percent share in the aluminum division of AMAX; Mitsui purchased shares in Anglo-Chemicals, a member of the South African Anglo American Group; Mt. Isa entered into a joint venture with ASARCO, a U.S. firm; NISSO-IWAI, a Mitsubishi affiliate, and Metalgesellschaft controlled Metalgesellschaft Ltd.; Mitsubishi also acquired shares in Triland Trading; and Consolidated Gold Fields, a British firm with massive South African holdings, controlled Tenant Trading with Marubeni. [106]

Prohibited from investing directly in South Africa, Japanese companies negotiated long-term contracts to purchase raw materials, especially iron and coal, there. These contracts contributed critically to the economic viability of several major South African development projects.

Japanese auto companies made a significant share of Japanese manufacturing investments overseas. Auto firms controlled almost 8 percent of the foreign investment and loans of the top 50 Japanese companies in 1975. An important share of this investment was in assembly plants in developing countries. Toyota, in particular, advanced into Africa. [107] Smaller Japanese firms, unable to compete through trade alone, invested overseas in last-stage assembly plants to secure markets. In the mid-seventies, they had larger foreign holdings than the much larger companies, Toyota and Datsun-Nissan, although the latter each exported twice as much from their domestic plants.[108]

The flow of Japanese capital abroad, like that of the F.R.G., was largely controlled by a handful of firms. Five commercial houses controlled almost half—43 percent—of the foreign investments and loans of the 50 largest Japanese companies. These top groups were Mitsui, Mitsubishi, Marubeni, C. Itoh and Sumitomo.[109] The next largest investors were the auto companies, but their share in overseas investments was small compared to the holdings of these giants.

Japanese banks, like those of the F.R.G., extended their operations overseas alongside and contributed to the rapid growth of direct foreign investments by Japanese industrial corporations.[110] Starting in the early '70s Japanese banks also entered the international money market through minority participation in consortium banks, mostly formed with European partners. They established even fewer overseas branch networks than their F.R.G. counterparts. They operated almost solely as wholesale banks through their ties on the international money market.[111] They created jointly-owned merchant banks with European banks: Sumitomo Bank with the British-Swiss Bank, Credit Suisse-White Weld; Mitsui Bank with the British Hambros; and the Industrial Bank of Japan with the F.R.G. Deutsche Bank.[112] The Mitsubishi Bank became linked to the Orion Bank, a consortium bank controlled by the U.S. firm, Chase Manhattan. By 1975, Japanese banks held over 18 percent of the assets of the top 300 banks in the world.[113]

Heightened Competition:

The growth of F.R.G. and Japanese industry and overseas investments led transnational corporations from these countries into direct conflict with U.S.-based transnationals. The changing positions of F.R.G. and Japanese transnationals among the top 500 companies in the world illustrated their increasing importance. In 1965, U.S. based firms constituted nine of the ten largest transnationals in the world. By 1977, this figure had dropped to seven. While U.S. corporations still dominated the top 15 places, primarily accounted for by their leading role in the oil industry, most of the other companies in the top fifty were non-American. Between 1970 and 1976, the number of U.S. companies in the top hundred dropped from 59 to 40, largely replaced by Japanese and F.R.G. firms.[114]

In the field of international finance, likewise, the U.S. banks' share in assets of the top 300 banks dropped. The Japanese share, in contrast, had risen to 18 percent, and that of the F.R.G. to 11 percent. Combined, the transnational banks based in these three countries held over two thirds of the assets of the top 300. Only French-based banks, with seven percent of the assets, were nearly as important; and, as noted above, some of the larger French banks had become closely allied with those based in the U.S. [115]

Growing production in the core capitalist nations, and increasing competition in the most important sectors of industry, sharply reduced the U.S. share of world trade. By the early '70s, the U.S. share of manufactured exports had dropped to a fifth of the total. Japanese and F.R.G. shares, in contrast, were rising rapidly. From 1963 to 1971, the Japanese share rose over 40 percent to account for 10 percent of all manufactured goods exports in the latter year. [116]

By the late '70s, the growing pressure for government protection by U.S. industries, especially textiles, televisions, auto and steel[117], underscored their weakness on international markets. When world demand began to fall with the 1974-75 recession, U.S. companies could no longer compete effectively in these areas, even within America. While they complained most about Japanese competition, the F.R.G. had also begun to penetrate the U.S. home market.

Summary:

The accumulation and reinvestment of capital, aided by rapidly expanding state capitalist expenditures on research and development, revolutionized industrial technologies in the core capitalist countries. They multiplied the size of investments required for basic industrial plants, reduced the relative amounts of labor employed per dollar invested, and rapidly expanded industrial productivity. This process fostered intensified concentration among the leading industrial firms in the core nations, and stimulated closer links between them and the largest national banks to ensure adequate finance. At the same time, it spurred the largest industrial conglomerates to compete in a global search for essential minerals and outlets for sale of their growing surpluses of manufactured goods, including machinery and equipment.

But this process did not proceed evenly and harmoniously among the core capitalist nations. The home industries of British and French firms had tended to stagnate. Over the years, they had invested much of their accumulated capital in the export sectors of their colonial holdings instead of renovating their outmoded domestic industries. U.S. transnationals invested the vast sums accumulated in World War II to buy up European industry, especially in England, gaining an entering wedge into their profitable African business. U.S. transnationals also bought into firms in the Federal Republic of Germany and Japan. The largest of these European rivals, however, collaborate closely with their national governments and the biggest national financial institutions, to stem the U.S. invasion while taking advantage of the U.S. invaders' technological contributions. By the 1970s, the F.R.G. and Japanese firms had gradually begun to squeeze the U.S. companies out. At the same time, their own accumulation and reinvestment of capital impelled their most powerful transnationals to scour the world for reliable sources of essential raw materials and markets in which to sell their burgeoning industrial output.

All these contradictory trends contributed to heightening the competitive effort of transnational corporations to penetrate more deeply into the Third World, especially Africa.

References

1. A. Nikolayev, *R&D in Social Reproduction* (Moscow: Progess Publishers, 1975, translated by Y. Shirokov) table 7, p. 144.

2. K. Pavitt, " 'International' Technology and the U.S. Economy: Is There a Problem?" *National Science Foundation, the Effects of International Technology Transfers of the U.S. Economy* (Washington, D. C.: July, 1974) p. 66.

3. *Ibid.*

4. *Ibid.*, p. 70. See also Y.S. Hsu, *The Impact of U.S. Investment in Europe* (New York: Praeger, 1973) p. 73ff.

5. Nikolayev, *R&D in Social Reproduction, op. cit.* p. 198.

6. D. Mezger, *Das Beispiel Kupfer* (Bremen: Bremer Afrika Archiv, 1977).

7. *Business Week*, Nov. 9, 1974; *Financial Times* (London), Mar. 4, 1977, p. 15ff.

8. See among others N. Girvan, "Economic Nationalists v. MNCs: Revolutionary or Evolutionary Change?" in C. Widstrand, *Multinational Firms in Africa* (Uppsala: Nordiska Afrikainstitutet, 1975).

9. P. A. Wellons, *Borrowing by Developing Countries on the Eurocurrency Market* (Paris: OECD, 1977), p. 61.

10. M. Odjagov, *United States Transnational Banking*, Report to the OECD, mimeo draft, Jan. 1977 (Paris).

11. *Ibid.*, p. 7-8.

12. Eg. *Business Week*, Oct. 24, 1977, p. 72ff.

13. Eg. *The New York Times*, May 23, 1977.

14. See R. Heller and N. Willat, *The European Revenge* (London: Barrie and Jenkins Ltd., 1975.) pp. 176-77. They assert:

The trouble is that (the chemical companies) have now become prisoners of their own strategies—forced to achieve high percentage utilization of huge plants if they are to attain profitability, yet equally forced for much of the time to accept ruinously low prices to keep that utilization high.

15. See, eg, R. Williams, *European Technology: The Politics of Collaboration* (New York: John Wiley & Sons, 1973) for discussion of the "technology gap;" and E.J.

Hobsbawm, *Industry and Empire* (Harmondsworth: Penguin Books, 1968) on the general decline of British industry in the interwar period. He writes that even by the early years of the century (p. 192)

Britain . . .was becoming a parasitic rather than a competitive economy, living off the remains of world monopoly, the underdeveloped world, the past accumulations of wealth and the advance of her rivals.

16. Hobsbawm, *Industry and Empire, op. cit.* p. 250 ff.

17. Rio Tinto Zinc, *Annual Report*, 1974.

18. See, eg., Government of Canada, *Foreign Direct Investment in Canada*, (Ottawa, Government of Canada, 1972); *Businessweek*, May 16, 1977, p. 59ff; and numerous others.

19. U.S. Department of Commerce, *Survey of Current Business, op. cit.*, Aug. 1961 and Oct., 1971.

20. Eg. J. J. Servan-Schreiber, *Le Defi Americaine*; and K. Blauhorn, *Ausverkauf in Germany?* (Munich: Moderne Verlag, 1967).

21. Re Lancia and VW, see Commision des Communaute Europeenne. *Les indices de concentration et leur application concrete au secteur de l'automobile dans las Communaute* in Collection Etudes, Series Concurrence, 1971, No. 17 (Brussels). Re Saab & Volvo, May 23, 1977, pp. 43-6.

22. *The New York Times*, June 5, 1977.

23. *Ibid.*

24. See A. and N. Seidman, *South Africa and U.S. Multinational Corporations* (Westport: Lawrence Hill and Dar es Salaam: Tanzania Publishing House, 1976).

25. Odjagev, *United States Transnational Banking, op. cit.*, p. 22.

26. Wellons, *Borrowing by Developing Countries on the Eurocurrency Market*, p. 58.

27. T. Hanley, U.S. Multinational Banking: Current and Prospective Strategies (New York: Salomon Bros., 1976).

28. Citibank, *Annual Report*, 1978.

29. The Economist Intelligence Unit, *The Growth and Spread of MNCs*, Quarterly Economic Report Special #5, New & Revised edition (London: 1971) pp. 58-9.

30. U.S. Department of Commerce, *Survey of Current Business, op cit.*, Oct., 1971.

31. For other examples, see Heller and Willat, *The European Revenge, op. cit.*: The Monopolies Commission (United Kingdom), *Metal Containers, A Report on the Supply of Metal Containers*, presented to Parliament in pursuance of Section 9, Monopolies and Restrictive Practices Act, 1948 (London: Her Majesties Stationery Office, 1970).

32. *Wall Street Journal*, April 25, 1975; May 7, 1975; June 19, 1975; July 15, 1975; July 25, 1975.

33. A. Seidman and N. Makgetia, *Transnational Corporations in South Africa* (New York, United Nations Center Against Apartheid, Notes and Documents, May, 1978) p. 27.

34. Odjagev, *United States Transnational Banking, op cit.* p. 31, Table 12.

35. Citicorp, *Annual Report*, 1977 (New York).

36. Mezger, *Das Beispiel Kupfer, op. cit.*, p. 154.

37. Department of Commerce, *Survey of Current Business, op. cit.* Sept. 1970.

38. *Ibid.*, Aug. 1961, and Oct. 1971.

39. K. Blauhorn, *Ausverkauf in Germany?* (Munich: Moderne Verlag, 1967).

40. F. Vogl, *German Business after the Economic Miracle* (New York: John Wiley & Sons, 1973) re the heirs of I. G. Farben; *Wer Gehört zu Wem*, Commerzbank, 1977 (Köln;

Commerzbank, 1977) re Volkswagen, AEG-Telefunken and other companies' ties to U.S. firms' foreign interests.

41. Deutsche Bundesbank, Monatsberichte, Nov. 1966, Jan. 1972, and Nov. 1974.

42. Capital (Köln) Aug. 78, No. 8.

42a. Vogl, German Business After the Economic Miracle, op. cit., p. 32.

43. U. Immenga, Participation by Banks in Other Sectors of the Economy (Brussels: Commission of the EEC, Series Concurrence, 1975) (translation by NSM).

44. Ibid. p. 35.

45. Commerzbank, Wer Gehört zu Wem, op. cit.

46. Centre europeen de l'entreprise publique, Les enterprises publiques dans le CEE (Paris: Dunod, 1967) pp. 286 ff.

47. Financial Mail (London), April 22, 1977.

48. Ibid.

49. Vogl, op. cit., pp. 114-5.

50. Information on shareholdings from Wer Gehört zu Wem, op. cit.

51. See among others, S. Rose, "The Misguided Furor about Investments from Abroad," in Fortune, May, 1975.

52. Vogl, op. cit. p. 110.

53. Holthus, Die deutschen Multinationalen Unternehmen (Frankfurt/Main: Athenäum Verlag, 1974) p. 7. (trans. by NSM)

54. Ibid., p. 11

55. Business Week, December, 1977.

56. Holthus, op. cit., p. 11.

57. Ibid. pp. 10-11; E. E. Keefe et al., Area Handbook for the F.R.G. (Washington, D.C. Government Printing Office, 1975) pp. 318-9.

58. Quoted in Frankfurter Algemeine Zeitung, "Blick durch die Wirtschaft," Oct. 26, 1974; (trans. by NSM)

59. Holthus, op. cit., pp. 17-19.

60. Ibid., pp. 73-4, 34.

61. See their annual reports, 1977.

62. Capital (Köln) Aug. 1978, No. 8.

63. See their annual reports, 1977.

64. J. Halliday, and G. McCormack, Japanese Imperialism Today (Hammondsworth: Penguin Books, 1973) p. 3.

65. Ibid.

66. C. Yanaga, Big Business in Japanese Politics (New Haven: Yale University, 1968) p. 266.

67. Halliday and McCormack, op. cit. pp. 107-8.

68. S. Sekiguchi, and K. Matsuba, "Direct Foreign Investment in Japan," in Japanese Economic Studies, Fall 1975 (IV.1), trans. by Hirokatsu Ogasawara. p. 15.

69. Ibid.

70. Mitsubishi Bank, Annual Report, April 1975-March 1976 (Tokyo).

71. Survey of Current Business, op. cit., Sept. 1975.

72. Sekiguchi and Matsuba, op. cit. p. 78.

73. Ibid.

74. The Oriental Economist, May 1975, pp. 6-8.

75. Ibid., p. 7.

76. Ibid.

77. Halliday and McCormack, op. cit. p. 110.

78. The Oriental Economist, May 1975.

79. Ibid.

80. *South African Financial Mail*, Japan Survey, Nov. 12, 1976.
81. *The Oriental Economist*, May 1975.
82. K. Kawahito, *The Japanese Steel Industry* (New York: Praeger, 1972) p. 56.
83. K. Imai, "Iron and Steel: Industrial Organization," trans. by Ogasawara, H., in *Japanese Economic Studies*, Winter 74/75 (III.2) p. 5.
84. *The Oriental Economist*, May 1975 pp. 7-8.
85. Sekiguchi and Matsuba, *op. cit.*, p. 69.
86. T. Ozawa, *Japan's Technological Challenge to the West, 1950-'74: Motivation and Accomplishment* (Cambridge: MIT Press, 1974).
87. Bank of Japan, Statistics Dept. *Economics Statistics Annual*, 1975.
88. Sekiguchi and Matsuba, *op. cit.*
89. *The Oriental Economist*, November 1975, pp. 16-7.
90. *The New York Times*, Nov. 23, 1977.
91. *Ibid.*
92. See for instance, Mitsubishi Heavy Industries, *Annual Report for the Fiscal Year ended 31 March 1976*.
93. *The New York Times*, 23 Nov. 1977.
94. Halliday and McCormack, *op. cit.* p. 17.
95. Kawahito, *op. cit.* p. 80.
96. *The Oriental Economist*, 3 Feb. 1977.
97. *The New York Times*, 23 Nov. 1977.
98. *Ibid.*
99. K. Yanaihara, "Japanese Overseas Enterprises in Developing Countries under Indigenization Policy—The African Case," trans. by T. W. Cleaver, in *Japan Economic Studies*, Fall, 1975 (IV.1).
100. Bank of Japan, Statistics Department, *Economic Statistics Annual*, 1975.
101. *The Oriental Economist*, Nov. 1976.
102. Halliday and McCormack, *op. cit.*, p. 31ff.
103. Yanaihara, *op. cit.*
104. See Kawahito, *op. cit.* pp. 76-80; M. Saito, "Japan's Overseas Resource Development Policy," trans by J. Uramatsu Smith, in *Japanese Economic Studies*, Summer 1975 (III.4).
105. Saito, *op. cit.*, pp. 39-49.
106. Mezger, *op. cit.*, p. 94.
107. *The Oriental Economist*, Nov. 1976, p. 3.
108. Compare *The Oriental Economist*, Nov. 1976, p. 3 re overseas investments with the same magazine, Feb. 1977, p. 3 re auto production for domestic consumption and export.
109. *The Oriental Economist*, Nov. 1976, p. 3.
110. *Ibid.*, pp. 6-7; see also Odjagev, *op. cit.*
111. See annual reports of the banks.
112. *The Oriental Economist*, Nov. 1976, p. 3.
113. Odjagev, *op. cit.*
114. J. E. Roemer, *U.S.-Japanese Competition in International Markets*, Institute of International Studies, Research Series, No. 22 (Berkeley: University of California, 1975) p. 1.
115. *South African Financial Mail*, April 22, 1976; *Fortune*, Aug. 1977.
116. Roemer, *op. cit.* p. 7ff.
117. See for instance, *Business Week*, May 16, 1977 and *The New York Times*, Oct. 7, 1977.

Transnational Corporate
Business in Africa 3

Nearly 50 African states, encompassing a land area and population roughly twice as large as the United States, attained political independence in the 1960s and the early '70s. Simultaneously, transnational firms were entering into a vigorous competitive scramble to reinvest their accumulating capital in rich mineral deposits and sell their mounting surplus manufactured goods in these new countries.

The collapse of outright colonial rule had changed the rules of the game. The transnationals were quick to design new techniques to attain their old goals. [1] Newly independent states proclaimed a desire to alter the distorted inherited political economies. Transnationals cooperated in such a way that corporate penetration often blended with new bureaucratic policies and agencies to foster greater external dependence. The deepening general crisis in the 1970s aggravated the resulting growth of inequality within and among the new states, further impoverishing the masses of the continent's inhabitants.

African State Intervention:

The umbrella of colonial rule had protected British, French and, in limited areas, other European firms from competition. In their mother countries' "own" domain, oligopolistic companies had emerged, setting aside rich minerals and vast stretches of agricultural land to be exploited as they chose. Colonial armies brutally crushed African resistance.

Even after African states won nominal political independence, the networks established by colonial firms still dominated the commanding heights that linked their externally dependent economies into the capitalist commercial world. [2] In the case of the former British colonies, that network remained firmly anchored in South Africa. Even though the new states established their own central banks, branches of Barclays, Standard, and sometimes National Grindlays, constituted their major commercial banks, fundamentally determining the amount and direction of credit and money supplies. Big British based trading firms handled exports and imports and internal wholesale operations, deciding what goods to import at what prices, and where and when to sell them throughout the country. Big British mining companies, sometimes together with U.S. capital, controlled the output of the mines and marketed it overseas. In east, central and southern Africa, European settlers, mostly British or of British ancestry, owned spreading tracts of the best agricultural lands.

Upon attainment of political independence, many African governments introduced increasingly direct interventionist policies. Frequently, responding to the revolution of expectations of their peoples, they claimed to embark on the path to "African socialism." More often than not, this was mere rhetoric. Most of the newly installed African bureaucrats introduced thinly disguised state-capitalist measures. They made few significant changes in the inherited sets of institutions which chained their countries' export-oriented political economies to the world capitalist commercial system. If anything, they augmented their countries' dependence on transnational corporate and financial institutions.

Most of the new governments adopted an orthodox western development program: expand exports and encourage import substitution industries. This basic formula was frequently accompanied by proposals for "Africanization," which in practice meant: oust visible foreigners in middle level positions in trade and real estate and let a handful of wealthy Africans take over their places.

The success of African government policies to expand exports were, of necessity, influenced by the characteristics of the particular mineral or agricultural product to which colonialism had geared their economies. A few benefitted, but many were adversely affected by the technological revolution in the core industrial nations.

Most African governments aimed to augment the output of export crops in hopes of earning added foreign exchange to finance the import of machinery and equipment to spread development. Their efforts were accompanied by limited land reform designed to encourage African farmers—rather than European settlers—to acquire permanent land holdings as incentives.* The peasants, as well as those estates that remained, did double, sometimes even triple, the output of cash crops for export.

---

*The argument was developed in line with the new conventional wisdom: Africans, given an opportunity, would respond like any (capitalist) "economic man" to adequate incentives.[3]

But for most, the anticipated multiplier effect failed to materialize. Growing competition among the producing countries frequently pushed prices down as world supply exceeded demand. Those countries which sold produce for which the core nations' technological advances had produced synthetic substitutes particularly suffered. The value of Tanzania's sisal exports plummeted when nylon was discovered to produce stronger, more durable rope. Egypt, Sudan, Uganda and Tanzania confronted lagging cotton prices as rayon, polyester and nylon fabrics came into vogue.

Transnational marketing firms still bought shiploads of African agricultural produce for sale overseas. They augmented their profits by playing off one country against another to buy their crops at the lowest possible prices. When Ghana organized a cocoa holdup* to stem the precipitous decline of cocoa prices in the mid-'60s, the big cocoa companies turned to other, more amenable producers. When instant coffees permitted use of less expensive African varieties, the companies encouraged Africans to expand their output in competition with Latin American growers. When liberation struggles disrupted Asian tea production, the transnational tea buyers fostered African output.

African expansion of export crops had another negative consequence. Food output was neglected as peasants were encouraged to forgo subsistence farming to plant crops for sales on overseas markets. Government ministries provided new tools, equipment, fertilizers, marketing facilities, credit and extension education to encourage growing numbers of male farmers to shift to coffee, cotton, tobacco, tea. The women, who grew most of the subsistence food crops, received little or no support.[4] As a result, country after country became increasingly dependent on the import of foodstuffs, often processed by transnational agri-business concerns in their factories back home.

The technologies utilized on the big mines, however, were far too complex and expensive for individual African would-be capitalists to take over. African governments sought to intervene more directly; not infrequently they bought shares of ownership in the local subsidiaries of the transnational mining companies. The mining conglomerates became increasingly willing to sell such shares, even a majority of them, to the African goverments. A leading European investment analyst termed this kind of government role "attractive," pointing out that it would "ensure that managerial control lies with the foreign investors

---

*Under Ghanaian government leadership, most of the major cocoa producing countries agreed to withhold their cocoa from the market to obtain better prices in a ploy much like that more successfully utilized a few years later by the oil producing countries.

and at the same time satisfy many of the requirements of 'national interest.' " African governments shared both the financing and the risks. They often helped obtain essential funds to meet the heavy costs of infrastructure—roads, ports, bridges—needed to ship out crude minerals. Typically, they reduced taxes to make their acquisition of shares more palatable to the foreign partner. Sometimes, they even provided part of the initial capital, although for the most part they paid for their shares out of future profits so they received minimal returns until the shares were paid for. Local governments also typically ensured favorable conditions for their transnational corporate partners by enforcing labor "discipline" and low wages.

The new governments usually left the management of the mines in the hands of the foreign partner. An UNCTAD report explained,[5]

In joint ventures and license contracts, ownership or control may formally lie with the local entrepreneurs. However . . . the technology suppliers may specify conditions that are so restrictive as to assure their virtual control over the enterprise and thereby individually influence the country's economy and social structure.

Technological changes in the core industrial nations influenced the consequences of the growing trend for government participation in mineral projects. Those countries producing valuable exports for which technological developments created new and rapidly expanding demand—like oil, uranium, and bauxite—had, at least temporarily, lucked out. They could take advantage of the growing competition between transnational corporations to raise prices, while expanding output to meet the growing demand in the new markets created. The per capita incomes of Nigeria, Libya and Algeria multiplied with the discovery and development of new oil reserves, especially after OPEC raised prices. The ensuing worldwide search for cheaper energy substitutes might eventually be expected to produce viable alternatives, but in the short run, these countries enjoyed unprecedented prosperity.

On the other hand, countries like Zambia and Zaire, whose mines produced copper, were less fortunate.[6] Copper had been Africa's largest single export, bringing considerable wealth to those countries in the '50s and '60s. Zambia enjoyed the highest per capita income in independent sub-Saharan Africa during the early post-independence years. In the late '60s, Zaire's government took-over 100 percent of the shares of its big mines. Zambia took-over 51 percent. Both governments accepted reduced tax revenues and current incomes in an effort to stimulate greater future output and foreign exchange earnings.

But the transnationals invested the capital they received in "compensation" from the African governments to develop new mineral deposits elsewhere. Anglo American Corporation and American Metal Climax, which sold 51 percent of their big mines to the Zambian government, for example, invested in expanding copper output in Botswana and Namibia.

The African governments had reckoned without the realities of the capitalist world market. U.S. and European fabricating firms introduced new technologies, enabling them to recycle copper to meet 40 percent of their demand. Aluminum and plastics provided cheaper substitutes for a variety of uses. By the mid-'70s, the world price for copper had fallen, in real terms, to an all time low. Both Zambia and Zaire had to borrow heavily from international financiers simply to cover the import of necessities while cutting back on projects to which they were already committed. Zaire borrowed hundreds of millions of dollars.[7] As copper prices plummeted and import costs rose, Zaire's corrupt, mismanaged economy faced bankruptcy in the late 1970s. Its transnational banking creditors cited this as a major reason why the International Monetary Fund should take action to "discipline" defaulting countries to ensure debt repayment to private lenders.

Throughout the '60s and '70s, whether they exported crops or minerals—almost without exception—the new African states sought to attract transnational firms to invest in their manufacturing industries, so long neglected under colonialism. They hoped for the increased production of goods and services and the employment opportunities which the construction of factories had brought to the industrialized countries of Europe and America. Almost every African government sought to create a hospitable investment climate to attract transnational corporate investment in the construction of import substitution industries. They financed the necessary infrastructure to encourage the transnationals to invest: water supplies, electricity, roads, port facilities. They introduced other measures to stimulate investments in industry: tax holidays, promises of low-cost labor, and even government purchases of shares in local factories.

The transnational manufacturing firms, embarking on fierce competition to sell their surplus output—including technologically advanced machinery and equipment as well as luxury and semi-luxury consumer goods—welcomed this opportunity to secure a foothold in the African markets by building last-stage assembly and processing plants behind tariff barriers erected by the new governments. This enabled them to sell capital-intensive machinery and equipment for the locally-built plants, and to continue to sell parts and materials to be assembled or finally processed for sale under a "made-in-Africa" label. The transfer of last-stage assembly plants to the new African countries was facilitated by the massive introduction of new technologies, including container ships and air freight, permitting fast, cheap and secure bulk shipping.

But for the most part, these new industries failed to initiate the desired industrial transformation. They typically[8] produced the wrong kinds of commodities—mainly luxury and semi-luxury items for those who could afford to buy them. Beer and cigarettes remained an important segment of local manufacturing industry. Expensive consumer durables—private automobiles, television sets, refrigerators and air conditioners—were imported as kits and assembled for sale to the small high income elite. The new industries tended to be relatively capital-intensive, based on the import of transnational corporate technologies, instead of focusing on providing jobs for growing numbers of urban unemployed. They continued to import parts and materials rather than contribute to development of domestic resources. Textile industries were built to process imported synthetic fabrics—instead of locally grown cotton—to produce high priced shirts and dresses that only the wealthiest ten percent of the population could buy. To top it all off, these new factories were typically located in and fostered the further growth of the inherited relatively modern export enclaves—contributing to the further underdevelopment and stagnation of the rural hinterlands.

The Drain Of Investable Surpluses:

The transnationals continued to siphon out a major share of the investable surpluses produced by the mines, the farms, and the factories of the new states. They drained off large amounts directly in the form of profits, interest, and dividends. Official U.S. data showed[9] that over the decade of 1965 to 1975, with the exception of 1968, U.S. firms—despite their relatively recent entry—shipped more capital out in a direct form every year from independent African countries than they invested there. In those years, U.S. corporations, alone, sent home $601 million, 25 percent more than they had invested. They drained out untold millions more through unreported profits of their affiliates based in other core industrial nations. In a growing number of cases, transnational firms disguised their acquisition of investable surpluses as managerial and licensing fees, or compensation paid by African governments for purchases of shares in the business.

Increasingly, the transnationals found new, indirect means of draining away a major share of the investable surpluses produced in Africa.

The primary one was through manipulation of the terms of trade. Their control of world markets enabled them to hold down prices paid to African countries for their crude exports. Oil, in the 1970s, became the most notable exception. The transnationals realized their profits when they charged high prices for the products fabricated from crude materials purchased from African countries at low prices. They also raised prices of equipment and parts sold to African states for further processing in locally-based plants, concealing the further outflow of profits and thus avoiding payment of taxes on them.

Through their control of the banking and financial sectors of most African countries, transnational banks influenced domestic credit and monetary policies to maximize their own global profits. Government ownership of some shares and/or participation by members of the local business community or government on the boards of directors of local branches did not really halt the parent firms from making the controlling decisions.

Over the years, the newly independent governments, faced with growing balance of payments deficits, found themselves increasingly saddled with foreign debts. Transnational banks played a key role as coordinators of industrial development and credits for the new states. As the governments exhausted their traditional sources of credit, they turned to the Eurodollar market for funds.[10] Those able to borrow the most, however, were not the "low income" but the middle and high income countries with visible resources which the international bankers assumed could be exploited to ensure repayment.[11] Global transnational financial institutions alternatively competed and collaborated to acquire this new business—and the debts of the African countries mounted, a new burden to be paid off by more urgent efforts to augment output and sell more raw materials abroad.

Growing Impoverishment: The "Have-Have Not" Gap:

In most African states, government intervention, far from initiating a process of transformation to build balanced integrated political economies, fostered the burgeoning of what in Africa became known as the "bureaucratic bourgeoisie."[12] Under the slogan of Africanization, parastatal managers, key government administrators and politicians frequently invested their legally-obtained high salaries (not infrequently along with not-so-legally-obtained additions[13]) and funds borrowed from the banks to buy up large farms, speculative real estate, and, in some cases, shares in local subsidiaries of transnational corporations. They exercised their influence at national and local levels to direct state actions to foster their private enterpreneurial activities. So-called "nationalization" programs, like that of Nigeria, requiring foreign firms to permit nationals to buy major shares of their local subsidiaries, accelerated the entrenchment of these emergent local capitalists in the "private" sector in close liason with the still dominant transnationals.

Widespread rhetoric focused on an alleged growing urban-rural gap, typically aimed at holding down the wages of lowpaid urban workers. Few governments seriously sought to capture and direct investable surpluses to a planned restructuring of productive sectors to spread employment opportunities throughout the countryside. Rather, they aimed primarily to ensure the continued profitability of factories, mines and estates in which the "bureaucratic bourgeoisie" had acquired personal stakes.

Despite innumerable government proclamations on the crucial importance of "rural development," extensive areas outside the inherited export enclaves continued to stagnate. Institutions handling marketing, credit and farm inputs typically remained directed to supporting export-oriented agricultural production.[14] Often large estates or "progressive"* African farmers controlled them, administering them primarily to cater to their own interests.

Women, in particular, tended to be excluded from so-called modern sector jobs.[15] Inherited stereotypical attitudes and institutionalized practices commonly relegated them to produce foodstuffs for their families, often using outmoded traditional techniques on less fertile land than that of the large estates.[16] Food output failed to expand rapidly enough to keep pace with growing populations. Nation after nation was forced to import growing amounts of processed foods for those who could afford to buy them. The drought of the early '70s, with its associated widespread famine, sharply exposed the insufficiency of local food production. Increasing numbers of African states had to spend precious foreign exchange to buy grain on the world market to avoid mass starvation.

Class stratification steadily deepened in expanding export crop regions. A few farmers became rich, while more and more peasants were squeezed out, forced to migrate to cities in search of cash employment. Tens of thousands of rural poor crowded into illegal urban squatter

*The term used in Africa, initially by colonial authorities, to refer to wealthier African capitalist farmers engaged in production of export crops.

compounds.* These settlements, without water, electricity, or schools, contrasted sharply with the modern glass-and-steel office buildings etched against new urban sky-lines. Urban populations mushroomed with a growth of 10 to 15 percent annually.

The Growing Crisis:

Africa, along with the rest of the western world, was deeply affected by the international monetary and economic crises of the 1970s. The re-emergence of the general crisis was, in fact, partly rooted in the post-World War II transnational corporate penetration of the newly-independent countries of Africa, as well as the rest of the Third World. Their continued drain of profits, interest, dividends, compensation and high salaries for their managerial personnel, together with their indirect drain of surpluses through manipulation of terms of trade, further narrowed potential African markets for their growing surpluses of in-creasingly sophisticated manufactured goods. Throughout the '50s and increasingly in the '60s, in a pattern reminiscent of the 1920s, mount-ing balance of payments deficits required country after country in Africa, as well as elsewhere in the Third World, to seek to reduce their imports and further expand their exports.[17] Many African states were forced to borrow funds, expanding their internal and external debt. In the late '60s and '70s, pressed by International Monetary Fund advisors and prodded by transnational banks, many introduced "austerity" pro-grams and devalued their currencies. They raised taxes, especially those on middle and lower income groups. They reduced government expenditures on social welfare and economic infrastructure, except those designed to attract further transnational corporate investments. Monetary and fiscal measures tended to squeeze credit and cause unemployment, especially among smaller, locally-owned firms. De-valuation led to higher prices for imported goods on which their econo-mies had become increasingly dependent. This tended to aggravate inflationary pressures.

All these policies, combined, tended to shift.the burden of the crisis onto the shoulders of wage earners, cash crop peasants and small domestic businesses, slashing the real incomes of lower income groups, squeezing out more labor intensive enterprises, and aggravating grow-ing under- and unemployment.

---

*"Illegal" in that their inhabitants built their shacks on available land in accord with African customary law, instead of buying it as western imposed laws required.

Pursuing a variety of essentially state capitalist policies, most of the newly-independent African countries, by the 1970s, had become increasingly externally dependent, their fragile economies ever more characterized by instability and a growing gap between the "haves" and "have nots."[18] In many, the attempt to maintain a democratic facade gave way to military coups in a pattern all too reminiscent of the earlier Latin American experience.

Summary and Conclusions:

Transnational finance capital, pressured by the contradictory internal features of home economies, initiated a renewed aggressive competition to penetrate the vast African continent after World War II. The search was for new sources of raw materials and markets for mounting surpluses of technologically sophisticated manufactured goods. Many of the new independent African governments, seeking to attract foreign capital to build their neglected manufacturing sectors, spurred exports and further exacerbated their external dependence and the outflow of investable surpluses. Their efforts to increase bureaucratic participation in mining and manufacturing industries only marginally altered transnational corporate domination of the commanding heights of their inherited lopsided economies. As their balance of payments deficits mounted, they borrowed heavily on international capital markets. They adopted International Monetary Fund and transnational bankers' advice to pursue austerity policies which further impoverished the majority of their low income citizens. Unable to retain the facade of western democracy as opposition, spurred by unemployment and impoverishment, spread, increasing numbers succumbed to military rule.

References,

1. A. Seidman, "Old Motives, New Methods: Foreign Enterprise in Africa Today," *African Perspectives*, R. W. Johnson and C. H. Allen, eds., (Cambridge: University Press, 1970).

2. The material in this chapter, unless otherwise cited, is substantiated in A. Seidman, *Planning for Development in Sub-Saharan Africa* (New York: Praeger, and Dar es Salaam: Tanzania Publishing House, 1974).

3. Eg. W. O. Jones. "Economic Man in Africa," *Food Research Institute Studies*, (Stanford) May, 1960.

4. See E. Boserup, *Women's Role in Economic Development* (New York: St. Martin's Press, 1970); also N. J. Hafkind and E. G. Bays, eds., *Women in Africa: Studies in Social and Economic Change* (California: Stanford University Press, 1976). R. Maboza, in her

MA thesis examined the reasons for the exclusions of women even in a country claiming to assist rural development and women, based on her field study in Zamiba (International Development Program, Clark University, 1979).

5. UNCTAD, Trade and Development Board, Intergovernmental Group on the Transfer of Technology, TD/AC 11/10, Jan. 1973, p. 24.

6. The difficulties confronting countries seeking to reduce their dependence on copper exports are examined in a series of studies presented in A. Seidman, ed., *Natural Resources and National Welfare: The Case of Copper* (New York: Praeger, 1976). This is the source of information re the copper industry in this chapter.

7. P. Wellons, *Borrowing by Developing Countries on the Euro-Currency Market* (Paris: Development Centre of the Organization for Economic Cooperation and Development, 1977).

8. Eg., see A. Seidman, "Import Substitution Industrialization: The Zambian Case," *Journal of Modern African Studies*, Vol. XIII, No. 4.

9. U.S. Department of Commerce, *Survey of Current Business*, annually reports on overseas investments.

10. Wellons, *Borrowing by Developing Countries*, *op. cit.*

11. M. Odjagov, *Transnational Banking* (Boston: draft paper prepared for Development Center of Organization for Economic Cooperation and Development, mimeo, 1977).

12. R. Sklar, in *Corporate Power in an African State: The Political Impact of Multinational Mining Companies* (Berkeley: University of California Press, 1975), characterized the new parastatal managers in Zambia's mining economy as a "managerial bourgeoisie"; but in more agricultural countries, government personnel played a direct role.

13. *New York Times*, April 19, 1977.

14. See Seidman, "Import Substitution Industrialization," *op. cit.*

15. A. Pala and A. Seidman, "A Proposed Model of Women in Development," paper presented to Wellesley Conference on Women and Development, June, 1976.

16. M. Lofchie, "Political and Economic Origins of African's Hunger," *Journal of Modern African Studies*, Vol. 13, 1975; and N. Ball, "Understanding the Causes of African Famine," *ibid.*, Vol. 14, 1976.

17. For data, see International Monetary Fund, Annual Reports: for general discussion, see Seidman, "Planning for Development," *op. cit*; and for details of copper case, see Seidman, ed., "Natural Resources and National Welfare: The Case of Copper," *op. cit.*

18. eg. A. Seidman, "The 'Have-Have Not' Gap in Zambia"; (Lusaka: University of Zambia) mimeo, 1974.

PART II
The Renewed
Scramble for Africa

Why South Africa   4

After World War II, transnational corporate finance capital focused its
expansion in Africa on, above all, South Africa. Firms from all the core
capitalist countries played a complex role in tranforming South Africa's
mineral-based economy into a modern, industrial, increasingly militarized state. The forms their penetration took varied, combining direct
investment, mobilization of international credits, provision of technology and managerial assistance. Their involvement escalated, at
least until the 1976 Soweto uprising and the economic downturn of the
mid-1970s. Three times as much foreign capital was invested in South
Africa in the first two decades after World War II as in the entire
pre-War era. The official South African Census of Foreign Transactions
Liabilities and Assets (see Table 4-1), the latest comprehensive survey
available, shows foreign investment totalled R9163 million in 1973—
more than three times the 1956 total of R2757 million, and almost
double the 1968 total of R4990 million.[1] In 1976, foreign investmen
constituted almost a fourth of all investment in the country.[2]

Transnational corporate investment grew most rapidly in manufacturing and finance. By 1973, these two sectors accounted for, respectively, a third and a fourth of total foreign investment. Foreign holdings
in manufacturing had overshadowed those in mining even as early as the
mid-1960s. In 1973, mining made up barely a third of total foreign
investment, only slightly more than in trade. In addition to investing
disproportionate amounts in South African manufacturing industries,
the transnational corporations effectively reversed the sectoral pattern
of foreign investment previously apparent in South Africa and still
prevalent elsewhere on the continent.

The transnationals frequently invested in collaboration with South
African state, as well as private, capital. The Census reported most
"direct" foreign (i.e. foreign-controlled)* investment in the private sec-

*The Census defined direct investment as total investment by foreigners who retain a
"controlling interest in organizations in South Africa and investment in those organizations by persons in foreign countries;" and non-direct investment as all foreign liabilities
and assets not covered by the term "direct investment."

Table 4-1.

Foreign investment in the private sector in South Africa (including Namibia) as of December 31, 1973
(Million rands)

	Agriculture	Mining	Manufacturing	Utilities	Construction	Trade	Transport	Finance, insurance, real estate	Community, social personal services	Individuals and organizations not included elsewhere	Total
Direct Investment	42	420	2,458	1	61	798	109	1,489	5	68	5,451
EEC	25	256	1,590	1	48	477	75	1,173	1	39	3,685
Rest of Europe	2	6	213	—	11	68	—	51	1	5	357
North and South America	6	157	608	—	1	234	27	154	3	15	1,205
Non-direct investment	5	928	1,177	332	6	235	75	789	29	136	3,712
EEC	3	570	745	228	3	136	59	510	16	78	2,348
Rest of Europe	—	191	117	94	—	18	4	79	13	4	520
North and South America	—	112	154	10	1	33	3	90	—	13	416
Total investment	47	1,348	3,635	333	67	1,033	184	2,278	34	204	9,163
EEC	28	826	2,335	229	51	613	134	1,683	17	117	6,033
Rest of Europe	2	197	330	94	11	86	4	130	14	9	877
North and South America	6	269	762	10	2	267	30	244	3	28	1,621

Source: Republic of South Africa, *The Second Census of Foreign Transactions, Liabilities and Assets, 31 December 1973:* Supplement to the South African Reserve Bank *Quarterly Bulletin,* March 1976.

tor; but it used the term "private" for the state-controlled parastatal or state corporate sector, which spearheaded the country's industrialization.

Table 4-2A.
Role of Foreign Capital in Financing Gross in South Africa Domestic Investment 1968-1977

	Capital inflow from rest of world[1]	Gross Domestic investment[2]	Foreign capital as percent of gross domestic investment
1968	340		
1969	176		
1970	427	3,149	13.6
1971	438	3,695	11.9
1972	628	4,243	14.8
1973	214	4,850	5.4
1974	761	5,976	12.7
1975	746	7,868	22.2
1976	989	8,913	11.1
1977	278	8,994	3.1

Notes: [1]Long term capital inflow
[2]Total fixed investment

Source: South African reserve bank, *Quarterly Bulletin of Statistics*, Sept., 1978

Table 4-2B.
Role of state sector in fixed capital stock in South Africa (percentages)

Period	Public authorities	Public corporations	Private business enterprises	Total
1946-1960	40.3	4.5	55.2	100.0
1961-1970	43.3	5.8	50.9	100.0
1970	44.1	6.9	49.0	100.0
1971	44.4	7.1	48.5	100.0
1972	44.9	7.4	47.7	100.0
1973	44.9	8.1	47.0	100.0
1974	44.8	8.7	46.5	100.0
1975	44.8	9.6	45.6	100.0
1976	45.2	10.3	44.5	100.0
1977	45.4	11.1	43.5	100.0

Source: South African Reserve Bank, *Quarterly Bulletin of Statistics*. Sept. 1978

Transnational corporate involvement in South Africa, then, mushroomed during the very years when independent governments took power and began to compete for investment, particularly in industry. The reasons for this are complex. On the one hand, they relate to the specific,

racist features of South Africa's political economy, and the interventionist role of the state. On the other hand, they reflect the "bounded
rationality" of corporate managements.** In the context of the pressures
to expand internationally, the overwhelmingly white male corporate
managers of U.S. and European transnationals apparently concluded that
South Africa's (white) business leaders behaved rationally in terms they
understood.

This chapter will discuss these factors in more detail. First, it provides
a brief historical survey, to explain the peculiar characteristics of the
South African political economy that so attracted transnational corporations. It then reviews more closely the scope as well as the reasons for the
changing pattern of transnational corporate involvement in the decades
following World War II.

The remaining chapters of Part II examine in depth the transnational
corporations' contribution to South Africa's military-industrial growth in
the 1960s and '70s, and, briefly, its implications for independent Africa.

South Africa's Racist State Capitalism

Over the centuries following their first landing, white settlers employed military force and played one African group off against another to
impose their minority rule. A review of South African history shows that
they did not, however, institutionalize racism as an end in itself. Rather,
they adopted the ideology of black inferiority as a convenient rationale for
the systematic exercise of state power to coerce the African majority into
one of the lowest-paid labor forces in the world. Cheap labor ensured the
profitability of the diamond and gold mines. The accumulation and
reinvestment of these profits in partnership with foreign finance capital
led to the emergence by World War II of a handful of domestic, oligopolistic "mining finance houses." After the War, these collaborated with the
state and transnational corporations to build the leading industrial economy on the continent: a regional imperialist subcenter, apparently
capable of providing transnational investors with a disciplined, cheap
labor force, valuable raw materials, and entree to the markets of the
entire southern African region. That history has been thoroughly docu-
mented elsewhere.[4] This review seeks merely to portray the features that
apparently made South Africa the most attractive investment climate for
transnational finance capital on the continent in the post World War II
decades.

***

**Drawing on Cyert, March and Simon, Evans[3] points out that corporate managers'
decisions are rational "only within the cognitive boundaries created by the information
available to the decision-maker. What information is available depends on who makes
the decision and where it is made."

In the mid-19th Century, diamonds were discovered in South Africa's Transvaal. As in the gold rush that transformed the western United States, thousands of European and American adventurers poured in to seek their fortunes. At their urging, the colonial state barred Africans from owning diamonds, forcing them to participate in the industry solely as poorly paid workers.

With the discovery of gold a few years later, the settlers' demand for cheap (black) labor mushroomed. The South African gold veins ran deep and scattered in the earth, requiring masses of low-cost human labor as well as expensive equipment to turn a profit. Under the protective umbrella of British colonial rule, South African capital, accumulated from the diamond mines, combined with U.K., U.S. and German finance to monopolize the gold industry. Throughout the rest of Africa, mining investments were virtually all foreign-owned, at least through the 1960s. In South Africa, locally based mining finance houses retained (white) control of the mining industry from the start, despite the continued participation of international finance capital. (In fact, the forerunners of two big British imperial banks, Barclays and Standard, got their start from the accumulation of profits reaped by financing South African gold mining. [See below, pp. 95, 205-6]) Most overseas investors placed their capital indirectly, through the stock market or as loans; settler interests held onto essential control in close partnership with transnational finance capital.

The earlier European settlers in the Transvaal, the Afrikaners* were initially excluded from this alliance. Most were farmers. They viewed the expansion of mining interests controlled by English settlers as a threat to their own claim to African lands and labor. Moreover, the mining firms for the most part imported their tools and other inputs from English factories. The Afrikaners looked to the mines to stimulate development throughout the region, providing them with an additional source of income, but they did not want to be controlled by the British. At the turn of the Century, these conflicts led to the Boer War. The British won, and in 1910, English and Afrikaner provinces were united in the Union of South Africa.

Despite bitter internal differences, whites—English and Afrikaner —united closely and effectively against the black majority from an early date. The Africans had not merely suffered in silence, as their lands were conquered and they were forced to labor for the invaders.[5] For over 300 years, they fought back despite their lack of weapons comparable to

---

*The name Afrikaner was adopted by the descendants of Dutch settlers on the Cape, who sought to assert the validity of their claims, backed by military force, to African lands.

the Europeans', ending the armed struggle only in the early 20th Century. They continued to resist even then, seeking through non-violent means to achieve equal rights in their own land. Faced with the Africans' determined opposition to oppression, the British colonial government sought after the Boer War to heal the division among whites by the 1910 Act of Union. The Union's basic premise was that "civilizing" the Africans required them to work at wages below the poverty line, assuring the profits of the white-owned farms and mines.

A series of colonial regulations, in both Afrikaner- and British- ruled areas, had given settlers control over the land while using state power to force Africans to work for them. At the same time, the rapid growth of the labor force on the mines created new markets for the white-owned farms, enabling the larger white farm-owners to make more profits and expand their acreage. The 1913 Land Act restricted African land ownership to "reserves" comprising less than 13 percent of the young nation's entire land area. Africans became strangers in the land of their birth. Independent black farmers were labelled "squatters" and forced from lands their families had lived on and worked for generations. For many, the alternative to starvation was the acceptance of a low-paid job on a white farm. [6]

Simultaneously, the expansion of the larger farms squeezed less successful white farmers, mostly Afrikaners, off the land, pushing them into the cities. There, they formed a "poor white" population, unable to compete with the growing numbers of Africans who, despite racist restrictions, had obtained education and skills. But the poor whites retained political influence. They agitated for a stricter "Color Bar," to prevent blacks from filling better jobs.

Through most of this period, gold prices remained low. The mine companies showed a profit only by holding down their workers' wages. After World War I, they tried to reduce labor costs by promoting a few Africans, just a small minority of all African workers, to the skilled jobs which higher-paid white workers had historically reserved for themselves. In 1920, the black miners closed down the mines, calling for higher wages and an end to the Color Bar; the government crushed their strike brutally. Two years later, the white miners struck. [7] They proclaimed a workers' state, under the slogan, "for a White South Africa." They demanded the exclusion of blacks from all but the most unskilled jobs. The army smashed the strike, and some leaders were hung.

But the mining companies had learned their lesson. Next time, they feared, the whites might join the far larger number of African miners to establish a real workers' state and, once and for all, end the companies' extraction of profits. They restored the Color Bar throughout the mines, in a deliberate effort to win the support of the whites against the black miners.

At the next elections, the Afrikaner electorate rallied to vote the forerunner of the Nationalist Party into office. The new government systematized and institutionalized the Color Bar in all sectors: laws excluded blacks from skilled jobs; reserved certain government posts for whites; and prohibited blacks from supervising whites. Whites got new educational privileges. State and corporate policies aimed to separate white workers from black, so that the whites would defend the racist system designed to hold down black wages. The ideology of race had always formed part of the colonial legal order; now it was further reinforced, to underwrite the creation of a highly paid, white "aristocracy of labor."

The new government also planned to stimulate industrial growth to provide adequate employment and higher incomes for white workers. It created the Iron and Steel Corporation (ISCOR) and the Electricity Supply Commission (ESCOM), and offered an array of inducements to attract domestic and foreign capital into manufacturing.

Although state intervention did foster some manufacturing growth, mining and agriculture formed the backbone of the South African economy until after World War II. The Great Depression of the 1930s sharply revealed the country's external dependence. At the outset, it brought the economy to a halt, but currency devaluations in Europe and the U.S. soon raised the value of gold, attracting a new inflow of capital to the gold mines. During World War II, the South African government backed Britain, although many whites dissented. (The government detained a number of future leaders of the Nationalist Party for pro-Nazi allegiance, some for as extensive acts of sabotage.) The war furthered manufacturing growth by cutting imports of European manufactures.

By the time the Nationalists came to power in 1948, the basic racist pattern of development had been set. A profitable marriage between Afrikaner farmers, privileged white workers and the British mining entrepreneurs had long since been cemented. It ensured that white South Africans, whatever their antecedents, enjoyed living standards among the highest in the world. They might engage in internecine strife; but most were anxious to present a united front against black demands for freedom and equality.

Systematic institution of racist laws had coerced the African majority into a low-paid labor force. They denied Africans the right to own land except in scattered, overcrowded reserves. Africans could only earn a living, however inadequate, by migrating in search of jobs in the "white" urban areas, mines and farms. Often laws required their families to stay in the reserves. The Color Bar put into law the practices of white trade unions and employers, excluding African men from industry except as low-paid, unskilled workers. African women rarely found any place there: they were expected to grow foodstuffs in the reserves to supplement the grossly inadequate wages of their husbands, or work as domestic servants in white households. In 1950, over 70 percent of Africans living in the major industrial areas reportedly received incomes below the minimum estimated as essential simply to survive. Over 60 percent could not even afford to pay rent. [8]

After World War II, the people of Africa demanded political independence. But the Nationalist Party, elected to office by the white minority in 1948, asserted its determination that, in South Africa at least, white domination would remain supreme. There, the minority government pledged, transnational corporations and domestic investors need not fear expropriation or other efforts to re-orient the economy to meet the needs of the majority of the population.

The regime's policy was two-pronged. First, it reinforced the migrant labor system to ensure cheap African labor. In this context it introduced a range of direct incentives and sanctions to increase manufacturing investment. An expanded industrial sector would ensure higher living standards for white South Africans, increased military might to employ against black resistance, and reduced dependence on foreign interests.

To maintain a cheap labor force, the regime adopted apartheid, which extended and made more rigid the system of racial oppression established over the centuries of European settlement. Although it officially aimed at total segregation of Africans and whites, the lands allocated the African population were so infertile, underdeveloped and limited in size that black workers had no choice but to migrate to "white" areas, seeking any kind of job at subsistence wages or less. Even official commissions exposed the fact that the African lands could never support the entire African population. The fragmented, overcrowded reserves—renamed Bantustans or Bantu homelands (incorporating the incorrect and insulting Afrikaner term for Africans, "Bantu")—were never expected to be anything other than a vast labor reserve, from which unemployment and hunger would drive able-bodied men, and some women, to work as cheap contract labor for the white-owned farms, mines and factories.

The regime proceeded to systematically remove blacks from urban industrial centers, where their aspirations for liberty might trouble whites or scare off foreign investors. Many of the uprooted African families had lived in the cities for generations; now they were forced into "homelands" they had never before seen. The regime tried to break down African unity by forcing them back into "tribal" groups, although alienation of land and capitalist industrial development had long undermined the political-economic foundations of pre-colonialist society. A century of capitalist development had plunged Africans into the melting pot of proletarianization; the process could not be reversed. Yet new laws stripped Africans of even the mockery of citizenship previously permitted; they now enjoyed "citizenship rights" only in the "independent" Bantustans. If they could find a white employer, they might migrate to the prosperous "white" cities or estates. For those who remained behind—women, the unemployed, old men and children—life became a grinding round of poverty, hunger, and death: a slow, less visible form of violence, which has been compared to Hitler's genocidal program.

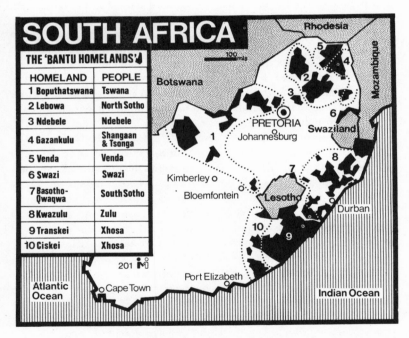

SOUTH AFRICA

THE 'BANTU HOMELANDS'

HOMELAND	PEOPLE
1 Boputhatswana	Tswana
2 Lebowa	North Sotho
3 Ndebele	Ndebele
4 Gazankulu	Shangaan & Tsonga
5 Venda	Venda
6 Swazi	Swazi
7 Basotho-Qwaqwa	South Sotho
8 Kwazulu	Zulu
9 Transkei	Xhosa
10 Ciskei	Xhosa

Enforcement of apartheid required that the population be categorized by racial group: African, Coloured, Asian, White. Legal differentiation and the pass system were rooted in the previous century, but after 1948 the white-minority regime broadened and rigidified them. "Experts" decided on border-line cases, even declaring in some instances that parents and children or brothers and sisters were of different race. Members of different groups could not marry or live together. The regime required Africans to carry passes signed by a white employer, certifying their right to live in a given urban area. If an African lacked a properly endorsed pass, at any time, for any reason, he or she was subject to criminal charges and, as a minimum, deportation to the starving homelands. Often fines or jail sentences were also imposed.

Africans had long been denied educational equality. A few, however, had achieved qualifications as doctors, lawyers and in other professions. The Nationalists now restricted all Africans to "Bantu Education," designed to provide only those rudiments of instruction—hours in class on gardening or housework, for instance—considered necessary for docile, skilled or semi-skilled workers. (In part, Bantu Education policies were based on the concepts developed in the latter 19th and early 20th Century for educating U.S. blacks.)

The state also introduced new measures to encourage investment in manufacturing. Neither domestic nor foreign private entrepreneurs would invest in basic manufacturing without extensive state support: short-term profits were highest in light industry based on imported parts and materials. The South African regime acted as an aggressive partner to the transnational corporations and mining finance houses anxious to expand their holdings in more basic industries.

State investment in South Africa was not new. Beginning in the colonial era, the government had subsidized the construction of ports and railroads, to enable the mine companies to ship minerals to their overseas customers. It set up the Land and Agricultural Bank in 1912 to assist white farmers, and helped them establish cooperatives, agricultural and processing firms. Government subsidies and agricultural regulatory boards ensured an expanding market for farm products at steady prices. These measures discriminated against Africans. They were designed to ensure the consolidation and growth of the largest white-owned farms to meet the demand created by the employment of hundreds of thousands of workers on the mines, as well as to supply the growing overseas markets of the British Empire. In the 1920s, the government established parastatals in the steel industry and electricity production, to provide jobs for whites and stimulate industry.

The Nationalist regime introduced typical state-capitalist planning procedures. It set targets for annual production increases in each sector. It emphasized the growth of basic industries, seeking to provide incentives as well as to pressure transnational corporations to extend their investments from last-stage assembly and processing plants to vertically integrated industries providing a wide range of basic industrial products. The regime broadened the parastatal structure, held through its overall holding company, the Industrial Corporation of South Africa. Each of the leading parastatal groups had its own complex of affiliates and subsidiaries, many of them part-owned by domestic and foreign private firms. Among the largest parastatals:

—ISCOR, the iron-and-steel corporation, produced almost three fourths of the steel consumed in South Africa in the 1970s. Transnationals and mining finance houses invested heavily in its largest subsidiaries, and transnationals provided it with the technologies needed to compete internationally.

—ESCOM, the electricity utility, undertook, with transnational corporate assistance, to construct a national grid of thermal and hydroelectric power plants, as well as the Koeberg nuclear plant.

—SASOL produced oil and petrochemical by-products from coal, using technology supplied by U.S. and F.R.G. transnationals (a project of particular importance as the regime faced an oil boycott and had no known natural oil reserves).

—The Industrial Development Corporation (IDC) was related to the colonial development companies established by the British throughout Africa, investing in diverse manufacturing industries.

—The South African Railways and Harbours Corporation (SAR&H) owned the most extensive rail network in Africa, and operated and modernized South Africa's port facilities.

—Sentrachem, in which the state owned a minority share, worked with transnational chemicals corporations to help establish a domestic chemicals industry.

Through this spreading parastatal empire, the South African regime multiplied its investments in manufacturing, to spur industrialization of the economy. It created the Council for Scientific and Industrial Research (CSIR) to develop and adapt technologies. By the early 1970s, the CSIR had an annual budget of $10 million and a staff of 600.[9]

In 1964, the government established a wholly-owned parastatal, Armscor, which contracted with hundreds of private and parastatal firms to produce parts and equipment for its growing military machine. It drew on the expanding national industrial base, built up with the eager participation of transnational finance capital, to achieve an increasingly self-reliant, capital-intensive capacity for production of military hardware.[10]

Growing Popular Resistance

The African majority never submitted docilely to the renewed onslaught of their rights. The African National Congress (ANC), a broad united-front group established in 1912, shorty after the founding of the Union of South Africa, had over the years organized African resistance to the exploitative political-economic system. Through the 1950s, it united wider and wider segments of the population—not only Africans, but also Coloureds, Asians and some whites—to struggle against apartheid. Mass demonstrations and strikes spread across the country.

The minority regime retaliated by imposing a series of oppressive laws, backed by growing police and military force. The Suppression of Communism and Terrorism Acts were catchalls, directed against any group which expressed opposition to increasingly stringent racist measures. When the courts did not find defendants guilty, new judges were appointed. Detention laws made possible the jailing of opponents for unlimited periods.

In 1961, Africans protesting the pass system were gunned down at the Sharpeville and Langa townships. Over 100 people were killed. The regime outlawed both the ANC and a group that had split from it, the Pan-Africanist Congress. Organizers were detained, tortured, sentenced under laws that made simply speaking out for change illegal; strikers were deported to the Bantustans or jailed; peaceful demonstrations were fired on. The people in the liberation movement realized that determined and wanton terrorism by the regime doomed continued non-violent efforts to promote change. They began to organize to fight for their rights through armed struggle.

At first, unused to clandestine operation, the newly established underground movement suffered tremendous setbacks. The regime raided a farm, Rivonia, and captured—almost accidentally—many important leaders of the ANC and allied organizations. They received long jail sentences, even life imprisonment (and for political prisoners in South Africa, there is no parole). Nonetheless, the ANC and its armed wing, Umkhonto we Sizwe ("Spear of the Nation") continued to mobilize the people for guerilla warfare, to struggle for full liberation.

African Poverty, Corporate Profits

In the context of this increasingly oppressive apartheid system, transnational corporations vied to expand their investments, especially in the strategic manufacturing industries. Several contradictory factors apparently persuaded the corporate managers to collaborate in a "triple alliance" with the South African parastatals and the mining finance houses.

First, the corporations' bottom line was profit; and profits in South Africa ranked among the highest in the world until the economy began to stagnate in the mid-1970s. U.S. manufacturing corporations with investments in South Africa, for example, reported[11] that they remitted home a share of profits equal to 16-18 percent of their invested capital annually from 1970 to 1974. They reinvested an additional share, ranging from 6 to 12 percent of their invested capital, to expand output in South Africa. Averaged and added together, the rate of profit may be estimated at 25 percent—far higher than the average reported for the rest of Africa.* U.S. firms in mining and smelting and oil refining reported profits in some years of over 40 percent. When the South African economy moved into crisis in the mid-'70s, manufacturing profit declined, and so did the rate of remittance to the U.S. Nonetheless, some manufacturing transnationals in strategic industries reported continuing high rates of return and augmented their investments. (See below, Ch. 7 for examples).

The high transnational corporate profits in South Africa resulted primarily from relatively low costs. First, black workers' wages were exceptionally low compared to those the transnationals paid in their home factories. (See Table 4-3) This was especially true in mining. Managers of some firms in relatively labor-intensive manufacturing industries—notably auto and electrical appliances—explicitly cited this factor to explain their expanding investments. The wages of manufacturing workers in South Africa rose in response to inflation and the strike wave of the early '70s. Yet they remained not only well below wages in the developed capitalist countries, but also, for the vast majority of black workers, below the bare minimum needed to support themselves and their families. Spokesmen for the regime argued that Africans' wages need only support the (male) workers themselves. Women and children, they claimed, could support themselves by farming back in the Bantustans. They ignored the fact that only about a third of all Africans actually lived in the Bantustans; of those who did, only about a tenth, at most, might hope to scrape a subsistence livelihood from the land.

---

*Manufacturing subsidiaries throughout the Third World often conceal profits by over invoicing (listing prices above world levels) for inputs bought from parent companies, particularly when taxes on reported profits are high. Real profits in Africa were probably significantly higher than reported.

Table 4-3.

	1970	1971	1972	Year 1973	1974	1975	1976
Whites							
Average Earnings (R)	3,244	3,572	3,797	4,180	4,767	5,377	5,867
Percentage Change(%)	—	10.1	6.3	10.1	14.0	12.8	9.1
Consumer Price Index	100.0	106.1	113.0	123.7	138.1	156.7	174.2
Real Earnings (R)	3,244	3,366	3,360	3,379	3,452	3,431	3,368
Percentage Change in Real Earnings (%)	—	3.8	(0.2)	0.6	2.1	(0.6)	(1.9)
Coloured							
Average Earnings (R)	931	1,061	1,156	1,325	1,497	1,727	1,895
Percentage Change (%)	—	14.1	8.9	14.6	13.0	15.4	9.7
Consumer Price Index	100.0	105.9	112.8	124.7	139.9	159.2	175.9
Real Earnings (R)	931	1,002	1,025	1,063	1,070	1,085	1,077
Percentage Change in Real Earnings (%)	—	7.7	2.2	3.7	0.7	1.4	(0.8)
Asiatics							
Average Earnings (R)	1,044	1,209	1,335	1,521	1,741	2,049	2,367
Percentage Change (%)	—	15.8	10.4	13.9	14.5	17.7	15.5
Consumer Price Index	100.0	105.9	112.9	124.3	139.3	158.4	175.3
Real Earnings (R)	1,044	1,142	1,182	1,224	1,250	1,294	1,351
Percentage Change in Real Earnings (%)	—	9.4	3.6	3.5	2.1	3.5	4.4
African							
Average Earnings (R)	476	518	577	686	861	1,095	1,269
Percentage Change (%)	—	8.8	11.4	18.9	25.5	27.2	15.9
Consumer Price Index	100.0	105.8	112.8	124.9	140.5	159.9	176.3
Real Earnings (R)	476	490	512	550	613	685	720
Percentage Change in Real Earnings (%)	—	3.0	4.5	7.4	11.5	11.7	5.1

Source: South African Institute of Race Relations, *Survey of Race Relations, 1977*, p. 206.

Various South African agencies advanced estimates of the amount a hypothetical African family would need for bare survival, the "Poverty Datum Line" (PDL). One of the more conservative, the Johannesburg Chamber of Commerce, concluded that a family of five would require a bare minimum of R123,38 a month in 1976, slightly under the *average* African wage at the time. But the Chamber admitted that a somewhat higher figure, the "Minimum Living Level," was closer to a realistic minimum. In 1976, that figure totalled R137,76, about R11, or almost 9 percent *more* than the average African wage that year.

Table 4-4.

Johannesburg Chamber of Commerce Estimates of the Poverty Datum Line (PDL) and Minimum Living Level for a Family of Five, November 1976

Components	Costs	
	Rands	*Percent of PDL*
Food	69.95	56%
Clothing	16.75	14
Housing	12.40	10
Fuel and Light	7.79	6
Transport	8.50	7
Taxation	1.91	1
Cleaning Materials	1.66	1
Medical Expenses	1.00	1
Education	3.72	3
Sub-Total: Poverty Datum Line	123.38	100%
Furniture	2.23	2
Crockery, Cooking Utensils, etc.	0.98	1
Writing Materials	3.51	3
Amusement and Sport	1.63	1
Personal Care	2.49	2
Savings for Emergencies	3.54	3
Total: Minimum Living Level	137.76	112%

Source: Institute of Race Relations, *A Survey, op. cit.*, p. 202.

The Institute for Planning Research at the University of Port Elizabeth calculated the PDL somewhat more liberally.* It maintained that the hypothetical budget should vary according to location. An average of its several community estimates indicated a PDL for an average family of six (one person more than in the Johannesburg Chamber's estimate) of R134,65 a month in 1976. The Institute recommended adding another 50 percent to reach what it called the "Household Effective Level," bringing what here will be termed a Minimal Health and Decency Level for a family of six to R201,98 a month. Africans wages in 1976 averaged R126, about R75 or 41 percent below this figure. A majority of the workers earned even less.

*Many such estimates actually argued that Africans could live on incomes lower than those of whites, Asians or Coloureds (in South Africa, even statistics are divided by race). Apparently, the assumption is that Africans neither desire nor need living standards comparable to those of other groups.

Still more important, from the point of view of transnational corporate investors, African wages in South Africa remained far below those of their employees doing comparable work in their home countries. This remained true even after African workers won increased wages in the 1970s.

Table 4-5.
Average Monthly—Earnings in South Africa compared to the United States and the United Kingdom, 1975 and 1976

	1975 (U.S. dollars)	1976 (U.S. dollars)
South Africa—White	$806	$880
Coloured	259	284
Asian	307	355
African	163	189
United States	726	779
Ratio of average U.S. wage to average African wage	4.45:1	4.12:1
United Kingdom	388.80	460.8
Ratio of average U.K. wage to average African wage	2.38:1	2.44:1

Sources: On South African wages: Institute of Race Relations, *A Survey*, op. cit., p. 206; calculated into dollars at the IMF exchange rate for 1976 of U.S. $1.15 per Rand; U.S. average wage: *U.S. Statistical Abstract, 1978* (Washington, D.C.: Government Printer, 1978, p. 414, calculated on the basis of a 40-hour week; U.K. average: Central Statistical Office, *Annual Report of Statistics, 1977* (London: Her Majesty's Stationery Office, 1977), p. 175; calculated into dollars at the average exchange rate for 1976 of U.S. $1.80 per Pound Sterling.

Transnational manufacturing corporations were not attracted to South Africa solely because they could pay African employees low wages, although this was a factor for firms with relatively labor-intensive plants. But firms that operated plants characterized by advanced technologies and capital-intensive machinery and equipment, employing mainly more skilled (white) workers, benefited more from the fact that the low-paid African labor force reduced the costs of local infrastructure and inputs.

As anti-apartheid criticism mounted in the 1970s, transnational corporate spokesmen claimed that their South African affiliates paid

higher wages and provided better working conditions for their employees than did local South African firms. The U.S. government under
President Carter vetoed efforts of the African states and the majority of
United Nations members to end further trade and investment by transnationals in South Africa.[12] Administration representatives insisted
that transnational corporate investments provided a lever for improving
wages and working conditions for black workers. In an effort to convince
the U.S. public that corporations should be encouraged to remain and
even expand their holdings in South Africa, over 100 U.S. firms signed
the so-called "Sullivan Principles" in the late-'70s. The principles
were a pledge to provide equal pay for equal work for all their employees
and to begin to upgrade their black employees into more skilled jobs.
They had actually been revised to render them acceptable to the South
African regime.[13] The guidelines called for:

1. Non-segregation of the races in all eating, comfort and work facilities;
2. Equal and fair employment practices for all employees;
3. Equal pay for all employees doing equal or comparable work for the same
   period of time;
4. Initiation and development of training programs that will prepare, in substantial numbers, Blacks and other non-whites [sic] for supervisory, administrative, clerical and technical jobs;
5. Increasing the number of Blacks and other non-whites in management and
   supervisory positions;
6. Improving the quality of employees' lives outside the work environment in
   such areas as housing, transportation, schooling, recreation and health
   facilities.

The Sullivan Principles required neither that signatory firms pay a
minimum living wage to black workers, nor that they bargain collectively with African trade unions. No enforcement mechanism was con-
templated. On the contrary, the U.S. Chamber of Commerce mounted
an effective lobby in 1978 to prevent Congress from passing legislation
to establish an agency for monitoring its enforcement.[14] Instead, the
Arthur D. Little Company agreed to check up on U.S. corporations'
compliance. Its reports seemed designed, however, to obscure rather
than expose the corporations' behavior. The two reports[15] published by
mid-1979 relied *solely* on figures submitted voluntarily by the com-

panies, with no independent, on-the-spot assessment at all. *

The governments of the European Economic Community (EEC) followed the U.S. lead by formulating a code of conduct for the South African operations of their transnational corporations. That code provided for equal pay for equal work and promotion of black workers. It went further, to recommend that black workers be given the right to organize and bargain collectively in recognized trade unions, and that European transnationals pay wages at least 50 percent higher than the PDL, that is, black wages should reach a minimal health and decency level. Contrasting with the warm reception given the Sullivan Principles, the South African authorities criticized the European code strongly. Elements of the South African press characterized it as "socialist" because it proposed minimum wages and support for African trade unions. [16] Yet even the European code, while urging firms to "abolish any practice of segregation," stressed that they should do so only "in so far as they are free to." In other words, it encompassed no serious challenge to the underlying apartheid system.

Promises of equal pay for equal work appeared unlikely to lead to much improvement in the wages of blacks, for, typically, the transnational corporations hired blacks and whites in separate job categories. Most blacks remained employed in unskilled and semiskilled positions, while whites were hired at higher pay for semiskilled, skilled or supervisory work. The discriminatory, industry-wide and government-backed

*In addition, the reports used vague, naive criteria to evaluate the integration of posts and upgrading of blacks. Three quarters of reporting firms claimed non-segregated facilities. But Little failed to investigate whether blacks were in fact able to use white facilities. (In Zambia, even ten years after Independence, white miners kept private clubs or restricted "their" areas to management personnel—excluding all but a tiny handful of blacks.) Almost all the firms claimed that all South African employees were eligible for the same benefits. But the Little report failed to note that this could easily be rendered meaningless. In the case of pensions, for instance, apartheid ensured that blacks seldom held jobs for nearly as long as whites or reached advanced positions— making them, in most cases, ineligible. As a rule, other benefits are reserved for management, effectively excluding the vast majority of black workers, most of whom were still relegated to unskilled jobs. (The sole exception was housing, a benefit usually reserved for blacks, an indication rather of their low wages than of corporate generosity.) Only 33 firms claimed to recognize unions. Of these, the majority of unions were for whites only. Most of the rest were "integrated," which, under South African law, guaranteed white members a dominant position. The reports gave no detailed or concrete figures on wage levels by race. They presented all data in the aggregate, releasing no details about individual companies. Categories were ill-defined and tables nearly incomprehensible. As a result, the reports gave the impression that the companies behaved quite well—although details on employment by single firms, when published elsewhere, as in the case of G.M. itself, revealed a far less rosy picture.

contracts between white unions and corporations created legal obstacles to upgrading black workers. In some cases, promoting blacks violated South African law. None of the codes of conduct proposed concrete goals or timetables for upgrading black workers, although these had long been recognized as essential in implementing affirmative action in the U.S.

It remained difficult to obtain accurate information about wages paid by transnational corporations to their South African employees. The South African *Financial Mail* suggested that transnational parent corporations themselves did not always know the facts about their South African employees' wages and working conditions.[17] In these circumstances, it appeared unlikely that parent companies would apply serious pressure on South African affiliates to pay significantly better wages or improve working conditions for their black workers. When a U.S. embassy official visited Port Elizabeth, where U.S. auto, tire and electrical firms were important employers, black workers "complained of inadequate training, job reservation, lack of union status, arbitrary promotion, abuse by S.A. foremen and job insecurity."[18]

The *Financial Mail*[19] reported that, despite the codes, foreign firms had done little more than South African companies to improve the working conditions of black employees. The Color Bar continued to operate "in one form or another, on practically every shop floor in the country." Wages remained "painfully low." Men and women were still "crowded together in bleak compounds." Managements exhibited a "great deal of inertia" in making training facilities available to Africans. "Hardly a week goes past" without allegation of victimization of African workers, not only for joining unions, but even for daring "to question the behavior or policies of managements" as members of the officially sponsored works or liaison committees.

In South Africa, the weight of the law and state power established and maintained the apartheid system, the Color Bar (in practice, at least), and the Bantustans, to enforce the economic inequality and exploitation of blacks. Two decades of rapid expansion of transnational corporate investments coincided with the increasing impoverishment of the black population. Available data[20] showed that, with the multiplication of transnational corporate holdings, in the 1960s and '70s, black workers, far from advancing up the national employment ladder, as a whole had been further downgraded by the end of the '70s. Africans won some wage increases in the 1970s. In that decade, the percentage rate of change for African wages exceeded that of whites. But because African pay started at such abysmally low levels, the gap in cash terms between black and white wages actually increased. From 1973 to 1976, for example, in the period of growing African pressure and highest wage increases, the *gap* between the wages of Africans and whites in manufacturing jobs rose from R316 to R445.[21]

At the same time, the proportion of Africans in almost every class of skilled position compared to whites declined between 1970 and 1978[22], despite the claims of the regime and transnational investors to the contrary. African participation in the administrative, executive and managerial category dropped from 2.9 to 0.4 percent. Among professionals, semi-professionals and technical staff, the African figure dipped from 29 to 26 percent. The miniscule proportion of African artisans and apprentices, mainly located in the Bantustans, dropped from 2.5 to 2.1 percent. African clerical workers fell from 13.4 to 13.2 percent of all clerical staff. The worsened position of Africans reflected in part the regime's plan to "whiten" South Africa's urban areas, where "black managers are not all that welcome."

The South African regime's institutionalization of poverty for the black labor force enabled it to create other attractions for transnational corporate investors. The parastatals sold them basic inputs at or below cost. Iscor, the iron and steel parastatal, depended on annual subsidies to keep the price of domestic steel at levels competitive with world prices. Escom, the state electricity corporation, charged lower rates to industry and mining than to private consumers. In part, the parastatals held their prices down by paying their African employees particularly low wages. The state could afford to hold down corporate taxes, since it refused to provide adequate social security, health care or education for the black majority. At the same time, tax concessions encouraged the introduction of machinery and equipment, partially to reduce the economy's dependence on black labor. Thirty percent of the cost of machinery could be deducted from taxable company profits. The effective tax rate paid by U.S. firms in South Africa through the '60s was estimated at a mere 22 percent of net income. Furthermore, double-taxation agreements with all the core industrialized nations provided that, if firms paid taxes on profits in South Africa, they would not again be taxed for those profits in their home countries.[23]*

While effectively denying normal services to blacks, the South African state could, and did, spend a disproportionate amount of its tax income to build up the social and economic infrastructure of the "white"

---

*In this way, taxpayers in the U.S., U.K. and other nations with such agreements with South Africa effectively subsidized investments there.

urban industrialized areas. On the one hand, this added to the profitability of manufacturing investment, as firms did not themselves have to provide water and energy, transport linkages or skilled (white) labor. Transnational corporate investments to take advantage of these provisions further aggravated the already grossly uneven pattern of development between South Africa's urban centers and the rest of Southern Africa. On the other hand, transnational managerial personnel, and their families, could enjoy the comfortable (lily-white) surburban surroundings provided them; it was just like living "at home."

Markets for Manufactured Goods

Transnational corporate managers, especially from manufacturing firms, optimistically eyed South Africa, with its rich mineral and agricultural resources and its high-income white population, as a tempting market for the sale of their sophisticated technologies. They saw South Africa's four million whites, although they comprised only a fifth of the population, as a significant market for high-priced consumer goods. Those four million whites boasted per capita incomes as high as any in the core capitalist countries. With the exception of Nigeria, the population of nearly 20 West African states, in contrast, averaged only about two million persons, with a per capita income little over $100.

The South African regime, parastatals and private industry in all sectors, moreover, were eager to buy the surplus sophisticated machinery and equipment the transnational manufacturing firms sought to sell. The mining companies proposed to spend three fifths of an R150-million, 10-year development program on mechanization in the '70s. After 1974, South Africa's wealthier white farmers multiplied their purchases of large, 200-Kw tractors tenfold, substantially reducing dependence on African labor.[24] Iscor and Sasol, the chemicals parastatal, both expanded rapidly throughout the '60s and '70, buying the most modern technologies available.[25]

After World War II, the regime progressively raised tariffs to stimulate and protect manufacturing firms that expanded their domestic production for the local market. In the early 1960s, duties were gradually raised on cars that contained more than stipulated percentages of imported parts. By 1976, 66 percent of cars, by weight, had to be made of locally produced parts in order to escape high tariffs.

The regime's rapidly expanding military became one of the most important components of the internal market. The military budget multiplied more than six times in the years between the Sharpeville massacre and 1970; and then increased more than fourfold by 1977/8, to reach almost $2 billion. [26] The military formed a particularly important market for technology, as the regime sought to replace its scarce white manpower with military machinery and mechanized equipment. The share of the defense budget allocated for "armament procurement and special equipment to replace obsolete gear" reached 50 percent by 1973. [27] In that year alone, almost $300 million was to be spent on aircraft, with over $100 million for ammunition and for electrical equipment, including radio and radar.

The regime took steps to stimulate the local manufacture, where possible, of essential parts and equipment for the military. A parastatal, Armscor, handled domestic military procurement. By 1978, Armscor had contracts with 1200 firms. Of these, 400 relied "to a significant extent" on military production. [28] Strict secrecy laws, however, made it impossible to determine to what extent individual transnational corporations engaged in manufacturing for South Africa's military machine. Furthermore, a number of transnationals which did not sell their output directly to the military produced inputs of critical importance for military equipment. Others supplied licenses needed for production within South Africa of a wide range of military equipment.

In 1977, following the U.N. Security Council's imposition of an arms embargo, the South African regime announced that it would not hesitate to take over the plant of any transnational corporation which refused to produce strategic materials upon request. This implied that the South African affiliate of any transnational corporation might, at any time, be required to produce military or related supplies for the regime. [29]

The Pattern of Growing Competition

In the 20 years of world-wide protest against apartheid following the Sharpeville Massacre, international finance capital intensified its competitive efforts to expand trade and investments in South Africa. It is hardly conceivable that the corporate managers believed that the South African regime sought to create a democratic or free private enterprise economy. Simply to sell their products or to invest, transnational corporations had to collaborate closely with the parastatals and the powerful mining finance houses.

The growing competition among transnational corporations for a stake in the emerging South African regional subcenter in the '60s and '70s dramatically altered the relative status of South Africa's major trading partners and the pattern of foreign investment. The lead in trade of the U K., as the former colonial power, diminished rapidly as rival

Table 4-6.
United States and British investment in selected southern African countries, by sector, and as percent of their investments in total Africa.

Sector*	U.S. investment in South Africa & Namibia (1976)		British investment, end 1974, in:			
			South Africa		Southern Rhodesia	
	$mn.	% of U.S. investment in total Africa	£mn.	% of U.K. investment in total Africa	£mn.	% of U.K. investment in total Africa
Mining and smelting	(D)	(D)	90.8	69.5	9.6	7.3
Petroleum	(D)	(D)	n.a.	n.a.	n.a.	n.a.
Manufacturing						
Total	705	78.2	712.2	71.1	65.6	6.5
Food products	102	(E)	109.0	53.7	8.6	0.4
Chemicals and allied products	95	84.3	105.1	73.9	9.2	6.5
Primary and Fabricated metals	48	35.8	—	—	3.5	—
Machinery (including electrical)	167	97.7	215.3	90.9	8.6	3.6
Transportation equipment	85	(E)	34.0	(C)	—	—
Other manufacturing	210	66.1	210.6	70.9	14.3	6.0
Transportation, communication and public utilities	1	1.0	—	—	—	—
Trade	204	66.7	99.2	32.5	16.9	5.5
Finance and insurance	−12	—	24.2	93.1	—	—
Other industries	66	30.7	45.8	34.2	—	—
TOTAL, all industries	1,665	37.3	997.2	57.5	113.6	6.5

Notes: (D) Concealed by source to avoid revealing individual firms.
(E) Data revealing to Africa outside South Africa and Namibia concealed by source to avoid revealing individual firms.
(C) Investment in Africa outside South Africa not given.
*As data for U.S. and Britain comes from different sources, categories may not be exactly the same for the two countries.

Sources: Calculated from U.S. Department of Commerce, *Survey of Current Business*, August, 1977; U.K Board of Trade, *Trade and Industry*, Feb. 21, 1977

transnationals vied to sell advanced machinery and equipment to the racist regime, its parastatals and private industry. Although British companies still provided the largest share of foreign capital, U.S. and F.R.G. transnationals, in particular, expanded their investments more rapidly to secure their hold on the market, particularly in the strategic sectors.

The U.K retained its position as South Africa's main export market into the 1970s, buying over a fifth of its total sales (about two thirds of them crude metals and mineral products. See Table 4-6). But the U.K. lost first place as South Africa's primary source of overseas purchases. At the same time, its share in total foreign capital invested in South Africa dropped from about a fourth of the total in the 1950s to about 18 percent in the '70s. Nevertheless, British transnationals still invested more than half of all their capital in the entire African continent in South Africa. At the end of 1974, direct British investment in South Africa totalled £997 million, compared to £737 in the rest of the continent.[30] Over a thousand British firms, including almost every one of the top companies, owned assets in South Africa, either directly or through affiliates. Many of their investments dated back to the days of outright colonial rule. Over the years, many British firms entered into joint ventures with South African parastatal and private firms. The tradition of mutually beneficial collaboration was reflected in shared company managements and boards of directors. After World War II, the growth of state capitalism in the U.K. led to direct British government ownership of important investments in South Africa, especially in iron and steel, chemicals, oil refining and transport.[31]

U.S. transnationals, expanding their interests in the region, had ousted British firms to take first place in the sale of machinery and equipment to South Africa by the 1970s. They still purchased barely a tenth of South African exports; but their purchases had begun to include key items like steel.[32] U.S. firms simultaneously expanded their investments to become close rivals to British investors as South Africa's second most important source of foreign capital, providing about 17 percent of the total in the 1970s. U.S. direct investment in 1977[32] totalled $1.8 billion, about 40 percent of all U.S. investment in Africa. This figure excluded extensive indirect investments through affiliates in Canada and Europe, particularly the U.K.[33] If oil investments were excluded, then well over half of all U.S. investments on the entire African continent were in South Africa.

Over 400 U.S. companies had acquired direct interests in South Africa[33] by the early '70s. Only 13 of these, among the largest corporations in the U.S., controlled over two thirds of total U.S. assets there

Table 4-7.
South Africa's Exports to and Imports from its Main Trading Partners, by value and as a percentage of total, 1956, 1966, and 1976

Country	1956				1966				1976			
	Exports		Imports		Exports		Imports		Exports		Imports	
	Value ($1000)	%	Value ($1000)	%	Value ($1000)	%	Value ($1000)	%	Value ($1000)	%	Value ($1000)	%
Africa	192,880	17.4	83,123	11.2	274,785	16.2	172,613	7.7	680,923	9.9	458,277	0.5
United Kingdom	203,699	29.2	438,250	59.6	564,975	33.3	628,507	27.3	1,502,004	22.0	1,544,950	17.5
Federal Republic of Germany	51,377	4.9	89,359	12.1	96,474	5.6	246,380	10.7	734,479	10.8	1,586,377	17.9
France	43,374	4.1	24,460	3.2	54,759	3.2	57,678	2.5	237,864	3.5	383,065	4.3
Japan	23,455	2.2	33,166	4.5	115,992	6.8	126,113	5.5	790,243	11.6	899,619	10.2
United States	80,598	7.7	277,701	37.7	218,793	12.9	407,818	17.6	689,490	10.1	1,899,859	27.5
TOTAL	1,036,190	100.0	735,380	100.0	1,687,691	100.0	2,303,753	100.0	6,813,040	100.0	8,813,509	100.0

Sources: Republic of South Africa, Foreign Trade Statistics, Vol. I Imports and Exports, 1966 and 1976 (Pretoria: Government Printer, 1976); South African Customs and Excise, Foreign Trade Statistics, Import Statistics of the Union of South Africa, 1956, Vol. I, Vol. II (translated to U.S. dollars using International Monetary Fund, Financial Statistics, 1956, 1966, 1976).

through branches, subsidiaries and locally owned affiliates.[34] U.S. data indicated that U.S. firms continued to expand their South African investments even after the Soweto uprising and despite the general stagnation of South African industry. A U.S. Department of Commerce survey showed U.S. firms spent about $230 million to expand their plant and equipment in South Africa in 1978, and planned to spend another $277 million the following year.[35]

Until the mid-1970s, U.S. transnationals maintained a higher degree of direct control over their South African and Namibian investments than did British firms. Four out of five U.S. dollars invested in South African manufacturing remained directly controlled by U.S. owners. Even in mining, where the South African mining finance houses had attracted a considerable amount of foreign capital while retaining control of management, more than half of U.S. capital remained under U.S. direction.

As world-wide anti-apartheid criticism mounted in the late 1970s, however, some leading U.S. firms sold a majority share of their holdings to South African partners, establishing a pattern resembling that of their British rivals. This tactic rendered their continued participation in South African business less visible and reduced their direct responsibility for the wages and working conditions of African employees—a particular point of criticism of U.S. firms in South Africa. Meanwhile, they continued to play a major role through their control of technology and access to world markets and finance.

Following the Soweto uprising, the South African regime accelerated its efforts to persuade U.S. business interests to increase trade with and investments in South Africa. It arranged to invite hundreds of U.S. businessmen to conferences in New York and Houston to discuss South Africa's prospects.[36] Speakers at the Houston conference included the general secretary of the white Trade Unions Congress of South Africa, and the secretary of the black National Union of Clothing Workers (Lucy Mvubelo). Presumably they hoped to help U.S. businessmen convince anti-apartheid activists that U.S. investors could have a major impact on labor relations in South Africa while expanding their holdings there.[37] The South African information scandal exposed the expenditure of tens of millions of dollars by the South African regime to influence U.S. voters against critics and to pay for the support of U.S. news media.[38] The U.S. Chamber of Commerce itself took part in organizing opposition to efforts by critics of apartheid to reduce contacts with South Africa.[39]

As their role in the capitalist world expanded in the late '60s, transnational corporations from the Federal Republic of Germany

(F.R.G.) accelerated investment in South Africa.[40] By the 1970s, the F.R.G.'s status vis-a-vis South Africa had altered dramatically. In the '50s, F.R.G. firms bought less than one twentieth of South Africa's exports, and supplied barely a tenth of its imports. As a result of F.R.G. transnationals' upsurge over the next 20 years, the F.R.G. became South Africa's second largest foreign supplier (after the U.S.), providing about a fifth of its imports. The F.R.G. bought over a tenth of South Africa's exports, considerably less than Britain and marginally less than Japan, though more than the United States. (See Table 4.6)

Simultaneously, the value of F.R.G. assets (direct investments, shares and credits) multiplied about 20 times, reaching DM 4.5 billion in the mid-'70s; in direct investment, the F.R.G. ranked just after the U.S. After Europe and Brazil, South Africa became a principal recipient of F.R.G. capital, and accounted for at least a third of all F.R.G. investments and loans in Africa.[41] Unlike their U.S. competitors, however, F.R.G. investors left a major share of their capital under South African control. Many simply purchased subscriptions to Deutschmark bonds sold by the F.R.G banks for the South African regime and its state corporations (mainly ESCOM, ISCOR, and the Railways and Harbors Corporation). F.R.G. firms held less than a fifth of all their assets in South Africa directly. Nevertheless, about 400 sales and service organizations representing F.R.G. manufacturers furnished technological skills and sold machinery and equipment. F.R.G. transnationals' largest direct holdings were in the automotive industry, chemicals and engineering.[42]

The F.R.G. government played a direct role in the mounting efforts of F.R.G. firms to profit from South Africa's industrial growth. It owned shares in several leading companies with interests there, including Volkswagen (20 percent), Urangesellschaft (over half) and Salzgitter (100 percent).

The rapid post-War recovery and expansion of Japan's oligopolistic corporate structure made it a prime market for South Africa's raw materials. Japan had been only a minor buyer of South African exports in the '50s. By the '70s, it had moved up to second place, next to Britain, purchasing a little over 11 percent of total exports. Japanese imports of South African chrome, manganese and asbestos amounted to 54 percent, 44 percent and 33 percent of Japan's total purchases of these items in 1973 alone.[43] Japan had become Iscor's largest customer for iron exports. Simultaneously, Japan multiplied its sales to South Africa almost 30 times, to capture just over a tenth of the import market.

Unlike the U.K., the U.S. and F.R.G., Japan's government prohibited direct investment in South Africa, because of apartheid. But

Japanese firms provided South African companies with licenses to manufacture Japanese models, especially in the auto and electrical industries, and continued to ship them parts and equipment. About 70 Japanese firms established representative offices in South Africa.[44] Japanese companies also supplied equipment for construction and expansion of South African-owned factories.

French transnational corporations had, by the mid-'70s, acquired only 5 percent of all foreign investment in South Africa. Their relative sluggishness probably reflected their heavy involvement in formerly French areas in Africa, as well as their relatively weak position in the growing transnational corporate competition. But French firms contributed aggressively in the exploration for and refinement of oil in South Africa, and joined in constructing two big hydroelectric projects, the dam on the Orange River and the tunnel under the Fish River. A French consortium, formed by Framatome, Spie-Batignolles and Alsthom, won the contract to build the big new nuclear power plant at Koeberg.

French transnational corporations' main role as collaborators with the South African regime, however, was in the military field.[45] South African firms made Panhard armored cars under French license. At least until the late '70s, French firms regularly sold Alouette and Super-Frelon helicopters there. France claimed to differentiate between arms that "might be used for repression" and other military equipment. This distinction seemed rather tenuous: French companies were allowed to supply the South Africans with Mirage III fighter-bombers and Mysteres, as well as Daphne submarines. In 1969, two French firms joined the South African Council for Scientific and Industrial Research to develop an all-weather surface-to-air missile system.

Switzerland's role among competing transnational corporations as a "neutral" center of financial transactions was illustrated in South Africa. The Swiss government published no official statistics on investment there. Transnationals based in Switzerland often used funds originating elsewhere to finance their South African subsidiaries. The Swiss firm Nestles, for example, drew widely on capital from the U.S. and Britain. In 1976, however, Swiss investments in South Africa were estimated at about R480 million, about 4.5 percent of foreign capital there,[46] nearly as large a share as the French. Most of it was in manufacturing. More important than Swiss investments, however, was the Swiss banks' aid to South Africa in selling gold, as well as in mobilization of international credits. They facilitated the rapid expansion of foreign exchange earnings needed by the South African regime to finance continued imports of machinery and equipment, military supplies and oil, in the growing political-economic crises of the 1970s.

In sum, transnational firms from all the major capitalist nations contributed to the dynamism of South Africa's economy in the post Sharpeville era. U.S. and F.R.G. companies, however, gradually took the lead from British investors, especially in strategic, fast-growing manufacturing industries. French firms traded and invested less, but made a special contribution to the regime's military build-up. Japanese industrial groups, prohibited from direct investment, expanded trade and licensed South African partners to produce their models. The most important role of the Swiss was in banking, particularly in the sale of gold. By competing to find new sources of profit in South Africa, transnational corporations ensured thorough attention to the requirements of the regime.

Economic Stagnation

Several basic contradictions characterized the structure of South African industrialization, spurred by transnational corporate investments. First, as in other regional subcenters, the potential benefits were denied to the majority of the population. The regime explicitly utilized the racist system of apartheid to exclude the black majority except as low-cost labor. As industry expanded, the incomes of workers in manufacturing and throughout the economy remained static or dropped in real terms. South African manufacturers had to sell their goods in the limited (white) luxury market, to the military, in neighboring countries or overseas. Transnational investors cooperated with South African capital to produce luxury autos and armored cars, while black workers packed into decrepit trains for unbearably long commutes to and from work. Equipment supplied by the transnational corporations produced electricity for the military; but Soweto, a city with over a million (African) residents, and most other African townships, went without electricity.

Production of sophisticated luxury and military goods tends to capital intensity. To compete in export markets, moreover, corporations introduced the latest, most capital-intensive technologies. To facilitate implementation of its plans to "whiten" urban areas, the regime encouraged this tendency.[47] As a result, South African manufacturing grew steadily more capital intensive, contributing to rising black unemployment, which escalated particularly in the latter 1970s.

The transnational corporations' participation in South Africa's industrial transformation was integrally tied in with—in fact, in part built upon—that nation's domination of neighboring countries. Official statistics partially concealed these relationships. U.S. and European statistics followed the lead of the South African regime by incorporating Namibian data together with South African after the mid-'60s. In addition, after the U.N. declared a boycott on the illegal Rhodesian regime, transnational corporations employed innumerable devices to conceal their activities there. South African trade figures frequently incorporated Rhodesian data. They also included the trade of politically independent Botswana, Lesotho and Swaziland without separate identification, because those countries remained members of the South African Customs Union until the mid-'70s.

Despite the effect of these manipulations in obscuring the facts, available evidence shows that South African economic expansion, and the transnationals' resulting profits, depended heavily on the exploitation of neighboring countries. In the first place, surrounding nations provided additional low-cost labor reserves. As South Africa's manufacturing industries expanded, increasing their labor requirements, they employed ever greater numbers of South African blacks, despite the regime's efforts to restrict them. Increasingly, South Africa's labor recruiting agencies contracted with workers to migrate from all the neighboring countries to work on South Africa's mines and farms, so that labor shortages would not push wages up. In the early '70s, about 80 percent of the workers on South Africa's mines came from neighboring countries. Only after the independence of Mozambique and Angola, and the rise in unemployment in South Africa as the political-economic crisis spread in the mid-'70s did more South African blacks go to work in the mines. The share of foreign mine workers fell to about half. (See Table 5-3)

Secondly, as the import-substitution capacity of the South African market became saturated in the late 1960s, South African manufacturing industries, in which transnationals shared, intensified their efforts to sell their output throughout the region. The importance of this expanded market cannot be overemphasized. The domestic South African market remained limited, not because its population of 24 million-plus was so small, but because the wages of the African majority were systematically held below the poverty line. South Africa's traditional export markets in the developed nations of western Europe, North America and Japan were effectively open only to raw and semi-processed materials, in a typical neo-colonial pattern. In exchange, South Africa purchased the capital and intermediate goods and equipment required to build up its own manufacturing industries.[48] In contrast, South Africa's exports to "the rest of Africa" (including a sizeable but unknown share to Southern Rhodesia) consisted primarily of manufactured goods, many of them produced with transnational corporate financial and technical assistance. In 1975, South Africa sold to "the rest of Africa" over half its chemicals exports and about three fourths of its exports of machinery and equipment (73 percent); plastics and rubber products (89 percent); stone, cement and glass products (77 percent); and transport machinery and equipment (73 percent). South African imports from the rest of Africa consisted of crude mineral products (26 percent), light consumer goods and processed and semi-processed agricultural and timber produce. Many of these imports were produced by firms with South African links who shipped them to South Africa for final processing and sale. The "rest of Africa" was the only area of the world with which South Africa reported a trade surplus. If Botswana, Lesotho, Swaziland and Namibia were included in the "rest of Africa," the neighboring countries' importance as a market for South African manufacturing would be shown to be still greater.

Thirdly, many transnational corporations used South Africa as their headquarters for investments in surrounding countries. Transnationals with regional head offices in South Africa collaborated with the mining finance houses and parastatals to mine copper, iron, chrome, diamonds, uranium and other metals and minerals throughout southern Africa. Their projects provided raw materials for processing in South Africa's new factories, as well as for sale overseas to augment the companies' profits and contribute foreign exchange earnings to the South African regime. At least 18 of South Africa's top industrial companies had major affiliates in Southern Rhodesia.[49] Of these, eight had major ties with transnational firms. The largest banks in the neighboring countries were affiliated to transnationals, typically operating through their regional head offices in South Africa.

As the general crisis deepened in the 1970s, its impact spread throughout southern Africa, affecting not only South Africa, but also its neighbors. In 1978, about a fourth of the capacity of South Africa's industrial productive capacity lay idle.[50] South Africa's official labor policies inevitably threw the burden of the crisis onto the black population—always last hired and first fired.[51] Unemployment mounted among the blacks. The South African regime grossly under-represented black unemployment. It ignored altogether unemployed black women.[52] By 1977, however, unofficial unemployment estimates indicated that two million South African blacks—one out of four members of the labor force—were jobless. Increasing numbers of unemployed were shipped off to the Bantustans where—without any form of social security or welfare payments—they faced slow starvation. Thousands more migrant workers were shipped back to swell the ranks of the unemployed in the neighboring countries.

Table 4-8.
Estimates of unemployment, 1970 to 1976

| | Unemployed (1000s)[1] | | | % of total |
	Urban Areas	White Rural Areas	Homelands (includes cumulative increase in underemployment	labor force
1970	227	25	32	20.4
1971	201	81	124	19.8
1972	226	138	227	20.9
1973	175	191	258	20.3
1974	128	257	325	20.8
1975	113	315	377	20.6
1976	151	377	396	21.0
1976 Sept. 30	180	389	418	22.4
1976 Dec. 31	222	401	437	

Sources: Institute of Race Relations, *Survey of Race Relations,* 1977, based on P. J. Van der Merwe, Black Employment Problems in South Africa (Pretoria: Nov. 1976) table 6; and C. Simkins, "Measuring and Predicting Unemployment in South Africa 1960-1977," unpublished paper, Mar., 1977, table 20.

Stepped-up military production had played a critical role, strengthening the regime's ability to maintain apartheid while expanding the domestic market. But it also increased state expenditures. To avoid discouraging continued investment, the regime raised taxes on lower- and middle-income groups, further limiting the domestic market for consumer goods.[53] Meanwhile, escalating government debt combined with heightened spending on military hardware to stimulate inflation. Rising prices for oil, as well as heavy machinery and equipment, which the regime imported for massive projects designed to strengthen the economy and/or the military, spurred domestic inflation still further. The cost of living more than doubled between 1970 and 1978.[54]

The pattern of dependent development established in South Africa by the alliance of transnational corporations, the state and mining finance houses rested, like similar developments in Brazil, on the continued poverty and oppression of the majority throughout the region. In South Africa, blacks were excluded except as cheap workers; in the rest of the region, the development of underdevelopment was furthered.

Responses to Crisis

The African population organized increasingly effective resistance to apartheid in the 1970s. The liberation of Mozambique and Angola and the rising tide of armed struggle in Zimbabwe and Namibia gave new impetus to the movement. The regime's soldiers and police gunned down unarmed students in the streets of Soweto in the 1976 uprising. In the following years, reports of armed resistance to the police and army in the cities and countryside—spearheaded by Umkhonto we Sizwe—surfaced more and more frequently, despite the effective censorship of the South African press.

Confronted with mounting internal resistance and growing international criticism, the regime made some placatory gestures. It altered the derogatory name of the "Bantu Administration Department" to "Department of Plural Relations."* It began to encourage the emergence of a black "middle class," in hopes of gaining support for the status quo. It permitted a handful of wealthy black businessmen to expand their activities. The few blacks with sufficient incomes to buy long-term leases might acquire a degree of residential security. A wealthy handful could enter elite restaurants and hotels in white areas. Perhaps more significant, the regime began to foster the establishment of a relatively stable strata of skilled workers. Although these concessions affected only a fraction of the black population, many elements in the white community opposed them; in any case, implementation rarely, if ever, equalled original promises.

Despite these reforms, the basis system of apartheid remained unaltered. The regime continued to base its policies on the Bantustans and the pass laws. Its position was clear. It hoped to create the illusion of change, without fundamentally altering the underlying institutionalized structure of white privilege and black exploitation.

Summary

After World War II, the Nationalist regime systematically intervened in the economy. It collaborated with the oligopolistic mining finance houses to build up a military-industrial complex that ensured perpetuation of the rule of white mine, farm and factory owners, buttressed by an "aristocracy" of white workers. The black majority of the population was condemned to provide plentiful low-cost labor.

State spending on industry, infrastructure and the military, in the context of low wages, guaranteed high profits for transnational corporate investors. They viewed South Africa as a particularly safe environment for their investments. They flocked there, competing to multiply their investments as repression grew and the struggle for

---

*Percy Qoboza, editor of the banned *World*, quipped that he went into detention a "Bantu" and came out a "Plural."[55]

liberation was forced underground in the '60s. At the same time, their investment in the most technologically sophisticated sectors—especially manufacturing—aggravated the contradictions inherent in South Africa's economic growth. On the one hand, they contributed to the spread of capital-intensive technologies throughout the economy, which reduced employment among the African population, further narrowing the already sharply limited domestic market. On the other, they collaborated with South African parastatals and mining finance houses to penetrate the economies of neighboring countries, aggravating the pattern of uneven development and underdevelopment in the southern third of the continent.

By the 1970s, these contradictory features had culminated in stagnation throughout the South African economy and much of the adjacent region. The downswing reflected and contributed to the spread of the re-emergent general crisis that engulfed the capitalist commercial system. Simultaneously, African resistance, spurred by the Soweto uprising, mounted.

Only the growing international monetary crisis granted a coincidental reprieve to the beleaguered regime. International investors, seeking a haven from wildly fluctuating currencies, turned more and more to the purchase of gold. The prices of South Africa's major export sky-rocketed to nearly $800 an ounce, more than 20 times its 1970 value, in early 1980.

Nevertheless, the underlying contradictory features built into the structure of the South African minority regime's domination of its own population and neighboring countries throughout the region, spurred the continuing spread of the political economic crisis. The rest of this part details the role of transnational corporations in strengthening the racist minority's role, in the context of deepening contradictions and mounting black resistance.

References

1. South African Reserve Bank, Quarterly Bulletin of Statistics, Dec. 1970.

2. South African Reserve Bank, Quarterly Bulletin of Statistics, June, 1976.

3. P. Evans, *Dependent Development—The Alliance of Multinational, State, and Local Capital in Brazil*, (Princeton: Princeton University Press, 1978).

4. N. Parsons, *A New History of Southern Africa*, (London: MacMillian, forthcoming); J. and R. Simons, *Class and Colour in South Africa, 1850 to 1950*, (Harmondsworth: Penguin African Library, 1969); Leonard Thompson, Monica Wilson, ed., *The Oxford History of South Africa*, (Oxford: Oxford University Press, 1969, 1971); M. Benson, *The African Patriots* (Harmondsworth: Penguin African Library, 1969); D. H. Houghton, *The South African Economy*, (Cape Town: Oxford University Press, 1973).

5. See N. Parsons, *A New History of Southern Africa, op. cit. passim.*

6. See S. Plaatjie, *Native Life in South Africa,*(London: P.S. King, third edition, 1920).

7. F. A. Johnston, *Class, Race, and Gold: A Study of Class Relations and Racial Discrimination in South Africa,* (Boston: Routledge and Kegan Paul, 1976).

8. South African Institute of Race Relations, *Survey of Race Relations in South Africa,* (Pietermaritzburg: The Natal Witness, 1956/7) p. 170.

9. State of South Africa, *Economic Financial and Statistical Year Book for the Republic of South Africa,* (Johannesburg: Da Gama Publishers Pty. Ltd. 1973).

10. *Guardian* (London) Dec. 5, 1973.

11. U.S. Department of Commerce, Survey of Current Business, Aug. 1974.

12. *New York Times,* Aug. 8, 1976.

13. Subcommittee on African Affairs, (Chairman, Senator Dick Clark), *U.S. Corporate Interests in South Africa,* report to Senate Committee on Foreign Relations, (U.S. Government Printing Office, Washington, D.C., 1978) p. 166.

14. *South African Financial Mail,* Apr. 7, 1978.

15. Arthur D. Little, Inc. *Second Report on the Signatory Companies of the Sullivan Principles,* (Philadelphia: Dr. Leon H. Sullivan, Zion Baptist Church, corner Broad and Venango Streets, 1979).

16. *South African Digest,* Oct. 7, 1977.

17. *South African Financial Mail,* Mar. 4, 1977.

18. Cable from Ambassador Bowdler to the U.S. State Department, "Subject: Black Attitudes Toward Foreign Investment," reprinted in full in *Southern Africa Magazine,* April, 1978.

19. *South African Financial Mail,* Oct. 7, 1977.

20. Republic of South Africa, Department of Labor, Manpower Survey, 1978.

21. Institute of Race Relations, *A Survey of Race Relations, op. cit.* 1977, p. 234.

22. *South African Financial Mail,* Feb. 17, 1978.

23. *South African Financial Mail,* Feb. 11, 1979.

24. South African Reserve Bank, Quarterly Bulletin of Statistics, Sept.

25. *South African Digest* (Pretoria: Government Printer) Sept. 30, 1977; *South African Financial Mail,* Apr. 7, 1979.

26. Institute for Strategic Studies (London), *Survival,* June-July, 1972.

27. *Financial Times* (London) July 5, 1978.

28. Investor Responsibility Research Center, Corporate Activity in South Africa: General Motors Corp. Sales to Police and Military, 1979 Analysis 6. Supplement No. 16, May 1, 1979 (Washington, D.C. IRRC, 1522 K Street, NW.)

29. *Washington Post,* Nov. 16, 1977.

30. United Kingdom Board of Trade, *Trade and Industry,* Feb. 25, 1977.

31. *South African Financial Mail,* May 12, 1978.

32. U.S. Department of Commerce, Survey of Current Business, Aug. 1977.

33. List of U.S. companies in South Africa, issued by U.S. Consulate in Pretoria.

34. Corporate Information Center, National Council of Churches, *Church Corporations and South Africa* (475 Riverside Drive, New York, 1973).

35. *Africa News* (Durham, North Carolina) Nov. 13, 1978.

36. *South African Financial Mail,* June 9, 1978.

37. *South African Digest,* June 8, 1979.

38. *South African Financial Mail,* April 7, 1978.

39. *Ibid.,* May 12, 1978.

40. *Star* (Johannesburg), weekly airmail edition, Feb. 15, 1975; Supplement on West Germany, Oct. 4, 1974; W. Schneider-Barthold, der Wirtschaftsbeziehung der BRD zur RSA (Deuschen Institut für politik, Berlin, 1976).

41. *South African Financial Mail*, Supplement on West Germany, Oct. 4, 1974, *Times* (Johannesburg) Oct. 26, 1975; *Star* (Johannesburg), weekly edition, Feb. 15, 1975.

42. *South African Financial Gazette*, July 21, 1974.

43. Asahi Shimbun (Japan) August 25, 1973.

44. *Management* (South Africa) April, 1973.

45. Reuters, report from Cape Town, Apr. 11, 1975; *Rand Daily Mail* (Johannesburg) April 7, 1975.

46. G. Rist, "Relations Between Switzerland and South Africa," United Nations Unit on Apartheid, Notes & Documents, 9/74, May, 1974.

47. *South African Financial Mail*, Feb. 17. 1978.

48. See Republic of South Africa, Monthly Abstract of Trade Statistics (Pretoria: Government Printers).

49. Association of Rhodesian Industries, Registrar of Rhodesian Manufacturers, 1976 (Bulawayo: Belmont Printers, 1976); and *Who Owns Whom*, 1977 (London, 1977).

50. *South African Financial Mail*, April 13, 1978.

51. *South African Financial Mail*, April 10, 1978.

52. *South African Financial Mail*, Feb. 10, 1977.

53. *South African Financial Mail*, April 21, 1978.

54. The consumer price index, April 1970=k100, reached 210 by May of 1978; reported in *South African Financial Mail*, June 30, 1978.

55. *The New York Times*, June 24, 1979.

Diamonds and Gold   5

Southern Africa's mineral wealth had long attracted international interests. By the 1960s, geological exploration of the region had been extended further than in any other part of the continent. South Africa boasted the largest and most varied *known* mineral resources of any region in the world outside the Soviet Union and the U.S. In addition to gold and diamonds, it exported copper, nickel, tin, manganese, asbestos and zinc. It possessed a third of the world's known reserves of uranium: the largest known deposits of chrome and vanadium; antimony, flurospar, titanium, and vermiculite; and produced over 80 percent of the western world's platinum. It owned extensive reserves of coal and iron ore. The only important minerals not discovered in large quantities were oil, bauxite and molybdenum.

Under colonialism, giant imperial firms blasted out rich minerals throughout the African continent, shipping them back to their home countries to be smelted, refined and fabricated into the machinery and appliances of the industrial world. After independence, nationalist groups, commonly acting through the state, often took a substantial share, even a majority of the equity of the international companies' local subsidiaries. Nevertheless, in virtually every case, the transnationals continued to control the sources of international capital, the supply of up-to-date technologies, and the international commodity markets; typically, too, they provided management. This enabled them to cream off the investable surpluses. As a result, in most cases, increased investment in African mines after independence failed to contribute to significant industrialization. [1]

The rich gold mines of the Transvaal, in contrast, were transformed into the financial backbone of industrialization in South Africa. Given low wages (which the colonial state assured), the mines were vastly profitable. They formed the single most important source of primary capital accumulation for a handful of huge domestic groups. From their inception, these "mining finance houses" cooperated closely with international finance capital, obtaining initial credits from banks such as

Barclays, Standard, and the Deutsche Bank. In fact, they provided an early stimulus for the emergence of these as transnational banks in the modern sense. But the orientation of the mining finance houses remained domestic: they joined with the racist state to develop manufacturing as well as the mining of base minerals in South Africa, diversifying and expanding their sources of profit.* Despite the fixed gold price after World War II, starvation level wages paid to black miners ensured mining finance houses of the profits they continued to funnel into the growth of the manufacturing sector. In the economic crisis of the late 1970s, the soaring price of gold, complemented by the expansion of other mineral exports (especially uranium), paid the regime's mounting oil and military bills, and saved the South African economy from total stagnation.

A century after the gold rush of the late 1800s, South Africa's mining industry was openly "controlled by seven major groups of financial houses."[3] Three had been founded in the earliest days by South African diamond magnates—Gold Fields South Africa (GFSA) by Cecil Rhodes; Rand Mines by Alfred Beit; and Johannesburg Consolidated Investments (JCI) by Barney Barnato. German banks, including the Deutsche Bank and the Berliner Handesgesellschaft, initially controlled two, founded in the days of the German intrusion in South West Africa (now Namibia) before World War I. One, Anglo-American Corporation, originally financed by British and U.S. capital[4], was destined to grow into the largest of them all.

The mining finance houses—despite their international linkages—remained the core of the national South African bourgeoisie throughout the quarter of a century following the Second World War. The South African companies, by reinvesting their profits, obtained the dominant share of South Africa's mining business by the mid-20th Century. In 1918, four out of every five dollars in profit were still being remitted abroad. By 1965, this had dropped to about one out of four.

Although the transnationals, eager to share in the huge profits to be made by employing low-paid black labor to mine the nation's known valuable mineral deposits, continued to expand their investments over the years, the mining finance houses retained local control. Foreign shareholdings and remitted profits increased in absolute terms, although not as rapidly as did those in manufacturing. Many foreign investors held their capital indirectly in the form of minority shares in

---

*In Brazil, mineral wealth was reported to be the original source of only one—albeit the most powerful—of the domestic industrial-financial groups that joined the militarized state and transnational corporate affiliates to achieve industrial transformation.[2]

the South African mining finance houses. British investments provided over half the total, but U.S. capital became increasingly significant. Many foreigners invested indirectly through the London Stock Exchange or the money markets of London, New York or continental Europe. They multiplied their investments in mining especially rapidly as the international monetary crisis matured and gold prices soared in the late 1970s.

Anglo-American and the Other Groups

The Anglo-American Group, the largest mining finance house, typified the symbiotic relationship that grew up between foreign transnational corporations and banks and the South African state and domestic capital. Anglo was founded just after World War I[5] by a South African diamond magnate, Ernest Oppenheimer, in collaboration with a U.S. bank, Morgan Guaranty, the U.S. firm, Newmont Mining, and the National Bank of South Africa. The National Bank had originally been founded (in 1890) as a central bank for the Boer's Transvaal Republic, but the British, in effect, confiscated it after the Boer War, and transformed it into a private bank. It proceeded to take over several smaller banks, becoming the second largest bank in South Africa (after Standard), and the only major one still in South African hands. In 1918, Oppenheimer obtained a seat on its board, and the relationship between the bank and his mining finance house flourished. In 1918, the National Bank established links to Barclays Bank. Barclays, a London bank, had accumulated its initial capital through the "triangle trade:" financing shipment of African slaves to the Americas; sugar, cotton and tobacco to Britain; and British textiles and manufactured goods to Africa and America. (In fact, Barclays' founder owned a Jamaican slave plantation.[6]) In 1925, the National Bank, Barclays and two other colonial banks merged to form Barclays DCO, one of the earliest transnational banks that operated throughout the British empire in response to the needs of imperial trading and mining corporations. Oppenheimer retained his seat on the board of the new bank, and it remained closely wed to Anglo. It provided Anglo with invaluable international contacts, particularly as Anglo's U.S. partners dropped out in the wake of the white miner's revolt on the Rand in 1922. Harry Oppenheimer, the current chairman of Anglo, inherited his father's place on Barclays International's board. Barclays continued to do a large share of its business in southern Africa.

By the 1970s, Anglo-American had grown into an international conglomerate,[7] although its South African gold mines still provided its financial foundations. Anglo affiliates penetrated throughout southern Africa in mining, a limited amount of manufacturing, trade, finance and real estate. An Anglo affiliate managed the huge copper mines that dominated Zambia's economy. Anglo became the largest foreign investor in Southern Rhodesia, with interests ranging from coal mines to sugar plantations. It opened mines in Botswana, Swaziland, and Namibia, in virtually every case exporting unrefined material to Europe, the U.S. or Japan. The assets of Anglo's group members totalled nearly $10 billion in the late 1970s.

One Anglo affiliate, De Beers, controlled 85 percent of the international production and sale of rough diamonds; Oppenheimer chaired both companies. De Beers mined diamonds in South Africa, Namibia, Lesotho and Botswana. It bought them from Zaire, Ghana, the Central African Republic and Sierra Leone. It shipped its diamonds to London to be sold, cut and polished, mostly in Israel and Belgium. Israeli cutters, who sold 52 percent of the world's cut and polished diamonds, became particularly close to the company. Together, Israel and Belgium annually exported cut diamonds worth over $1 billion. [8]

In addition to Barclays, Anglo had two other major foreign associates. Charter Consolidated, a British transnational, affiliated to the Anglo Group, acted as its agent in London. Charter's quoted and unquoted investments totalled about a billion dollars. Most were located in England and South Africa, but it also held interests in Asia, Australia, continental Europe, North America and independent Africa. The Anglo-American Corporation and Charter made joint investments throughout the world. Together, they obtained 34.75 percent of Hudson Bay Mining and Smelting in Canada. Charter also owned smaller interests in a number of other transnational corporations, including the U.S.-controlled Falconbridge Nickel and several of the larger U.S. oil companies.

Anglo-American became so closely interlocked with the U.S. firm, Engelhard Minerals and Chemicals (EMC) by the 1970s, that it was hard to tell where one began and the other left off. Engelhard mined and marketed ores, metals and non-metallic minerals, and refined and traded precious minerals for industry. As a result of a complex series of stock transactions between 1969 and 1972, the Anglo-American Group came to own about 30 percent of Engelhard's common and 20 percent of its preferred stock. [9] The companies shared directors.

EMC's founder, Charles Engelhard, an avowed supporter of the South African regime, remarked in 1966 that Vorster's policies were "as much in the interests of South Africa as anything I can think of or suggest." [10] He took a seat on the board of Wenela, the agency which recruited Africans as migrant workers for the South African gold mines. He arranged a $35-million loan to tide the regime over the capital outflow that followed the massacre at Sharpeville. But Engelhard did not neglect U.S. politics: he was a generous contributor to the Democratic Party, a close friend of Presidents Kennedy and Johnson, and represented the United States at independence ceremonies in Gabon, Zambia and Algeria, and at the coronation of the Pope in 1963.*

Although Engelhard died in 1971, the company continued his tradition of strong ties to the U.S. government as well as South Africa. J. G. Harlan, who became an Engelhard vice-president in 1969, had held various high U.S. government posts until then. He continued to serve on various special official U.S. commissions while rising to senior vice president in the company, consolidating his relationships with top-ranking U.S. personnel, particularly those dealing with mineral reserves. Undoubtedly these contacts facilitated efforts to convince U.S. officials to strengthen reliance on South Africa's "strategic" resources. This position was presumably backed up by another Engelhard board member with extensive links to the U.S. government, J. T. Connor. Connor sat on the board of the Chase Manhattan Bank, one of the largest U.S. banks, which itself developed extensive South African connections.

The interests of the U.S. mining transnational, American Metal Climax (AMAX), also became increasingly interlinked with Anglo's in the 1960s and '70s. In fact the companies acquired substantial shares in each other. They invested jointly in Zambia's copper mines. Together, they developed the Selebi-Pikwe mine in Botswana, shipping concentrates to an AMAX refinery in the U.S. and then selling the copper to Metalgesellschaft of the F.R.G. (with which AMAX had ties; see below, p. 248). AMAX and Anglo, with a number of other companies, developed the Tsumeb copper mine in Namibia. Like Engelhard, AMAX shared personnel with the U.S. government. One director, W.A.M. Burden, served with various defense agencies from 1939 to 1952, and was Ambassador to Belgium from 1959 to 1961. In the 1970s, he became Chairman of the Institute for Defense Analysis and Director of the Council on Foreign Relations.

Anglo forged a number of additional international connections, as well as building a network of smaller affiliates and subsidiaries throughout Africa, the Americas, Europe and Australia. It shared directors with top international mining companies, including the Brit-

*In 1978/9 when Harvard University planned to call a library after Engelhard, students forced a name change because of his South African connections.

ish Rio Tinto Zinc. It established ties with the Dresdner Bank, one of the F.R.G. Grossbanken. (An Anglo director acted as advisor to the bank.)

Using the vast accumulations of capital it extracted from the low paid African workers it employed on its South African mines, Anglo collaborated closely with the South African parastatals and transnational corporate interests to develop key sectors of South Africa's basic manufacturing industries (See Ch. 7 below). At the same time, it continued to expand, undermining the independence of other mining finance houses while working ever more closely with the ruling Afrikaner interests. It acquired 47 percent of the Johannesburg Consolidated Investment (JCI, or "Johnnies"). When the Afrikaner group, Federale Mynbou, took over the General Mining and Finance Corporation (GMFC or GenMin), Anglo also obtained a substantial share. Two Anglo directors sit on GenMin's board.

The other mining finance houses, while less extensive than Anglo, also spread into many fields in partnership with transnational banks and corporations. The U.K. firm, Consolidated Gold Fields (CGF) in the 1970s still owned almost half of the shares of the second largest, Goldfields of South Africa (GFSA). This group, too, held interests throughout southern Africa and the world. Consolidated Gold Fields owned 85 percent of the Ascan Corporation in the U.S.

Formed at the turn of the century by German banks, including the Dresdner Bank, working through a London-based consortium, GenMin became the only finance house controlled by a local group generally recognized as Afrikaner. GenMin's close ties with the other mining finance houses illustrated the increasingly intertwined relationships between British and Afrikaner capital in South Africa. Any distinction between them had almost lost its meaning. GenMin retained particularly close links to the South African regime, as shown by the many directors it shared with parastatals, including ISCOR, the government's Iron and Steel Corporation; and SASOL, the government's oil-from-coal venture.

The remaining groups—Johnnies, Union Corporation, Anglovaal, and the Rand Corporation—were considerably smaller and almost continually the object of takeover bids. Originally the property of Engelhard, the Rand Corporation did, in fact, merge with one of South Africa's largest manufacturing conglomerates to form Barlow Rand in the early 1970s.

Regardless of their origins, the mining finance houses came to form a network of linked holdings and joint ventures at all levels. GenMin, for example, owned almost a third of Union Corporation, in which Barlow

Rand and the Anglo associate, Charter Consolidated, also held interests. Each group held shares in gold mines controlled by others; they invested together in platinum, copper and other mines throughout southern Africa; and they worked together to develop South African manufacturing. [11]

Profits and Poverty

Two years after the Soweto uprisings, Anglo's chairman, Oppenheimer, insisted once again that the major factor working for a merger of black and white interests in South Africa was "the growth of a powerful modern free enterprise economy."[12] In reality, the network formed by the mining finance houses and their transnational partners conformed in no way to the competitive model suggested by his rhetoric. And the habits of the mining firms with respect to their African employees were hardly likely to encourage conciliation. Analysis of their profits, and the wages and conditions they considered appropriate for their workers, underscores the fundamental conflict between these representatives of "powerful modern free" enterprise and the impoverished black working class.

Before 1971, the gold price was fixed at $32 an ounce. At this rate, wages on the South African mines had to be reduced to starvation levels for the companies to turn a profit. By employing migrant labor, outlawing unions and strikes, (treating both with utmost brutality), and isolating workers in giant compounds, the mining finance houses, aided by the state, created conditions conducive to the continued accumulation of capital. In the mid-'70s, when the world gold price soared as the currencies of the leading capitalist nations depreciated, the mining finance houses profited at fantastic rates. But they hardly improved the black miners' wages or working conditions. In 1974, the gold mines returned $2340 million in profits, almost two-thirds of their parent companies' total income. In 1978, when gold prices averaged $139 an ounce, profits reached more than 100 percent. In 1979, as gold prices more than doubled to over $400 an ounce, profits almost tripled. Early in 1980, the world gold price skyrocketed to over $800 an ounce, reflecting the uncertainty and speculation fostered by the intensified international monetary crisis.

The South African minority regime diverted a considerable share of these profits to finance the growing military expenditures needed to perpetuate its repressive regime. (See table 5.1) In 1978[13] the South African Treasury received almost a billion dollars from gold mines and leases.

Table 5-1.

Distribution of mine companies' profits* between dividends to shareholders, tax payments to the South African regime, and savings for reinvestment, 1971 to 1977.

	Number of mines	Dividends Percent	Taxation Percent	Saving Percent
All gold mines				
1976-77	45	29.7	35.4	34.9
1975-76	45	32.9	39.1	28.0
1974-75	45	35.2	48.4	16.4
1973-74	43	32.0	49.9	18.1
1972-73	43	33.0	44.9	22.1
1971-72	42	36.4	41.9	21.7
Metallic mineral mines, excluding gold				
1976-77	30	25.5	13.2	61.3
1975-76	30	30.3	11.1	58.6
1974-75	24	31.6	26.4	40.0
1973-74	21	37.5	27.3	35.3
1972-73	20	38.5	26.1	35.4
1971-72	19	40.9	34.5	34.6

Note: The net profits for the years 1971-72 to 1976-77 were distributed as shown in the table above. In evaluating these profits, it must be borne in mind that certain mines normally do not make provision for depreciation of fixed assets so that in the net profits as defined here, a measure of capital consumption is included.

Sources: Republic of South Africa, *A Survey of the Accounts of Mining Companies for the Years 1966-77 and 1975-76* (Pretoria: Government Printer, 1978)

Table 5-2.
Employment in South African mines, 1976

	GOLD MINES number	GOLD MINES %	COAL MINES number	COAL MINES %	ALL MINES number	ALL MINES %
Whites	38,697	9.6	9,168	10.9	95,734	13.0
Coloured	578	0.1	65	—	7,556	1.0
Asians	16	—	327	0.1	1,102	0.1
Africans	362,616	90.2	74,254	88.6	626,807	85.5
	401,907	100	83,814	100	733,193	100

Source: Financial Mail, June 10, 1977, published in Institute of Race Relations, *A Survey of Race Relations*, op. cit., p. 257

The thousands of black miners who dug the gold benefitted little from the booming gold prices. About half of all South African miners worked on the gold mines.

By the mid 1970s, wages constituted less than a tenth of the mining companies' total income. (See Chart 5.1) Over half the wage bill went to the white miners who comprised barely a tenth of the labor force.

To hold labor costs down, the companies hired blacks almost solely as migrant workers* on long-term indentures. As the manager of Wenela, the recruiting organization for the Chamber of Mines, put the issue bluntly:[14]

Our case has always been that we want peasant farmers as labor. Our wage isn't sufficient to meet the needs of a man and his family unless it is augmented by earnings from a plot of land in the man's homeland. A family man from Johannesburg, for instance, couldn't live on what we pay.

In reality, by the '70s, many migrants and their families had no choice but to subsist almost entirely on their wages. In particular, miners from South Africa—a growing proportion of the total in the 1970s—signed on because in the Bantustans they had no alternative means of earning a living: no land, no job, no chance of either.

The mines dehumanized the migrants, breaking down their resistance to low wages and intolerable conditions. The process began in the branches of Wenela, established to recruit Africans throughout the southern third of the continent. (Many Wenela branches were closed down after South Africa's neighbors attained independence.) Responsible for feeding and transporting its recruits, Wenela typically provided food of low quality and unsanitary and overcrowded accommodations. The process of dehumanization began with the medical examination needed to obtain a job: The men had to strip naked in large groups so the doctor could examine their heartbeats. The procedure "seems unnecessary except as a way of initiating the miners into a subculture which is deprived of any values about human dignity."[15]

On the mines themselves, working conditions were brutal:[16]

...it is perhaps easiest to start by thinking of a road laborer digging up pavement with a jack-hammer drill. Now imagine him doing that work thousands of feet underground, in intense heat, where he cannot even begin to stand upright and where the drill...has to be held horizontal and driven into the wall in front. Add to this picture the noise of a roaddrill, magnified several times by the confined space;...and the possibility that the roof of the mine might suddenly cave in under pressure.

*The authors wish to express their appreciation to James Goldstein and Robert Accola for much of the following material on migrant workers.

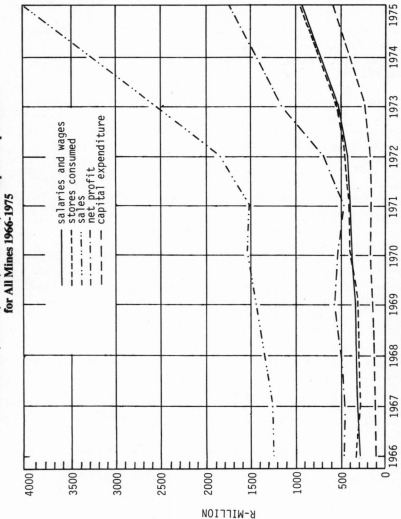

Chart 5.1.
Total Salaries, Stores, Sales, Net Profit, and Capital Expenditure
for All Mines 1966-1975

salaries and wages
stores consumed
sales
net profit
capital expenditure

R-MILLION

4000 3500 3000 2500 2000 1500 1000 500 0

1966 1967 1968 1969 1970 1971 1972 1973 1974 1975

Source: Republic of South Africa, Department of Statistics, *Mining and Financial Statistics, 1975*, Report No. 16-01-06 (Pretoria: Government Printer, 1975).

The South African mines had one of the highest accident rates in the world. The most dangerous were the "deep level" mines, tunnelled two or three kilometers underground. In these mines, the tremendous stress on surrounding rocks resulted in periodic rock fractures and collapses. These "rock bursts" caused the largest number of deaths on the mines, 262 of a total of 796 in 1976 alone. [17] Blacks with little training, working for long hours on the most difficult and dangerous jobs, made up by far the highest proportion of those killed or injured.

Miners on the job had to put up with harsh racist treatment from white supervisors. They worked a ten-hour day, six-day week. Their off hours afforded them little relief. The companies crowded them into large, fenced-in compounds, some housing as many as 8,000 men, far from their homes and families. Often 16 to 20 men lived crowded into a single room. The only relaxation available was drinking. These conditions inevitably undermined the stability of the miners' families.

The mining finance houses and the regime severely restricted the black miners' channels for complaints about the inhuman conditions on the mines. Unions seeking to organize migrant workers, in particular, were repressed brutally. The companies usually separated the workers by nationality or ethnic group as a tactic to hinder effective organization. Strikes by miners were illegal. The workers were expected to communicate their problems through the "indunas" (foremen) appointed by the companies for each separate ethnic group. Not surprisingly, the system did little or nothing to protect the workers. The indunas grew notoriously corrupt. In the mid-'70s, the companies introduced employee-management liaison committees to try to head off worker discontent, but these met little success.

Despite these measures, the black miners of South Africa have, over the years, repeatedly organized to demand improvements in their working conditions. [18] The companies have suppressed news of their efforts, but in some cases resistance became so widespread that the facts reached the public notice. In 1920, black workers shut the mining industry down entirely, demanding higher pay and an end to the Color Bar. In 1946, they again organized a massive, industry-wide strike. Both times, the regime and the companies reacted with customary brutality, clubbing and shooting miners, driving them back into the mines and jailing their leaders.

In the 1970s, serious labor unrest once more escalated on the mines as part of a nationwide pattern of mounting black demands for higher wages as living costs rose. On Sept. 11, 1973, the workers at Anglo-American's Carltonville Deep mines went on strike. Police "restored order" by killing 11 and wounding 27 others, firing "indiscriminately in darkness for nearly three hours at miners 'armed'—when they were armed at all—with sticks and stones."[19] In the next three years, over a 100 black miners were killed during strikes. In the mid-'70s, a government Commission of Inquiry[20] admitted:

The mineworker is becoming more and more aware of himself and the important part that he plays in the mining industry. He is aware of the enhanced gold price . . .that the industry is dependent on him and is very vulnerable—seen from the labor point of view.

The mining companies utilized various tactics to end the strike wave. One of the most important was to further segregate ethnic groups. As the Commission of Inquiry explained, otherwise "it is likely that the entire labor force will band together and the mine concerned will, therefore, be most vulnerable."

After Mozambique's liberation from the Portuguese, the Chamber of Mines took steps to reduce dependence on foreign labor. Mozambique's government itself had cut back on the supply of its migrants after independence. Moreover, the South African regime feared "communist" influences among the miners as a result of Frelimo's politicization programs. Malawi's government, too, cut back on migration after many migrant workers were killed in an airplane crash. On the other hand, the companies hoped that South Africans, faced with growing joblessness as the manufacturing sector stagnated in the mid-'70s, and encouraged by minor improvements in wages and working conditions, would prove a docile labor force.

The companies shortened the average length of stay on the mines required for South African miners from a year to about seven months. Most black South African miners still migrated from the Bantustans, so the regime introduced a new, if rather illusory, incentive. They no longer had to return to their 'homelands' at the end of their contracts, but might remain in the urban areas—if they found employment. This, of course, might induce them to sign on for another term on the mines.

The companies also raised wages to R57.20 for beginners—more than twice 1971 levels, but still below the 1975 Poverty Datum Line. At the same time, in absolute terms, the gap between black and white miners actually widened.[21]

As a result of these policies, the proportion of black miners from South Africa itself rose dramatically, from 20 percent in 1973 to just over 50 percent in 1977. In addition, the Chamber of Mines began to recruit in Southern Rhodesia in 1975. By 1977, over 20,000 miners on the South African mines came from that country. In 1976, however, new laws sharply reduced the number of Southern Rhodesian migrants.

In spite of these new tactics, unrest persisted on the mines. The companies began to purchase the most advanced technologies available in order to reduce dependence on black labor. Anglo-American, alone, planned to spend $1 billion between 1975 and 1980 on capital investments, a significant share going to mechanize its mines. Between 1973 and 1976, fixed capital stock in mining, overall, increased 28 percent, while employment fell two percent. [22] The transnationals played a dual role in the process of mechanization, both providing the needed technologies and assisting with finance.

The program aimed at two primary areas, stoping (extracting gold from the deep subterranean veins) and development of new mines. In stoping, introduction of tunnelling equipment and shuttle trains reduced the average crew from 25 to 10 men and raised output, offsetting the initial cost increase. [23]

Finally, the mining companies hoped to pacify black workers by hiring a few at high levels. This policy paralleled the transnational corporations' policies in other sectors. They aimed, on the one hand, to create a black skilled labor aristocracy that would defend the *status quo*; on the other hand, to relieve the shortage of white skilled labor and cut costs. As one observer said of Anglo-American's plans to break down the Color Bar, "then they can have the work now done by whites done by blacks, but at lower overall costs." [24] The shortage of qualified whites for the mines had emerged as early as 1970, [25] but nevertheless they retained their monopoly on all skilled jobs well into the '70s. With piece work bonuses and benefits, white miners averaged R1000 a month in take-home pay; some got up to R3000. In contrast, the vast majority of black miners received little over R60 a month in cash, plus accommodation and food, provided by the companies for roughly R50 more. Migrant workers received few sick benefits and no pensions.

The Chamber of Mines proposed repeatedly that a few blacks be promoted, while most remained poorly paid, unskilled migrants: [26]

...the top of the jobs pyramid must be stabilized and the workers should be South African blacks living with their families in or near the mines. The remaining portion of the pyramid, which will form the bulk of the labour force, will remain migratory for some time in the future.

Despite the marginal nature of these proposed changes, the white miners' unions resisted them with notable success. In any case, the

Table 5-3.
Where the Black Mine Workers Came From, 1960-1978

Country	1960 no.	%	1970 no.	%	1974 no.	%	1975 no.	%	1976 no.	%	1977[1] no.	%	1978 no.	%
South Africa (Transkei)	145,437	36.7	115,530	31.4	76,523	21.2	100,739	31.4	192,710	41.8	192,558 (88,733)	50.0	224,660[2]	53.4
Botswana			14,829	17.5	17,037	4.9	17,432	5.4	19,862	5.8	20,982	5.5	21,009	4.9
Lesotho	72,960	18.4	65,009	4.1	71,930	20.6	74,927	23.4	81,383	23.8	96,704	25.3	97,462	23.1
Swaziland			5,037	1.3	5,163	1.5	7,348	2.3	9,941	2.9	10,711	2.8	9,299	2.2
Mozambique	178,293	44.9	169,665	47.7	80,737	23.2	91,359	28.5	67,436	19.8	34,733	9.1	33,874	8.0
Angola					2,780	0.8	3,410	1.0	2,862	0.8	1,206	0.3	306	—
Malawi					94,728[3]	27.1	22,875	7.1	496	0.1	163	—	19,799	4.7
Zimbabwe							2,437	0.7	15,939	4.7	22,133	5.7	13,049	3.1
Total	396,690	100.0	371,070	100.0	348,901	100.0	320,536	100.0	341,099[1]	100.0	381,759	100.0	420,958[3]	100.0

Notes: [1] estimated

[2] After Transkei was granted illusory "independence", the Institute of Race Relations began to separate out its migrant labor to the mines; this was not continued in the Financial Mail Survey.

[3] The Financial Mail Supplement included Namibian migration data (1,500) and that is included in this total. The Institute of Race Relations did not report Namibian data separately, but included it in the data for South Africa, apparently.

Sources: Institute of Race Relations, *A Survey of Race Relations, 1961, 1970, 1977*; and Financial Mail (South Africa) "Mining Survey;" July 28, 1978.

companies apparently did not care to promote significant numbers of blacks to positions of real power. Anglo-American, for instance, claimed a liberal outlook, but its record was poor, even at its head office where there was "no reactionary white trade union...to resist any changes management wants to introduce." Pressured by black workers, a joint employee-management working party investigated the situation there in 1979.[27] It found that, "despite the stated intentions of the corporation," blacks remained relegated to much lower-level positions. Of the 347 employees in management at the head office, 346 were white, and none of the ten management trainees was black. Furthermore, nine of the 57 blacks in jobs comparable to whites received less pay. Between January 1976 and October 1978, 71 blacks were laid off—but no whites.

A strike at Anglo-American's labor relations showpiece, the Elandsrand gold mine[28] revealed the mining companies' inability to quell the black miners' militancy. The Elandsrand management had reportedly incorporated "all the best thinking by mine planners, personnel experts and architects in the 'single men's village.' " But, in April, 1979, the miners struck: Only 100 of the 4000 workers in the "model village" went to work, and they "battled" the company's security guards and police, plus a mine helicopter, for over two hours. The company labelled the strikers "rioters" and refused to allow journalists into the compound, but workers on the outside explained that the main grievances were low pay and poor food.

The Direct Involvement of Transnational Mining Firms[29]

A few huge British and U.S. transnational mining firms expanded and managed their own mines in South Africa, alongside of the mining finance houses. The country's rich mineral resources, given extremely low wages for black miners, promised high profits. Moreover, the companies felt safe from nationalization in South Africa, as their interests essentially coincided with those of the white-minority regime. In most other African countries where they invested, they seldom constructed plants to process ores beyond the first stages required for shipment at the lowest possible cost back to their home factories. In South Africa, in contrast, they built smelting and refining facilities in close collaboration with the South African mining finance houses. Increased processing within the country boosted its foreign exchange earnings, as well as stimulating local industry. The smelters and refineries, along with the mines, provided the transnationals with a welcome market for their surplus technologies. They also expanded their operations from their base in South Africa to invest, in collaboration with South African capital, in Namibia, Southern Rhodesia, Botswana and Zambia. In some cases, they shipped the ores back to South Africa for refining before exporting the metals overseas. (See Table 5.4)

Table 5-4.
Foreign investments in South African mines, including Namibia, December 31 1973

	rands (millions)	% of total mining investment
Direct	*420*	*31.2*
EEC countries[1]	256	18.9
Rest of Europe	6	—
North and South America[2]	157	11.6
Nondirect	*928*	*68.8*
EEC countries[1]	570	42.3
Rest of Europe	191	14.2
North and South America[2]	112	8.3
Total	*1,348*	*100.0*
EEC countries[1]	826	61.3
Rest of Europe	197	13.1
North and South America[2]	260	19.2

Sources: Republic of South Africa, Second Census of Foreign Transactions, Liabilities and Assets, 31 December, 1973, Supplement to South African Reserve Bank Quarterly Bulletin March, 1973.

Notes: [1]Includes England
[2]Primarily United States firms, either directly, or through Canadian affiliates

As in other industries, the British imperial companies had long been involved in South African mining. The British firm, Consolidated Goldfields, had been associated from the outset with Gold Fields South Africa, while Barclays was integrally linked with Anglo American. The output of the diamond and gold mines was traditionally sold through London, and most metals transactions were conducted through the London Metal Exchange. After World War II, however, U.S. firms—notably AMAX, Union Carbide, Newmont and Superior Oil's subsidiary, Falconbridge—became more and more involved. Where the British tended to leave management to the mining finance houses, the U.S. companies usually developed their own mines, frequently with minority South African participation.

Few F.R.G. transnationals invested directly in South African mining. Metalgesellschaft alone acquired extensive holdings in the mines of southern Africa, usually in collaboration with U.S. and South African partners. Similarly, Japanese companies, rather than become directly involved in mining there, signed long-term contracts with the mining finance houses for minerals (mostly iron ore and coal). This pattern conformed to the typical Japanese resource expansion program throughout Africa. It aimed to ensure Japanese factories of long-term supplies of raw materials with a minimum of Japanese investment. In the South African case, long-term Japanese contracts provided the essential markets and security for financing which, in several cases, enabled South African firms to develop new mines.

The British mining transnational, Rio Tinto Zinc, had traditional ties to Anglo-American and other South African mining finance houses. It also managed two major mining operations in southern Africa: Palabora, which mined and smelted magnetite, and the Rossing uranium mine in Namibia. Palabora employed over 3000 workers. An initial contract to supply Japanese firms with nine million tons of concentrates over 10 years ending 1976 provided an initial stimulus for the project. It returned high profits: In one year, 1974, net income totalled $66 million, 49 percent of the value of sales. Rio Tinto held 60 percent of Rossing. This project began to produce uranium from its deposit near Swakopmund in Namibia in 1976. British and French, as well as South African interests, helped finance Rossing, hoping to ensure regular uranium supplies for their nuclear power industries. The Federal Republic of Germany's government also participated initially, but domestic critics of apartheid forced it to back out of a major role. GenMin, the mining finance house associated with Anglo-American and the Afrikaner group, EVB, owned a substantial minority share. Rossing sold its output only to Nufcor, a South African parastatal.

From the early '60s, U.S. investments in South African mining and smelting grew rapidly. Direct U.S. investment in South Africa's mines and smelters doubled, from $78 million to $158 million, in the five years between 1968 and 1973. This represented a growth rate of 15 percent a year, compared to 5 percent in the rest of Africa; by 1973, U.S. investment in South Africa's mines equalled 28 percent of all U.S. holdings in African mining. U.S. companies officially reported average profits from the South African mines three times as high as from mining investments in the rest of Africa.[30] After 1973, however, the Department of Commerce suppressed data relating to U.S. mining investment in South Africa "to avoid disclosure of data of individual companies." (See above, p. 79)

By the mid-'70s, U.S. capital constituted about a fifth of all foreign funds invested in the mining sector. In contrast to British holdings, which were closely interwoven with South African interests, over half— 58 percent—of U.S. investments remained under direct U.S. control in the mid-'70s. When the gold price escalated in 1977-8, this proportion shrank somewhat as private U.S. investors purchased South African gold shares. Merrill Lynch, giant of the United States brokerage community, recommended that its clients purchase gold mining shares as the gold price soared in 1979. Though inflation was on the rise in South Africa, a Merrill Lynch spokesman explained, low cost labor would keep costs down:[31]

"The key to improved cost trends lies in the abundant flow of black labor now available to the mines. The number of blacks applying for work in the mines is well in excess of the jobs available."

U.S. mining firms continued to have a direct say in the operation of some of the largest base-metal mines. Like earlier investors in South Africa, they developed smelting and refining, as well as extracting minerals.

Besides Engelhard, two U.S. transnationals—AMAX and Newmont —became deeply involved in southern African mining and smelting. They, too, cooperated closely with the mining finance houses, particularly Anglo-American. In addition to capital and international contracts, they brought the most up-to-date mining technologies to these partnerships, making possible a reduction in the mines' dependence on African labor in the 1970s.

American Metal Climax (AMAX) actually came to own 10 percent of Anglo. In turn, Selection Trust, a leading member of the Anglo American Group, acquired an 11.8-percent share in AMAX. In the 1970s, this brought Anglo into close proximity with the largest firm in the world, Standard Oil of California, which held 20 percent of AMAX and was also deeply involved in South Africa's oil business. (See below, pp. 190-3) AMAX conducted its business throughout southern Africa in close collaboration with Anglo-American. Together, the two companies had developed the mines in then-Northern Rhodesia (now Zambia), turning them into some of the biggest copper producers in the world, (and providing a major early source of capital for Anglo). After independence, the Zambian Government took a majority share in an attempt to dam the massive outflow of investable surpluses engineered by the two mining companies, but was largely frustrated by their continued domination of international copper markets. The companies also largely thwarted attempts to raise the number of African managerial personnel. In Botswana, AMAX and Anglo collaborated to develop the Selebi-Pikwe mine. There, they gave a share to the government from the start; in return, Botswana provided infrastructure worth rather more than the value of its initial share. The companies continued to provide management, and refused to develop refining capacity. In cooperation with Newmont, AMAX also invested in Tsumeb, the giant copper mine in Namibia, and in O'okiep Copper which operated in South Africa and Namibia.

Newmont had long-standing ties to the white-minority regimes of southern Africa. A vice president had worked for eight years, from 1947 to 1955, as general manager of the Rhodesia Company. By the mid-'70s, the company reaped almost a third of its net global income from its holdings in four southern African companies: O'okiep, which it controlled; Palabora; Tsumeb; and Highveld Steel and Vanadium. Highveld produced basic iron and steel products in partnership with the South African parastatal ISCOR. Tsumeb and O'okiep both defied U.N. sanctions to operate in Namibia, illegally occupied by South Africa. O'okiep, which returned good profits (20 percent on sales in 1974), planned significant expansion in the mid-'70s in both the Cape Province and in Namibia, south of Windhoek.

A third U.S. mining transnational in South Africa played a particularly significant role. Union Carbide mined and smelted chrome in Southern Rhodesia, and in the mid-'70s opened a chrome refinery in South Africa. It produced about 20 percent of South Africa's chrome, exporting thousands of tons a year to the U.S. To protect these investments, the company engaged in politics in the U.S.

In 1971, it organized a powerful Congressional lobby to obtain passage of the Byrd Amendment. The amendment required the U.S. to continue importing chrome from Southern Rhodesia, in direct defiance of the U.N. embargo and official U.S. foreign policy. In the late '70s, Union Carbide supported efforts to pressure Congress into acceptance of the so-called "internal settlement" engineered for Zimbabwe by Ian Smith and the South African regime. Union Carbide's former president, Kenneth Rush, presumably used his government contacts to further the company's aims: he had been Ambassador to the F.R.G. and deputy secretary of Defence and of State in the early '70s.

Union Carbide's employment practices exemplify the relations between U.S. mine investors and black mine workers. In 1976, all but about 10 percent of Union Carbide's African workers earned less than a minimum health and decency living standard for a typical South African family. (See Table 5.5) In the United States, mine workers earned an average of over $1000 a month,[32] almost six times the average wage of black workers employed by Union Carbide in South Africa.

Union Carbide's employees in South Africa had no union. Instead, the company, in line with South African government policy, formed

Table 5-5.
**Wages and Employment Policies of Union Carbide's Two Largest
South African Subsidiaries (Ucar Minerals and Emsa),[1]
1976 compared to 1973**

Employment grade[2]	1973: BLACK EMPLOYMENT		1976: BLACK EMPLOYMENT		1976 WAGES		
	no.	% of total work force	no.	% of total work force	Rand per month	% of MEL[2]	% increase since 1973
11-14	0	0	48	7.2	R278-[3]	—	—
7-10	40	9.9	118	17.7	R168-222	144	148
3-6	48	11.8	155	23.2	R131-155	87-115	74
1-2	318	78.3	346	52.9		68-80	71
Total	406	25.0[4]	667	25.1			

Source: Investor Responsibility Research Center, "Corporate Activity in South Africa: Union Carbide Corp." Analysis E., Supplement No. 8 (Washington, 1977).

Notes: [1]Total Union Carbide employment in South Africa was 1800, two thirds black.
[2]In 1973, the MEL (Minimum Effective Level) was estimated at R141 a month. By 1976, it was around R193. It represents the minimum needed for any kind of reasonable living standard, and equals 150 percent of the PDL, which is the absolute minimum needed for survival.
[3]Not given.
[4]Estimated.

liaison committees, headed by white managerial personnel. Militance on South Africa's mines and pressure from the U.S. anti-apartheid critics led, nonetheless, to some increases in African wages in 1973-76. Most workers' wages barely kept pace with inflation but Union Carbide granted about a fifth of its African employees much larger wage increases, both absolutely and relatively, than it did the majority. This, of course, pulled up the average. It also appeared designed to contribute to creation of a new kind of black "labor aristocracy" to restrain further pressure for change.

As with other minerals, the search for "stable" cheap reserves of ore led U.S. and Japanese steel producers to South Africa. U.S. Steel, one of the two biggest steel companies in the U.S., established four subsidiaries there. It contracted to buy some three million tons of iron ore from South Africa each year for 15 years, beginning in 1978. In addition, its South African affiliates processed copper, zinc, ferrochrome and ferromanganese in South Africa itself. In contrast, the only large U.S. Steel company affiliate in independent Africa, in Gabon, (44 percent owned by U.S. Steel) merely exported manganese ore. In cooperation with AMAX, Newmont and Anglo-American, U.S. Steel also had an indirect share in Tsumeb in Namibia.

Japanese iron and steel firms hoped to take advantage of similar opportunities in South Africa. In 1971, they petitioned their government to lift its ban on direct investments there.[33] Although the government refused, the Japanese steel industry came to depend heavily on imports of iron ore and coal. Japan was ISCOR's largest export market by the 1970s. Japanese firms signed several long term contracts for iron ore from South Africa, and with an Anglo-American subsidiary in Swaziland. (See below, p.246)

French firms mostly refrained from direct involvement in South African mining, perhaps because they had extensive access to mines in the former African colonies of France. The French uranium firm, Minatome, a consortium formed by the Compagnie Francaise des Petroles, owned by the French government, and Pechiney Ugine Kuhlman, did, however, acquire a 10-percent interest in Rössing uranium. Minatome apparently hoped to ensure a steady supply of the mine's output for its nuclear industry back home. At the same time, French companies became increasingly involved in providing nuclear technology for the South African regime's program. Minatome also took minority shares in a number of companies producing uranium in independent Africa, and financed exploration for uranium in Mauritania.

As popular resistance increasingly threatened the minority regime, the transnational corporations tended to limit their development of new

mines to financing and indirect assistance. Instead of investing themselves, they would guarantee long-term markets, or provide loans. For
instance, in the late '70s, South African mines signed 10-year contracts
to supply France[34] and Belgium[35] with natural uranium. In both cases,
the European customers provided loans at little or no interest to finance
the initial expansion of the mines. In the Belgian case, the credit was to
be repaid by uranium shipments at prices below the world level. This
increasingly common form of financing was important as "an assurance
against the possible effects of any future embargo on trade with South
Africa."[36]

Regional Mineral Development

In the 1970s, the South African regime sponsored a series of strategic
regional mining projects, acting primarily through ISCOR to strengthen
the economy as a whole. The intensive prospecting and mining investment engaged in by transnational mining firms made these developments possible. In most cases, the state provided financing to further
South African independence from imports, stimulate investment, and
increase foreign exchange earnings; the transnationals gained assured
sources of cheap raw materials. Transnational engineering firms profited from construction of infrastructure. A number of companies found
welcome markets for technology in the new projects. These mining
developments gained in importance as the economy stagnated in the
latter half of the decade.

U.S. mining firms discovered massive deposits of copper, zinc, lead
silver and antimony in northwestern Cape Province in 1973/4. A number of transnationals, including Rio Tinto Zinc, Shell, U.S. Steel and
Falconbridge, in cooperation with the South African mining finance
houses, planned to invest there. Newmont, O'okiep and the South
African firm, Union Corporation, planned to invest R100 million in zinc
production. Phelps Dodge, one of the largest copper producers in the
U.S., began to develop the Aggeneys mine in 1977. It invited Gold
Fields South Africa to take over 51 percent of the project, in part to
blunt anti-apartheid criticism. The two companies' initial investments
totalled almost $200 million,[37] a particularly important boost to the
South African regime in a period of capital outflow following the Soweto
uprising.

Phelps Dodge's only productive investment in independent Africa
was its minor holding in Metal Fabricators of Zambia, a small copper-
wire fabricating plant. The Zambian government provided most of the

finance for that project, while Phelps supplied the management and equipment.[38]

A number of transnational mining companies also vied to participate in the regional development project undertaken on the initiative of the South African regime in the Richards Bay area.[39] The regime planned to expand the bay into a deep sea harbor, primarily to facilitate the export of coal from the Transvaal. Growing international demand for coal in the wake of rising oil prices spurred South African exports: contracts signed with the U.S., France, the F.R.G., Italy and Japan among others, led to a tenfold increase in South African coal exports between 1973 and 1976. Transnationals from Italy, Luxembourg, the Netherlands, the F.R.G. and Belgium constructed the harbor and developed the coal mines and slurry pipes to the bay. The Afrikaner group, GenMin and ISCOR, undertook the actual mining. The South African Railway and Harbor Authority financed the harbor's expansion with loans supplied by Eurodollar syndicates. In addition, two smelters were built at the bay, both with participation from a parastatal, the Industrial Development Corporation (IDC). The IDC joined with Alusuisse, the Swiss firm, to form Alusaf, to operate the country's first aluminum smelter. The R80 million investment made South Africa virtually self-sufficient in aluminium production.[40]* The Quebec Iron and Titanium Corporation, a Canadian subsidiary of a U.S. firm, joined the IDC and Union Corporation in a R200-million project to mine and smelt titanium and zirconium from beach sands north of Richards Bay.

Transnational corporate participation in the Sishen-Saldanha Bay iron ore project illustrated the increasing dependence of South African expansion of minerals production and processing on foreign technology, finance and markets. Japan reportedly signed contracts for over 40 million tons of iron over a 15-year period, starting in 1977. On this basis, the regime planned to establish a major mining, steel production, and exporting complex. ISCOR retained control, mobilizing about $200 million for the project in 1973-75 from U.S., U.K., F.R.G., Austrian and other European banks. It contracted with a number of transnational engineering and construction firms to build the needed infrastructure and plant. Significantly, almost all the companies involved had subsidiaries in South Africa. Spie-Batignolles, which helped the Cabora Bassa dam and the Koeberg nuclear power plant, undertook to construct the railway. SAGE, the South African subsidiary of General Electric, supplied 40 diesel-electric locomotives. The rails were bought in the

---

*Alusaf's attitude towards its black employees was illustrated during the 1973 strikes, when it called in the army to "maintain order."

F.R.G. and welded with British equipment. A U.S. firm provided the signalling system. The F.R.G. engineering company, MANN, erected the handling and shiploading equipment in the harbor, which a Dutch firm, Salcon, designed and coordinated. Voest, an Austrian parastatal, built a new steel plant for ISCOR. It installed an oxygen-blast system, the most advanced in the world, to make possible exports to Europe, the U.S., and elsewhere. (See below, p. 138) The entire project ran into trouble in the mid-'70s, however, as its costs soared to $1 billion, ISCOR had trouble borrowing more money, and anti-apartheid groups in Austria and the Netherlands inspired a certain nervousness among the transnationals involved.

Summary

Employing low-paid black labor, compelled by systematically imposed poverty to migrate from South Africa and beyond, South Africa's mines produced vast profits. On this foundation, primarily with financial assistance from imperial British and German banks, a handful of mining finance houses built sprawling industrial empires. Over the years, increasingly interlinked with the South African regime's parastatals, they came to dominate and shape the nation's racist political economy. Anglo-American, by far the largest, reinvested its profits at home and abroad to weave an international network closely intermeshed with U.S. and British transnational finance capital.

Far from improving the lives of their black workers, Anglo and the other mining companies recruited migrant blacks from throughout the southern region, openly paying them wages too low to support their families. When labor unrest, spurred by the spreading liberation struggles of the 1970s, threatened their profitable business, the companies devised new approaches. They recruited increasing numbers of South African blacks who faced prolonged unemployment as the economic crisis gripped the rest of the economy, paying them slightly better wages than before—although still below the poverty line. They admitted a few to the formerly lily-white "aristocracy" at the top of the labor pyramid, but the bulk of black miners had no choice but to migrate annually from their impoverished "homelands" to earn the meager wages offered. At the same time, the companies reinvested growing shares of their skyrocketing profits to purchase sophisticated machinery and equipment sold by eager transnational corporate salesmen, to mechanize their old mines and open new ones while reducing their dependence on increasingly restive black workers.

Transnational mining companies eagerly sought to participate in South Africa's profitable mining business. British and American companies, in particular, invested far more in South African mines than in the independent African states. From their headquarters in South Africa, they spread their holdings throughout southern Africa, typically in partnership with the South African mining finance houses. Conforming to South African labor policies, they reaped super profits by paying below poverty line wages. Furthermore, whereas they shipped the ores mined in independent African states back to their factories in Europe, the U.S., or Japan, they built extensive smelting and refining facilities in South Africa. They often shipped ores mined in neighboring countries back to their South African plants.

As the threat to white rule made the South African situation appear less "stable," the transnationals introduced tactics they had adopted in other Third World countries. Increasingly, instead of investing directly, they negotiated long-term contracts and partnership agreements, leaving the risk to the South African regime together with its parastatals and the mining finance houses. When the transnationals did participate directly, they established consortia in collaboration with local private or state firms, ensuring assistance with local financing and infrastructural costs. Their partners' regional development schemes provided welcome markets for their surplus technologies and capital. At the same time, their continued purchase of South African minerals and mineral products provided the steady inflow of foreign exchange and profits that continued to prop up the brutal apartheid system.

References

1. E.g. See A. Seidman, ed., *Natural Resources and National Welfare: The Case of Copper* (New York: Praeger, 1976).

2. E. Evans, Dependent Development - *The Alliance of Multinational, State and Local Capital in Brazil*, (Princeton: Princeton University Press, 1979), p. 158.

3. State of South Africa (Johannesburg: Da Gama Publishers, 1973)

4. R. First, C. Gurney, J. Steele, *The South African Connection* (London: Uarrice Temple Smith, Ltd., 1972).

5. For history of Anglo-American Corporation, see T. Gregory, *Sir Ernest Oppenheimer and the Economic Development of Southern Africa* (Cape Town: Oxford University Press, 1962); "Inside the Anglo Powerhouse," *Financial Mail* (Johannesburg) July 4, 1969; and A. P. Cartwright, *The Gold Mines* (Johannesburg: Purnell and Sons, 1962).

6. E. Williams, *Capitalism and Slavery* (New York: Russell & Russell, 1961).

7. For Anglo American Corporation's current holdings, see its current annual reports, published in South Africa, unless otherwise cited.

8. See United Nations, *World Trade Annual, 1973*, Vols. I, III.

9. For information relating to the U.S. companies, see the relevant annual reports,

reports to the U.S. Securities and Exchange Commission, and look up their top executives in *Who's Who in America* in relevant years. For company histories see Moody's Industrials.

10. Cited in First, et al, *The South African Connection*, op. cit., 132.

11. See A. and N. Seidman, *South Africa and U.S. Multinational Corporations* (Westport: Lawrence Hill & Co., and Dar es Salaam: Tanzania Publishing House, 1977) Ch.3.

12. *South African Financial Mail* May 26, 1978.

13. *South Africa Digest*, June 8, 1979.

14. *Forbes*, June 15, 1974, p. 40.

15. *Another Blanket*, p. 10.

16. F. Wilson, *Labour on the South African Gold Mines 1911-1969* (Oxford: Oxford University Press, 1972).

17. D. Massey, "Black Workers' Struggle and Management Response on the South African Mines," (Mochudi, Botswana: unpublished paper, 1978), p. 8.

18. For history of South African labor, including miners, see J. and R. Simons, *Color and Class in South Africa, 1850-1950* (Harmondsworth: Penguin African Library 1969).

19. *The New York Times*, Sept. 21, 1973.

20. Republic of South Africa, Report of the Inter-Departmental Committee of Inquiry into Riots on Mines in the Republic of South Africa, 1975. (unpublished) cited in Massey, "Black Workers Struggle. . . ." op. cit.

21. *Mining Journal*, Feb. 3, 1978, Supplement, p. 9; and *Optima*, Two. 1974, p. 85.

22. South African Reserve Bank, Quarterly Bulletin of Statistics, Dec. 1977.

23. *Optima*, One, 1975, p. 68.

24. *The New York Times*, Oct. 23, 1973.

25. *Economist*, June 6, 1970, p. 74.

26. *South African Mining and Engineering Journal*, April, 1975, p. 35.

27. *South African Financial Mail*, Mar. 16, 1979.

28. Reported in *Rand Daily Mail*, extra edition, Apr. 9 and 10, 1979.

29. Unless otherwise cited, see relevant companies' annual reports.

30. U.S. Department of Commerce, Survey of Current Business, August, 1974. (Washington, D.C.: Government Printing Office, annual).

31. *Boston Globe*, Sept. 23, 1979.

32. U.S. Statistical Abstract (Washington, D.C., Government Printing Office, 1979) p. 414.

33. *Africa Keizai Jijyo* (Japan), July 20, 1971.

34. *Die Welt* (Bonn) July 15, 1977.

35. *Blick Durch die Wirtschaft*, Feb. 10, 1979.

36. *Mining Journal*, Feb. 3, 1978.

37. *South African Financial Mail*, Oct. 1, 1976.

38. A. Seidman, ed., *Natural Resources and National Welfare: The Case of Copper* (New York: Praeger, 1976 pp. 30-31).

39. For further information on Richards Bay project, see *South African Financial Mail*, Special Supplement, March 5, 1976; U.N. Center Against Apartheid, Contribution of Transnational Corporations to South African Development Projects.

40. G. Rist, "Relations Between Switzerland and South Africa" United Nations Unit on Apartheid, Notes and Documents, Sept. 1974, May 1974.

Transnational
Agribusiness 6

Early Plantations

While British settlers and capital flooded the gold fields of the Transvaal in the late 19th Century, a few British firms introduced plantation agriculture in securely-held British areas like Natal. Some followed Cecil Rhodes' armies up north to plant spreading estates in Southern Rhodesia. They produced specialized plantation crops like sugar and tobacco for sale to the region's growing urban and mining population, as well as for export to England and Europe and, increasingly, the United States.

The British had varied experience throughout the continent. In West and parts of East Africa, the organized military strength of the Africans prevented the British trading firms and settlers from actually expropriating the Africans' land. Instead, they set up trading posts to buy tropical crops—cocoa, palm nuts, ground nuts, rubber—grown by the African peasants themselves. In East and Central Africa, British settlers, after pushing Africans off the best agricultural lands, hired them for a pittance to grow the produce they reaped for export throughout the Empire. In South Africa, the British trading companies at first imported shiploads of contract workers from India to reap the harvests. The land had been taken from the African peoples. To avoid further immediate conflict, which must have ensued if the Africans, who still had access to lands elsewhere, had been forced to work, the British imported Indians. The British colonial government was too deeply engaged in disputes with the Boers over the rich lands and mines of the Transvaal to take on another battle with African laborers. When the Asians' contracts ended, unable to pay their way back to their own colonialized homelands, they continued to work as low-cost labor to reap crops and profits for British agribusiness. Over time, they were joined by growing numbers of Africans, who were eventually forced off their own lands throughout South Africa once the British and Boers had settled their own disputes.

The big agricultural companies' southern African estates thrived. They had an expanding, ever-available supply of low cost labor. The mining finance houses' expansion of output and employment created an ever-growing domestic demand for their crops. They found a ready and expanding market for their produce in the industrializing states of Europe. Over time, they spread their business throughout Africa, sometimes on their own, sometimes by merging with companies already engaged in trade in tropical produce.

Elsewhere in Africa, the expanding trading agricultural firms restricted their business to buying or producing and shipping tropical crops to Europe and the U.S. for processing. They left the African economies, after almost a century of outright colonial rule, geared to the sale of one or a few low-cost agricultural raw materials on an uncertain world market. After independence, the new African states pressed the companies to increase local processing. They sought to augment local employment and foreign exchange earnings while laying the foundations for a deeply desired industrial transformation.

But by the years of independence, the agricultural trading firms had grown into transnational corporate conglomerates, manipulating global agribusiness networks. A number had merged with U.S.-based firms. Their parent companies owned factories in Europe and America which processed the coffee, cocoa, cotton, sugar, tea, oil seeds, and beef which they purchased at low prices from Africa and sold at high prices after processing to their home customers. Their corporate managers concluded that it was more profitable to shop around, playing the peasants of one African country off against another, buying their crops at the lowest possible prices for their factories back home. They no longer even risked their capital investing in plantations or up-country trading posts. Far less did they wish to invest in processing factories in African countries to produce foodstuffs, beverages and tobacco for sale abroad in competition with their own home industries. Only under growing pressures, typically spurred by the imposition of tariffs and not infrequently aided by African governments' investments, did they construct small plants to process a few agricultural products—sugar, cigarettes, bottled drinks—for local consumption.

But in South Africa, transnational agribusinesses reinvested a considerable share of their profits to build associated processing plants and factories. They not only sold their processed foodstuffs, beverages and tobacco products to those who could afford to buy them in South Africa itself; they also shipped them throughout southern Africa, undercutting the neighboring states' efforts to industrialize; and back to Europe, the U.S., and increasingly, Japan.

It is brutally ironic that, while the overwhelming majority of blacks in South Africa were literally struggling for survival on the verge of starvation, South African-based agribusiness was shipping valuable processed and unprocessed foodstuffs, including fruits and vegetables, overseas. The members of a typical African family counted themselves lucky to eat maize meal porridge daily, with meat perhaps once or twice a month. Fresh fruit was an unusual treat. Meanwhile, despite its industrial growth, agricultural products still constituted almost a fourth of South Africa's exports in the mid-'70s. (See Table 6-1)

Table 6-1.
Exports of Agricultural Produce from South Africa, 1976

Category of exports	Rands	% of total exports
Live animals, animal products	104,456,964	2.3%
Vegetable products	443,662,999	9.8%
Animal and vegetable fats and oils	19,781,934	0.4%
Prepared foodstuffs, beverages, tobacco	503,188,947	11.1%
Total agricultural exports	1,071,090,844	23.6%

Source: Calculated from Republic of South Africa, *Foreign Trade Statistics*, Vol. I, Imports and Exports, 1978 (Pretoria: Government Printer, 1978).

The post World War II expansion of transnational agribusiness in South Africa was inextricably linked to the further impoverishment of the black South African population. In the first place, they continued to hire hundreds of thousands of black workers for their plantations and factories at wages far below those paid in other sectors of the South African economy; and, secondly, they played a leading role, especially in the 1970s, in mechanization of agriculture, pushing increasing numbers of Africans into the ranks of the unemployed.

The Growing Impoverishment of Agricultural Workers

The transnational agribusiness firms paid their workers incredibly low wages, even in the 1970s when the farms had to compete in mining areas with the rising wages paid to black miners. African agricultural employees' wages did somewhat more than double from the early 1960s to the mid-'70s, the years when transnationals multiplied their investments in the apartheid system. But their yearly cash incomes remained barely more than five percent of that of white farm employees. Their *annual* cash income would hardly support the typical African family for a *month* in the urban areas. (See Table 6-2) To live, they depended on the pitiful housing and food provided by white farm owners, so they were essentially tied to the job—as long as it lasted.

Table 6-2.
Average Cash Earnings per year of regular farm employees, 1963-1974

	Whites	Colored	Asians	Africans
1963	1311.23	152.09	189.76	72.09
1964	1285.38	154.66	194.24	83.07
1965	1305.76	153.86	245.53	77.50
1969	1727.62	199.03	339.40	94.11
1971	2332.10	244.78	416.81	119.49
1972	2634.82	262.10	526.69	130.59
1973	2930.76	304.48	637.07	152.11
1974	3439.07	346.09	902.70	185.32
% of white earnings		10.1	26.3	5.4

Source: *Stats*, March, 1977, p. 46, presented in the Institute of Race relations, *A Survey 1977 . . .* op. cit., p. 256

Transnational agribusinesses profited, not only by paying low wages on their farms, but also from the fact that they paid their factory workers wages well below the average paid in other branches of the manufacturing sector. (See Table 6-3)

Table 6-3.
Average Monthly Wages and Employment of Workers in Agri-industry, 1976

	FOOD		BEVERAGES		TOBACCO	
	Average no. employed	Average wage per month (rands)	Average no. employed	Average wage per month (rands)	Average no. employed	Average wage per month (rands)
Africans	103,100	110	18,400	136	1,900	150
Asians	8,400	200	700	309	—	—
Coloured	25,900	132	3,400	148	1,000	143
Whites	22,400	517	4,600	516	800	467

Source: *Rand Daily Mail*, April 1, 1977.

Throughout the 1960s and 1970s, the biggest agricultural firms reinvested the profits they reaped from the overseas sales of crops produced by their low-paid black employees to buy machinery and equipment to mechanize their farms. [1] Their investments constituted an important market for the transnational manufacturing companies building up South African industry. The number of tractors per farm multiplied ten times from 1946 to 1970. In less than 15 years after World War II, the number of combine harvestors increased nearly sixfold. The introduction of weed sprays—conducted by airplane on the big plantations—sharply reduced the amount of labor required for weeding.

Increasing numbers of black agricultural workers were pushed into the ranks of the unemployed. Data on unemployment among agricultural workers was particularly inadequate (see pp. 77, 85 above on unemployment data). One report showed regular farm employment diminished from 720,265 in 1970 to 712,892 in 1974. Another estimated the decline was even greater, accompanied by a growth in the numbers of Africans who crowded into the subsistence farms in the Bantustants. (See Table 6-4)

Table 6-4.
Employment in Agriculture, Hunting, Forestry, and Fishing, 1970-1974

	Whites	African, Coloured and Asian				Total
		Regular	Casual	Subsistence	Fishing	
	1000's			1000's		1000s
1970	103.4[1]	(774.2)[1]	(192.0)[1]	705.5	(5.0)[2]	1780.1
1971	101.9	732.9	185.4	812.3	(5.0)	1837.5
1972	100.4	724.4	179.7	858.5	(5.0)	1868.0
1973	99.0	715.0	170.5	899.7	(5.0)	1827.4
1974	97.5	700.4	171.0	(853.5)[1]	(5.0)	1879.2
1975						(1862.6)
1976						(1862.6)

[1]The 1970 figure for whites is a corrected Census figure.
[2]Bracketed figures are either interpolations or mean figures.

Source: Presented in Institute of Race Relations, *A Survey,* op. cit. p. 254.

The estimated numbers of unemployed and underemployed agricultural laborers constituted about a third of the agricultural labor force throughout the 1970s.

Table 6-5.
Number of Unemployed and Underemployed Agricultural Workers and the Percent of the Labor Force, 1970-1976

	Number of unemployed and underemployed 1000's	% of labor force
1970	874	32.9
1971	977	34.7
1972	963	34.0
1973	746	28.4
1974	1008	35.1
1975	960	34.0
1976	948	33.7

Source: Institute of Race Relations, *A Survey,* . . . op. cit. p. 255.

Unemployed agricultural workers had three options. They could apply for jobs on the mines, but increased mechanization and unemployment rendered these jobs increasingly difficult to get. They could move illegally into urban areas in hopes of finding employment there, though stagnation of the industrial sector made that hope slim; and if they were caught by the police, they might well go to jail—perhaps to be sent back to work on farms as convict labor. Or they could join the reservoirs of underemployed and jobless on the overcrowded Bantustans.

The population of QwaQwa, for example, rose from 24,000 in 1970 to 190,000 in 1976.[2] The government's Economic Development Program Report[3] projected an increase of 4.8 percent in agricultural workers, a high proportion of them women, in the Bantustans. Given the already high level of malnutrition and disease in the overcrowded areas, this could only contribute to accelerating the pace of genocide by starvation.

Agribusiness and the Development of Underdevelopment

The major agribusiness firms—Unilever and Nestles, the British American Tobacco Company, Brook Bond-Leibig, Cadbury Schweppes and Tate and Lyle[4]—not only contributed to the intensified impoverishment of blacks in South Africa; their role there was simply a feature of the on-going process of development of underdevelopment fostered by transnationals throughout Africa. By the 1970s, they had expanded their industrial holdings in South Africa from plantations and simple agricultural processing plants to complex industrial conglomerates. In most of the rest of Africa, they continued to extract raw produce for shipment to their factories, not only in Europe and North America, but also in the South African regional sub-center. Only in a few independent African states did they establish even small-scale plants to process a limited amount of their output for local consumer markets. They marketed the foodstuffs and beverages they produced in their factories elsewhere—including South Africa—in the independent African states. These sales contributed to the irony inherent in the fact that the predominantly agricultural countries of Africa actually imported increasing amounts of foodstuffs—aggravating their balance of payments deficits and undermining their efforts to achieve self-reliant, integrated agricultural-industrial development.

The British firm, Unilever, was itself a holding company, the second largest firm in Great Britain, excluding oil companies. It had long dominated African agricultural exports, particularly from West Africa, through the United African Company (UAC).[5] By the 1970s, Unilever owned subsidiaries in Cameroon, Zaire, Ghana, Ivory Coast, Kenya, Malawi, Nigeria, Sierra Leone, and Zambia. Its Zairois subsidiary, Huilieries de Belges, owned hundreds of thousands of acres in plantations. It manufactured all kinds of goods for household consumption in 70 countries, had over 200 operating companies, and 150 factories. Its world sales almost equalled the total value of all African exports.

But Unilever had acquired more investments in processing and manufacturing in South Africa than in any other African country with the possible exception of Nigeria. In Nigeria, its holdings consisted primarily of plantations and meat-producing facilities, however, whereas those in South Africa included technologically sophisticated chemicals production and transportation business. Unilever also retained its Southern Rhodesian subsidiary as one of its principle holdings, despite United Nations sanctions against the illegal regime there.

In 1976, Unilever, with 10.9 percent of its capital invested in Africa, made 12 percent of its sales and reaped 24 percent of its operating profits (before taxes etc.) and 18.1 percent of all profit attributable to ordinary capital there. Though its sales had declined in 1978, it still reaped 9.3 percent of its operating profit and 15.9 percent of its profit for ordinary capital from a somewhat smaller proportion of its capital invested there.

In the 1970s, Unilever merged part of its interests with Nestles, the Swiss holding company that had developed extensive food industry interests, including milk, chocolate, soluble coffee, soups and frozen foods. Nestles owned 820 factories, sales branches, depots and operating units throughout the world. Together with Unilever, it initiated operation of a joint food business throughout the Federal Republic of Germany, Austria and Italy. To expand its sales throughout the Third World, Nestles vigorously advertised its powdered milk formula for infants to replace the much healthier breast feeding. Besides fostering unnecessary imports, evidence soon exposed the spread of preventable malnutrition and disease as African mothers sought to adopt the advertised "modern" ways.[6]

Nestles, like its partner, Unilever, purchased many of its raw materials from African states. It located most of its processing plants, however, in Europe and the U.S. where it sold most of its output. It built few manufacturing facilities in Africa. By far the largest were those in South Africa and Southern Rhodesia, where it processed almost the full line of its products.

The British sugar manufacturing firm, Tate and Lyle, still owned holdings throughout the former British Empire in the 1970s. They, too, were concentrated in southern Africa, particularly in South Africa and

Table 6-6.
Major Holdings of Some Agribusiness Corporations in Africa, 1976
(Percent of equity in local subsidiary in parentheses)

African Country	Unilever*	Nestles*	British American Tobacco Co. (BAT)	Tate & Lyle	Brook Bond Leibig	Cadbury Schweppes
South Africa	South Africa, Ltd. (100%) Glenton & Mitchell (100%) Hudson & Knight (100%) Lever Bros. (100%) Van den Bergh and Jergens (100%) T. Walls & Sons (100%) Elida Gibbs (100%) S.A. Warehousing Services (100%) Naire Industries (100%)	*Local processing of:* sweetened condensed milk; evaporated milk; pasteurized, sterilized milk and cream; milk powder; cheese and butter; cereals for infants; instant chocolate. *Local processing and imports of:* milk powder, instant coffee	Unico Holdings (58%) Alex Pirie & Sons (100%) Wiggins Teape Converters (100%) Wiggins Teape, Ltd. (100%) Lentheric (100%) Yardley of London (100%)	Pure Cane Molasses (100%) African Products (52.32%)	Brook Bond Oxo (100%)	Cadbury Schweppes Holdings (100%) Cadbury Schweppes (65%)
Rhodesia (Zimbabwe)	Rhodesia Ltd. (100%) Lever Bros. (100%)	*Local processing of:* condensed milk; milk powder; dietetic milk foods; cereal for infants; *imports others*	BAT Central Africa (85%) BAT Rhodesia (100%) Carlton Cigarette (100%) Export Leaf Tobacco (100%)	Rhodesian Sugar Refineries (50.13%) Hippo Valley Estates (10%)	Brook Bond (33.3%) Liebig's (100%) Lyons Brook Bond (33.3%) National Canners (100%)	Schweppes (55%)
Cameroons	United Republic of Cameroons, Ltd. (100%) Pamol (Cameroons) (100%) Pamol Plantations (100%)					
Congo (Braz)	Societe Commerciale du Kouilou Niari-Congo (96%) Peoples Republic of Congo- (Brazza), Ltd. (100%)					
Gabon	Gabon Ltd. (100%) Hatteret Cookson (99%)					
Ghana	Ghana Ltd. (100%) Lever Bros. (45%) UAC of Ghana (60%)	*Local processing of:* milk power, coffee; *imports others*	Pioneer Tobacco Co. (100%)			Cadbury
Ivory Coast	Ivory Coast Ltd. (100%) CFCI S.A. (99%)	*Local processing of* coffee, imports others				

126

Table 6-6. Continued

Country		Local processing				
Kenya	Kenya Ltd. (100%) East Africa Inds. (4%) Gailey & Roberts (100%)	*Local processing of milk powder, instant coffee; imports most of others*	BAT Kenya (60%)		Brook Bond Liebig (88.2%) Kabazi Canners (24.4%) Kitco (100%) Limuru Tea	Cadbury Schweppes Holdings (100%) Cadbury Schweppes (100%)
Malawi	Malawi Ltd. (100%) Lever Bros. (80%)				Lyons Brook (45.9%) Bond (33.3%)	
Mauritius			British American Tobacco Co. (100%)	Mauritius Molasses Co. (66.6%)		
Nigeria	Nigeria Ltd. (100%) Lever Bros. (60%) Pamol (100%) UAC (60%) Guinness (19%) Nigerian Breweries (22%)	*some local processing: of dietetic milk foods, imports all others*	Nigerian Tobacco (90%) Wiggins Teape (59%)	Tate & Lyle (60.46%)	Nigerian Canning (30%)	Cadbury (60%)
Sierra Leone	Sierra Leone, Ltd. (100%) UAC (100%)		Tobacco Co. (90%)			
Tanzania	Tanzania Ltd. (100%) UAC (100%)				Brook Bond Liebig (100%) Tanzania Tea Blenders (40%)	
Tchad	Republic of Tchad, Ltd. (100%) Brasseries du Logone (67%)					
Uganda	Uganda Ltd. (100%) Gailey & Roberts (100%)					
Zaire	Republic of Zaire (100%) Sedec s.a.r.l. (99%) Plantations Lever (98%) Compagnie des Margarines, Savons et Cosmetiques (100%)					
Zambia	Zambia Ltd. (100%) K. B. Davies & Co. (100%)		Wiggins Teape (100%)	Zambia Sugar (22.86%)	Lyons Brook Bond (40%)	Cadbury Schweppes (100%)

Notes: *Unilever and Nestles merged in 1970.

Sources: Annual Reports of companies, 1976.

127

Southern Rhodesia. In these countries, it had diversified its holdings from sugar into associated activities, including starch production in South Africa.

In the 1970s, the sugar firms in South Africa had to raise wages to compete with those paid on the mines, since they hired workers mainly from two increasingly important mine recruiting areas, Transkei and Pondoland. The sugar millers-cum-planters recruited labor through the Sugar Industry Labour Organization (SILO), hiring annually between 17,000 and 20,000 migrant workers from Transkei, alone. They were prohibited by law from housing more than 3 percent of their African laborers in married quarters, an aspect of the government policy of "whitening" the rural areas outside the Bantustans, so they paid their workers somewhat higher wages than private farmers who were still permitted to house whole families. By 1977,[7] cane cutters earned an average of R66 a month in basic pay, and between R50 and R66 a month in cutting bonuses, roughly the same as the underground mine workers' wage of R101. The companies had, however, successfully stimulated speedup among their workers to reduce costs. Whereas in 1972-3, the companies hired 4.6 men to cut 1,000 tons of cane, by 1977, they employed only 3.4—cutting their labor requirements by about a fourth for that job alone.

The British American Tobacco Company, more familiarly known in Africa as "BAT," initially began its operations on the continent during the colonial era in Southern Rhodesia. Over the years, it extended its operations throughout the British African colonial possessions, and branched out into several other fields besides growing tobacco. In the 1970s, however, its largest producing units remained those in South Africa and Southern Rhodesia.

In Southern Rhodesia, BAT's several subsidiaries continued to engage in production and export of tobacco, earning foreign exchange for the illegal Rhodesian regime despite the officially declared United Nations sanctions. (See below, pp. 262-3) In South Africa, BAT affiliates engaged in a variety of light manufacturing industries. One, Utico, employed about 3000 workers and produced about R50 million worth of cigarettes annually in the mid-'70s, presumably mostly processing tobacco grown on its Rhodesian plantations. Utico's Rhodesian operations continued to "churn out cash profits"[8] during those years, helping to offset the South African firm's financial difficulties. In 1978, however, BAT's Rhodesian operations, too, encountered problems as a result of the spread of guerrilla warfare. Yet they still produced over 40 percent of Utico's profits that year.[9]

Elsewhere on the continent, BAT worked out a variety of arrangements with independent countries. In 1976, Zaire, for example, took over BAT's business, and offered the British parent a 40-percent interest. In the same year, the Ghana government decreed that BAT should sell 55 percent of its tobacco subsidiary there to Ghanaian shareholders or the state. Nowhere, however, did BAT engage in as extensive industrial projects as it did in South Africa.

Brook Bond Leibig, another British food conglomerate, was formed as a result of a merger in the late '60s between the tea producing company, Brook Bond, and the meat packing firm, Leibig. By the late '70s, it still retained about a fifth of its assets in Africa. It owned several major holdings there, but, outside of Kenya, its most important ones remained those in southern Africa, especially Southern Rhodesia. Apparently Brook Bond-Leibig did not consider the ten-year-old United Nations sanctions against the illegal Rhodesian regime anything more than a nuisance, for its directors reported to their stockholders in 1976:

> Despite continuing local difficulties stemming from the political situation, our business in Rhodesia continues to prosper. Our canned meats and vegetables are of a high standard and the brands are market leaders, but it is on the ranching side that progress has been most marked. Since 1965 profits have been used to double the carrying capacity of the ranch, and the results so far have been most encouraging. We have an efficient, well controlled operation in Rhodesia, held back from achieving its full potential by sanctions and political uncertainty.

The British transnational drinks firm, Cadbury Schweppes, produced and sold soft drinks throughout the western world in the 1970s. Eight of its principal subsidiaries were located in African countries, two of them in South Africa, and one in Southern Rhodesia. In the mid-'70s, one South African affiliate took a stake in the local Coca-Cola bottling firm. In exchange the latter acquired its soft drink business on a franchise basis, and expanded its confectionary production.

The maverick British firm, Lonrho, became increasingly difficult to classify according to any particular economic sector. It started out as an agricultural business in beef ranching in Southern Rhodesia. By the '70s, however, it had mushroomed to become the largest industrial-finance holding company (excluding the mining finance houses and parastatals) in South Africa. Its South African holdings included a $3 million platinum refinery at Brakpan, with refined plantinum exports expected to be worth "at least $372 million by the late 1980s."[10] It

Table 6-7.
Principal Companies—Lonrho, Ltd., 1976

The following companies materially contributed to the assets and/or profits of the group.

Most of the subsidiary companies shown are themselves holding companies and there may be minority interests in their subsidiaries. The beneficial interest shown below represents the percentage of net profit for the year ended 30 September, 1976 attributable to the shareholders of Lonrho Limited after taking account of such minority interests. For acquisitions and disposals during the year the beneficial interest shown is that interest on an annual basis.

| | Country of Incorporation | Direct interest in equity | | Beneficial interest % | Principal activities |
		Lonrho Ltd. %	Lonrho and subsidiaries %		
African Commercial Holdings Ltd.	Zambia	100	100	69	Soft drink franchise and general trading
Afrima SZRL	Zaire		70	32	Motor trade
Ashanti Goldfields Corporation (Ghana) Ltd. (associate)	Ghana	45	45	45	Mining
Balfour Williamson Co. Ltd.	England	100	100	100	Export and confirming company
Brentford Nylons (1976) Ltd.	England		100	100	Textiles
Central Africa Co. Ltd.	England	100	100	100	Tea and wattle estates
Cominier S.A.	Belgium		54	60	Investment holding, motor trade and building
Consolidated Holdings Ltd.	Kenya		52	48	Newspaper and commercial printing, office equipment and import/export services
Coronation Syndicate Ltd.	South Africa		66	39	Mining
David Whitehead & Sons (Holdings) Ltd.	England		100	74	Textiles
Duiker Exploration Ltd.	South Africa		76	76	Mining
East African Tanning Extract Co. Ltd.	Kenya		100	100	Agriculture
Firsteel Holdings Ltd.	England		100	100	Engineering and specialized steel processing
John Holt & Co. (Liverpool) Ltd.	England		100	72	General trading, manufacturing, motor trade and wines
John Holt Ltd.	Nigeria		60	60	General trading and motor trade

Company				Country	Activity
Heinrich's Syndicate Ltd.	90	90	89	Zambia	Hotels and investments in breweries
Kaduna Textiles Ltd. (associate)		33	33	Nigeria	Textiles
Kenya Tanning. Extract Co., Ltd. (associate)		33	33	Kenya	Agriculture
J.L.P. Lebegue & Co. Ltd.		100	100	England	Wine shippers
Land Investment and Development Corporation Ltd.		100	100	South Africa	Property development and investment
London City & Westcliff Properties Ltd. (associate)		29	29	England	Property
Lonrho Exports Ltd.	100	100	100	England	Export and confirming company
Lonrho Insurance Services Ltd.	100	100	100	England	Insurance broking
Lonrho Investment Co. Ltd.	100	100	75	Rhodesia	Mining and motor trade
Lonrho (Malawi) Ltd.	100	100	98	Malawi	Agriculture and motor trade
Lonrho Sudan Ltd.	100	100	100	Sudan	Sudan representation and sugar development
Lonrho Zambia Ltd.	100	100	90	Zambia	Building, motor trade and newspaper printing
Louis Eschenauer S.A.		100	100	France	Owns Chateau Rausan-Segla and Chateau Smith–Haut-Lafitte vineyards
Motor Mart & Exchange Ltd.		70	67	Kenya	Motor trade
Nanyuki Textiles Ltd. (associate)		27	49	Kenya	Textiles
National Breweries Ltd. (associate)		49	44	Zambia	Brewing
Nyaschere Copper (Private) Ltd. (associate)	20	50	50	Rhodesia	Mining
Richard Costain Ltd. (associate)		20	20	England	Construction
South African Managed Industrial Corporation Ltd.		100	74	South Africa	Manufacturing
Swaziland Sugar Milling Co. Ltd.		99	65	Swaziland	Sugar estates
Tweefontein United Collieries Ltd.		59	57	South Africa	Mining
Volkswagen (G.B.) Ltd.	100	100	100	England	Motor trade
Wankel International		72	72	Luxembourg	Rotary engine patents/exploitation
Watergate Steam Shipping Co. Ltd.	100	100	100	England	Shipping
Western Platinum Ltd.		50	50	South Africa	Mining
Westland Motors Ltd.		100	100	Kenya	Motor trade

Source: Lonrho, Ltd., *Report and Accounts*, 1976 (London).

engaged in a wide variety of other South African businesses, ranging from manufacturing and mining to real estate. Its capital invested there totalled £396,760,000 in 1976. In that recession year, the year of the Soweto uprisings, it boasted a healthy 23-percent rate of profits before taxes. Its contribution to the South African government in the form of tax revenue totalled £45.9 million. [11]

Lonrho's almost meteoric rise on the South African scene was of particular significance because of the simultaneous expansion of its holdings elsewhere throughout the continent. By the mid-'70s, it had not only acquired many direct holdings in independent African states, but also held shares in other, mostly British companies, like the textile firm, David Whitehead & Sons, which in turn had additional long-standing investments in independent African countries. It is not possible to trace all Lonrho's African holdings, but its direct affiliates, including those based in Europe, are listed in Table 6.7.

In the early '70s, Lonrho's head, "Tiny" Rowland, boasted that he had established close ties with African leaders as a new approach to gaining profits in Africa. By the late '70s, he sought to use those ties to ensure that political economic changes in southern Africa would not upset his profitable business there. He turned his plane over to Ian Smith to fly to Zambia for private talks with President Kaunda and the Zimbabwean co-leader of the Patriotic Front, Joshua Nkomo. His company's extensive South African ties suggested, however, that he was far from a disinterested mediator; rather he was concerned to achieve the conditions necessary to continue to expand his octupus-like firm's activities.

Summary

In short, British, and increasingly, American, agribusiness continued into the 1970s to obtain low cost tropical agricultural produce from many African countries. But they showed little interest in building major industrial processing plants there. They carried on most of their manufacturing in their home countries. Only in South Africa did they construct a complex of integrated manufacturing and processing facilities. There, where apartheid coerced the black majority to work on farms and in factories at wages below the poverty line, these giant agriculturally-based firms contributed significantly to the South African regime's goals of attaining industrial growth.

References

1. Institute of Race Relations, *A Survey of Race Relations*, 1977, p. 255.

2. *Rand Daily Mail*, Feb. 11, 1977.

3. Republic of South Africa, Economic Development Program Report, 1977 (Pretoria, Government Printer, 1977) pp. 113-4.

4. Unless otherwise noted, the following information is from the annual reports of the companies and Moody's Industrials, 1978.

5. A. Seidman, *Planning for Development in SubSaharan Africa* (New York: Praeger, and Dar es Salaam: Tanzania Publishing House, 1974), Ch. 2.

6. "Infant Formula Topic of UN Talks," *Boston Globe*, Oct. 9, 1979.

7. Institution of Race Relations, *A Survey . . . 1977*, op. cit., pp. 256-7.

8. *South African Financial Mail*, Jan. 6, 1977.

9. *South African Financial Mail*, Jan. 12, 1979.

10. *Economist Intelligence Unit* (London) *Quarterly Economic Review—Southern Africa*, 2nd Quarter 1974.

11. Johannesburg Stock Exchange Handbook, Volume II, 1976, p. 150.

The Industrial Core

Upon independence, the new states of Africa all called for increased investment in manufacturing. Expanding this sector could lead to raised productivity and employment throughout the economy, providing more productive inputs as well as markets for agriculture and mining. But the transnationals located only a fraction of their new investments in manufacturing in the independent states. Few of the plants they constructed, furthermore, had any significant linkages to the local economy. Typically they merely assembled imported parts to produce luxuries for the small high-income groups, or they produced simple mass consumption goods (cigarettes, beer or textiles), importing the critical inputs. As a result, the new industries did not have the hoped for stimulating impact on the economy.

Transnational corporate investment in South Africa, in contrast, played a crucial role in facilitating real industrial growth, producing not only consumer goods for the high-income white population, but also sophisticated capital equipment and machinery for the big white-owned mines and farms. By investing, the transnationals responded to pressures exerted by the white-minority regime and the mining finance houses to widen the basis for white wealth and build the military and industrial might needed to combat the mounting armed struggle of the liberation movement.

By the 1970s, transnationals provided about 40 percent of all capital invested in the manufacturing sector of South Africa. They played a particularly important role in the sophisticated, strategic sectors: iron and steel, chemicals, auto, machinery and electrical equipment. They provided the linkages between manufacturing, mining and agriculture, which they neglected elsewhere on the continent. This chapter will consider transnational corporate investments in South African manufacturing in more detail, compared to their involvement elsewhere in Africa. (See Table 7-1)

Table 7-1.
The Overall Growth in Manufacturing Employment and Wages in
South Africa, 1960, 1973 and 1976

	1960		1973		1976		Percent of
	Numbers employed	Average monthly wage	Numbers employed	Average monthly wage	Numbers employed	Average monthly wage	Minimum Health and Decency level (1976)
Africans	357,00	R 29	645,000	R 72	708,200	R126	62.4
Coloured	125,800	R 47.58	197,600	R103	207,500	R154	76.2
Asians			68,200	R111	73,400	R183	90.5
Whites	208,900	R157.50	260,500	R388	275,400	R501	

Source: Institute of Race Relations, *A Survey of Race Relaions,* op. cit. 1962, p. 159; 1977, pp. 234-5.

Intensified Competition

Transnational corporate rivalry to penetrate the South African regional subcenter was sharply intensified in the 1960s and early '70s. British firms had played the primary role in providing technical assistance as well as finance and the necessary capital goods and equipment to build up South Africa's industrial base in the earlier years. As in other sectors, British firms tended to merge their interests with those of the South African mining finance houses and government parastatals, often retaining only a minority share. They continued, nevertheless, to provide technology and to sell vital capital goods and equipment, and to handle imports and overseas marketing for their South African affiliates. As economic crises enmeshed the British economy in the early '70s, British manufacturing firms invested especially heavily in South Africa. In 1974, British manufacturing investments[1] in South Africa and Namibia, combined,* totalled almost a billion pounds sterling (£997 million)—more than double the 1971 figure of £407 million. Over half was in basic industries: chemicals (11 percent); metal manufacture (12 percent in 1971; not given for 1974); and electrical engineering (18 percent). In contrast, British firms invested only 9 percent of all their capital in the rest of Africa in these industries.

After World War II, U.S. manufacturing firms also heightened their drive to invest in South Africa's manufacturing sector.[2] By 1976, South Africa ranked 14th internationally in terms of U.S. manufacturing investment. U.S. transnationals concentrated their investments in

*British statistics, like those of South Africa, combined Namibian with South African data after 1966.

newer, technologically more sophisticated industries, where their financial power and advanced technological expertise enabled them to compete most effectively with the British. In a number of industries—electrical, nuclear and computer technology, motor vehicles and petroleum refining—U.S. firms achieved a crucial, in some cases dominant, role.

U.S. investment in manufacturing in independent Africa remained, in contrast, marginal. Four-fifths of U.S. investment in manufacturing on the African continent as a whole were located in South Africa in the mid-'70s. Over 97 percent of U.S. investment in the production of machinery in Africa was concentrated in South Africa. And, in the mid-'70s, U.S. investors in manufacturing reaped from South Africa nine-tenths of all profits they made in Africa. U.S. firms directly controlled a higher proportion of their manufacturing investments than did British companies. [3]

A considerable but unreported amount of additional U.S. capital was invested in South African manufacturing industries through companies based in other countries—notably Canada, Britain, France and the F.R.G.—in which U.S. firms held shares. Aggregate data as to the full extent of this indirect form of U.S. penetration is unavailable. Instances are noted below in the discussion of specific sectors.

U.S. transnationals also helped Japanese affiliates assemble their products in South Africa, circumventing the Japanese government's ban on investment there. This pattern reflected the contradictory relationships that emerged between U.S. and Japanese industrial interests following the Vietnam War. U.S. firms producing for the domestic market complained bitterly about competing Japanese imports, while the largest U.S. transnationals acquired shares in Japanese companies and assisted them in penetrating the southern African market. Japanese firms became most heavily engaged in the South African auto assembly, electrical and rubber industries.

F.R.G. manufacturing investments in South Africa multiplied exceptionally rapidly in the late '60s and early '70s. By the end of 1975, almost two-thirds of net F.R.G. investment was concentrated in four branches: motor vehicles (23 percent); chemicals (19 percent); machinery production (17 percent); and electrical machinery (6.5 percent). [4] As elsewhere in the world, a handful of companies—Siemens, Volkswagen, Daimler-Benz, AEG Telefunken and a few others—dominated F.R.G. investments.

F.R.G. managers explicitly viewed South Africa, with its low wages and oppressed labor force, as an ideal "workshop" for production for sale in third-country markets. This was part of a general policy of rationalization adopted by F.R.G. companies, faced at home with the highest production costs in Europe as well as increasing freight rates.[5] The managing director of Siemens, South Africa, manufacturers of electrical appliances and equipment, asserted[6] that F.R.G. industrialists grouped:

South Africa, or rather southern Africa . . . among the top five or ten countries in which the breakthrough from export to broad and independent regional technological planning, assembly, service, repair, manufacture, and finally even research should be established.

Pursuing this policy of concentrating on regional subcenters, F.R.G. transnationals invested next to nothing in manufacturing in independent Africa, although they exported increasing amounts of manufactured goods to a number of countries, above all Libya and Nigeria.

French manufacturing firms did not invest as much in South Africa as did those based in the F.R.G. or the U.S. Nevertheless, heightened French interest found reflection, not only in their expanded trade, but also in increased French involvement in specific industrial projects.[7] Transnationals from other European countries, including Holland, Belgium and Switzerland, as indicated below, likewise contributed significantly to the growth of particular industries.

Steel and Heavy Engineering

South African government and financial circles considered the steel industry the backbone of industrial development. Its establishment was crucial to the indigenous transport and heavy machinery sectors. The state steel corporation, ISCOR, had been founded back in 1928 as a key feature of the minority regime's first attempts to create a national industrial base. Although ISCOR was legally established as a parastatal, private interests took up only a tiny percentage of the original share offering, and the regime retained firm control throughout its history. But ISCOR shared directors with the dominant South African firms, notably the Afrikaner group, Federale Mynbou. By the 1970s, ISCOR had grown into a giant holding company, with assets worth almost R3000 million and an annual output of over three million tons of steel.[8] It cooperated closely with a handful of large steel and heavy engineering firms, most of them affiliates of either the mining finance houses or foreign steel corporations.

ISCOR stimulated manufacturing by providing subsidized, low-cost steel inputs. South African steel was cheap by world standards:[9] 30 percent below British prices for angles, 20 percent less for plates, 25 percent less for cold rolled steel. Low wages were a primary factor in these low prices.

Table 7-2.
Wages of Workers Employed in the Iron-and-Steel Industry

	Average monthly wages 1976	Percent increase over 1975	Industry Percentage of Minimum Health and Decency level
Basic metal			
Whites	R633	12.0	(201.98)
Coloured	253	9.1	
Asians	265	14.7	
Africans	146	17.7	72
Metal Products			
Whites	593	13.8	
Coloured	221	28.5	
Asians	212	10.4	
Africans	142	25.7	70

Source: Institute of Race Relations, *A Survey*, 1977, op. cit.

As the economy stalled and inflation boomed in the late '70s, ISCOR pushed exports to "keep the mills going" and "earn much-needed foreign exchange."[10] ISCOR's export prices were substantially lower than those charged in South Africa; exports accounted for 40 percent of its production and 28 percent of its sales. In the 1970s, ISCOR found its largest export market in Japan, but targeted the U.S. for increased activity. As part of its export effort, it formed a steel trading corporation, ISKOOR, in collaboration with the largest Israeli steel processor, the Koor Group. Koor retained 51 percent; ISCOR held the rest. ISKOOR purchased steel on the world market for Israel, presumably buying as much as posible from ISCOR.[11] (It may also have served as a conduit for clandestine arms sales between the two countries.) In 1979, South Africa expected to earn some R400 million in foreign exchange from steel sales, 30 percent more than in 1978.[12] ISCOR also aimed to stimulate the South African economy by initiating several major projects, notably at Sishen-Saldanha and Richards Bay. (See Ch. 5 above).

Transnational corporations' cooperation ensured that ISCOR fulfilled its leading role in transforming the South African economy. Even before World War II, British steel firms provided technical assistance and capital for South Africa's infant industry, and a number became close partners of ISCOR affiliates. As a result, when the British ernment nationalized the steel industry, the anamolous situation in which ISCOR controlled British government capital in South A

Other transnationals, mostly from the U.S. and the F.R.G., became increasingly active in South Africa's steel industry, particularly in the major developments organized by ISCOR in the 1970s. A number of transnationals—notably British Steel, some Japanese companies (Nippon Steel, Mitsubishi Heavy Industries, Mitsui, Hitachi, Marubeni), [13] and the Austrian parastatal, Voest—provided the most up-to-date equipment and know-how needed for South African companies to "develop products competitive in the export markets of the world."[14] They sold South African steel producers such advanced systems as rolling mills, oxygen-blast furnaces, continuous casting equipment and computerized control systems. In no other sub-Saharan country, except, on a far smaller scale, in Southern Rhodesia, did these companies help build up an integrated steel industry, much less provide the latest technologies.

Transnational corporate banks supported ISCOR's efforts to build up the steel industry by arranging international loans. In 1975 alone, the net financial charges on ISCOR's accumulated foreign and domestic debt totalled R87 million, 40 percent more than its reported profits.[15] The South African regime acted as guarantor. In other words, the regime used its borrowing capacity to subsidize low-cost iron-and-steel production.

The most important foreign corporations in the South African steel industry were all British. In the mid-'70s, a network of partnerships bound virtually all the dominant British steel corporations to South African state and private interests. Transnationals of other nationalities played a less integrated and fundamental role, engaging primarily in the sale of sophisticated technologies or the purchase of iron ore and steel products.

According to the South African *Financial Mail*,[16] the British parastatal, British steel, still had "inextricable links" to South Africa in the late '70s. British Steel was formed through the nationalization of the 14 dominant British steel firms after World War II, and acquired their subsidiaries and affiliates in South Africa. These holdings linked it to practically all the largest private South African steel firms, as well as to ISCOR and Anglo-American. They were already valued at £25 million.[17]

In 1970, British Steel reorganized its South African interests. Although it retained the largest single share in these holdings, it effectively handed control over to ISCOR. This gave ISCOR more power and

Table 7-3A.
Affiliates of the British Steel Corporation

A. In South Africa

Corporation	Holding	1975/76 Employment[1]	1975/76 Sales[1] R100	Activity
British Steel Corp. (S.A. Sales) Pty. Ltd.	100%	n.a.	3000	Metal service center and offices. [1] 1970s: supplied high-level technology to local steel industry, "frequently enabling them to develop products competitive in the export markets of the world." Set up six continuous casting machines for ISCOR. [2] Sales throughout southern Africa.
IPSA (International Pipe and Steel Investments, South Africa	35%	n.a.	n.a.	Remaining shares held by Anglo-American (15%) and ISCOR. Owns 52% of Stewarts & Lloyds of South Africa; 56% of Dorbyl.
Stewarts & Lloyds of South Africa	via IPSA: 23% direct	12000	179000	Blast furnaces, rolling mills, steel works plumbing and heating equipment. [1] 1978: Rank by assets—30; assets—R147 mn. [3] Commissioned a high-speed weld mill for steel tube production. To invest R15 mn. over following four years. (These investments allowed it to reduce its tax rate from 30.5 to 18 percent, indicating significance to regime.) [4] Returns: 1974/75—over 23%; 1977—14,8%. [5]
Dorbyl	via IPSA	20000	18000	Shipbuilding, repairing railroad equipment. [1] Heavy engineer-

Consolidated Metallurgical Industries	10%	n.a.	n.a.	ing subsidiary: Vecor, with two plants, at Vanderbijlpark and Vereening. 1978: Rank by assets—17; assets—R210 mn.[3] Increased shares in companies in auto industry. Took over minority shares in Busaf, SA Instrumentation; and Steel. Took over Wheel & Axle from British Steel. Took over Broderick Investments to complement Vecor. Expected to move further into the "heavy-vehicle and motor component industries."[4]
Lexa Advisors	100%[6]	n.a.	n.a.	Acquired share in 1976. Allegheny Ludlum Industries (U.S.) also had shares. Commissioned a new ferrochrome plant near Lydenburg in the mid-'70s.
South African Manganese, Ltd.	3%[6]	n.a.	n.a.	Renamed Samancor in mid-'70s. ISCOR owned 45 percent. World's largest exporter of manganese; also owns extensive manganese reserves and produces manganese alloys.[7]

Sources: [1] Dun and Bradstreet, *Principal International Business, 1975-1976, The World Marketing Directory* (New York; 99 Church St., 1977).

[2] *Financial Mail* (Johannesburg), August 21, 1977.

[3] "Top Companies," Supplement to the *Financial Mail* (Johannesburg), April 21, 1978.

[4] *Financial Mail* (Johannesburg), January 19, 1979.

[5] *Financial Mail* (Johannesburg), January 8, 1978.

[6] British Steel Corporation *1972/73 Annual Report and Accounts* (London, 1973).

[7] *Financial Times* (London), September 1, 1977.

flexibility to build up the domestic steel industry and, through it, to influence the entire southern African economy. [18] As a result of these transactions, Britcor South Africa acquired 35 percent of International Pipe and Steel Investments (IPSA). The remaining shares were held by ISCOR and Anglo-American. In turn, IPSA controlled Stewarts & Lloyds, the largest South African manufacturer of tubes and pipes, and Dorbyl, South Africa's biggest structural engineering company. Both Stewarts & Lloyds and Dorbyl (both ranked in the top 50 South African industrial firms) expanded their investments in 1978. Dorbyl took over several firms producing parts and equipment for the auto industry. It expanded its ship-repair capacity because, according to its chairman, "we believe both the government and related authorities value the strategic importance of the undertaking."[19] A British Steel agent, SA Sales, or Britsteel, also imported advanced technologies for local sale.

British Steel found its South African operations very profitable. Stewarts & Lloyds returned almost 15 percent on invested capital in the midst of 1977 (a depression year)—a good rate by European standards, although down from the 1974-75 high of over 23 percent. These profits undoubtedly contributed to British Steel's refusal to divest its South African holdings, as demanded by anti-apartheid groups. Instead, as the South African *Financial Mail* remarked,[20] it continued to be "very much a force in our own steel and engineering manufacturing industry."

British Steel confined its investments in independent Africa essentially to the import of parts and materials, and construction. In Mauritania, it participated in a consortium exporting crude iron ore; in contrast to its South African activities, the project did not involve local steel production, remaining an enclave isolated from the economy of Mauritania and the region. The construction firm, Dorman Long, held most of British Steel's other African holdings. Only in Southern Rhodesia, although on a smaller scale than in South Africa, did British Steel cooperate with the Rhodesian regime's steel parastatal, Risco, to develop an integrated steel industry. (See Tables 7-3A and B)

Guest Keen and Nettlefolds (GKN), Britain's largest private manufacturer of steel products and one of the world's largest engineering groups, became, like most British transnationals, heavily involved in South Africa. (See Table 7-4A) In 1976, it sold over a seventh of its world output in southern Africa. It owned no manufacturing investments elsewhere on the continent, although it distributed its products throughout Africa. Many were presumably produced in South Africa, where GKN had four subsidiaries manufacturing a range of equipment, from heavy construction machinery to office furnishings. In the early

Table 7.3B.
British Steel Corporation Affiliates in Africa Outside South Africa

Name of Company	Percentage of equity held	Activity
Southern Rhodesia		
The Rhodesia Iron and Steel Co. Ltd.	28	The major Rhodesian steel producer; shares held by illegal Rhodesian regime.
Lancashire Steel (Rho.) (Pvt.) Ltd.	100	
Unisteel Central Africa (Pvt.) Ltd.	100	
Ghana		
Dorman Long (Ghana)	67	Sale of imported materials and construction.
Mauritania		
Societe Anonyme des Mines de Fer de Mauritanie	19	Export of crude ore, in association with other transnational corporations
Nigeria		
Dorman Long and Amalgamated Engineering Ltd.	95	Sale of imported materials and construction

Source: British Steel Corporation, *1972-73 Annual Report and Accounts* (London: 1973).

70s, GKN employed about 3500 South Africans. GKN Mills, near Johannesburg, had 900 workers, about two thirds black. Most Africans were unskilled laborers, earning an average of 14 pence an hour. The highest paid Africans earned £23 a week as truckdrivers—less than the lowest white wage. Both the GKN Mills medical assistance scheme and its provident fund excluded African employees. [21]

Among the major steel firms not enveloped in the partnership of British and South African capital were subsidiaries of Demag, (See Table 7-4B) itself a subsidiary of the F.R.G. transnational, Mannesman, AG. Its involvement went back to the 1930s, when it built ISCOR's first mill. In response to the regime's incentives, Demag began to produce heavy plant equipment locally. It looked on South Africa as a base for exports throughout the region, selling to Mozambique and Angola before independence, and to Southern Rhodesia despite U.N. sanctions. [22] Over half its South African employees earned less than the PDL in 1973. [23] Neither Demag nor Mannesman owned any additional production facilities in Africa in 1976. Yet Mannesman's sub-Saharan sales totalled hundreds of millions. [24]

A number of smaller South African companies, mostly associated with mining finance houses, and other foreign firms invested in the

Table 7-4A.
Guest Keen and Nettlefolds (GKN) holdings in South Africa, 1977

Company	Percentage held	Activities
Guest, Keen & Nettlefolds South Africa (Pty.) Ltd.	100	Holding company
GKN Mills	majority	Manufacturing heavy construction equipment, including cement shutters for dams & tunnels
GKN Sankey	majority	Manufacturing office furniture, partitioning and shelfing.
GKN Twisteel	majority	Manufacturing steel flooring
GKN Walter & Deane Combined Reinforcing Services	majority	Distribution of general engineering equipment and steel reinforcement systems.
Borg-Warner S.A. (Pty.) Ltd.	20	
Guetro Industries (Pty.) Ltd.	50	Affiliated to Dorbyl, in turn affiliated to British Steel through Ipsa. Produces components for the auto industry.

Source: Guest, Keen and Nettlefolds, Ltd., *Annual Report, 1976* (London: 1977); *Financal Mail* Johannesburg, January 19, 1979.

Table 7-4B.
Demag/Mannesman Subsidiaries in Africa

Company	
South Africa	
Demag Industrial Equipment	Capital of R200000
Plastic Technical Services	Capital of R100000
Algeria	
Sprior Algerie SARL	Sales outlet

Source: Demag, *Annual Report, 1975*

engineering industry, without engaging in large-scale production of basic inputs. They aimed increasingly to adapt imported technologies to local requirements—a crucial aspect of the industrial transformation process in developing countries. Many imported and/or manufactured a limited range of machinery for the mines, agriculture and construction. Several of the transnationals involved are listed in Table 7-5. Their South African holdings were, for most, their only productive investments in Africa.

The British giant, Metal Box, represented an exception. As in Britain, where it held a hugh share of the market, Metal Box produced a variety of containers and packaging materials in South Africa. From that base, it expanded into Southern Rhodesia, despite U.N. sanctions,

Table 7-5.

Selected Firms with Holdings in South African Engineering and Construction, 1975/76

Name of Parent Company	South African Affiliate	Sales (R000)	Employment	Activities
U.K.:				
Acrow Engineers	Acrow Engineers	8,000	500	Lumber and allied woodwork; asbestos
APV Holdings Ltd.	APV Kestner S.A.	45,000	220	Manufacture of industrial machinery
B. Elliot & Co.	Elliot Machine & Tool Mfg. Co.	n.a.	n.a.	Manufacture of machine tools
Hadon Carrier	Air Conditioning & Engineering Co.	3,000	600	Ventilation contractors
Hall Engineering Holdings	BRC Weldmarsh	n.a.	n.a.	Metalworking machinery
Parkinson Cowan	Parkinson Cowan	1,500	136	Manufacture of industrial heat treatment equipment
Powell Duffryn	Hamworthy Engineering Africa	n.a.	n.a.	Manufacture of heating equipment
Samuel Osborn	Samuel Osborn	n.a.	500	Construction equipment
Vickers	Vickers	n.a.	n.a.	Engineering contractors
U.S.:				
Columbus McKinnon	McKinnon Chains S.A.	4,000	n.a.	Manufacture of chains
Macdem Holdings	McKechnie Bros.	30,000	400	Manufacture of non-ferrous metal products
Masonite Corp.	Masonite (Africa)	180,000	3,000	Manufacture of masonite and insulation boards
Norton Co.	Norton Co.	15,000	1,250	Manufacture of grinding wheels, coated abrasives, hand tools, construction equipment
Otis Elevator	Otis Elevator	21,000	1,800	Manufacture of elevators and escalators
H.H. Robertson Co.	Robertson (Africa)	n.a.	700	Manufacture of building materials
F.R.G.:				
Klein Schanzlia & Bocker AG	KSB Pump	n.a.	120	Manufacture of pumps, compressors, valves
Canada:				
Massey Ferguson	Massey Ferguson	38,000	1,500	Manufacture of agricultural equipment

Source: Dunn and Bradstreet International Business, 1975-76; The World Marketing Director) New York: 1977).

as well as Lesotho and Namibia. It also established four much smaller subsidiaries in independent African countries, in partnership with local private or government interests. (See Table 7-6)

Table 7-6.
Metal Box Affiliates in Africa, 1976

Affiliate	% Owned	Activity
Metal Box South Africa	58.99	1975/76 sales—R48 million; employment—over 8000
Metal Box Central Africa (Southern Rhodesia)	91.80	Shares held 80% by British parent 20 percent by South African subsidiary
Metal Box Kenya Ltd.	74.48	
Metal Box Tanzania Ltd.	50.00	
Metal Box Nigeria Ltd.	60.00	
Metal Box Toyo Glass Nigeria Ltd.	53.45	

Source: Metal Box, Annual Report and Accounts, 1976.

Chemicals

Development of the chemicals industry constitutes a critical component of any modern industrialization program. After independence, most new states of Africa continued to rely on imports for fertilizers and pesticides, as well as explosives for the mines—although a number exported the raw materials used in these chemical products. At the same time, they accelerated the import of all kinds of plastic products. In most African countries, the "chemicals industry" involved little more than last-stage processing of imported goods for cosmetics and synthetic textiles.

The transnationals underwrote the production of the basic chemicals required to build modern industry in South Africa alone. There, they found additional markets, as the regime's demand for ammunition, nerve gas, napalm and tear gas climbed.* In South Africa, the chemicals industry originated through the collaboration of British and South African capital to produce explosives for the mines and, later, fertilizers for white-owned estates. After World War II, a pattern of development evolved parallel to that of the steel industry. The regime invested in the expensive, capital-intensive production of basic chemicals, in cooperation with the mining finance houses and established British interests. South African firms relied on transnational corporations for sophisticated equipment and know-how, as well as marketing and financial contacts. To a greater extent than in the steel industry,

---

*Evidence suggested that the regime's troops may have used nerve gas produced by the chemicals industry in attacks on refugee camps at Cassinga in Angola.[25]

because of the larger economies of scale characteristic of the basic chemicals industry, they continued to rely more heavily on imports. The transnationals became more and more involved in production of chemical consumer goods in South Africa after Sharpeville, using cheap inputs ensured by state investments and hoping to expand sales in markets elsewhere in Africa.

Low wages prevailed for African workers: in 1976, Africans made up half the industry's work force of 75,000, and earned, on average, R147 a month. Although this was 30 percent more than in 1975, it was still below the minimum health and decency level. Unskilled workers averaged only R86. [26]

Two of the largest British transnational corporations held important shares in the two dominant private South African chemicals corporations: British Petroleum, a British parastatal, in Sentrachem; and Imperial Chemicals Industries (ICI) in AECI, closely linked to Anglo-American. The third major South African chemicals company, SASOL, a South African parastatal, provided cheap basic inputs from its giant oil-from-coal plants (discussed below, pp. 189-90).

A merger between several South African companies and a subsidiary of British Petroleum (B.P.) under the sponsorship of the South African parastatal, IDC created the new chemicals parastatal Sentrachem. B.P. retained a minority share (20 percent), as did the South African regime. Between 1972 and 1976, Sentrachem's assets more than doubled, to R175 million; its profits rose five-fold, to R25 million. In 1976, it employed 4700 workers, and ranked among the top 20 industrial corporations in the country. [27] Much of its growth was due to its transnational ties; an advertisement claimed the company "depends to a great extent on international links in order to stay abreast of an industry of great technological depth and rate of change." [28] An observer emphasized that foreign companies had not only "provided production and marketing know-how, they have also made direct capital investments in Sentrachem's chemicals plants." [29]

AECI reflects the contradictory alliance between the mining finance houses and the transnationals. It was formed before World War II by ICI and De Beers, a member of the Anglo-American Group; each held 42½ percent. ICI's chairman became AECI's deputy chairman. AECI was founded to produce dynamite for the mines, but over time expanded into fertilizers, plastics and polyvinyl chloride, an important basic chemical. It maintained its position as "sole supplier" of explosives to the Chamber of Mines, [30] however, and constructed munitions plants for the South African regime. By 1977, it ranked fifth among industrial corporations in South Africa. It employed 8700 Africans, four-fifths of them as migrant workers.[31] In 1978, AECI proclaimed a "reformed" industrial relations system, establishing a Central Co-Ordinating Committee comprised of representatives of African workers and of management. But this group would not be represented on the industrial council that actually determined African wages and conditions, because, an AECI spokesman declared, they would be allowed only as "observers," and, "We don't want them there as second-class citizens."[32]

AECI and Sentrachem collaborated on critical chemicals projects, including a R350-million plant to produce fuel from corn and sugar cane in 1979. Sentrachem initiated this project after Iran imposed an oil boycott on South Africa; it could play an important role in supplying the military. AECI and Sentrachem cooperated, at the same time, to avoid the tendency toward over-capacity, resulting from the large scale of modern chemical technologies and the limited size of the South African market.[33]

ICI is the largest chemicals firm in Britain. By the 1970s, South Africa had become its second largest export market, after the U.S. It owned other holdings there besides its share in the AECI. ICI (South Africa), a relatively small but highly profitable part of ICI's business, ranked as one of South Africa's largest companies in the mid-'70s. It held three subsidiaries, including one in Angola, and marketed basic chemicals, resins, dyes and plastics that could not be manufactured economically in South Africa. ICI affiliates in other African countries, in contrast, contributed only marginally to industrial development.

Although Sasol, Sentrachem and AECI effectively monopolized heavy chemicals production in South Africa, a host of transnational corporations, mainly from the U.K., F.R.G. and U.S., established smaller affiliates there, primarily to retain a foothold in the southern African market. (See Tables 7-7A and B) For the most part, they controlled their South African subsidiaries directly from overseas. They manufactured a limited range of products, depending in part on imported materials, as well as marketing finished goods purchased from the parent company.

U.S. chemical companies acquired only a small share of the South Afrcan market, although all the larger companies had sales offices there and four had production facilities. This relative weakness apparently reflected several factors. South African firms, closely linked to British interests, dominated the industry. The explosives requirements of the mines provided a strong internal demand for their operations, and they enjoyed the support of the South African regime. Furthermore, U.S. companies in chemicals are not as large as in other technologically

sophisticated sectors. Only DuPont ranks among the 50 largest companies in the world, although four chemicals companies from other
countries made the list. One reason may be that the U.S. chemicals
industry has become, more and more, a sideline of the petroleum and
mining conglomerates.

In contrast, three transnationals, Hoechst, Bayer and BASF, all
listed among the 50 largest in the world, dominate the F.R.G. chemicals industry. (Hoechst and BASF are larger than DuPont, and all four
are larger than ICI.) The chemicals industry is one of the F.R.G.'s
principal areas of foreign investment, and accounts for about a fifth of
all F.R.G. holdings in South Africa.

The three major F.R.G. chemicals companies located in South Africa
all but one of their producing subsidiaries in Africa. Hoechst had two:
Hoechst South Africa (wholly-owned), and Safripol, in which Sentrachem held 49 percent. Safripol produced high density polyethylene and
polypropylene. Demand for these ingredients in plastics grew rapidly in
South Africa, as in all industrialized countries, in the 1960s and 1970s.
Despite South Africa's economic problems after 1973-74, Safripol's
sales increased steadily. By 1976, it had R8.5 million in capital,
although it employed only 470 workers, reflecting its capital-intensive
nature.[34] Hoechst South Africa, with the same amount of capital in
several plants, employed almost 800 workers to produce plastics,
synthetic fibers, paints and pharmaceuticals. In 1976, Hoechst
claimed its most skilled African employees earned R800 a month, six
times as much as an apprentice "straight from the bush" (sic). The
company did not specify how many in fact earned this amount. Three
years earlier, two-thirds of its black workers had earned less than the
PDL.

Hoechst employed over 4000 workers on the entire continent in the
mid-'70s (a little over 2 percent of its world-wide employment), mostly
in sales agencies. It sold about 6 percent of all its output in Africa but
imported three-fourths of its sales there from the F.R.G. Its only
manufacturing affiliate in Africa outside South Africa was located in
Lagos, Nigeria. Its 60-percent holding in the equity of the Nigerian
plant represented little more than 10 percent of its investment in its
wholly-owned South African subsidiary. The Nigerian subsidiary's
sales came to three-fourths those of Hoechst South Africa, but it
imported a much higher proportion than did the latter. The Nigerian
plant employed only 340 workers.

FBA Pharmaceuticals, a subsidiary of Bayer, manufactured insecticides in Johannesburg. It had installed capacity to produce the nerve
poisons Tabun, Sarin and Soman.[35]

Table 7-7.

Transnational Corporate Investments in the African Chemicals Industry

A. In South Africa.

Country/Company	Affiliate	% Owned	Activity
U.K.:			
Imperial Chemicals Industry (ICI)	AECI	42½	42½% owned by De Beers; remainder by S.A. public. Produces a wide range of industrial chemicals, explosives and fertilizers. Fifth largest firm in South Africa. (See pp. 147-8)
	ICI (South Africa)	100	Holds ICI interests in South Africa. Three subsidiaries ICI Pharmaceuticals; Optilon Africa; ICI (Angola); plus minority share in AECI. Markets basic chemicals, resins, dyestuffs and plastics.
British Petroleum (B.P.)	Sentrachem	20	S.A. regime also had a share, through a parastatal. Assets: 1972–R71mn.; 1976–R175 mn. Profits: 1972–R5 mn.; 1976–R24 mn. (See text, pp. 190-1, 194)
British Oxygen	African Oxygen	majority	Sales R30 mn. in 1976; over 4000 employees. Holding company for British Oxygen's affiliates in Angola and Southern Rhodesia.
U.S.:[1]			
Dow Chemicals			Reported a "sales office and small warehouse employing a total of 39 people" in 1979.[2] Did not report what was being sold; may have been nerve gas.[3]
Borden Group of Companies	Borden Co.	majority	Wholesale of chemicals and food products; 1976 employment—70; sales—R10 mn.
Bristol Myers	BM Group	majority	Maufactures pharmaceuticals, toiletries and household supplies. 1976 employment—385.
Miles Laboratories	Miles Laboratories	majority	Manufacturers of pharmaceuticals and drugs. 1976 employment—100.
Squibb Corp.	Squibb Laboratories	majority	Manufactured pharmaceuticals. 1976 employment—100.
F.R.G.:			
Hoechst	Hoechst South Africa	100	Manufacturers and imports plastics, synthetic fibers, paints and pharmaceuticals. Capital stock (1976)—R8,5 mn.; 1976 sales—

150

Company (Home Country)	Major Known affiliate subsidiary	% owned by parent firm	Activity
			R51 mn, 24 percent more than 1975. Commissioned two new plants in 1976. 1976 employment—800.
	Safripol	51	49 percent held by Sentrachem. Produces high-density polyethylene and polypropylene (inputs in plastic) 1976 capital—R8,5 mn. 1976 employment—468.
Bayer	FBA Pharmaceuticals	majority	Capacity to manufacture insecticides, including the nerve gases: Tabun, Sarin and Soman.
Badische Analyn & Soda-Fabrik (BASF)			Produces printing ink. Participated in a joint venture with AECI to produce formaldehyde, kaurit urea, potash and paraffins. 1975 sales: R30 mn. 1973—over half its African workers earned under PDL.

Notes: [1]U.S. companies with sales offices in South Africa included: Anchem Products (Pennsylvania); Abott Laboratories; Colgate Palmolive; Parke, Davis Laboratories; Eli Lilly; Smith, Kline and French; Wyeth International.
[2]*Dow Today*, quoted in South Africa Digest 1/26/79.
[3]*Africa News*, Sept. 18, 1978.

Sources: Annual reports of companies cited; Johannesburg Star, August 29, 1976; fn. 25.

Table 7.7B.

Major Producing Subsidiaries[1] of Transnational Chemicals Corporations in Independent Africa

Company (Home Country)	Major Known[2] affiliate subsidiary	% owned by parent firm	Activity
Imperial Chemicals Industry (U.K.)	Magadi Soda Co. (Kenya)	100	Manufacture of soda ash
British Petroleum (U.K.)	(See BP in Ch. 8 below)		(Engage in oil exploration, production, marketing)
Hoechst (F.R.G.)	Nigerian Hoechst	60	Manufactures Mowilith, dispersions, pigment preparation, surfactants 1977 sales: $6.48 million, employment: 391

Notes: [1]All major companies listed in 7.7A had sales organizations in independent African states; but very few had producing units.
[2]As reported in parent companies annual reports.

Sources: Companies' annual reports.

Transport

All of independent Africa suffered from inadequate transport systems. The transnational mining and agro-business firms built infrastructure solely to ship out their crude minerals and agricultural produce, while lack of access to the rural areas beyond the export enclave hindered trade and development. Transnational manufacturing companies, seeking to retain their hold over national markets, limited their local production of vehicles to assembly of private autos and trucks from imported kits. Personal cars represented a convenience for a few African and expatriate businessmen and bureaucrats, but they made no real dent on the pressing need to transport people and goods as part of national efforts to spread specialization and exchange. Instead, the import of automobile kits cost valuable foreign exchange. The new auto plants had virtually no effect in stimulating development throughout the economy, as the only local input was (mostly low-paid) labor. Bus and truck assembly made better sense from the perspective of national transport requirements, but maximization of their contribution to long-term development required ever greater integration into the national economy. Here again, the transnationals preferred to import ready-to-be assembled kits from their plants back home or in regional subcenters like South Africa.

In South Africa, on the other hand, transnational corporations responded to the minority regime's incentives to invest heavily in the manufacture of equipment to meet the full range of transport needs, especially for the white community. In particular, transnationals developed South Africa's auto and trucking industry. By 1970, it accounted for 7 percent of the GNP and 14 percent of total capital investment, and made extensive use of local parts and materials. All the major transnational auto companies were involved.

Four factors stimulated transnational corporate competition for the motor vehicle market in South Africa. First, the regime encouraged the industry as its "chosen instrument for achieving the crucial sophistication of industrialization"[36] by pressuring manufacturers to use domestic inputs. After 1966, cars with less than two-thirds local content, by weight, faced high tariffs. This policy ensured increased demand for local manufacture, especially for steel, machinery, electrical, glass and petroleum products. In turn, locally-based auto producers obtained access to the protected market. Second, the industry is relatively labor-intensive, so that the low wages of African workers formed a major attraction for transnational investors. Despite increases in the 1970s, average wages for Africans in the transport industry remained well below the minimum health and decency level. Moreover, industrial stagnation in the mid-'70s led to heavy lay-offs among black workers.

Table 7-8.
Employment and Wages in Transport Industry,
1976 Compared to 1975

| | Average Employment, 1976[1] | | | Average Monthly Wage, 1976[2] | |
| | | Decrease from 1975 | | | Increase/decrease |
	number	number	percent	Rands	from 1975 (%)
Whites	46,600	2,800	−5.6	552	+11.1
Coloureds	15,100	800	−4.9	168	−1.2
Asians	5,500	100	−1.9	234	−19.2
Africans	76,400	6,900	−8.3	132	+6.0
Total	145,400	10,500	−6.7		

Source: Institute of Race Relations, *A Survey of Race Relations, 1976, op. cit.*

Notes: [1]Motor Industry
          [2]Transport Industry

Third, accelerated industrial development provided an expanding market, particularly in the regime, its parastatals and military machine. Transport needs expanded as agricultural, mining and manufactured output multiplied. The rich white market still consumed a considerable share—there were 2.5 persons per vehicles in the white community in the late 1970s, compared to 125 per vehicle among Africans. Furthermore, the regime explicitly proposed to reduce its dependence on military imports. The relatively limited number of troops available relied on modern air, land and sea transport to shift rapidly from one trouble spot to another, throughout southern Africa. The growing domestic auto industry had a guaranteed market, supplying the military and police with trucks and Land Rovers, as well as motors and other inputs for tanks, planes, ships and weaponry.

Fourth, the transnationals used their productive plant and low-paid labor force in South Africa to produce entire models as well as spare parts and equipment for sale throughout southern Africa, and even to lower their costs to facilitate their competitive expansion in Europe and North America.

By 1975, over ten producers had entered the South African market, and smaller firms could not attain needed economies of scale. The crisis of the late '70s, combined with high oil prices, revealed the industry's weaknesses. Shrinking export and domestic markets slashed profits.

The transnationals with relatively small subsidiaries began to sell majority shares to South African partners. This meant, on the one hand, that the transnationals maintained their income from licensing and sale of parts and technology, while avoiding direct involvement in potential losses. On the other, they hoped to reduce criticism by opponents of apartheid in their home countries. In this climate, Illings, a subsidiary of Anglo-American, initiated an aggressive expansion campaign. In less than two years, it consolidated several smaller, less profitable lines to corner a fourth of the market.

Illings already produced Mack trucks and Mazda cars on license. In 1976, it purchased Chrysler South Africa, while the U.S. parent retained 29 percent. Chrysler had built its first plant in South Africa in 1958. In the mid-'70s, it moved to a new factory on the border of the Bophutatswana Bantustan to take advantage of the "large, readily available source of unskilled labor."[37] At the same time, Chrysler employed about 2000 workers, just over half blacks, to produce 25,000 vehicles a year. In 1972, Chrysler South Africa began to assemble Mitsubishi's "Galant" cars and trucks;[38] Chrysler owned 15 percent of Mitsubishi Motors in Japan. Illings consolidated production of Mitsubishi and Chrysler models with its Mack and Mazda production to form the Sigma Motor Corporation (SMC).[38a]*

Sigma then took over a subsidiary of the French firm, Peugeot-Citroen, for $34 million. Peugeot Automobile Afrique had captured only a fraction—less than 6 percent—of the South African market by the early '70s, although its only other African plant, in Nigeria, was expanding. Sigma cut costs by moving the production of Peugeot models onto its own lines.

Finally, Sigma merged its commercial vehicle operations with Leyland Motor Car of South Africa in 1978. Leyland's parent, British Leyland, had been nationalized by the British government two years earlier, to rescue it from economic difficulties caused by stagnation and foreign competition. British Leyland acquired a 49-percent interest in the new firm, the Sigma Leyland Motor Vehicle Company, while Anglo-American held 51 percent.

Leyland South Africa, like most British subsidiaries in that country, had always forged close ties to local capital. Before it merged with Sigma, Sanlam, a large Afrikaner insurance house, had become a major shareholder. In 1972, Leyland South Africa employed 4500 workers in all its South African plants. It produced both cars and trucks, and

---

*In 1979, Chrysler in the U.S. claimed to be on the verge of going out of business, unless it received heavy U.S. government assistance.

imported Land Rover Kits from the U.K. for assembly and sale to the South African police. In contrast, British Leyland's subsidiaries in independent Africa only assembled imported parts, probably including some from South Africa. Leyland South Africa refused to assign blacks to supervisory jobs, and it paid very low wages—black skilled and semi-skilled workers averaged less than the Poverty Datum Line, about R40 a month. Apparently, British Leyland hoped to avoid criticism by the "anti-apartheid lobby in Britain" over such policies, by selling a majority share to Anglo-American, while still "reaping profits from its partnership with Sigma."[39]

In 1979, the U.S. company, International Harvester, agreed to assemble Mitsubishi and Mack trucks for Sigma at its Pietermaritzburg plant. Earlier, the plant had operated at only 30-percent capacity; the new arrangement would double output. Sigma also planned to invest R5 million to open additional branches in South Africa, Botswana, Lesotho and Swaziland, and to import new machinery and top-level staff.[40]

General Motors and Ford, the two companies that dominated the U.S. auto market—Chrysler came third—had established subsidiaries in South Africa in the 1920s. In compliance with the regime's policies, they greatly expanded their productive capacity after World War II, even exporting parts to Europe and the United States itself, as well as throughout southern Africa. Despite the recession of the mid '70s, their substantial shares in the South African market protected them from serious losses, and both announced that they intended to expand their holdings.

General Motors (G.M.) is the largest non-oil corporation in the world, with investments on every continent. It has extensive contacts with the U.S. government, and shares directors with the Chase Manhattan and Morgan Guaranty banks, U.S. Steel and 3M, as well as other transnationals involved in South Africa. In 1974, the sales of its South African operation alone, over 30,000 cars and trucks, equalled in value those of the 563rd largest U.S. firm,[41] although they accounted for only 4 percent of G.M.'s international output. In 1975, G.M. South Africa ranked 17th in assets and sales, and 34th in employment, in that country. Two years later, its fixed investments had risen to over $220 million,[42] mostly invested after Sharpeville. In 1979, it announced plans to spend a further $20 million to modernize its plant.[43] Its holdings included three factories near Port Elizabeth for manufacturing and assembly. To comply with local content policies, it produced basic components, including radiators, engines, batteries, spark plugs, springs and sheet metal components. G.M.'s "Ranger" model was designed in South Africa and sold worldwide, and it also exported parts from South Africa to European affiliates. In addition, G.M. South Africa produced locomotives at Port Elizabeth. To satisfy the regime, its principal customer, it produced 30 to 35 percent of the locomotives locally. G.M. also admitted selling trucks to the South African police and army after the UN imposed a mandatory embargo on arms sales to the regime.[44]

In 1967, the chairman of G.M. wrote[45] that:

General Motors policy has always been to conduct its affairs in each country as a good citizen of that country. This...includes respect for, and adherence to, the methods of conducting business and the commercial, social and cultural traditions of the country.

G.M. applied this policy more consistently in South Africa than anywhere else on the continent. In independent Africa, it established only assembly plants and sales agencies. In South Africa, in contrast, it certainly played the "good citizen"—from the regime's point of view. It complied with the local content program, helping to achieve a degree of industrialization unequalled on the African continent. It assured the regime's military forces of the mobility needed to battle popular resistance. Dealers in Chevrolet, the G.M. model, worked to raise R1 million to provide entertainment and recreation for the regime's soldiers.[46]

In the late '70s, the company complied even more directly with the regime's military plans. A secret company memorandum, delivered by hand to G.M.'s Detroit headquarters, explained that G.M. South Africa had been designated a "National Key Point." This status meant that the military would take it over in case of national emergency because of its strategic importance G.M. did not plan any attempt to block such a move. Instead, it encouraged its white personnel to join the "G.M. Commando" to guard its plants in an "emergency" situation. This was necessary, as the memo explained, because of the scarcity of skilled whites:[47]

...compulsory military service is applicable only to White male citizens. The concept of utilizing plant personnel in a dual function is related to the fact that key skills, technical and managerial expertise are concentrated in the same population group from which defence requirements must be drawn.

In the 1970s, G.M. tried to counter criticism of its involvement in apartheid by promising to improve its labor policies. In 1976, a board member, the Rev. Leon Sullivan, introduced a set of guidelines purporting to ensure equal pay and promotion for black workers in South Africa. Unfortunately, as pointed out above, these were totally inadequate. G.M. claimed to have adopted the guidelines, giving them wide publicity, but they made little real difference to its employees. In 1976, G.M. employed 3575 workers. In a country where 90 percent of all workers are black, only 18 percent were African (up from 10 percent in 1972), and 55 percent, Coloured. The rest were whites. Just three Africans and 58 Coloured workers held salaried posts. Only 36 Africans and 440 Coloureds earned over $1.18 an hour; only 73 whites earned less.[48] In other words, G.M. South Africa upheld the racist policy of keeping blacks in poorly paid, unskilled jobs. Then, in the 1976 recession, G.M. laid off 40 percent of its African workers and 30 percent of its Coloured workers, compared to 14 percent of its white workers. By January, 1978, a tenth of its workforce of 3675 was African, down to 1972 levels.[49] Four Africans were salaried—not as powerful executives, however, but as a nurse, a clerk, a personnel officer, and a computer operator.

In the U.S., G.M. has never "been in the forefront of helping solve social problems."[50] On the contrary, the parent company had been criticized for lack of mobility from semiskilled to skilled jobs, the scarcity of minorities and women in skilled trade and supervisory positions and its anti-union stance. More work stoppages have occured in its plants than in those of any other company.

Like G.M., Ford developed in South Africa its largest holdings in Africa. It founded Ford South Africa in 1923 through its Canadian subsidiary. This allowed it to take advantage of Empire and then Commonwealth trade preferences. (As early as 1923, two-thirds of Ford Canada's exports went to South Africa, Australia and India.)[51] Ford South Africa expanded most rapidly in the 1960s, in compliance with the local content program. By 1970, it owned a manufacturing and assembly complex for cars, vans, tractors and trucks, Although its sales of cars and commercial vehicles represented less than 3 percent of Ford's total sales outside the U.S., it supplied 18 percent of the South African market.[52] In 1972, Ford South Africa began to seek export markets for its Cortina light pick-up truck, "designed and developed" in South Africa.[53] The regime designated Ford, like G.M., a National Key Point, because of its military importance.

When the president of Ford visited South Africa in 1978, he pledged to increase investments in Ford South Africa[54] despite growing criticism of apartheid following the Soweto uprising and the regime's increased brutality against the population. Ford's strategy for dealing with criticism of its role in South Africa paralleled G.M.'s: it tried to turn attention to its treatment of employees, ignoring its strategic role in support of the apartheid system.

Actually, Ford's labor policies did not differ significantly from those of other relatively labor intensive manufacturing firms in South Africa. In all, the company employed about 4000 workers in the 1970s, many of them in administration sales, and distribution. Three-fourths of its hourly-paid production workers, about 1050 employees, were black, most of them in the lowest wage categories. (See Table 7.9) As the economic crisis spread throughout the economy in 1975-6, Ford, like GM, laid off hundreds of workers. The South African Institute of Race Relations declared, following a 1979 study of Ford's South African labor policies, that its practices "make a mockery of the aspirations of the Sullivan Principles."[54a]

Table 7-9.
U.S. Auto Firms' Employment, by Race

Employment	General Motors (1976)			Ford (1977)
Category	White	Coloured	African	Black
Total hourly-paid workforce	989	1954	630	1050**
% of hourly-paid workers in given wage categories*				
1-4	1%	47%	77%	66%
5-8	12	41	26	24
9-12	87	11	4	10
Salaried Workers (number)	n.a.	58	3	55
Apprentices	n.a.	n.a.	n.a.	25

Notes: *G.M. wage categories in South Africa, in U.S. dollars per hour:

	White	Coloured	Asian
Category 1	—	0.77	0.78
Category 4	0.93	0.91	0.89
Category 8	1.43	1.36	1.35
Category 12	2.94	—	—

**In 1972, Ford employed almost 4000 workers, almost 8 percent of whom were Africans, and two-thirds, Coloured.

Sources: G.M.—Prepared statement of AA Cunningham, General Manager, G.M. Overseas Division, to U.S. Senate, Subcommittee on African Affairs of the Committee on Foreign Relations, 94th Congress, Sept. 22, 1976; Ford—World (Johannesburg), May 31, 1977; Corporate Information Center, National Council of Churches, Church Investments, Corporations and South Africa (New York, 1973).

Ford enjoyed close ties to the U.S. government, as well as other transnational firms, sharing directors with Citicorp and Morgan Guaranty. Its only other factory in Africa was located in Egypt, where it assembled vehicles.

F.R.G. auto companies, with Volkswagen and Daimler-Benz in the forefront, expanded their South African operations rapidly as part of their world wide growth in the years following 1965. As noted above (pp. 27-8) VW was an F.R.G. parastatal. Daimler-Benz was controlled by F.R.G. transnational banks: The Deutsche Bank owned 28.5 percent, and a holding company owned by the Commerzbank, Deutsche Bank and Bayerische Landesbank owned 25.2 percent. The Kuwaiti government owned 14 percent.[55]

By 1974, more Volkswagens were sold in South Africa than any other make. The company complied with the local content program, developing significant linkages with other sectors of the economy. In 1976, though it cut back on employment, it invested another $11 million. In that year, it still employed 982 white staff and 4340 workers: 1019 whites, 843 Coloureds, and the rest Africans. No Africans held jobs in the top four employment grades.[56] The company still paid its unskilled African workers a minimum wage of R0.76 per hour. Even assuming a 40-hour week, this was still 12 percent below the Poverty Datum Line; and most auto plants at that time operated a shorter work week.[57]

Volkswagen established sales and repair facilities in most African states. Its only other major assembly plant in Africa, however, was in Nigeria. There it assembled some 16,244 vehicles, almost entirely from imported parts and materials. The Nigerian plant produced less than half the number of vehicles turned out by the South African subsidiary, but the Nigerian company imported completed vehicles as well, which the South African regime prohibited. Volkswagen of South Africa exported vehicles throughout southern Africa[58], and had a branch in Namibia.[59]

Two other F.R.G. firms, Deutz and Daimler-Benz, concentrated, respectively, on tractor and truck production in South Africa. Both the South African and the Southern Rhodesian armies used Daimler-Benz UNIMOG trucks. Klockner-Humboldt-Deutz and another F.R.G. firm, Mann, supplied the South African army with armored locomotives.[60] Both Deutz and Daimler Benz had assembly plants or sales agencies in a number of other African countries (See table 7.10), but conducted manufacturing operations in South Africa, alone. Deutz's managing director explained that, because of rising labor and freight costs in the F.R.G., it planned to concentrate manufacture of components in its foreign plants with the lowest costs. From there, it planned to export parts to assembly centers around the world. He emphasized that Deutz viewed the relatively cheap labor and materials available in South Africa as "an advantage."[61]

Table 7-10.

Transnational Auto Companies' Investments in Africa, mid 1970s

Company	S.A. Affiliate	Activities	Other African Activities[3]
U.K.			
British Leyland (nationalized by U.K. government, 1976)	Sigma Leyland Motor Vehicle Company	British Leyland owned 49%; Anglo-American owned 51%. Before 1978 takeover, British Leyland subsidiary produced trucks and autos; imported Land Rover kits for assembly and sale to S.A. Police. Complied with local content program.[1] 1972 employment—4500	Assembly plants in Ghana, Tanzania, Malawi, Zaire, and Zambia (subsidiaries)—using imported parts, probably in part from S.A., especially in southern Africa.
Brockhouse & Co.		Subsidiary manufactured motor vehicle bodies. 1976 employment—400	
Robert Hudson	Robert Hudson & Sons	Manufacture of railroad & pneumatic equipment. 1975/76 sales—R16 mn.; employment—750	
U.S.			
G.M.	G.M. South Africa (founded 1926)	Largest U.S. industrial corporation. In S.A., manufacture and assembly of cars, trucks and components. Sales of trucks to S.A. military. Also production of locomotives, mostly for sale to regime. Complied with local content program. Exports to Europe, Southern Africa. Assembled cars for Isuzu, G.M.'s Japanese affiliate. 1977 fixed investment—$220 mn. 1978 employment—3574 (African employment—375) 1976 sales—38,000 cars & trucks. In 1975, G.M. South Africa was equivalent, by assets, to 17th largest S.A. firm; by employment to 34th largest.	Assembly plants in Zaire and Kenya; latter in cooperation with Kenyan government.
Ford	Ford South Africa (founded 1923)	Manufacture and assembly of cars, trucks, components and tractors. Complied with local content program. Exports to Europe. 1976 employees—4500? 1976 sales—over 35,000 cars & trucks	Truck assembly plant in Egypt (joint venture with government); to build diesel engine factory in Egypt.

Company	Subsidiary	Activities	Other African involvement
Chrysler	Sigma Motor Co. (SMC) Chrysler founded subsidiary, 1958; sold it to Anglo-American affiliate, 1976; retained 29 percent of shares.	Produced various models in plant in Bophutatswana border area. Complied with local content program. Assembled trucks for Japanese affiliate, Mitsubishi. 1972 employment—2000. SMC now produces Chrysler models.	Only sales
International Harvester	International Harvester S.A. Pan Africa Industries	After 1979, assembly of Mitsubishi and Mack trucks for Sigma Corp. in Pietermaritzburg, doubling output to about 60% capacity. Planned to invest R5 mn. in S.A. to open additional branches in S.A., Botswana, Lesotho and Swaziland. 1975-76 consolidated sales R 36 mn. consolidated employment—1200	Sales
F.R.G. Volkswagen (V.W.) [20 percent owned by F.R.G. government, 20 percent by Niedersachsen]	Volkswagen of South Africa	Complied with local content program. 1976 employment—5322. Owned a branch in Nambia and exported thorughout southern Africa	Assembly of imported parts in Nigeria; output of about 16000 vehicles a year, about half its S.A. production.
Daimler-Benz	United Car & Diesel Distributors of S.A.	United Car & Diesel Distributors owns Car Distributor Assembly of South Africa (100%). Supplies UNIMOG trucks to both S.A. and Southern Rhodesian military. 1976 Consolidated profits—C. $210 mn. 1976 consolidated sales—C. $940 mn. employment n.a.	Assembly of knockdown kits in Nigeria, Zaire, (Angola), Kenya, Tanzania, Malagasy and (Mozambique)
Deutz	n.a.	Produced the first wholly S.A. made tractor in 1974. Parent firm supplied armoured locomotives to regime. Planned world-wide exports from South Africa.	Marketing agencies in Zaire, Algeria and Morocco.
BMW	n.a.	Relatively new involvement. Planned to export from S.A. to Australia, New Zealand, the Far East and South America, as well as independent Africa.	n.a.

Japan			
Toyota	Toyota South Africa	Toyota owns no shares in this company, because to do so would violate Japanese government policy, but provides it with parts, licenses, patents, managerial and techological advice. 1974—opened a new, R1.8-million plant for trucks. Most truck parts imported.	n.a.
Nissan Motors		First began shipping parts for assembly of its Datsun cars at Rosslyn, a border area near Pretoria, in 1966. Licensed a new engine-manufacturing plant in 1973. Financing (about $17 mn.) channelled through its U.S. subsidiary. 1974 employment—4500. Refused to allow formation even of Works Committee.	n.a.
Mitsubishi		Trucks and Galant model cars assembled by Chrysler, which owns 10 percent of Japanese company; new trucks by International Harvester under contract with Sigma Corp., cars by Sigma itself.	n.a.
Isuzu		G.M. owns 34 percent of Isuzu, and assembles Isuzu trucks at its plant in Port Elizabeth.	n.a.
Honda/Yamaha/Suzuki		Assembly of motorcycles (since late '60s and early '70s)	
France			
Peugeot-Citroen	Sigma Corp.	Before sale to Sigma, subsidiary (Peugeot Automobile Afrique) supplied about 5% of S.A. market. Still produced by Sigma.	Sales and assembly in Franco-phonic Africa
Renault [owned by French government]	n.a.	n.a.	n.a.

Notes: [1] i. e. South African regime's program, imposing high tariffs on cars produced less than 66 percent, by weight, in South Africa.
[2] n.a.—unavailable
[3] Most companies sold their products throughout Africa; but few established productive facilities.

Sources: Annual reports of companies; and Dunn and Bradstreet, Principal International Busines, 1975-76: The World Marketing Director (New York; 1977).

162

In the 1970s, Japanese[62] auto firms' specialization in small cars paid off as oil prices rose. Their South African sales boomed, threatening such established firms as G.M. and Ford. Although the Japanese government banned direct investment in South Africa, Japanese auto companies licensed local plants to produce their models there in order to capture a larger share of the market. Their associates tended to pay even lower wages than other transnational auto companies in South Africa. Mitsubishi and Isuzu models were assembled in the plants of their U.S. affiliates, G.M. and Chrysler. Datsun-Nissan funnelled investments through its U.S. subsidiary to set up a plant employing 4500 workers. It captured the third largest share of the South African market.

The largest Japanese auto firm, Toyota, established a South African franchise-holder, Toyota South Africa, so that technically it made no direct investments. Johannesburg Consolidated Investments, the mining finance house, helped with local credits. An Afrikaner family, the Wessels, owned two-thirds of the business. The Japanese firm provided the expertise, patents and blue prints, management skills and personnel training, and new production techniques. Toyota captured the third largest share of the South African truck market, selling more trucks than cars. Since the local content program did not apply to trucks, Toyota South Africa imported most of the parts from Japan. To further evade restrictions, it began to assemble combined car-truck models.

In 1974, Toyota South Africa's net taxed profits reached $5.5 million, 50 percent higher than in 1972.[63] One reason was low wages: Its minimum wage was a third lower than that of G.M. or Ford. It moved its plant to Prospecton, a border area, and its workers to Umlazi, a rather distant black township. Their families often had to live still further away, in remote Bantustans. In 1972, Toyota's starting wage was 22 cents per hour, but the bus ride to the plant from Umlazi cost 20 cents. In 1974, after the workers struck, Toyota raised the starting wage to 41 cents—still below the Poverty Datum Line. Independent Africa represented one of Toyota's major growth targets. Its plants there, however, operated solely to assemble knock-down kits.

Besides selling trucks, locomotives, engines and parts that had both civilian and military applications to the regime, transnational transport manufacturers produced equipment designed expressly for military use. Thanks to these activities, South Africa could manufacture armored cars, tanks, airplanes and rocket boats by the 1970s. The conditions of secrecy surrounding these activities rendered it difficult

Table 7-11.
Military Transport Equipment Supplied by Transnational Corporations

	Source	Remarks
Road Transport:		
Trucks	G.M., Ford, Deutz	Deutz supplied UNIMOG, which the Rhodesian regime also used.
Land Rovers	British Leyland	Assembled from imported kits for use by the police.
Armoured cars	Panhard (France)	As of 1974, still required imported axles, motors and chassis.
Railroad		
Armoured locomotives	Klockner-Humboldt, Deutz	G.M. also produced locomotives (30-25 percent local content), which it sold mostly to the regime.
Air		
Helicopters	Messerschmidt-Bülkow-Blohm (F.R.G.)	Affiliated to Boeing
Airplanes	Avions, Marcel, Dassault	The Mirage F1 and Mirage 3 have been produced on license by Atlas, a parastatal (subsidiary of ARMSCOR), at the rate of about six planes a month since 1977. Components had to be imported (mostly jets and electronic equipment). Before 1977, South Africa had bought 48 Mirage F1s. After 1977, France cut off direct exports of parts, and a number of F1s had to be grounded. South Africa began to rely more on the Mirage 3, which is older and so the equipment is easier to replace. Israel's "Kfir" model is based on the Mirage 3.
	Impala/Lockheed	n.a.
Naval		
Rocket Boats	Israel	n.a.

Source: U.S. Military in S.A.; Frankfurter Rundschau, July 13, 1978; Münchner Merkur, 22/23, Jan. 1977; Neue Zürchner Zeitung, Sept 29, 1977 and Sept. 19, 1974; Die Neue, (West Berlin), 3/28/79.

Notes: In 1978, South Africa reportedly bought "weapons and other military equipment" worth about $340 mn. overseas, despite the mandatory embargo on arms sales to the white-minority regime. (Die Welt (Bonn) Dec. 20, 1978). n.a. = not available.

to identify the roles of particular transnationals. The regime still depended on imports of key inputs from the parent company in several instances, however. For instance, it had to purchase jet engines and electronic equipment for its Mirage planes overseas. Most South African production of military transport equipment took place under license from transnational corporations. (See Table 7-11) Since Israel had obtained licenses to produce a number of similar models, it supplied South Africa with a number of the necessary inputs after the western nations finally agreed to stricter enforcement of the arms embargo in 1976.[64]

Electrical Equipment and Machinery

Transnational corporations vied to build up the electrical equipment and appliance industry, vital for manufacturing the sophisticated, capital-intensive machinery which increasingly underpinned the rule of the white minority. Utilization of electric power permitted reduced dependence on imported oil, utilizing water power, coal and uranium which abound in South Africa. In addition, systematic electrification of the economy permitted increased automation, facilitating the regime's efforts to overcome a chronic shortage of skilled labor without upgrading blacks. The military also needed electrical equipment for communications and radar as well as modern weaponry and transport equipment. The industry's potential military significance was suggested by the fact that all four U.S. electrical firms with major South African affiliates also ranked among the top 25 arms contractors for the U.S. governments.

Transnational electrical manufacturers set up relatively large plants in South Africa to take advantage of economies of scale. They found markets in the military, parastatals, and private industries, as well as in production of consumer durables for the wealthy white minority. They also sold their output in other southern African countries. At the same time, they profited from low wages. Although blacks in the industry earned slightly more than in other basic metals and machinery sectors, whites still received almost four times as much.

Both British and U.S. companies had established South African subsidiaries well before World War I, but U.S. firms soon assumed the lead in this industry. Though smaller, British affiliates in South Africa were nevertheless substantial. The General Electric Company (South Africa), a subsidiary of the British General Electric Company (GCE) owned plant worth about $110 million in 1978. It sold equipment worth

Table 7.12.

Black Electrical Workers' Average Monthly Wages in 1976 in Rands Per Month as a Percent of Whites' Average Wage

Electrical machinery industry	average monthly wages (rands)	as percent of whites' wages (%)
Whites	548	100.0
Coloured	182	33.2
Asians	190	34.7
Africans	158	28.8

Source: Department of Statistics, South Africa, 1976, reported in Institute of Race Relations, *A Survey . . . op. cit.*, p. 236.

R3000 million in 1976, much of it imported, and produced transformers, consumer and light industrial goods, and telecommunications equipment.[65] In 1978, GEC sold 50 percent of its South African GEC affiliate to the South African conglomerate, Barlow Rand.[66]

Another British firm, Plessey, owned a number of South African subsidiaries. One, Plessey South Africa Holdings, employed 3600 workers in the mid-'70s to produce semi-conductors and related devices.[67] Plessey had no other African subsidiaries. GEC had only two, in Zambia and Nigeria, neither approaching the South African one in size.

U.S. electrical companies' early establishment[68] in South Africa reflected their initial lead in global expansion. General Electric (GE), the largest electrical firm in the U.S, ranking fifth among U.S. industrial corporations in the 1970s, opened operations in South Africa in 1898. South African General Electric (SAGE) became South Africa's largest electrical company. It manufactured and imported a wide range of consumer and capital goods, including electrical controls (used in ISCOR plants) and capacitators. SAGE provided control relay panels for the Cabora Bassa Dam when the minority regime viewed that project as crucial to continued Portuguese colonial rule.

SAGE employed almost 2000 workers in South Africa in 1976. Of these, 1306 were black, but less than 70 held salaried posts. Only one black worked at the "professional and management" level, compared to 262 whites. SAGE took advantage of the apartheid system to set up a small plant (162 workers) on Bophutatswana in 1976, where it paid wages lower than in its other factories. Two years later, General Electric sold its consumer goods lines in South Africa to a South African firm, Defy, in which it acquired a 23.5-percent holding.[69] But it continued to profit from sales of parts and materials, as well as technologies, in a pattern similar to other transnationals. Its own employment in the more capital intensive industrial machinery and equipment industry dropped to little over 200. GE's activities in independent African states, like those of most other U.S. firms, were limited primarily to sales.

International Telephone and Telegraph (ITT) invested extensively in South Africa over the years. Its most important affiliate, Standard Telephone and Cable (STC) was held through ITT's British subsidiary of the same name. STC, one of South Africa's largest manufacturing concerns, produced mostly communications equipment. In 1976, it reported that 70 percent of its total sales were made to the South African government[70], including the police. STC also equipped and provided engineers to operate the Simonstown Naval Base. In the early '70s, it paid white employees, on average, four times as much as blacks. In 1977, ITT sold a majority share in STC to a local electronics concern, but retained a 36-percent interest and continued to provide technology, know-how, and the needed imported parts and equipment.

Another ITT affiliate, ITT Supersonic Africa, owned a plant in South Africa and acted as marketing agent for a Southern Rhodesian subsidiary, the Supersonic Radio Manufacturing Company. ITT had acquired a number of subsidiaries in independent Africa, but had encouraged integrated manufacturing only in South Africa and Southern Rhodesia.

Sperry Rand and Westinghouse both owned manufacturing and sale subsidiaries in South Africa. Sperry Rand sold R7.5 million worth of aerospace, communications and agricultural equipment annually in South Africa in the mid-'70s. Much of Sperry Rand's civilian aerospace equipment was used for military purposes in the U.S., raising questions about the end use of similar equipment sold in South Africa. The company's only other reported activity in Africa was the construction on contract of a plant in Nigeria.

Electrical equipment had become, by the 1960s, one of the main fields of international expansion for F.R.G. firms. They focused on South Africa as one of their leading regional headquarters. Within a decade, South Africa represented Siemens' largest investment area after Austria and Brazil and the F.R.G., itself. Siemens South Africa typified the close links forged between F.R.G. and local state and private capital: IDC, the South African parastatal, the Afrikans Federale Group and South African Mutual Insurance owned substantial minority shares. (As noted above, p. 27, Siemens itself is linked to the Deutsche Bank.) Siemens, SA. was Siemens' fifth largest subsidiary, with annual sales of R180 million. In its seven plants, it produced electrical components, data systems, and telecommunications, power and medical equipment. It supplied a third of all the post office and railway signalling equipment required by the regime, and, like SAGE, provided equipment for the Cabora Bassa Dam. Siemens also provided technical assistance and equipment for the South African nuclear power program.[71]

In 1976, Siemens South Africa employed almost 7000 workers. 54 percent were black, working for a maximum of R1,70 and a minimum of R0,56 an hour. The average was just under R0,90 an hour,[72] or R112 a month for a 40-hour week. This was below the health and decency level. Although Siemens sold 10 percent of its output in Africa and Australia, it constructed its only manufacturing plants in Africa in South Africa.

The second and third largest F.R.G. electrical firms, AEG-Telefunken and Bosch, both had small subsidiaries in South Africa. AEG-Telefunken had historic links to the U.S. firm, General Electric. GE still owned 15 percent of its equity, when, in the mid-'70s, its South African subsidiary had become a major producer of electrical equipment there.[73]

As in the auto industry, Japanese electrical companies licensed local firms to produce their models. Here, too, the Japanese partners profited from the provision of the necessary technological and managerial expertise and components. The largest Japanese companies in the industry—Hitachi Electric, Tokyo Shibaura Electric (an affiliate of General Electric), and Matsushita, among others—gained a foothold in this way in the South African market. (see Table 7.12) Mostly they sold radios and other consumer goods, although Tokyo Shibaura also supplied the parastatal, ESCOM, with hydroelectric power generators for the billion dollar Orange River dam.[74]

French companies were able to compete effectively only in the newer fields of the South African electrical industry, where other companies were less well established. The French consortium, Telspace, won the contract for South Africa's first telecommunications satellite-earth station. According to the South African press, the fact that the French government and transnationals had supplied arms to the South African military tilted the regime towards acceptance of the French bid.[75]

Transnationals based in the smaller countries—Philips (Holland) and Brown Bovari (Switzerland)—also established South African subsidiaries. Philips South Africa, associated with the Afrikaner firms, Sanlam and Volkskas, operated three factories, with sales, apparently largely of imported items, representing a major share of Philips sales in Africa, Asia and Australia.[76]

Transnational Corporate Investments in African Production of Electrical Equipment and Appliances

Parent Company	South African Affiliate	Activities	Other African Activities
U.K.:			
General Electric Co. (GEC)	GEC (South Africa)	1975/76 sales—R3 billion, apparently largely imports.	Last-stage assembly plants in Zambia & Nigeria
Plessey	Plessey South Africa	Controls a number of subsidiaries. One employed 3500 to produce semi-conductors and related devices. Also owned 74% of Tellurometer, a firm operating in England.	None.
U.S.:			
General Electric	SAGE	Established in 1898; now largest S.A. electrical company. Manufactured wide range of household appliances, industrial controls (used by ISCOR) and capacitors, and imported additional consumer and capital goods. Manufactured railway locomotives for S.A. regime, produced relay panels for Cabora Bassa. One of five companies selected by regime to manufacture television sets in 1970s. Employment (mid-1970s): 1945 (1249 blacks) New plant in Bophutatswana opened 1976, employed 163 at wages below company average to produce housewares. 1978: Sold consumer goods production to S.A. firm, Defy, while retaining 23.5%.	n.a.
Internat'l Telephone & Telegraph (ITT)	Standard Cable & Telephone (STC)	Held through ITT British subsidiary of same name. Produced electrical equipment. 1976—70% of output sold to regime. Supplied communications equipment to police and Simontown Naval Base; also recruited engineers for base. 1978—ITT sold to a South African firm, but retained 36 percent.	
	ITT Supersonic Africa	Initially formed as marketing agent for ITT's Southern Rhodesian subsidiary, Supersonic Radio Manufacturing Co. Manufactured radio equipment in low-wage "border area" in Pietermaritzburg.	Supersonic Radio Mfg. Co. (Rhodesia) assembled radios etc. others, n.a.

169

Sperry Rand	Sperry Rand South Africa	Sales of aerospace, communications and farm equipment; some with military applications. 1975/76 sales-R7 mn.; employment over 400	Contracted to construct a plant in Nigeria.
Westinghouse	Westinghouse	Production of earthmoving and railway signaling equipment. Consolidated employment—750. Westinghouse was also associated with Framatone, the French firm leading a consortium to build the Koeberg nuclear power plant (see below, p. 176).	
F.R.G. Siemens	Siemens South Africa (Siemens owned 52%; IDC (a S.A. parastatal) —24%; remainder owned by Sanlam & the Federale Group.)	Mid-'70s: Owned seven plants with almost 7000 workers. Produced electrical components, data and telephone systems, power and medical equipment. Produced a third of all Post Office telecommunications and railway signalling equipment. Built transmission system linking Cabora Bassa to S.A.'s electrical grid. Siemens South Africa was Siemens's fifth largest subsidiary in sales; fourth largest area of investment.	No production facilities, but sold 10 percent of international output in Africa & Australia.
AEG-Telefunken	AEG-Telefunken (G.E., a U.S. firm, owned 15 percent of AEG parent company)	Manufacture of electrical equipment and appliances. introduced color T.V. system (PAL-system), and helped set up T.V. network. Also provided components for Project Advocaat, the military communications system.	n.a.
Steinmuller	—	Contracted to supply R100 mn.-worth of boilers for Kriel & Endrina thermal power stations; as part of deal, to begin local production of equipment and seek export markets.	
Bosch	subsidiary	n.a.	Has an affiliate in Southern Rhodesia.
France: Telespace	—	To build S.A.'s first satelite-earth station, to provide telephone, telegraph and telex channel all over the world, plus one T.V. channel via the Atlantic.	n.a.
Holland:			

another.

Switzerland:

Brown Boveri — Two subsidiaries, producing power distribution and transport equipment.

Involved directly and thorugh BBC Mannheim (F.R.G.) and Cie. Electromecanique (France) both of which are major corporations in their own right. Together, these firms are supplying six 360 000-Kwh sets for Kriel and Grootvlei stations. Also supplied a huge rectifier for Alusaf.

No producing affiliates; but supplies electric power generating systems for major infrastructure projects.

Japan:

Hitachi Electric — The largest Japanese firm in the field. Began exports to S.A. in 1960s; in 1970 opened an assembly plant in Pinetown, Durban, managed by United Electronics Corp. (a S.A. company) for radios, hi-fis and other equipment. Sold hydroelectric power generating equipment to ESCOM for Orange River Development Project.

n.a.

Matsishita Electric Co. — Established assembly plant in 1972 as minority partner with Barlows Mannufacturing, a member of Barlow Rand Group. Provided technology for colour T.V. production.

Tokyo Shibaura Electric (G.E., U.S. owns 10%). — Second largest electricla machinery manufacturer in Japan. Began assembly and sale of "Toshiba" brand appliances in 1970 in association with Gallo African Co. of South Africa.

Supplied hydroelectric power generating equipment for Orange River development Project.

Sharp Corp. — Franchised SESA to assembly record-players, radios, minicalculators, etc.

Pioneer Electric Co. — Built assembly factory at Capetown in late '60s to produce stereos. By 1970, supplied 50% of S.A. hi-fi market; South Africa had become Japanese firm's largest market after the U.S.

Source: Annual Reports of companies; and Dunn and Bradstreet, Principal International Business, 1975-76, op. cit.

Brown Boveri and its two giant subsidiaries, the Cie. Electromecanique of France and BBC Mannheim of the F.R.G., concentrated on
the sale of major electricity generating systems to ESCOM. Brown
Boveri also had two South African subsidiaries, its only productive
affiliates in Africa, but it expanded its sales of electrical equipment in
independent African states which sought to improve the infrastructure
they inherited from colonialism. In 1976, for example, it sold giant
turbosets to the Libyan power station at Derna, and four gas turbines to
the Nigerian National Electric Power Authority.

Computers

South Africa has modernized and streamlined its pass and influx
control system, with computers that flash out reference numbers, photo-
copies that are relayed by telephone and other inovations reminiscent of
George Orwell's *1984*.[77] The pass system underpins apartheid and
since 1967, computers supplied by transnational corporations have
handled millions of registration numbers, assigning one to each adult
African, with their associated fingerprints and domiciles. Computerized control points (cynically titled "Aid centers" by the regime) caught
38,500 persons violating the pass laws in 1976 alone, leading to their
expulsion to the Bantustans. The regime also used computers to set
rates and collect the high rents charged in the townships.[78]

The introduction of computers enabled the regime to accumulate the
data needed for its system of easy identification and control. It provided
a large section of the furiously growing South African market for computer supplies and services.

The minority regime also counted on computers to replace white
workers, helping resolve the critical shortage of skilled labor power
without promoting blacks. Automation and control systems in production combined with computerization of clerical jobs to reduce the
demand for trained employees.

ICL conducted its main African business in South Africa, but it had
established subsidiaries in other African countries, too. These in
cluded Southern Rhodesia, despite U.N. sanctions, as well as Kenya,
Nigeria, Tanzania and Zambia.

IBM's subsidiary, IBM South Africa, employed 2600 workers,[79]
mostly whites, as sales and service personnel. About a third of its sales
were to the regime or its agencies. In response to criticism of its role in
South Africa, IBM's chairman declared[80] in 1977 it would not sell
computers when they might be "used to abridge human rights" but:

...we do not see how IBM or any other computer manufacturer can guarantee that they will not be...we do not and cannot control the actions of our customers, and it would be grossly misleading to espouse a policy that we cannot enforce.

In 1977, in accordance with the U.N.'s mandatory embargo on arms sales to South Africa, the U.S.-imposed limits on the export from the U.S. of services or equipment to South Africa's military. Nevertheless, IBM's South African affiliate announced plans to supply components and services for military and police computers as long as spare parts were available. Even if IBM did not, the police and military used commercial models similar to those acquired by corporations and other government agencies. The South African regime established a network among its departments to handle all official computer work jointly. As long as any computer services were sold to South Africa, whether to the public or private sectors, it was difficult for the U.S. government to prevent them from being used for military purposes.

Table 7-14.
Uses of Computers by South African Government

Department or Parastatal	Use of Computers in:
Defense Department	Early warning system; underground nerve-center, Northern Air Defense Sector; satelite radar station near Botswana and Mozambique borders; Mobile Radar Unit
ARMSCOR (arms manufacture)	'various' purposes (top secret)
Atomic Energy Board	Pelindaba nuclear research project;
UCOR (Uranium Enrichment Corporation)	Velindaba nuclear enrichment project
Department of Justice	Financial and statistical purposes
Department of Prisons	Financial purpose
Department of Interior	Book of Life and passbook control
Department of Labor	In control of terms and conditions of work
East Rand Bantu Administration Board	Administration of pass laws
Bantustans	For administrative purpoes
Local municipal administrations	Administration

Source: R. Leonard, *Computers in South Africa: A Survey of U.S. Companies* New York: The Africa Fund, 198 Broadway, New York, NY 10038, 1979).

The F.R.G. firm, Siemens—which already produced electrical equipment in South Africa (see above, p. 167)—began marketing large-frame computers there in 1971. It installed one in ISCOR's steel mill at Vanderbijlpark, and provided another to the city of Capetown.[81] In 1978, Siemens advertised that its computer installations were "backed by 6700 employees" and "nationwide facilities for manufacturing and service." It also purchased a South African firm, Sati, which produced a locally-designed small computer, Isis.[82]

Nuclear Technology

In 1977, satellite reconnaissance discovered an installation in the Kalahari Desert of Namibia which resembled a testing facility for nuclear explosives. In response to the concern expressed by several governments, the South African regime claimed it had no plans to produce atomic weapons. But it later denied it had promised the U.S. government never to do so, and refused to sign the Nuclear Non-Proliferation Treaty.[83] Analysts were convinced that the minority regime would probably soon develop the capacity to produce nuclear bombs, on the basis of its general nuclear power program. They underscored the fact that there is no such thing as a solely "peaceful" nuclear technology.[84]

By contributing essentially to the development of an integrated sophisticated manufacturing sector, transnational corporations laid the foundation for the white-minority regime's attainment of nuclear power. The fact that a number of transnationals engaged in local production of electrical equipment as well as industrial chemicals and other machinery, enabled South Africa to advance in this, the most sophisticated technological field of all.

Transnational corporations, sometimes in consortia and sometimes in competition, supplied the regime with the technologies needed in all stages of nuclear weapons production, from uranium enrichment to reactors. For many manufacturers of nuclear technology, South Africa —along with other regional subcenters including Brazil, Taiwan, Israel and Iran—represented a new and expanding market. After public sentiment mounted against nuclear power in their home countries, the transnationals became increasingly eager to sell their nuclear technologies in these nations. Parastatals usually financed the deals. The transnationals' home governments frequently supported them in obtaining multibillion dollar credits.

South Africa had additional attractions. With access to Namibia's Rossing mine, it possessed the world's fourth largest known uranium reserves. Uranium had long been produced as a by-product of the gold mines. The regime was anxious to swap crude 'yellow cake' either for enriched (refined) uranium or nuclear technology. It sold uranium to England and provided 40 percent of the F.R.G.'s uranium needs. Belgium and France also signed long-term contracts to import uranium from South Africa in the late '70s.

The South African regime sought transnational corporate collaboration, sometimes with and sometimes without their home government's participation, to sell uranium to augment its foreign exchange earnings; to ensure enriched uranium for its domestic nuclear power plants; to reduce further its necessity to import oil; to obtain potential for producing nuclear weapons; and last, but not least, to acquire an important lever for political bargaining to gain international support for the perpetuation of its oppressive regime.

The United States government and private firms first became involved in the South African nuclear business back in 1952 when the first South African uranium plant was opened under a tri-partite agreement between the British, the U.S. and South African governments. At that time, U.S. and Britain were the sole purchasers of South African uranium. South Africa bought its first nuclear reactor, Safari I, from the U.S. in the early '60s. It was installed with the aid of the U.S. corporation, Allis Chalmers. South African nuclear scientists were invited to the U.S. Atomic Energy Commission laboratory at Oak Ridge for training. The U.S. firm, Forxboro Co., sold two large computers to the South African Pelindaba research center in 1973, computers which probaly could not have been obtained elsewhere. [85]

In 1974, the Oak Ridge-based U.S. Nuclear Corporation exported 45 kilograms of enriched uranium to a research reactor in South Africa, after the Nuclear Regulatory Commission* obtained South African agreement that it would not used it for nuclear weapons. The U.S. again provided enriched uranium to South Africa in 1975 and 1976. It initially pledged to sell more to the French American-built nuclear plant to be completed in South Africa by 1984. In all, the U.S. had sold or was committed to selling 300 pounds of weapons-grade uranium from which 15 atomic bombs could be produced. [86] The U.S. delegation to the United Nations explicitly insisted that nuclear cooperation be left out of the 1977 mandatory United Nations embargo on the sale of military equipment to South Africa. Only in 1978, did the U.S. government officially terminate its own agreement to sell further enriched uranium to the South African regime.

By the 1960s, F.R.G. firms had mastered the intricacies of nuclear power production, and were seeking new sources of uranium as well as markets in which to sell their nuclear technologies. An F.R.G. parastatal, Urangesellschaft, GmbH, joined the British Rio Tinto Zinc and South African capital to invest DM 70 million in the Rossing Uranium

*The U.S. agency which grants licenses for exportation of nuclear material.

mine in Namibia. The Minister of Economic Cooperation declared, however, that his government feared its "support for the uranium project would be bound to damage West Germany's reputation in Black Africa."[87] Nevertheless, the F.R.G. did contract to buy almost half its natural uranium from South Africa.

In 1973, F.R.G. firms, including STEAG (Steinkohlen-Elektrzitats AG, a branch of Ruhrkohle) and Gesellschaft fur Kernforschang, started to explore the possiblity of collaboration in developing the uranium enrichment process in South Africa. STEAG, an F.R.G. parastatal, signed an agreement with the South African state-controlled Uranium Enrichment Corporation (UCOR). After criticism in the F.R.G., STEAG limited its role to making the feasibility study of the project. The pilot plant at Pelindaba was completed in 1976. A plan to build a much larger plant at Valindaba to export enriched uranium was shelved, however, when anti-apartheid critics managed to prevent transnational corporations from providing finance and marketing connections. The regime still planned to produce enriched uranium process for its own use as Valindaba, using the "Helikon" process developed at Pelindaba. This process required the import of "very sophisticated axial-flow compressors."[88]

The efforts of three international consortia to sell the reactors for South Africa's nuclear power plant at Koeberg illustrated the intensity of international competition in the nuclear market. One consortium consisted of General Electric (U.S.); Rijn-Schelde Verolme; Vereinigde Bedrivjven Brodero, Ingenieursbureau Comprimo (Holland); and Brown Boveri (Switzerland). The second was formed by Kraftwerk-union, a joint venture of Siemens and AEG-Telefunken. The French companies, Spie-Batignolle and Alsthoms (construction) and Framatome (nuclear technology) made up the third group. The Creusot-Loire group owned Framatome, but Westinghouse, the U.S. firm, held 15 percent.* South Africa awarded the deal to the consortium led by Framatome, apparently because of French military assistance.[89] Westinghouse provided much of the technology.

The transnational suppliers of nuclear technology found few customers elsewhere in Africa. Westinghouse did receive a contract from Morocco in 1977 to construct a "modern integrated air defense system" including radar, communications and control systems for over $200 million.[90]

---

*Westinghouse had controlled Framatome with a 45-percent share of its equity until the French government forced it to reduce it to 15 percent in the early 1970s.

Rubber

Transnational rubber corporations vied to develop the manufacture of finished rubber products in South Africa, although some owned rubber plantations or bought natural rubber from independent African states. Firestone, one of the largest U.S. rubber companies, manufactured tires and tubes in two plants in South Africa. Its only major holdings in independent Africa were rubber plantations: two huge ones that dominated the economy of Liberia for almost half a century, and another, in Ghana, which it purchased at bargain-basement prices after the overthrow of the President Kwame Nkrumah in 1966.* In addition, Firestone had small rubber factories in Ghana and Kenya, the latter based mainly on imported raw materials.

Dunlop (U.K.) and Goodyear (U.S.) likewise had built huge tire factories in South Africa, apparently planning to export their output throughout southern Africa. Japanese rubber companies, wishing to invest in South Africa, like other Japanese firms had to circumvent their government's prohibition. At first, the dominant Japanese firms, Bridgestone Tire, Yokohama Rubber and Toyo Tire, were content to export to South Africa, capturing 10-15 percent of the market with their relatively low cost tires.[92] Pressured by the U.K. and U.S. transnational with large South African holdings, they combined to establish a R20 million rand plant in a low-wage border area near Durban in a joint venture with two South African firms associated with Anglo-American, Foremost and Syfrets. (Table 7-15)

Summary and Conclusion

The white minority regime in South Africa sought, above all, to build up its basic manufacturing industries to augment its wealth and strengthen its economic and military capacity. Particularly in the 1960s after Sharpeville, transnational manufacturing firms, sometimes in competition, sometimes in consortia, collaborated with the parastatals and mining finance houses to mold South Africa into an increasingly dominant regional subcenter. Their accumulation and reinvestment of capital in expanded development and output of sophisticated capital

*The International Monetary Fund had insisted on the sale of state-owned projects as part of the price for lending funds to the new military government; and the latter sold the state-owned rubber plantation, together with the factory which had just been completed, to Firestone just as the new rubber trees were about to begin to produce.[91]

Table 7-15.
Transnational Corporate Involvement in African Rubber Industry, mid 1970s

Parent Company	South African Affiliate	Activity	Other African Activity
U.K.:			
Dunlop Holdings Ltd.	Dunlop South Africa (Parent owned 70%)	Two plants (at Durban and Ladysmith) produce tires, flooring, belting, hose, sportswear footwear, products. Diversified into sports accessories in mid-'70s. Late '60s—paid African workers half of Coloured and a third of white wages.	Dunlop Rhodesia (100%)—produces tires, flooring, general rubber, rubber products. Dunlop Zambia and Dunlop Nigerian Industries produced primarly tires from imported materials (to avoid tariffs).
U.S.:			
Goodyear Tire & Rubber	Goodyear S.A.	Produces tires, tubes etc. at Uitenhage. Employment—c. 250 in 1970s.	Smallscale tire and tube production in Zaire and Morocco.
Firestone Rubber	Firestone S.A.	Manufacturer tires and tubes at Port Elizabeth and Brits. Employment—C. 2500 in 1970s. 1975/76 sales—R30 mn.	Owned two rubber plantations in Liberia. After coup against President Nkrumah, acquired formerly state-owned plantations & tire/tube factory at Bonsaso in Ghana. Also built a tire/tube plant, to process imports, at Kenya.
U.S./Japan Bridgestone Tyre Yokohama Rubber Toyo Tyre B.F. Goodrich Goodrich owned 33.6% of Yokohama, making possible its investment via U.S.)		Under pressure from other producers, established R20-mn. plant in low-wage border area near Durban, in joint venture with S.A. firms Foremost and Syfrets (associated with Anglo-American).	Goodrich owned a rubber plantation in Liberia. Other holdings not known.

Source: Annual reports of companies and Dunn and Bradsteet, *Principal International Business, 1975-76* op. cit.

equipment in their home countries pressured them to seek new markets for their mounting surpluses of advanced machinery and equipment. They viewed South Africa as a "stable" area where their factories would not be threatened by expropriation or radical interference with their managers. They sought to profit from the vast reservoir of low cost African labor created by the systematic imposition of apartheid. The more labor-intensive firms hired large numbers of African workers at wages below the poverty line, a fraction of what they would have had to pay employees in their home countries. Some shifted their plants to the border areas next to the Bantustans to take advantage of the still lower wages available there. More capital-intensive firms, while hiring mainly skilled (white) workers, profited from the ready supply of low-cost infrastructure and local inputs made possible by the systematic depression of African living standards.

The South African regime played one transnational off against another to encourage them to invest more. It employed typical state-capitalist measures, including extensive parastatal participation to provide low-cost industrial and infrastructural inputs, along with a range of tax incentives. The big mines and estates, along with multiplying military expenditures, guaranteed a basic domestic market. The growing regional domination exercised by South Africa seemed to transnational corporate managers to open vistas of a market spreading throughout the southern third of the vast continent, an area as large as the continental United States.

But transnational corporate investments in manufacturing, although they helped the regime to build the most advanced industries on the continent, did not contribute to balanced, integrated "development" capable of self-sustaining growth. Instead, they actually intensified the underlying contradictions that riddled the national economy and finally brought to a halt its vaunted "growth miracle." The transnational manufacturing firms' rapid industrial expansion particularly aggravated the conditions of the inherently narrow domestic market.

Apartheid had been created as a device to exclude the workers, the black majority, from any role in the political economy except as a low-cost input: labor. Only a pitiful minority of blacks ever earned incomes sufficient to buy the luxury cars, refrigerators and stereos manufactured by transnational affiliates in South Africa. The heavier industries could only sell part of their output to mechanize and automate South African mines, agriculture and factories. Large sectors of industry, notably auto and electrical appliances, produced primarily for the luxury white market and the military. To fill in the gap between their output and the local market, the transnationals had anticipated expanding their exports, counting on low domestic wages to enable them to maximize their global profits. But their introduction of the most capital-intensive technologies contributed to putting increasing numbers of blacks out of work. Moreover, the luxury and export markets were particularly sensitive to recessions: In the mid-'70s, South Africa's economy fell into persistent crisis. The manufacturing industries, except those contributing directly to the regime's plans for strategic economic and military expansion, slumped, operating at less than two-thirds of capacity. Black unemployment became chronic.

At the same time, the concentration of transnational manufacturing investments in South Africa aggravated the underdevelopment of the rest of southern Africa. The transnationals sought to sell the goods manufactured in their South African factories, discouraging industrial development in the neighboring countries. Even local handicraft industries were squeezed out of business by the spread of goods mass-produced in their South African plants. Where the transnational firms did build factories in independent African countries elsewhere to maintain a foothold in tariff protected markets, they designed them to assemble and/or process imported parts and materials (not infrequently from South Africa) to produce luxury items for the limited high-income groups. They contributed little to augmenting productivity in the mines or African-owned farms by producing needed inputs. They failed to stimulate the output of locally produced materials and parts. They provided relatively few local jobs. They drained away surpluses and foreign exchange needed for more productive investment to meet the needs of the local populations. Increasing numbers of young men from countries neighboring South Africa were forced to migrate to its mines and white-owned farms in search of cash employment.

But the spread of unemployment among South African manufacturing workers in the 1970s forced more and more South African blacks to seek lower-paying jobs in the mines. The migrants from neighboring countries found themselves increasingly excluded, forced to seek work in their home economies.

The temporary "miracle growth" of South African industry, spurred by transnational corporate investments, strengthened the apartheid regime, reduced its dependence on black labor, and intensified the repression of the South African population. At the same time, it distorted and underdeveloped the economies of the neighboring southern African states. Meanwhile, the transnational, in collaboration with the South African mining finance houses, continued to cream off the profits.

References

1. United Kingdom, Board of Trade: *Trade and Industry* (London: Her Majesty's Stationery Office, 1974).
2. The aggregate data relating to U.S. investment in manufacturing is from the U.S. Department of Commerce, *Survey of Current Business*, annual report of U.S. overseas investments unless otherwise cited. The issue containing this report usually appears in August, September or October of each year.
3. Republic of South Africa, Second Census of Foreign Transactions, Liabilities and Assets, 31 December, Supplement to South African Reserve Bank, Quarterly Bulletin of Statistics, March 1973.
4. W. Schneider-Barthold, *Die Beurteilung der Wirschaftsbezeihung der BRD zur RSA* (West Berlin: Deutschen Institut für Entwicklungs-politik, 1976) p. 41ff.
5. *Star* (Johannesburg) Sept. 24, 1973.
6. W. E. Wentges, "Deutsches Investment in Südafrika: Eine 'Case Study'—Siemens," paper presented to seminar of F.R.G. industrialists, Köln, Nov. 4, 1976.
7. See U.N. Center on Transnational Corporations, Activities of Transnational Corporations in Southern Africa and the extent of their Collaboration with Illegal Regimes, adopted May 6, 1977, reprinted by UN Center Against Apartheid, Notes and Documents, Nov. 21, 1977.
8. For materials relating to specific companies, unless otherwise cited, see their annual reports, published in the country of their home offices.
9. *South African Financial Mail*, Mar 2, 1979.
10. *Financial Times* (London) Sept. 23, 1977, quotes an ISCOR spokesman.
11. ISCOR, Annual Report, 1974.
12. *South African Financial Mail*, Mar. 2, 1979.
13. *South African Financial Times*, May 20, 1974.
14. *South African Financial Mail*, Aug. 21, 1977, refers specifically to British Steel.
15. *South African Digest*, Feb. 22, 1974.
16. Aug. 21, 1977.
17. R. First, C. Gurney and J. Steele, *The South African Connection* (London: Maurice Temple Smith, Ltd., 1972).
18. *Ibid*.
19. *South African Financial Mail*, Jan. 19, 1979.
20. August 21, 1977.
21. Wages and Conditions of African Workers Employed by British Firms in South Africa, Fifth Report from the Expenditure Committee, Session 1973-4, (London: Her Majesty's Stationery Office, 1974), Ch. 7.
22. *Star*, Nov. 12, 1971; *South Africa Digest*, Feb. 22, 1974.
23. "Survey of Wages and Working Conditions of German Firms in South Africa," released by Lenelotte von Vothmar, M.P., Bundeshaus, Bonn, Dokumentation B/RS/2/73. The average wage the companies surveyed—including all major F.R.G. investors in South Africa—paid African workers was R45 per month. The PDL for the relevant areas was R78-100 per month. (See pp. 70-71 above for discussion of PDL) The figures were obtained by investigations conducted by two social scientists who spent four months in South African examining working conditions of Africans employed by European firms. Not a single F.R.G. company supplied data officially. The results are therefore based on surveys of workers and individual company officials whose anonymity had to be assured.
24. Mannesman AG (F.R.G.), *Bericht über das Geschäftsjahr 1976*.

25. *Africa News* (Durham, North Carolina) September 18, 1978. See also SIPRI Yearbook 1978 (Taylor & Francis, London, 1978.)

26. South African Institute of Race Relations, *A Survey of Race Relations*, 1977, p. 243.

27. *South African Financial Mail*, April 21, 1978.

28. *South African Financial Mail*, May 20, 1974.

29. La Revue Francaise, *La Revue Francaise Looks at South Africa*, (Paris, 1975) p. 104.

30. *Evening News* (London), Feb. 19, 1974.

31. *Rand Daily Mail*, April 1, 1977.

32. *South African Financial Mail*, June 16, 1928.

33. See, e.g. *South African Financial Mail*, "Special Survey: Top Companies." April 23, 1976.

34. *Star* (Johannesburg) Aug. 29, 1976.

35. *Evening News* (London) Feb. 19, 1974.

36. First, et., *The South African Connection, op. cit.* p. 95.

37. Corporate Information Center, *Church Investments, Corporations and South Africa, op. cit.*, p. 58.

38. Y. Kitizawa, From Tokyo to Johannesburg (New York: Interfaith Center on Corporate Responsibility, 1975) p. 20.

38a. *New York Times*, Nov. 4, 1979. This report indicated Chrysler was to receive 35 percent of the profits of the enlarged project.

39. *Business Week*, Aug. 21, 1978.

40. *South Africa Digest*, Aug. 10, 1979.

41. *Fortune Magazine*, "The Second 500 Largest Industrial Corporations," June, 1975.

42. Litvak, DeGrasse, McTigue, *South Africa: Foreign Investment and Apartheid* (Washington: Institute for Policy Studies, 1978) p. 47.

43. *South Africa Digest*, Aug. 19, 1979.

44. Investor Responsibility Research Center, Corporate Activity in South Africa: General Motors Corp. Sales to Police and Military 1979 Analysis G, Supplement No. 16, May 1, 1979 (Washington: Investor Responsibility Research Center, 1979).

45. F. Donner, *The World-Wide Industrial Enterprise: Its Challenge and Promise* (New York: McGraw Hill, 1967) p. 87.

46. *GM Bowtie*, (South Africa: Chevrolet Dealers of South Africa, 1975).

47. General Motors South Africa (Pty) Ltd., Inter-Office Memo: published by Interfaith Center on Corporate Responsibility, National Council of Churches, May, 1978.

48. Prepared statement of A.A. Cunningham to U.S. Senate Subcommittee on African Affairs of the Committee on Foreign Relations, Sept. 22, 1976 in U.S. Senate Subcommittee on African Affairs, Hearings, Sept. 1976 (Washington, D.C.: Government Printing Office, 1977) p. 448.

49. Karen Rothmeyer, American Committee on Africa, telephone interview with R. Cordova, Jan. 9, 1979.

50. Interview with Herbert Davis, United Automobile Workers, U.S., by R. Cordova, Jan. 9, 1979.

51. Y.S. Hsu, *The Impact of U.S. Investment in Europe* (New York: Praeger, 1973).

52. *Business Week*, Aug. 21, 1978.

53. Corporate Information Center, *Church Investments, Corporations, and South Africa*, op. cit.

54a. *Africa News*, March 17, 1980.

54. *The New York Times*, Jan. 17, 1978; see also Jan. 20, 1978.

55. Commerzbank, Wer Gehört Zu Wem (Köln: 1976).

56. V.W. AG, *VW in Sudafrika*, May, 1976.

57. South African Institute of Race Relations, *A Survey of Race Relations 1976*, *op. cit.*, p. 245.

58. *U.S. News and World Report*, Jan. 16, 1978, reports that as a result, V.W. exports from the F.R.G. to those regions was declining.

59. *South Africa Digest*, Oct. 17, 1976.

60. *Stern* (F.R.G.), No. 32, 1977.

61. *Sunday Times* (South Africa) Oct. 14, 1973.

62. R. Kopler, "Deutsche Manager sind Schlimmer als die Südafrikanische" Informationsdienst Südliches Afrika (Bonn, No. 4, April 1979).

63. For information re Japanese auto companies, see Yoko Kitizawa, *From Tokyo to Johannesburg* (New York: Interfaith Center on Corporation Information, 1975) unless otherwise sited.

64. *Die Neue* (West Berlin) July 23, 1979: Frankfurter Rundschau, July 13, 1978.

65. Dunn and Bradstreet, Principal International Business 1975-76: The World Marketing Director (New York: 1977) p. 1175: Handelsblatt (Hanover) Apr. 22, 1978.

66. Handelsblatt, April 22, 1978.

67. Dunn and Bradstreet, Principal International Business, 1975-6. *op. cit.*

68. Unless otherwise cited, information re U.S. electrical companies from their annual reports or the Corporate Information Center, Church Investments . . . .*op. cit.*

69. *Africa News*, Nov. 13, 1978, Vol. XI, No. 20.

70. ITT in South Africa, (New York: International Telephone and Telegraph, May, 1976).

71. Informationdienst südliches Afrika (Bonn), Dec. 12, 1977.

72. Wentges, "Deutsches investment in Südafrika . . ." *op. cit.*

73. *Sechaba*, Nov.-Dec., 1975.

74. *South African Financial Gazette*, May 21, 1971; *Nihon Kogyo Shimbun* (Japan) Aug. 23, 1973.

75. UN Center on Transnational Corporations, Activities of Transnational Corporations in Southern Africa . . . .*op. cit.*

76. *South African Financial Mail*, Supplement: South African Philips Survey, July 29, 1977.

77. *South African Financial Mail*, Mar. 24, 1978.

78. IBM in South Africa, (New York: New York Council of Churches, 1972) p. 3. Unless otherwise cited, this and company reports are the source of materials re computerization in South Africa.

79. Dunn and Bradstreet, Principal International Business . . .*op. cit.*

80. IBM Annual Meeting, April, 1977.

81. *South African Financial Mail*, March 14, 1975; Sunday Times (South Africa) Apr. 6, 1975.

82. *South African Financial Mail*, Feb. 10, 1978.

83. *The New York Times*, Oct. 25, 1977.

84. F. Vayrynen, "South Africa: A Coming Nuclear Weapon Power?" in Instant Research on Peace and Violence, Vol. 7, No. 1.

85. *The New York Times*, Apr. 23, 1975.

86. Vayrynen, "South Africa: A Coming Nuclear Weapon Power?" op. cit.

87. Blick durch die Wirtschaft, May 23, 1979.
88. *Financial Times* (London) Feb. 17, 1978.
89. *South Africa Digest*, June 19 and July 30, 1976.
90. *The New York Times*, Oct. 11, 1977.
91. For discussion see A. Seidman *Ghana's Development Experience, 1951-1966* (Nairobi: East African Publishing House, 1978).
92. *Star* (Johannesburg) Dec. 26, 1971.

The Oil Majors   8

The Majors' South African Oil Business

Six of the world's biggest transnational oil firms became deeply involved in South Africa's military-industrial build-up, despite the fact that that country had no known natural oil reserves of its own. In 1973* three U.S. oil firms alone had already invested $274 million in South Africa—12 percent of their investments in oil on the whole African continent. That investment was more than all U.S. oil investments in Nigeria ($250 million) in the year of 1977[2] when that country was rapidly becoming one of the most important suppliers of U.S. oil imports.

As in the case of other manufacturing industries, the oil companies in Nigeria and elsewhere in independent Africa concentrated on pumping out crude oil for their refineries at home. Only under intense government pressures did they agree to help build small refineries for domestic consumption in Africa itself.

In South Africa, on the other hand, the oil majors collaborated closely with the parastatals, not only to build refining complexes and distribute oil products throughout the southern African region, but also to manufacture petrochemicals and produce oil from coal. They assisted the South African regime to violate United Nations sanctions to ship oil to Southern Rhodesia. They enabled South Africa, itself, to continue to buy essential crude oil after the oil producing countries, through OPEC, had agreed to impose an embargo.

Like every other modern industrial economy, South Africa needed oil to fuel its transport system, industrial sector, chemicals production, agricultural machinery, and fishing and shipping fleets. Above all, in the 1970s, it had to have oil for the capital-intensive military equipment

---

*1973 was the last year for which official data was reported. Thereafter the U.S. Department of Commerce "suppressed" data as to U.S. petroleum investments to "avoid identification of specific companies."[1]

and machinery required to safeguard its minority rule. As *Paratus*, the journal of the South African Armed Forces, pointed out, the concept of "mobile warfare . . . has made petrol a critical item in the time of operations."[3]

Under South African law, oil was considered a "munition of war." As the U.S. transnational parent firm, Mobil, was informed by South African lawyers[4] when its South African affiliate refused to answer the U.S. government's questions about its role in South Africa:

As oil is absolutely vital to enable the army to move, the navy to sail and the air force to fly, it is likely that a South African court would hold that it falls within . . . the definition of munitions of war.

South African legislation made it illegal for an oil company operating in the country to refuse to supply the South African armed forces.[5] All six oil majors in South Africa—Shell, BP, Mobil, Caltex* and Total—regularly sold oil products to the military.[6]

Why the Majors Invested

The oil majors invested heavily in South Africa's oil business for a number of reasons. Given the relatively capital-intensive nature of refineries and petro-chemicals industries, the low wages of black labor provided only a partial explanation—certainly not the primary one. Blacks typically constituted less than half of their labor force.

The South African regime gave generous concessions, including tax advantages and the construction of extensive infrastructure to stimulate the oil companies to invest. As in the case of other manufacturing industries, too, the pleasant surroundings available to the families of the white managers of the oil majors' South African subsidiaries undoubtedly contributed to their eagerness to set up shop in the white urban areas.

But the more persuasive explanation probably lay in the companies' expectation that by investing in South Africa they could sell their products throughout southern Africa and even further north. South Africa's fast growing manufacturing industry necessitated a simultaneous expansion of available refined oil products, as well as the possibility of utilizing petrochemicals. Undoubtedly, the fact that the oil majors had links through shares in and joint directors with other

---

*A merger of the overseas affiliates of two U.S. firms, California Standard Oil and Texaco, that would undoubtedly have been prohibited by U.S. anti-trust law if it had been consummated in the U.S. itself.

transnational industrial corporations involved in South Africa further stimulated their interest. Their growing investments may have led, in turn, to still closer linkages.

The South African regime's expansion of its military establishment further enlarged the regional oil market. Industries might utilize other forms of energy for many purposes, although they had to use some form of oil for lubrication. But South Africa's growing numbers of tanks, ships, trucks and airplanes could use no substitute for petroleum. The South African minority's reliance on mobility and capital-intensive military technologies intensified their necessity for augmented supplies of imported and refined oil products. These the oil majors were happy to sell—indeed, South African laws required them to do so.

Tied to the expanding military market, the oil company managers publicly argued for the importance of maintaining relations with South Africa's militarily powerful regime for strategic reasons: After the Suez Canal was closed in 1967, the firms shipped oil from the mid- and far-East around the Cape. South African military strength, they stressed to U.S. government officials, would help to secure these strategic routes. [7]

Furthermore, South Africa's regime encouraged transnational investments in ship building and repair facilities which the oil majors viewed as important to their long distance oil haulage. Thus South Africa's military expansion, primarily aimed at perpetuating its own repressive rule, provided both an attraction and—in the view of their managers—a mutually beneficial protection against disruption of their profitable oil business.

The oil companies probably viewed the separation of their refining and manufacturing capacity from their producing wells in Africa as a positive advantage. Extensive evidence suggests that the oil majors pioneered in locating their refineries in countries separately from those where they drilled their wells in order to perpetuate their control. [8] No government could easily nationalize the entire business, and would have to remain dependent on the transnational firms for at least some aspects. In the South African case, this argument appeared stronger insofar as the regime pledged both stability and protection of private interests. And the fact that the South African regime had to depend on the companies' willingness to continue to import crude ensured that it would have to remain sensitive to their concerns.* On the other hand,

---

*It is interesting to contrast this to the Brazilian case where Petrobras, with its own oil wells, developed its own refining and distributing capacity, creating "a crisis for the multinationals . . ."[9]

from the South African government's perspective, the more the companies could be persuaded to invest in refining and distribution in South and southern Africa, the more they would have a built-in interest in continuing to supply oil imports.

Exploration for Oil

The South African government remained eager, however, to discover sources of crude oil more immediately under its own direct control. It encouraged as many oil firms as possible to compete to discover oil by encouraging widespread exploration efforts throughout southern Africa. Almost all the majors became involved, including among U.S. firms, Amoco, Mobil, Chevron-Regent, Esso Exploration, Placid Oil, Gulf Oil, Syracuse Oil, and the Superior Oil Company of Houston (which controlled the Canadian firm, Falconbridge, which was linked to Anglo-American Corporation). The British Petroleum Company (BP) in which the British government held a majority of shares, joined a consortium with Shell and the French state-owned firm, Total, to prospect a large area off the Cape coast up to the border of the Transkei. Together with Shell, BP also developed a large concession in Namibia. Two major shipping companies, the British Cayzer, Irvine & Company, and the South African state-owned shipping firm, Safmarine, formed a joint operation to establish a fully equipped oil base at Mossel Bay. Even in 1977, long after the possibilities of discovering oil appeared exhausted, the South African regime spent R28 million more on oil prospecting. [10] But all these explorations failed.

To compensate, the South African government made every effort to reduce its dependence on oil by intensive development of other energy sources, including hydroelectric and nuclear power. Partly as a result of transnational corporate contributions of the most advanced technologies in these fields, it successfully reduced its dependence on oil to less than a fourth of its total energy needs,* probably the lowest level achieved by any industrial economy in the world. But its demand for that irreducible minimum remained.

In the 1960s, to guard against the possibility that an oil embargo might be imposed, the South African government introduced measures to build up oil stockpiles. In 1967, an American firm, Fenis and Scission, received the first contract to complete underground storage facilities. [12] The South African regime had requested the transnational

---

*The *South Africa Digest*, a government publication, claims oil provides only 20 percent of the nation's meeds. [11]

oil companies to "hold large stocks at their own expense. This requirement was, indeed, made a condition of the franchise given to oil companies to build or expand refineries."[13] The regime's own *South Africa Digest* reported[14] in the late '70s that the stockpiles then totalled about 18 months' supply.

Oil-From-Coal

Transnational corporations helped South Africa acquire the essential technology to build SASOL to produce oil from its vast coal reserves. In 1955, it completed SASOL I, which used the Fischer-Tropsche method developed in Germany between the two world wars. It produced about one percent of South Africa's current oil requirements.[15]

The government initiated a second project, SASOL II, in the 1970s, for completion by 1981. The largest industrial complex in the nation, its early cost estimates reached R2,458 million in 1977. It was to be financed from three sources: R1,666 million from the Government's Strategic Oil Fund, R492 million in the form of export credits provided by transnational firms, and R300 million from Parliamentary appropriations.[16] The regime expected the two SASOL projects, together, to produce about 13 percent of the nation's oil requirements.

U.S. and F.R.G. transnationals sold South Africa the essential advanced technology to build SASOL II.[17] A U.S. engineering firm, Fluor, undertook the basic construction contract. Another U.S. firm, Raytheon, subcontracted for about $350 million of the construction operations through its subsidiary, Badger. A third U.S. firm, Honeywell, provided much of the essential electrical equipment.* The Lurgi Company of Frankfurt, F.R.G., engineered and supplied the gasification and other major equipment. Deutsche Babcock, F.R.G. also participated in the construction.

Anti-apartheid critics in the F.R.G raised serious questions as to whether the high cost of the second SASOL project, which far exceeded the estimates of their experts, might not in fact conceal construction of nuclear facilities.[18] The fact that both Fluor and Badger had engaged in nuclear construction in projects in the U.S. itself tended to lend credence to this suspicion, since they were the major construction firms building the highly secret project in South Africa.

---

*Ironically, in 1979, the U.S. government apparently permitted initiation of negotiations with the South African regime to acquire the oil-from-coal process, rather than obtaining it directly from the U.S. companies engaged in constructing the South African project.

In the late '70s, the revolution in Iran led to the cut-off of South Africa's major source of imported oil. Skyrocketing gold prices increased the regime's foreign exchange earnings, so it planned to expand SASOL II still further, expending almost R4 billion on the highly secret project. By 1978, more than 230 contracts, accounting for 60 percent of the cost, had been placed with South African consultants and contractors. These included subsidiaries of transnational firms like British Steel Corporation's affiliate, Dorbyl. But overseas transnationals continued to play the major role in providing critical technical guidance and key imported inputs. Fluor was again selected as contractor for phase three and four extensions for SASOL II. [19]

Fluor's South African business accounted for 13 percent of its 1978 world wide turnover. [20] Fluor framed a consortium contract with the South African affiliate of Babcock & Wilcox, Dillinger Engineering & Contracting, General Erection and Roberts Construction for supply of labor and construction services. Siemens participated in the construction of the coal mine. [21]

Transnational Corporate Oil Refineries [22]

While many firms futilely explored for oil throughout southern Africa in the 1960s and early '70s, six majors financed the expansion of South African oil refinery capacity, until it almost equalled, if it did not surpass, the refinery capacity of all other African countries combined. The majors imported crude from their wells in other Third World nations, including independent African states, and refined it in South Africa for sale throughout the southern region.

Eight major oil companies engaged in refining and/or distributing oil products in South Africa. Six were completely foreign-owned. One was largely foreign owned, and the eighth was the parastatal, SASOL.

By the 1970s, four subsidiaries of transnational oil firms, Mobil, Shell, British Petroleum, and Caltex, supplied 75 percent of the total regional demand for petroleum products. Each supplied 18 to 22 percent of the market. CPF, a subsidiary of the French national petroleum firm, Total, supplied 10 percent. SASOL, Trek (a locally-controlled company), Esso and Sonap (backed by Portuguese interests) accounted for between 2 and 4 percent each. These firms, working singly or in consortia, built all of the oil refinery capacity in South Africa.

The British Petroleum Company (BP), in which the British government held shares, helped build up South Africa's petro-chemicals industry as well as its oil refinery capacity. It owned 20 percent of the shares of the South African parastatal, Sentrachem, and helped Sentrachem acquire technologically advanced inputs to develop the industry. By the mid-'70s, BP, together with Shell, controlled almost a fourth of the South African oil products market. Shell-BP also constructed a lubricating plant and a tanker terminal at Reunion, a few miles south of Durban. The Shell/BP refinery, SAPREF, had the biggest output of any single commercial South African refinery, next to the huge state controlled NATREF. Shell-BP owned or supplied about 1700 service stations throughout southern Africa. Shell also engaged in coal mining.

Shell and BP each owned 18 percent of Trek Beleggings Beperk. This joined them, not only with the South African parastatal, the Industrial Development Corporation (which retained 9.5 percent) but also with the Afrikaans mining finance house, General Mining. Trek owned or supplied another 193 service stations in South Africa. [23]

In the rest of Africa, Shell-BP confined its activities primarily to exploring for and producing crude petroleum and distributing refined products, imported from its refineries elsewhere, including South Africa. It built small refineries only for domestic consumption in those independent African states where it appeared necessary to preserve its control over oil wells and/or markets, or where the local government financed much of the cost. In 1979, the Nigerian government, incensed at BP's continued sales of crude—including supplies from Nigeria—to South Africa, nationalized Shell-BP's Nigerian wells.

U.S. oil giants invested more capital in their South African business than in any other single African state. Next to manufacturing, oil had become the most important sector of U.S. investment in South Africa by 1973. Four U.S. firms, Caltex (Standard Oil of California and Texaco) Mobil, and Esso, together, controlled almost half of the South African market for petroleum products by the 1970s. Caltex and Mobil owned two of the largest refineries in the country.

Standard Oil of California, by the 1970s the biggest company in the entire world, shared ownership of the Caltex oil refinery in South Africa with Texaco. Although U.S. anti-trust legislation would not have permitted such a combination to operate in the United States itself, it did not prohibit it abroad.

In 1975, Standard Oil of California acquired 20 percent of the common stock of AMAX which, in close cooperation with Anglo-American Corporation, had extensive investments throughout southern Africa. (See above, pp. 97, 110-11). Standard Oil owned extensive operations in the rest of Africa, as well, although it did not issue as detailed reports on its continental activities as did Mobil and Texaco.

Texaco engaged primarily in exploring for and producing crude oil and importing and selling refined petroleum products through widespread marketing networks in many independent African states. It pumped oil from wells in Nigeria, which it owned jointly with the Nigerian government, and explored for more in Gabon, Niger, Mauritania, Mali and Egypt. In 1979, the Angolan government licensed it to search for oil there. Texaco supplied about 11 percent of the West African petroleum products market in the mid-'70s. Its sales volume had continued to rise despite increasing costs, government mandated restrictions on consumption, and the nationalization of its marketing operations in several countries.

But Texaco's biggest involvement in oil refining in Africa was in the South African plant it owned through Caltex, together with Standard Oil of California. In 1975, Caltex initiated expansion of its operations, aiming to almost double its output to 100,000 barrels a day by 1978. Caltex also owned 23.8 percent of Mobil's lubricating oil refinery in Durban.

Mobil boasted[24] in 1979 that it had begun its South African operations in 1897 when a predecessor company, Vacuum Oil, established a branch in the British Cape Colony. Today, "two Mobil subsidiaries, both incorporated in South Africa, are engaged in refining crude oil, manufacturing and blending lubricants, and marketing petroleum products. Total assets in wholly owned operations amount to about $426 million."

One subsidiary, Mobil Oil Southern Africa, with its headquarters in Cape Town, marketed a full range of petroleum products, including fuels, lubricants, asphalt, and special products like international jet fuels and international bunkers. It owned and supplied 1350 service stations. It claimed to control an estimated 21 percent of the 1977 inland market for all oil products.

The other subsidiary, Mobil Refining Company Southern Africa, owned a 100,000-barrel-a-day refinery at Durban, and held a 32.9 percent equity interest in South African Oil Refinery. In addition, Mobil carried on other relatively minor activities in South Africa like road surfacing, and marine insurance.

In late 1978, a Mobil subsidiary, Condor Oil, opened an oil recycling plant which provided about 6 percent of South Africa's lubricating oil needs. Mobil staff designed and engineered the plant for which 90 percent of the materials were provided by South African based industry. Presumably, Mobil imported the rest through its own transnational corporate connections.

In 1976, a United Church of Christ publication, *The Oil Conspiracy*,[25] exposed the "paper-chase" set up by Mobil South Africa to sell its oil products in Southern Rhodesia despite United Nations sanctions. Mobil

South Africa sold a bulk consignment of oil products to a South African intermediary, usually part of Freight Services, Ltd., which resold it via further South African intermediaries to GENTA, a Rhodesian government agency responsible for importing all Rhodesia's oil requirements. GENTA finally sold the oil to the oil majors' own Rhodesian subsidiaries, including one belonging to Mobil itself, for distribution in Rhodesia. After 1976, evidence emerged to show that South African subsidiaries of Shell, BP, Caltex and Total engaged in similar methods of supplying oil to Rhodesia.[26]

In 1976, Mobil incorporated its Namibian operations, which it had previously conducted from its South African office, as a separate company. Its Namibian assets, worth about $6 million, included inland depots, about 70 service stations, and a coastal terminal at Walvis Bay. Elsewhere in Africa, Mobil's oil wells, principally in Libya and Nigeria, produced about 9 percent of its world-wide output. Mobil refined about 8.8 percent of its world wide refined products in Africa. Its South African refinery produced almost 90 percent of this total.

Compagnie Francaise des Petroles, partly owned by the French government, originally had complete control of Total South Africa. In 1969, however, it sold a block of shares in Total to a local Afrikaner house, Volksas. Total owned a 30-percent interest in the state oil refinery, NATREF, SASOL (52.5 percent) and the Iranian National Oil Company (17.5 percent) owned the remaining shares.*

Total explored for oil in many independent African states, mostly former French colonies. It pumped crude from its wells in Tunisia and Algeria. These, together, produced about 10 percent of its world-wide output. Algeria produced far more than Tunisia. Total built small-scale refineries in Morocco, Senegal, Ivory Coast, Gabon, the Malagasy Republic and Southern Rhodesia (though it claimed the last had ceased operations). But Total, like its British and U.S. transnational competitors, refined far more oil in South Africa than anywhere else in Africa. Its South African refinery produced twice as much output as its next largest in Ivory Coast. (See Table 8-1)

The Majors' Labor Practices

Oil refineries and petrochemicals industries are highly capital-intensive. They require primarily highly skilled labor, a category from which the South African union contracts and custom, as well as government policies, systematically excluded African workers. In 1978,

---

*What happened to this holding after the Iranian coup has not been reported.

Table 8-1.
The Oil Majors' Business in South Africa Compared to Independent African States[1]

Oil Major	South African Holdings[2]	Holdings in Rest of Africa
British Petroleum (1975) (U.K.)	Oil refinery (50%); African Lubricants (34%); Trek Petroleum (20%); Sentrchem (20%); BP Southern Africa	Burundi; Cameroon; Kenya (includes refinery, 13%); Libya; Gabon; Ghana; Nigeria; Rwanda; Rhodesia (21%); Sudan (50%);Nigeria (wells, 50%);Sierra Leone (refinery, 7%); Senegal (refinery, 12%); Tunisia; Morocco (50%); Gabon (refinery, 3%); Ivory Coast (refinery, 10%; sales, 50%); Malagasy (refinery, 6%); Niger; Togo (storage, 20%; distribution, 100%); Volta
Mobil (1975) (U.S.)	Mobil Refining Co. Mobil Oil Southern Africa (marketing)	*Exploration:* Egypt, Tunisia, Libya, Nigeria *Marketing:* Cameroon, Ivory Coast, Canaries, Equatorial Africa, East Africa, Ghana, Volta, Kenya, Liberia, Malawi, Mali, Niger, Nigeria, Senegal, Sierra Leone and Gambia, Sudan, Tanzania, Togo, Tunisia *Producing and marketing:* Egypt, Libya, Nigeria
Texaco (1977)[1] (U.S.)	Caltex (50%) refinery and distribution	*Marketing:* Maili; West Africa; Ivory Coast, Ghana (60%); Gabon (90%); Upper Volta; Nigeria; *Exploration:* Egypt; Niger; Gabon: Zaire *Exploration and producing:* Nigeria, Angola (also may have other holdings in independent Africa through Caltex, but information re details not available)
Standard Oil of California (U.S.)	Caltex (50%) refinery and distribution	Details not available
Total (French) (1975)	30% of NATREF	*Exploration:* Angola (50%); Senegal (36.50%); Kenya (70%); Somalia (50%) *Crude oil:* Algeria (142,055 bls/day); Tunisia (532 bls/day) *Refining and marketing:* Morocco (6.5%); Senegal (11.83); Ivory Coast (10.8%); Gabon (n.a.); Southern Rhodesia (plant not in operation, 5.3%); Malagasy (7.5%) *Other marketing networks:* details unknown

Notes: [1]Unless otherwise noted in parentheses, holding is 100%
[2]Shell owns other 50%

Sources: Company's annual reports of dates indicated.

Mobil Oil, proclaiming its non-discriminatory labor practices,[27] reported it employed 3036 persons, of whom only 46.6 percent were "non-white" and of these little more than half (roughly a fourth of the total labor force) were "black;" presumably African.* This was the outcome of what Mobil announced in 1972 as a vigorous policy of upgrading blacks.**

Mobil argued[29] that, since lack of education was a key barrier to upgrading blacks, it helped to overcome this barrier by providing black parents with jobs so their children would not have to leave school to avoid being a burden on their families. Mobil's spokesmen conveniently neglected to point out that the government policy of segregated education and pathetically inadequate finance for black public schools was the real cause of lack of educational qualifications among blacks.

Mobil also failed to explain that the oil majors, by introducing advanced technologies, actually contributed to reducing overall employment. Speaking elsewhere, a Mobil representative illustrated this[30] by describing his firm's steps to upgrade Africans in the relatively unskilled work of a petroleum depot. The company reduced the number of white workers from seven to one supervisor, who was ultimately to be phased out. Meanwhile, the number of blacks was increased by only three persons, from 37 to 40. The manager asserted, "The rate of pay wasn't a factor. There was a fairly high rate of turnover among whites." But his own figures showed that the number of workers—now all but one black—doing the same amount of work as before had been reduced by almost 18 percent. In other words, he expected fewer blacks to do the same job the whites had done before, another way of getting more output for less money. The whites were released to assume skilled jobs elsewhere in the economy, while overall employment was reduced.

Texaco, in publishing data purporting to prove it had upgraded African workers from 1962 to 1977, demonstrated the longer run implications of these kinds of labor practices. While the company increased output over the 15 years, it cut back on total employment by several hundreds of workers. Furthermore, it reduced the proportion of blacks from 62 percent of the labor force in 1962 to 41 percent in 1977.[31]

The majors in some instances actually perpetuated the ethnic segregation which the South African racists sought to preserve as a basic

*Apparently Mobil's South African managers had adopted the South African government's divisive racist nomenclature, rather than including all persons of Asian and mixed ancestry as blacks.

**Prior to that, in eight years from 1962 to 1970, Mobil South Africa had trained 992 whites for highly skilled jobs, but only 4 Africans and 22 Asians and Coloureds.[28]

feature of their divide and rule program. Thus Mobil, accepting the myth which the regime sought to institutionalize through bantustanization, declared, the "black population . . . is not homogeneous—but, on the contrary, consists of nine ethnic groups or tribes . . . Between them and the other non-whites, there are strains and stresses arising from their different histories and cultures." Therefore, it praised its company policy of segregating these alleged tribal groupings in an age-old technique designed to hinder worker solidarity: "At our Durban refinery, for example, we have . . . been required to compose each shift of members of the same tribe."[32]

Evading OPEC's Oil Boycott

The Organization of Petroleum Exporting Countries (OPEC) decided, in the mid-'70s, to impose an oil boycott on South Africa. But the oil majors claimed the crude they continued to import was from their wells in non-OPEC countries. Until 1978, Iran was the only country willing publicly to defy the OPEC agreement to boycott South Africa. Iran's National Iranian Oil Company owned 17.5 percent of the South African Oil Refinery NATREF (see above, p. 191) The Shah's government apparently expected, in return, a guaranteed supply of uranium for its expanding nuclear capacity. Whether big oil firms in addition shipped in crude they pumped from wells in other countries was impossible for outsiders to determine. As one UN report emphasized:[33]

It was difficult to compile statistics on South Africa's oil supplies because the oil-exporting countries frequently depended on the multinational oil companies for information concerning the destination of their oil. Crude oil was sometimes carried to South Africa by ships belonging to multinational companies with subsidiaries in South Africa, having been purchased in Middle Eastern countries which were members of OPEC, and which had recently attempted to enforce an oil embargo against South Africa. One or more of the parent oil companies were clearly undermining the policy of various Middle Eastern OPEC members by failing to inform them that their oil was being exported to South Africa.

With the fall of the Shah in Iran, and the new government's declaration that it would end sales to South Africa (as well as cancellation of its plans to construct new nuclear power facilities), it was expected that South Africa would suffer shortages of crude—unless the oil companies shipped in supplies from elsewhere.

How South Africa obtained its oil after the new Iranian government declared its determination to end shipments is not clear. Bits and pieces of evidence emerged suggesting the transnationals continued to assist South Africa to overcome the impact of the OPEC boycott. Shell apparently had a contract with Bahrein to ship oil to its South African refinery. And South Africa appeared to be able to buy crude at 60 percent more than OPEC prices by purchasing it on spot contract at Rotterdam.[34] South Africa's Globe Engineering Works at Cape Town reported that it serviced the U.S. tanker *Atlantic*, the French tanker *Jade*, and the British tanker *Lima*,[35] suggesting South Africa maintain close on-going links with transnational oil firms engaged in shipping crude.

The president of the Deak Perara Group, the leading retailer in gold and foreign currencies operating through 58 agencies and banks world wide, reported that some OPEC countries were violating the boycott. He claimed South Africa was exchanging gold bullion for Saudi and Kuwaiti supplies: "I wouldn't care to speculate on what exchange rate for bullion is being used," he added.[36]

But most of the evidence tended to confirm reports by the *Financial Mail* that for "the oil majors, with supply commitments to their SA refining and marketing subsidiaries, the loss of Iran has forced drastic rescheduling of their supply chains."[37] The Mail added, "The base load of SA's crude oil requirements is probably being carried by sources to which the oil majors have access with a reasonable prospect of medium to long-term on a contractual basis. In addition to these limited sources, the oil companies and SASOL will probably negotiate term contracts with international brokers and take their chances on the spot market."

The *Mail* suggested that the oil majors were not acting without their government's support. It reported that, when the Big Four summit of the heads of government of France, West Germany, Britain and the U.S. met in Guadeloupe in January, they "huddled" on Rhodesia, Iran, oil and South Africa, and proposed that "Britain and the U.S. would guarantee South Africa's annual oil imports of 15 million tons for an indefinite period. In return, Pretoria would resume full diplomatic pressure on Salisbury to bring about a peaceful solution there."[38] The *Mail* argued[39] that "It is unlikely that the . . . Congress would allow the White House to ship domestic U.S. oil abroad," but U.S. Energy Secretary James Schlesinger declared, "there was 'substantial evidence' that petroleum products that normally would be going to the United States have been diverted to Europe by oil companies looking for higher profits."[40] Privately, U.S. officials reportedly said that 200,000 barrels a day were involved. How much of this might be going to South Africa remained unknown.

The British government, on the other hand, openly announced that it planned to sell some of its North Sea Oil to South Africa, replacing it with supplies from other sources, including independent African countries. This was undoubtedly a factor in Nigeria's nationalization of BP's Nigerian assets. The international oil companies, according to the South African *Financial Mail*[41] seemed to be using their position as suppliers of a "scarce and strategic commodity" to muscle in on South Africa's coal industry. BP, Shell and Total had obtained an allocation of almost half of South Africa's lucrative coal exports, apparently on the assumption that "The more business the oil majors can do in SA . . .the less inclined they will be to close SA's oil tap."[42]

Summary

The globe-encircling oil majors enabled South Africa to overcome what might have been the major block to its continued economic and increasingly military domination of southern Africa: its lack of viable crude oil reserves. With the South African regime's encouragement, many firms explored extensively in a fruitless effort to help overcome this handicap. Others provided the necessary sophisticated technologies to enable South Africa to produce oil on an increasing scale, using its own vast supplies of coal. Perhaps most important, a handful of oil majors, collaborating with South African private and parastatal firms, built extensive oil refining capacity and the foundations of a petrochemicals industry in South Africa. These firms continued to ship in crude oil from their wells around the world, including some in Africa itself. While Iran officially remained the most important supplier until 1979, experts argued persuasively that the transnationals could—and probably did—ship in oil on their own or chartered tankers, even from oil producing countries which sought to adhere to the OPEC boycott of South Africa. The fact that the South African regime continued to obtain oil suppies after the fall of the Shah's government tended to support this argument.

The explanations for the big companies' expanded investment in South Africa's growing military-industrial complex differ at least in emphasis from those of manufacturing firms. The low cost of black labor explained relatively little, since the majors introduced increasingly capital-intensive machinery which required relatively few workers, mainly skilled; over half their employees were white.

The primary reason undboutedly lay in two interrelated factors; first, the companies' investments seemed to guarantee their ability to enter into the regional market, particularly that created by the growth of South Africa's military-industrial might. Their growing linkages with domestic private and government firms both grew out of and contributed to this likelihood. Secondly, the companies probably considered their investments in refining and manufacturing in "stable," militarily strong, white-ruled South Africa, geographically separated from their producing wells in independent African states, a protection against the dangers of nationalization.

References

1. U.S. Department of Commerce, Survey of Current Business, Aug., 1974.
2. Ibid., August, 1978.
3. Major J. A. H. J. Smith, Verspreiding van Petrol tydens Operasies', *Paratus*, Aug. 1973, p. 23, translated in Martin Bailey and Bernard Rivers, *Oil Sanctions Against South Africa* (New York: Center Against Apartheid, United Nations Department of Political and Security Council Affairs, Notes and Documents, June, 1978), p. 19.
4. Extract (Section 3.3.3) from legal opinion prepared by Hfayman Godfrey & Sanderson (Johannesburg) for Mobil, dated July 14, 1976 (submitted by Mobil as part of its evidence to the United States Senate, Sept. 17, 1976); cited in Bailey and Rivers, Oil Sanctions Against South Africa, *op. cit.*, p. 19.
5. Legislation on "conditional selling" is embodied in the National Supplies Procurement Act, No. 89 of 1970, cited in Bailey and Rivers, *op. cit.*, p. 20.
6. Testimony, Dec. 1, 1977, cited in Bailey and Rivers, *op. cit.*, p. 20. *South Africa Digest*, Mar. 2, 1979.
7. See Association of Concerned African Scholars, Western Massachusetts branch, U.S. Military Involvement in Southern Africa (Boston: South End Press, 1978) for discussion.
8. H. O'Connor, *World Crisis in Oil* (New York: Monthly Review Press, 1962).
9. P. Evans, *Dependent Development-The Alliance of Multinational, State and Local Capital in Brazil*, (Princeton: Princeton University Press, 1979), pp. 266-7.
10. *South African Financial Mail*, Mar. 10, 1979.
11. *South Africa Digest*, March 2, 1979.
12. *Southern Africa* (London) Apr. 24, 1967.
13. P. Odell, *Oil and World Power: Background to the Oil Crisis* (Harmondsworth: Penguin, fourth edition, 1975).
14. Nov. 10, 1978.
15. For discussion, see Bailey and Rivers, *Oil Sanctions Against South Africa, op. cit.*, pp. 51ff.
16. Ibid., reference 98.
17. Informationsdienst Südliches Afrika (Bonn) Dec., 1977.
18. *Ibid.*
19. *South African Financial Mail*, Mar. 2, 1979.
20. *Ibid.*, Mar. 16, 1979.
21. *Ibid.*, Mar. 2, 1979.

22. Unless otherwise cited, the following information relating to individual companies is from their respective annual reports.

23. *South African Financial Mail*, Feb. 10, 1978.

24. Mobil Corporation, *What Mobil is Doing in South Africa* (New York: Mobil, 150 East 42 Street, 1979)

25. New York: June 21, 1976.

26. Rivers and Bailey, *Oil Sanctions Against South Africa, op. cit.*, ref. 127.

27. Mobil Corporation, *What Mobi is Doing in South Africa, op. cit.*

28. Corporate Information Center, *Church Investments, Corporations and South Africa*, (New York: National Council of Churches, 475 Riverside Drive, 1973).

29. Mobil Corporation, *What Mobil is Doing in South Africa, op. cit.*, p. 7.

30. *Wall Street Journal*, Mar. 16, 1978.

31. Texaco, *Texaco Star*, No. 4, 1977.

32. Mobil Corporation, *What Mobil is Doing in South Africa, op.cit.*, p. 7.

33. United Nations Document, Anti-Apartheid Committee, A/AC.115; SR.361 (Engl., p. 7).

34. *South African Financial Mail*, Feb. 9, 1979.

35. *South Africa Digest*, May 18, 1979.

36. *The New York Times*, June 27, 1979.

37. *South African Financial Mail*, Feb. 9, 1979.

38. *South African Financial Mail*, Jan 12, 1979.

39. *Ibid.*

40. *Washington Post*, May, 1979.

41. *South African Financial Mail* Jan. 12, 1979.

42. *Ibid.*

Transnational Finance Capital

The transnational banks constituted the core, as well as the most advanced elements, of transnational finance capital. Their vigorous competitive growth in South Africa financed the expansion of the South African military industrial complex in the 1960s and 1970s. On the one hand, their presence facilitated the accelerated penetration of associated transnational firms into the region. On the other, their desire to discover profitable new outlets for mounting accumulations of capital stimulated them to mobilize vast sums to help the minority regime surmount the political and economic crises of the 1970s.

It became increasing difficult to obtain hard facts about the nature and extent of transnational industrial firms in South Africa in the 1970s as they sought to conceal their activities from anti-apartheid critics. But it was far more difficult to gather relevant data about the expanding involvement of transnational banks there. In the late 1960s, their traditional practice of maintaining highly confidential relations with their clients was reinforced by the growing criticism of anti-apartheid groups.[1] Moreover, money is a fungible commodity; it was extremely difficult to monitor transfers between parent transnational banks and local branches, and between local affiliates and private and state agencies.

Available evidence, nevertheless, exposed the predominant, if contradictory, role of transnational banks and associated institutions. While facilitating industrial investments and credits, sought by the South African regime to strengthen its independence, they enmeshed its economy ever more tightly into the world capitalist commercial networks, aggravating its economic disproportions and external dependence. A small handful of powerful transnational banks held about two-thirds of the assets of the biggest 20 banks in South Africa, (See Table 9-1) a far higher percentage than foreign firms held in any other sector of the economy. They participated in a full range of financial services for private, parastatal and governmental activities, providing

Table 9-1.
Assets of South African banks with major shareholdings, 1976

Name of Bank	Assets in Rands	Rank*	% of total assets of top 20 banks	Foreign shareholder (% held, if known)
Primarily foreign-held banks:				
Associated with Barclays,				
Anglo-American Corp. (AAC)				
Barclays (c)	2,611	1	23.0	Barclays (UK) (63%) AAC group (17.5%)
Westbank (a)	311	7	2.7	Barclays (UK)
Barclays (Merchant) (m)	171	12	1.5	Barclays (UK)
UAL (a)	226	11	1.9	AAC & Lazard Bros. (UK); Barclays minority holding
Total associated with Barclays & AAC	3,319		29.2	
Associated with Standard				
Standard	2,330	2	20.5	Standard (UK)**
Standard merchant (m)	302	8	2.7	"
Stannia (Hp)	282	9	2.4	" (Nedbank holds minority share)
Senbank (m)	336	6	2.9	" (minority holding)
Total associated with Standard	3,251		28.6	
other:				
UDC (g)	161	16	1.4	affiliated to United Dominion Insurance (SA-15)
Hilsam (m)	126	17	1.1	Hilsam (UK), a Citibank affiliate
Citibank (m)	117	19	1.0	Citibank (US)
French (c)	115	20	1.0	Banque de l'Indochine (France)

202

	519		4.5	
Total other primarily foreign-held banks				
Primarily South African-held banks:				
Volkskas (c)	1,500	3	13.2	
Trust (g)	996	4	8.8	
Nedbank (g)	949	5	8.3	AAC (8%); Old Mutual Insurance (SA-15)
Boland (g)	250	10	2.2	
Rand (g)+	169	13	1.5	
Santam (g)	166	14	1.5	
Bank of Johannesburg (g)	165	15	1.5	
Credcor	122	18	1.1	
Total, Primarily South African Held Banks	4,317		37.7	
Total, Primarily Foreign-Held Banks	7,089		62.3	
Total Assets, top 20 banks	11,255			

Notes: *In terms of assets.
  **Standard, U.K., is controlled by Midlands (U.K.)
  + Bankrupt in 1977
  (c) commercial bank
  (g) general bank
  (m) Merchant bank
  (Hp) hire-purchase

Source: South African Financial Mail, Supplement April 23, 1976; Foreign ownership is from *Who Owns What in World Banking* (London Financial Times) 1974.

commercial and merchant banking, discounting and leasing, insurance and pensions, and mutual funds.

The British banks were by far the largest and most influential. They had planted their roots in South Africa back in the colonial days, and had become closely intertwined with the domestically-based mining finance houses. (See Chapter 4 above) After World War II, some of the biggest U.S. banks had begun to penetrate the British banks' near-monopoly, both to facilitate their U.S. industrial clients' entry and to partake of the profitable business generated by industrial growth. By the late 1960s and '70s, European banks, especially from the Federal Republic of Germany, had become increasingly involved, although they tended to act solely as wholesale banks* working through the existing South African banking structure.

The same big banks played a predominant role in independent African states, but in none did they contribute much to the mobilization and reinvestment of capital to build up the local economy. They rarely provided credit needed for local projects. They almost never set up branch networks in rural areas which might serve peasant farmers or small scale industrial establishments. Nor did they provide significant assistance to African governments seeking to restructure their political economies to attain industrial development and self-sustaining growth. Instead, they mainly financed production for export and import trade, and served to facilitate the drain of investable surpluses in the form of profits, interests, dividends, and high salaries by the transnational firms engaged in extracting crude materials and selling manufactured goods.

In South Africa, in contrast, the transnational banks financed the industrial transformation of the apartheid political economy. They provided the financial networks that played a crucial role in helping South Africa emerge as the regional subcenter. Their own reports implied that they continued to funnel capital into Southern Rhodesia, despite United Nations sanctions. (See Ch. 11 below)

Two British banks, Barclays and Standard, remained by far the largest transnational banks operating in South Africa throughout the postwar period. Their eight domestic affiliates still controlled almost two thirds of the assets of the 20 largest South African banks in the

---

*Retail banking involves provision of normal banking services: mobilizing savings through deposits, arranging routine credits, etc. In wholesale banking, foreign banks provide international contacts for domestically based banks, helping to arrange international credits and establish local contacts for their transnational corporate clients. In most cases, the wholesale bank does not establish a local branch network.

mid-'70s. Both banks had funnelled British capital into the profitable mining business of the Transvaal back in the 19th Century. Over time, pressure from the South African regime and their subsidiary banks' desire for local ties led them to sell shares on the Johannesburg Stock Exchange, but in both cases the parent banks retained a majority control. Subsidiaries of three other transnational banks, Hilsam (U.K.), Citibank (U.S.), and the French Bank had entered the ranks of the top 20 South African banks by the 1970s, as well. Although their combined assets constituted less than 5 percent of the total, they played an increasingly important part in mobilizing international funds and establishing valuable international ties, especially with U.S. industrial firms. Other European and U.S. banks established wholesale relations with domestic and foreign bank affiliates located in South Africa.

The British Banks

Barclays Bank remained South Africa's leading bank. By the 1970s, with over a thousand branches spread throughout the country and Namibia, its South African profits still comprised over a tenth of the profits of its British parent, and a third of those of Barclays International. The South African bank's share of the latter declined as Barclays' overseas affiliates expanded business elsewhere outside England more rapidly.

Table 9-2.
Net Profits before taxes of Barclays' Bank, South Africa, as percentage of profits of Barlcays' Ltd., of United Kingdom, and Barclays DCO, International

	Barclays, S.A., net pre-tax profits (R Million)	As percent of Barclays Ltd., U.K.'s profits (%)	As percent of Barclays DCO/International's profits (%)
1970	16	12.1	64.
1971	19	10.7	55.8
1972	25	10.6	39.6
1973	26	9.0	36.1
1974	31	11.9	32.9

Source: South African Financial Mail, Special Supplement, Jan. 30, 1976.

Barclays bank helped finance Anglo American Corporation at its birth, and remained closely tied to it as it grew into the dominant mining finance house in South Africa. (see pp. 95-9 above) Anglo remained one of Barclays South Africa's biggest customers in South Africa and its largest South African shareholder. In 1976, Barclays purchased Wesbank, the seventh largest South African bank, in which Anglo already owned 70 percent of the shares. This transaction augmented Anglo's ownership of Barclays, South Africa from 15 to 32 percent. Barclays South Africa provided one of the many links between Anglo and other South African mining finance houses; directors of three of them, Barlow Rand, Anglovaal, and Union Corporation, also sat on its board.

Although Barclays South Africa remained Barclays International's largest single subsidiary, the latter nevertheless conducted extensive operations in other African states. In 1976, the largest included holdings in Ghana, Nigeria, Zambia and Egypt. It also owned several smaller affiliates in southern Africa, including Botswana, Lesotho, and Swaziland. Barclays Bank's Southern Rhodesian associate owned over $R141 million worth of assets, including 37 branches and 50 fixed and mobile agencies. (See Ch. 11 below).

Barclays South Africa had forged innumerable ties with other South African banks. It owned a minority of shares in the merchant bank, Union Acceptance Ltd. (UAL), the 11th largest South African bank in terms of assets. Anglo American Corporation had established UAL in 1955 in collaboration with the London-based merchant bank, Lazard Brothers. In the 1970s, UAL merged with two South African banks, Nedbank and Syfrets, under the overall control of the Nedbank Group, creating a domestic merchant bank conglomerate, Nedsual, with total assets of R2 billion—greater than all the other merchant banks put together. (For Nedsual's role in Southern Rhodesia, see Chapter 11 below).

The bank which has today grown into the Standard Chartered Bank of England[3] was born in South Africa during the gold rush back in the 19th Century. Its head office was later transferred to England. Its South African business, nevertheless, continued to expand until, by the time of the 1961 Sharpeville Massacre, it had about 350 branches. In the 15 boom years that followed, Standard's South African branches more than doubled in number to reach almost a thousand, with a full branch at Windhoek in Namibia. A fifth of Standard's world-wide profits still originated in South Africa. It remained one of South Africa's major agents for selling gold. Despite United Nations sanctions, Standard's activities continued to reach into Southern Rhodesia after UDI. (See Chapter 11 below) Like Barclays, Standard had extended its holdings into the rest of Africa, but its South African business remained by far its most important activity on the continent.

Hilsam, the third largest transnational bank in South Africa, was established in 1960 by the British Hill Samuel Group[4] to conduct merchant banking business. Merchant banking remained its most im-

Table 9-3.
Standard and Chartered Bank Group Holdings in Africa,
1975[1]

	South Africa	Other Africa
Standard and Charter (1975)	Standard Bank, SA (73.09%) Standard Bank Investment Corp. (73.09); Consumer Finance & Leasing (73.09%); Standard Bank Fund Managers (insurance—73.09); Standard Bank Financial Services (73.09%) Computer Leasing; (19%)	Southern Rhodesia (Standard Finance); Export Credit Insurance (12.6%); Nigeria (51%); Zambia (Commercial Bank); Industrial Credit Co. (50%); Sierra Leone (92.08%); Swaziland (60%); Uganda (51%); Mozambique (33.65%); Ghana (87.5%); Angola (33.65%[2]); Malawi (25.5%); Zaire (25.89%); Kenya (National Industrial Credit)

Notes: [1]The type of bank holding is commercial unless otherwise noted; and the percentage holding is 100% unless otherwise noted in parantheses).
[2]Since 1975, nationalized.
m-merchant bank
a-acceptance bank

Sources: Annual report Standard and Chartered Bank, 1975.

portant activity, but it also entered into insurance and pension fund business. In 1973, it initiated a program for domestic servants' pensions through its wholly-owned susidiary, the African Pension Trustees (APT).[5] Employers paid into the scheme primarily to attract and hold servants: if employment was terminated for any reason within ten years, the employee received no benefits—the employer kept the total contribution, plus interest. After ten years of steady employment, the servant became entitled to half the contribution. Only after 20 years, did he or she qualify for the full sum, a lump-sum payment of R480 plus interest. With inflation of 10 to 15 percent a year, this total meant little to the former employee, but the combined accumulated funds gave Hilsam a tidy sum for investment in other sectors of the apartheid economy.

South Africans held a majority of equity in the UDC, South Africa's 16th largest bank, but it remained, nevertheless, affiliated to the British bank, the United Dominions Trust. An affiliated institution,

UDC, Ltd., operated in Southern Rhodesia. The British parent had several smaller affiliates in other former British colonies engaged in financing agricultural and trading activities dating back to the Empire days.

The U.S. Connection[6]

Reflecting and facilitating the U.S. transnationals' growing penetration of the South African political economy after World War II, the three largest banks in the U.S. began to acquire links to the South African business world, some direct, others through relationships with British banks. The second largest bank in the U.S., Citibank, had emerged as the fourth largest foreign bank in terms of assets in South Africa by the 1970s, although it ranked only 19th among the 20 largest South African banks.

Citibank* set up its first South African branch in 1958. By 1976, it had established eight banks in major industrial centers throughout the country. It had also acquired an additional channel into South Africa's lucrative banking field when, in 1963, it purchased 16⅔ of the shares of the U.K. firm, M. Samuels. This gave it access to the Hill Samuel Group's South African and Rhodesian affiliates. In this way, Citibank, the leading Rockefeller bank in the U.S., established the South African contacts it used to aid U.S. industrial firms finance their South African investments. Almost all the major U.S. transnationals with investments in South Africa had directors sitting on Citibank's board, as well as important links with U.S. government agencies. [7]

Citibank's overseas holding corporation, Citicorp, began in the same period to open its doors for business in a number of independent African states by purchasing shares in British and French banks with long established branch networks throughout the continent. It bought 49 percent of the British bank, Grindlays, sharing control with Lloyds (the fourth largest British bank which owned another 41 percent). [8] Grindlays had branches in several African countries, including Kenya and Zambia. It established a Southern Rhodesian affiliate by taking over the Ottoman Bank there in 1969, three years after UDI. (See below p. 274)

Citicorp also purchased 49 percent of the Banque d'Afrique de l'Ouest, a big French bank with affiliates in almost every former French African colony. But Citibank financed significant industrial growth only in South Africa and, to a lesser extent, in Southern Rhodesia. In the independent African states, most of its loans went primarily to foster

---

*At the time it was called the First National City Bank of New York.

the extraction of crude materials and the sale of goods manufactured in its clients' home factories.

The Chase Manhattan bank, a second big Rockefeller bank and the third largest bank in the United States, opened its first branch in South Africa in 1959. In 1965, after it had established three branches there, Chase purchased a 15-percent stake in the British Standard Bank, giving it direct access to the latter's African network. Chase executives joined Standard's board of directors, and a Chase officer served with Standard's central management group in London. Chase merged its South African branches with those of Standard, South Africa. Chase, like Citicorp, had interlocking directorships with many of the largest industrials expanding their business in South Africa.[9]

In the early '70s, when Standard opened a branch in the U.S., the Federal Trade Commission required Chase to divest itself of Standard's shares. It then opened a representative office in South Africa, headed by an officer who formerly worked with Standard's South African affiliate.

The Bank of America, the largest United States Bank—in fact, the largest bank in the world—never opened its own branches in South Africa. However, its British partner, Kleinwort-Benson, helped the South African government establish its own merchant bank, giving it an on-going indirect relationship with South Africa. French Bank, although ranking only 20th and holding about one percent of the assets of the top 20 South African banks, was the fifth largest transnational bank affiliate there. By 1976, it had opened seven offices in South Africa's main towns, as well as one in Windhoek. The bank experienced steady growth in volume of deposits and profits through the mid-'70s.[10] It was affiliated to the Banque de l'Indochine of Paris. Like French firms with business in other sectors of South Africa's economy, the Banque de l'Indochine shared ownership in the French Bank with several local partners, including Union Corporation, the Old Mutual and the Messina Development Co., an Anglo American Group member.

Facilitating the Accumulation and Reinvestment of Domestic Funds:

In South Africa, the transnational banks' affiliates operated in various ways to mobilize domestic capital and direct its reinvestments to facilitate the industrial transformation of the apartheid system. Each year, their commercial banks advanced billions of rands—almost R4 billion in 1975 alone,[11] despite the onset of the recession—to those sectors that the minority regime slated for expansion.

An unknown percentage of these loans went directly to the South African government. South African law required commercial banks to buy bonds to finance its growing expenditures, including its military buildup. In 1978, the South African arms parastatal, ARMSCOR, floated R40 million in loans on the domestic capital market. It planned to borrow R30 million more, with the banks' assistance. [12]

How much transnational banks' local affiliates loaned to the South African regime for military purposes remained unknown. Barclays South Africa advertised a purchase of South African Defense bonds worth R10 million. Anti-apartheid critics in England objected strenuously, and British government officials called in the parent company's officers for questioning. Frank Dolling, chief executive of the South Africa Group, asserted that "Barclays was deeply concerned at the insensitive nature of the investment in Defense Bonds and at the nature of the publicity given to it by their South African subsidiary." He gave his assurance that "the bank will do whatever possible to ensure such action will not happen again."[13] The Rand Daily Mail reported,[14] however, that the Register of Financial Institutions had characterized Barclays' pledge "to keep tighter control over its South African subsidiary's Defense Force links as 'virtually meaningless.' "

Other transnational banks did not publicize their purchases of South African Defense Bonds, although South African law required the banks to buy them.

Beyond loans for direct military purposes, the commercial banks and their affiliates contributed far more extensive credit facilities to the South African regime for general purposes. This, of course, released other government funds for military expenditures. Table 9-4 shows the sources of credit for the regime. The banking sector clearly provided a major share of the short-term credit, made a significant share of the long-term loans, as well, since in South Africa, banks sponsored pension and insurance plans. The loans made by the transnational bank affiliates cannot easily be separated out, but, since they controlled about two-thirds of the assets of the 20 largest banks, they undoubtedly played an important role in providing these large amounts of credit.

As part of its effort to attract foreign capital after Sharpeville, the South African government encouraged the growth of merchant banking. Merchant banks typically take part more directly in the ownership and management of corporate enterprise than do commercial banks. The transnational banks' merchant affiliates not only provided long-term loans to private and public sectors in South Africa, but also financed equity capital of transnational corporate affiliates and domestic firms. [15]

Table 9-4.
Ownership distribution of domestic marketable stock debt of central government

SHORT TERM[1]

End of	Public Debt Commissioners[2]	Banking sector[3]						Other banking institutions	Building societies	Insurers and private pension funds	Other identified	Uniden-tified	Total
		Reserve bank	Commercial banks	V.F.C. and discount houses	Merchant banks	Other	Total						
1971	29	64	362	231	6	182	846	9	98	6	19	26	1,033
1972	24	38	469	243	62	150	963	36	124	4	21	13	1,185
1973	18	302	446	253	61	151	1,212	48	99	6	21	-26	1,379
1974	9	321	385	269	69	155	1,199	57	48	8	18	-28	1,310
1975	113	279	626	326	106	226	1,562	60	37	10	45	-1	1,826
1976	190	311	977	417	118	294	2,118	71	50	22	27	19	2,497
1977	323	297	1,248	506	105	301	2,456	67	132	24	32	21	3,054

LONG TERM

End of and long	Public Debt Commissioners[2]	Banking sector				Unit trusts	Other banking institutions and buildings societies	Insurers	Private pension funds	Other identified	Uniden-tified	Total	Total Short term loans
		Reserve bank	Commercial banks	Other	Total								
1971	2,844	80	20	7	107	49	18	287	232	114	-3	3,648	4,681
1972	2,899	86	92	90	269	48	48	419	338	149	94	4,264	5,449
1973	3,012	63	114	82	259	41	60	488	416	164	98	4,538	5,917
1974	3,242	70	79	97	246	34	49	555	490	171	47	4,835	6,145
1975	3,385	145	144	115	404	30	52	690	610	250	12	5,433	7,259
1976	3,542	165	82	101	348	11	38	874	755	236	13	5,816	8,312
1977	3,892	137	132	174	442	1	130	1,060	937	337	123	6,923	9,976

Notes: [1]i.e. with outstanding currency not exceeding 3 years.
[2]Including the Department of Posts and Telecommunications as from April 1, 1974.
[3]See definition on pages 5-25.

Source: South African Reserve Bank, Quarterly Statistical Bulletin, Dec., 1978.

Transnational financial institutions helped mobilize the smaller savings of individuals through insurance and pension programs. By 1976, when the South African government passed a bill paving the way for domestic ownership of the majority of shares of all insurance companies in South Africa, life insurance companies there had accumulated assets worth more than R4 billion. About 14 percent of this, almost R500 million, was held by South African affiliates of transnational life insurance companies. [16] Barclays' Bibsal had become the third largest insurance broker in the country, offering over 100 kinds of insurance through its extensive commerical bank network. Standard Bank's South African subsidiary had also entered the insurance brokerage business.

Transnational financial institutions broadened the scope of their activities in the 1960s and 1970s by putting up the foreign exchange required to buy heavy industrial equipment, and leasing it to the South African private and parastatal sectors. The South African Finance Charges Act did not govern leasing rates, so banks charged two to three points more than the commercial banks' prime lending rates. The transnationals' larger size and international connections gave them an advantage over domestic banks in this lucrative field. Their purchases assisted their transnational clients to sell their heavy equipment and machinery, while enabling South African firms to acquire advanced technologies.

As the South African economy stagnated in the late '70s, the regime sought to encourage further transnational corporate expansion by providing a discount on rands—called "financal rands"—provided by banks for investment purposes. By March, 1979, estimates [17] of the amount of authorized financial rands, ranged from R75 million to R175 million. Transnational corporations receiving these discounted rands did not publicize the transactions; but "market rumor" identified Volkswagen, Pilkington, BMW, IBM, AECI and Siemens. Transnational parent banks played a key role in the business. Overseas, the industrial parent company bought financial rands with a foreign currency from the parent of a South African bank. Then, in South Africa, the bank supplied the equivalent rand amount to the company's local affiliate.

Smaller South African banks feared the added leverage this procedure bestowed on the bigger transnational banks. A Reserve Bank proposal to turn over to the private banking sector the foreign currency proceeds from krugerrand and diamond sales, as well as public corporation and municipal borrowings (totalling about R3 billion a year) was delayed. The small banks reportedly feared the inovation would strengthen Barclays and Standard, as the Chamber of Mines (Kruger-rand sales) and DeBeers (diamond sales) conducted the bulk of their business with them. Several smaller South African banks requested the regime not to let go of the krugerrand and diamond receipts for fear they would "be at the mercy of Barclays and Standard whenever they need to buy dollars."[18]

The transnational banks' South African commercial bank affiliates participated in shaping the nation's banking system to conform with apartheid. They accepted deposits from Africans—their small personal savings or limited black businesses' accounts—but invested them almost solely in white-owned business. Barclays South Africa, for example, revealed that blacks had deposited some R88 million in its branches in one year, but its chief executive argued that, although a bank should lend to a community from which it received its deposits, "one has to accept that the black businessman is largely unsophisticated" and "there is a lot of danger here."[19]

In the mid-'70s, as part of the apartheid stategy of building a client black capitalist class, the South African government permitted the first predominantly African-owned bank, the African Bank of South Africa, to open a branch in one of the Bantustans. Blacks owned 75 percent of the new bank's shares. The rest were held by Barclays, Standard, Nedbank Trust, and Volksaas.[20] The board of directors consisted of 7 blacks and 3 whites representing the five participating banks. The new bank was restricted to operating solely in the impoverished Bantu-stans.[21] In 1977, Stanbic, a Standard affiliate, purchased 30 percent of the shares of the New Republic Bank, chartered as the Indian Bank. By supporting the creation of a separate but dependent banking system, the transnational banks helped to shape the economy further along apart-heid lines.

Wholesalers of Credit to South Africa

In the late '60s, additional transnational banks expanded their South African ties. They operated primarily on a wholesale basis, carrying on their South African business through existing British and South African banks, rather than establishing their own local branches.[22] Even Barclays appeared to be moving more and more in that direction. The trend might have been explained in part by South African governmental pressure on the banks to establish 50 percent local participation, and in part by the banks' own desire to avoid the growing criticism of anti-apartheid groups in their home countries.

The Grossbanken of the Federal Republic of Germany—the Deutsche Bank, Dresdner Bank and Commerzbank—became increasingly in volved in South Africa alongside of F.R.G. transnational industrial firms expanding their business there. More than any other transnational banks, the Grossbanken were tied directly to the transnationals based in their homeland that invested in South Africa. (See Ch. 2, above) The Commerzbank and the Deutsche Bank, together with the Bayerische Landesbank Gerozentrale, for example, directly and through holding companies, owned substantial shares in the big transport machinery manufacturer, Daimler Benz. The Dresdner Bank owned 25 percent of the only F.R.G. transnational mining firm, Metalgesellschaft, which had become especially active in Namibia. Dresdner Bank acquired a sizeable share of the machinery and equipment firm, Degussa. The Berliner Handels-und Frankfurter Bank owned over 10 percent of the engineering firm, Deutsche Babcock.[23] The Deutsche Bank, the largest holder of industrial shares among the F.R.G. banks, was founded by Georg von Siemens in 1870, and retained close contacts with the Siemens' electrical company as it expanded on a global scale over the following century. A Siemens representative still sat on the bank's board in the 1970s.

Before the 1960s, reflecting the disruption of their business by their homeland's defeat in World War II,* F.R.G. banks had only a few commitments in South Africa, including only one commitment to Anglo American Corporation. By the beginning of the 1970s, however, F.R.G. financial interests assisted South African parastatals in offering stock on the F.R.G. market almost annually. For the most part, they conducted their business in South Africa through agencies or representative offices. The Dresdner Bank set up a representative office in Johannesburg which it later shared with the European Banking Consortium (EBIC-see below p. 217). The Commerzbank shared an office with Banco di Roma and Credit Lyonnaise. It also set up an agency, the Koller and Bauhaus Trust Co. in Namibia.

Although their deepest thrust paralleled that of the largest F.R.G. industrial firms which had begun to invest heavily in the South African regional subcenter. F.R.G. banks simultaneously began to penetrate the largest independent African countries. All three Grossbanken established representative offices in Cairo. The Deutsche Bank purchased minority shareholdings in banks in Casablanca, Dakar, Libre-

---

*As noted in Chapter 4, several German banks had provided initial finance for two mining finance houses in South Africa: Anglovaal (The Deutsche Bank) and General Mining & Finance (Dresdner Bank).

ville, Lome, N'Djumana, Rabat and Yaounde. (See Table 9-5) The Dresdner Bank acquired a tiny (0.4 percent) investment in the Banque Nationale pour le Developement Economique in Rabat. The Commerz-bank handled its Libyan business through a representative office in Beirut, Lebanon, and participated in the Misr International Bank, SAE, of Cario, as well as two Moroccan banks. But, like their British and French predecessors, the F.R.G. banks sought primarily to establish contacts for the probable expansion of sales of F.R.G. manufactured goods, and the purchase of raw materials in independent African states. They did little to finance the growth of manufacturing industries there.

Table 9-5.
**Known Holdings of Federal Republic of Germany's Grossbanken
in banks in Africa outside South Africa, 1976**

	Holdings (percent of shares)		
	Deutsche Bank	*Commerz-bank*	*Dresdner Bank*
Banque Commerciale Congolaise	3.1		
Banque Commerciale de Commerce Morocco	7.1	*	
Banque Nationale pour le Developpement Economique	0.4	*	*
Banque Tchadienne de Credits et de Depots (Chad)	7.5		
Societe Camerounaise de Banque (Cameroons)	5.0		
Societe Ivoirienne de Banque (Ivory Coast)	12.0		
Union Gabonais de Banque (Gabon)	8.0		
Union Senegalaise de Banque pour le Commerce et l'Industrie (Senegal)	1.9		
Union Togolaise de Bank (Togo)	18.0		
Societe Financiere de Developpement (SOFIDE) (Zaire)		**	
Union Internationale de Banques S.A. (Tunisia)		*	

*Unspecified shareholding.
**Also acts as representative bank.

Sources: Annual reports of the banks, 1976.

Three Swiss banks, the Swiss Bank, the Union Bank, and the Swiss Credit Bank, became increasingly important in arranging finance for the South African economy through the Zurich Gold Pool. Alfred Schaefer, Chairman of the Board of the Union Bank, declared, "We consider some countries, such as South Africa, . . . which in other quarters are perhaps not much liked, as absolutely respectable members of the world community."[24]

Credit Suisse set up its own representative office in Johannesburg. By the mid-'70s, it had established only one representative office (in Cairo) in the almost 50 independent African states. Credit Suisse was the largest single shareholder in White Weld, a British merchant bank that became active in underwriting loans to South Africa in the 1970s.

The Japanese government prohibited direct loans as well as investments in South Africa.[25] It halted efforts by Japanese banks and business houses to lend Japanese funds to South Africa through the Japanese International Bank, a London-based subsidiary. Japanese firms were permitted, however, to borrow from their domestic banks to finance exports to South Africa. The Bank of Tokyo established a representative office in Johannesburg to service the growing Japanese commercial interests there. Loans by Japanese banks to finance construction assembly plants in South Africa in return for the purchase of South African goods were considered "trade" and therefore in compliance with the goverment's policy of "non-investment."[26]

As part of their overseas expansion in the 1970s, several Japanese banks participated in consortium merchant banks with European banks already deeply involved in South Africa. Such consortia were formed by Sumitomo and Credit Suisse-White Weld; Mitsui Bank and Hambros; and the Japanese Industrial Bank and Deutsche Bank. They aimed at "advancing securities underwriting businesses overseas."[27] It was possible for these banks to contribute through these channels to loans mobilized by European banks for South Africa.

International Banking Consortia

International banking consortia emerged as an important feature of international financial support for South Africa in the 1970s. Initially formed to enable their participants to compete against the growing penetration of U.S. banks into Europe and elsewhere, these consortia established representative offices in Johannesburg to enable their member banks to service their transnational corporate clients' South African investments. Among those represented in South Africa by the 1970s were the Associated Bank of Europe (ABECOR) and European Banks International Company (EBIC), as well as the Commerzbank-Credit Lyonnaise-Banco di Roma group, and the Berliner Handels-und Frankfurter Bank. Each in turn had affiliated subgroups.

Several banks participated in ABECOR, the largest European group, which took over the Johannesburg office of the Dresdner Bank. Barclays' 1975 Annual Report emphasized that "The strength of ABECOR is unique, not only in its resources, which in combination total more than U.S. $172,000 million, but in depth of international financial knowledge and speed of action which it provides through the 11,000 offices of its member banks in some 129 countries. ABECOR member banks included: the Algemene Bank Nederland, Netherlands; Banca Nazionale del Lavoro, Italy; Banque Bruxelles Lambert, Belgium; Banque Nationale de Paris, France; Barclays Bank, U.K.; Bayerische Hypothean-und Wecheel-Bank, F.R.G.; the Dresdner Bank, F.R.G. The Banque Internationale, Luxembourg and Osterreische, Landesbank, Austria, were associate members. The Banque de las Societe Financiere, Europeenne, Paris, was a special associate.

The managing director of the Dresdner Bank explained that an international consortium of this kind "acts as an information center, to pull in other business for the group, and to liaise with local correspondent banks and customers." "European banking consortia and banks represented in South Africa" he added, aim "primarily at raising foreign capital and a variety of medium-term bank facilities for government, local authorities, public utilities and large corporations."[29]

The second biggest consortium, the European Banking International Corporation (EBIC) established its representative office in Johannesburg in 1969. Its member banks included: Amsterdam Rotterdam Bank, Netherlands; Creditanstalt Bankverein, Austria; the Deutsche Bank, Federal Republic of Germany; Midland Bank, United Kingdom; the Societe Generale, France; and the Societe General de Banque, Belgium.

Mobilizing Foreign Capital

As the political economic crisis shook South Africa in the mid-'70s, it was forced to borrow heavily overseas. It desparately needed additional foreign funds to finance the rising costs of its continued oil imports, its expanding military purchases, and its strategic economic development programs designed to make its minority-ruled economy more self-sufficicent. By the end of 1978, South Africa's overall foreign debt had jumped to at least $11.5 billion. (See Table 9-6A) The major transnational banks—with vast accumulations of capital piling up in the Eurocurrency market—sometimes cooperated, sometimes competed to mobilize the international capital required to finance South Africa's pressing needs. Their role in this crisis pointed up sharply the contradictory characteristics of the South African model of dependent development and its growing dependence on international finance capital.

The transnational banks' eagerness to lend funds to South Africa in the mid-'70s constituted an integral feature of their response to the re-emerging general crisis of capitalism. Faced with a pervasive economic slowdown, coupled with inflationary price increases that threatened to wipe out profits at interest rates prevailing at home, they sought new, more profitable areas in which to invest their mounting accumulations of surplus investable funds. While they expanded their loans to high income independent African states with adequate mineral riches to ensure ultimate repayment, the sums they advanced were mostly paltry compared to those they poured into South Africa.

Table 9-6A.
Estimated International Loans to South Africa, 1974-78
(total exposure in billions of U.S. dollars)

All Major Banks	1974	1975	1976	1977	1978
(including U.S.)	2.7	4.8	7.0	8.0	7.4
U.S. banks	N.A.	1.2	2.2	2.3	2.0
IMF	0	.094	.459	.459	.381
Bond Issues					
(U.S. and Other)				(estimate) 1.7	
Foreign Government Trade					
Expansion Credit Agencies				(estimate) 2.0	
TOTAL				(estimate) 11.5	

Table 9-6B.
Estimated transnational bank loans to major African borrowers, 1978
(total exposure in billions of U.S. dollars)

	All major banks[1]	U.S.
World	N.A.	217
Africa (estimate)	34. plus	9. plus
South Africa	7.4	2.0
Nigeria	1.8	0.6
Algeria	5.7	1.8
Liberia	6.3	2.2

[1]Banks from G-10 countries; Canada, Belgium-Luxembourg, France, F.R.G., Italy, Netherlands, Sweden, Japan, U.K. and U.S.A. The four other countries included in survey are Switzerland, Austria, Ireland and Denmark.

Sources: Estimated by William Raiford, Foundation for Foreign Policy Studies, 1979, from U.S.—Federal Reserve Board *Country Exposure Survey.*

G-19 + 4—Bank for International Settlements (BIS) Quarterly Series. The BIS also has a "maturities" series which has slightly higher figures. This series more closely corresponds to earlier series.

South Africa's minority regime pledged security for repayment of loans at rates of interest far above those available in the ailing cities and stagnating industries of the transnationals' homelands. And the regime backed its pledge with some of the world's most valuable minerals. The value of South African gold and uranium, mined by low paid black workers, could only be expected to go up in the context of the growing international monetary and energy crisis.

In all, 36 banking groups participated in the business of mobilizing Eurocurrency credits for South Africa from 1972 to 1976.[29] These included most of the major financial institutions in the international capital market. Banks from six countries—Britain, the F.R.G., France, the U.S., Switzerland and Luxembourg—were the most active bond sales managers or lenders. (See Table 9-7) The banks frequently organized consortia for particular loans. Typically, one of the larger transnationals would act as lead bank for major loans, bringing together banks from several other countries as participants. The transnational banks even helped South African municipalities to borrow in the syndicated credit markets. There, six months rates at 6.5 percent with spreads of 1.75 percent permitted them to borrow more cheaply than on the bond market.[30]

The distinction between loans to the private and public sectors was seldom clear in South Africa. The South African government parastatal, the Industrial Development Corporation (IDC), for example, obtained transnational bank assistance to float foreign loans for private businesses.[31] On the other hand, information about loans to private borrowers by transnational banks was seldom publicized. The South African Reserve Bank put the total foreign credit extended to the private sector at $5.8 billion in 1975,[32] more than that to the public sector that year. But no details were revealed as to what banks or borrowing firms were involved.

In 1977, the Bank of America, which admitted outstanding credit to South Africa worth $188 million, explained that over half represented short-term loans to commercial banks, while over a quarter of the rest constituted loans to private and public corporations for "trade-related purposes or financing of industrial development projects." The largest recipient of the remainder was the South African government, which borrowed short-term funds to ease pressure on the balance of payments.[33] If this breakdown was typical for all lenders, the total of loans reported for the private sector by the South African Reserve Bank—which did not include loans made to commercial banks—was significantly understated.

Table 9-7.

Banks which provided international credits for South Africa, 1972-1976

Country	Institutions	Number of Commitments in which participated
Federal	Westdeutsche Landerbank Girozentrale	10
Republic of	Commerzbank A.G.	13
Germany	Dresdner Bank A.G.	9
	(Deutsche Bank)	11
	Berlmar Hendels und Frankfürter Bank (BHF)	6
England	White Weld Securities	10
	Hill Samuel	9
	Strauss Turnbull and Co.	7
	Delta Trade Co. Ltd.,	5
	Barclays Bank International Ltd.	5
	Hambros Bank Ltd.	4
France	Credit Commerciale de France	15
	Credit Lyonnais	9
	(Société Générale)*	5
	Paribas	4
Italy	Banco Commerciale Italiana	4
	Banco di Roma	4
Belgium	Kredeitbank N.V.	8
	Bondtrade	7
Netherlands	Algemene Bank Nederland N.V.	7
Luxembourg	Kreideitban Luxembourgaise SA	12
Switzerland	Union Bank of Switzerland	10
United States	Citibank	10
	Manufacturers Hanover	8
	Kidder Peabody	8
	Chase Manhattan	3

*Information tables do not identify this as Société Général (Belgium) or (France).

**Credit Commerciale is owned 4 percent each by: Continental Illinois Corporation; Canadian Imperial Bank of Commerce; Schweizerische Bankverein; Schwezerisch Rücker-versicherungs-Gesellschaft; Banco Espanol de Credito.

Source: :William Raiford, unpublished paper, 1977.

In the late '70s, several factors combined to change the pattern of bank loans to South Africa. First, the Soweto uprisings and heightened repression against blacks, as they intensified their struggle for liberation, finally led the international bankers to question the political stability of the minority regime. Secondly, critics of apartheid overseas campaigned against continuing bank loans, pointing out that they represented a vital prop for the whole apartheid system. Third, South Africa's balance of payments, adversely affected in the mid-'70s by the rising price of oil and arms imports, as well as the falling price of crude exports as recession gripped the capitalist world, began to improve as the international monetary crisis pushed up the price of gold. Nevertheless, available data showed that South Africa's government and private sector borrowing from all sources remained at about an estimated $11.5 billion through 1978. (See Table 9-6) Banks themselves continued to lend $7-8 billion. Transnational bank loans to South Africa, alone, equalled about a fifth of all loans made to almost 50 independent African countries that year.

South Africa's credit rating in international capital markets, as reflected in the shortened term of loans and higher interest rates, declined. An opinion survey of bankers in 1978 classed South Africa among the countries most likely to have trouble borrowing.[34] But, by mid-1978, as gold prices rose, bankers began, once again, to claim that five-year high-interest loans to South Africa were still a good risk.[35]

The impact of the anti-apartheid campaign against banks in the major lending countries did have some impact. Chase Manhattan and Citibank, which had been among the leading banks mobilizing funds for South Africa, as well as a number of U.S. regional banks, agreed not to lend additional funds directly to the South African government.[36] Both declared, however, that they would continue to lend funds to the private sector, echoing Oppenheimer's myth that continued economic expansion would ultimately help the blacks. The Bank of America insisted it would continue to lend money to both the private and state sectors.[37] The Chairman of the European American Banking Corporation (SABC) assured the World Council of Churches that it would in the future only facilitate loans to finance the sale of goods to South Africa. This appeared to reflect both the political situation, and the fact that the Corporation had already become heavily committed to South Africa.[38]

The extent to which the bankers' concessions would significantly restrict their role in financing the minority regime's needs remained unclear. The close interlinkage between parastatal and private sectors (indeed, in South African government statistics, the parastatals are included in the private sector) ensured that loans to private industry would boost public enterprise. Loans directed to financing international trade, furthermore, likewise contributed to strengthening the entire economy. Money is fungible: funnelled into one part of the system, it could easily be transferred to others. Foreign loans to any part of the apartheid economy helped to finance and strengthen the entire military-industrial complex.

The domestically based transnational banks' affiliates, especially those of Standard and Barclays, provided an additional, less visible conduit for transnational bank funds. In 1977, alone, they advanced more than a billion dollars ($1058 million)[39] to finance the purchase of machinery and equipment which they then leased to parastatal and private corporations. Affiliates of transnational merchant and other banks found it increasingly lucrative to use their foreign ties to finance both imports and exports by obtaining international credit. They also took advantage of the daily differences in the floating exchange rates of major currencies.[40] Since the South African regime kept interest rates high to combat inflation, borrowers used international bank contacts to obtain cheaper funds through lines of credit overseas. Eurodollar credit in the late '70s was 1 to 2 percent cheaper than local rates for loans of six months to a year. The larger banks and firms had access to acceptance credit in New York at still lower rates.[41]

The South African minister of finance used tax powers to encourage this use of foreign credit for domestic productive activities.[42] South African importers borrowed an estimated R2 billion for these purposes in 1978. The South African *Financial Mail* characterized these loans as so important that a small decline might "knock the foreign exchange reserves clean out of the window."[43] The South African regime's use of export credit to finance SASOL II (its gigantic oil-from coal-project), when direct foreign loans did not appear forthcoming to finance its construction, further underscored the importance of this type of credit.

The boom in gold prices in the late '70s reduced South Africa's need to borrow long term funds. At the same time, the resulting improvement in the balance of payments convinced some European and U.S. bankers that South Africa's credit worthiness was improving. The acclaim with which the South African press welcomed the news that Swiss and F.R.G. banks had loaned $280 million, allegedly for the black townships, however, illustrated the South African regime's desire for continued foreign credit, and recognition of its essential role in sustaining its military industrial complex. The State radio broadcasting company declared that these funds "will bolster our foreign exchange reserves and help to support the recovery momentum at a juncture when it has shown signs of flagging."[44] South Africa needed further loans to repay past loans together with high interest charged by transnational banks.[45] It also sought to maintain its international credit lines as a sign of its continued acceptance and creditworthiness in the eyes of the capitalist world's businessmen.[46]

At the same time, the transnational banks sought to weaken anti-apartheid criticism by lending funds to the Urban Foundation, allegedly helping South African blacks to acquire 99-year leases (not outright ownership) of homes in the townships adjacent to white areas. "American loans" of some R30 million enabled black borrowers to pay interest rates reduced from 10.5 percent to 8.75 percent for this purpose. The foreign loans covered only a five-year period, "after which it is hoped black incomes will have risen sufficiently to permit borrowers to pay the going (South African) interest rate without undue hardship." Almost three years after the Soweto uprisings, however, the program "marched slowly": By April, 1979, only residents of the tiny luxury suburb of Dube in Soweto had borrowed funds under the scheme. By May 1st, only one 99-year lease-hold had actually been "purchased," and only 16 applied for. This should not have come as a surprise. The cheapest Soweto house cost R4000, which, toegther with R1000 for improvements, required an income of R156 a month; and "monthly repayments over 30 years would be roughly R39, money that would cut into the living standards of the family to the extent of producing malnutrition."[47] The transnational banks claimed, nevertheless, that their loans now contributed directly to social advance. The total loans they provided for this program were insignificant compared to the hundreds of millions they still poured into the continued expansion of the South African military-industrial complex.

Throughout 1978, South Africa's parastatals shopped about for further loans from abroad, receiving encouragement especially from the F. R. G. and Switzerland. "These countries—and most notably (West) Germany—are the only two where effectively public deals have been arranged for South African borrowers in the last few months. The reception for Deutschmark placements by South African borrowers has improved considerably in recent months."[48] The F.R.G. banks reportedly loaned about 63.3 percent of the total public sector foreign debt of the regime of R5.1 billion at the end of June, 1978. Swiss banks' loans brought the portion up to 77.3 percent of the total.[49]

Among parastatals which had successfully borrowed funds in the F.R.G. were[50] the South African Railways and Harbors (DM 40 million); ESCOM, the electricity supply corporation (DM 20 million); and the City of Johannesburg (DM 50 million at 7.7 percent). ISCOR, the Iron and Steel Corporation, and the Industrial Development Corporation also placed loans. Most F.R.G. loans had an effective interest rate of about 8 percent. In contrast, similar F.R.G. loans to other countries were made at 6 percent. But the rates to South Africa had gone down: Johannesburg had paid 18 percent in October, 1976. Because South African loans were limited to less than five years, the bankers concluded there was "no particular political risk." Their renewed interest was ascribed to the accumulation of surplus funds in Europe, a perceived improvement in South Africa's economic position, and its repayment of earlier loans. As the F.R.G. commercial journal reporting this new situation declared,[51] "In banks and stock market circles, the talk is of a great faith in the future of the country (South Africa), which cannot be simply dropped overnight by the Western world, for political and strategic reasons." Because of "understandable political considerations," nevertheless, bank consortiums did not take up "large" new issues from South Africa. ESCOM, for example, had to make two separate private placings, worth DM 20 million, in one day. This size "did not have to be registered in the subcommittee of the central capital-market commission."

Home Government Insurance and Guarantee Programs

As the general crisis deepened in the core industrial nations in the mid-'70s, their governments extended guarantees of export credits in an effort to stimulate the export of accumulating surpluses of manufactured goods in the increasingly competitive world market. These guarantees became an important factor reducing transnational bank risks on short term trade credits upon which South Africa's regime came to rely increasingly heavily. Transnational banks' home governments not infrequently guaranteed, insured, or in some cases even discounted loans for goods sold to South Africa as part of their export promotion progams.

The Export Import Bank (Eximbank) of the United States, despite a ban on direct Eximbank loans to South Africa in 1964, insured or guaranteed about three-fourths of a billion dollars ($691 million) worth of trade with South Africa from 1972 to 1976.[52] Additional export credits were insured in 1977 and 1978. Another U.S. government agency, the Commodity Credit Corporation, financed $46.2 million worth of U.S. agricultural exports to South Africa in the same period. In late 1970s, opponents of apartheid persuaded the U.S. Congress to pass an amendment prohibiting continued Export-Import guarantees and insurance. The U.S. corporate-supported South African lobby, however, convinced Congress to add a rider: If the U.S. concerns involved had adopted the Sullivan Principles, the prohibition would be lifted. The U.S. Chamber of Commerce had already thwarted Congressional efforts to create a commission to monitor the implementation of the Sullivan Principles in South Africa, rendering this prohibition essentially meaningless—assuming the marginal improvements called for under the Principles warranted the amendment at all. (See pp. 73-4 above)

The Federal Republic of Germany's export insurance system, administered by two private insurance companies, Hermes Creditversicherung AG and Deutsche Revisions und Treuhand-AG,[53] increased guarantees of loans to South Africa by 36 percent from 1970 to 1975.[54] In 1976, Hermes guarantees of export loans to South Africa almost tripled, reaching DM2.3 billion by the end of the year. They rose another DM 475 million in the first quarter of 1977. World-wide, in contrast, the value of these guarantees grew only 42 percent. The share of "developed" countries, in which South Africa was included, actually declined by 7 percent.[55]

These guarantees primarily facilitated the finance of export of capital equipment by major F.R.G. companies operating in South Africa for sale to utilities owned by the regime. One, for example, guaranteed a loan of $210 million (DM515 million) to Deutsche Babcock to provide steam-generating equipment for SASOL II. The U.S. Exim bank had turned down guarantees for SASOL because of their strategic implications. An F.R.G. interministerial committee, representing the Departments of Economics, Finance, Foreign Affairs and Economic Cooperation, had to agree to guarantees of loans exceeding DM 6 million, so it was evident that these loans had been approved by the government at the highest level.

In late 1977, the Federal Republic of Germany, under heavy antiapartheid criticism, appeared likely to require that firms with plants in South Africa must acquiesce to the EEC labor code to qualify for further export guarantees, and to pledge that goods would not be transshipped to Southern Rhodesia.[56] As the limit on loans to be guaranteed was R18 million per transaction, however, the president of the South African branch of the F.R.G. Chamber of Trade and Industry declared, "The practical effect will be relatively small." A South African-based F.R.G. banker added, "R18 million (is) a lot of money, besides, I understand Bonn will be prepared to allow exceptions."[57]

Transnational banks located in South Africa's other major trading partners overseas had access to a variety of government supported export programs.[58] Information about the amount of credit insured, guaranteed or financed by these agencies is not as complete as that for the U.S. Eximbank or the Hermes program.

The loans made for exports under the United Kingdom program (Export Credit Guarantees Department, ECGD) were covered by an unconditional guarantee covering all risks. Bank loans could be subsidized.

France encouraged exports by providing low-cost medium and long-term export credits with a special (4.5 percent) discount rate for exports to countries outside the European Common Market. All major French banks provided credits of varying duration for French exporters. A specialized bank, Banque Francaise du Commerce Exterieur (BECE) facilitated exports through acceptances, discounts and guarantees. About 30 percent of all French exports are supported by provision of these credits, but no breakdown by country is available.

The Japanese government permitted its banking community to finance the growing trade with South Africa. The Ministry of International Trade and Industry (MITI) funded a variety of export insurance prorgams. In 1976, MITI spent Y13,610 billion on these programs, but again the data on specific countries involved was not available.

The International Monetary Fund to the Rescue

As the economic crisis spread from the western capitalist core nations to engulf South Africa in the mid-'70s, it confronted mounting balance of payments deficits. It could no longer sell enough exports to pay for its continued imports of machinery and equipment, oil and growing military supplies on which the minority regime remained dependent. The International Monetary Fund stepped in to help it stave off disaster. The Fund sent a team to South Africa to review its economic situation. Elsewhere in Africa, the Fund's experts typically insisted that governments facing chronic balance of payments deficits must cut back on government spending and devalue their currencies. In South Africa, ignoring the exploitative system which condemned the black majority to perpetual poverty, they gave the minority regime's economic program a clean bill of health. On this basis, as the Soweto uprisings rocked the country, the Fund loaned the minority regime $366 million by the end of 1976.[59] By the first quarter of 1978, South Africa owed the Fund $485 million. It only gradually reduced this debt, despite soaring gold prices, as it continued to spend heavily to buy oil, military supplies and machinery and equipment overseas. By January, 1979, it still owed the Fund $353 million.

Selling South Africa's Gold

Gold was always the backbone of South Africa's economy. The profits accumulated from the sale of gold financed the growth of the dominant mining finance houses. They also provided essential tax revenues for the South African government. In the late '70s, as South Africa's industrial sectors stagnated, the boom in gold prices—reflecting the breakdown of the international monetary system under the impact of the re-emerging general crisis of capitalism—once again seemed likely to strengthen the minority regime.

Transnational banks handled most of the sales of South African gold. In the 1970s, about 80 percent of South Africa's gold was sold on the Zurich Gold Pool established by three Swiss banks, the Swiss Bank, the Union Bank, and the Swiss Credit Bank. The Swiss banks purchased on their own account all the gold the South African Reserve Bank offered them. They added some of the gold to their own stocks for their investment requirements, and sold the rest. The South African governmet could thus unload large quantities of gold without fear of depressing the world price. It could also insist on payment in the currency of its choice. In this way, the Swiss banks provide South Africa with a major source of external finance.

Of the five brokers who handled buying and selling of the rest of South Africa's gold in London, four were owned by transnational banks: the Standard and Chartered Group purchased the oldest, Mocatta and Goldsmith in 1973. Samuel Montagu was wholly taken over by Midlands Bank. Rothschild and Sons became linked to the National Westminister through the Westminister International and Johnson Mathey and Co. and carried on its buillion trade through its Johnson Matthey subsidiary.

During the crisis of the mid-'70s, the transnational banks enabled South Africa to borrow funds using gold as security through "gold swaps."[60] The first of these reportedly arranged by the Zurich Gold Pool members in 1976, was for about $500 million at about a 5-percent interest rate for three months. The second involved about $390 million. Since the amounts involved constituted a large percentage of the Swiss banks' total assets, it appeared probable that the syndicate had tapped the wider transnational bankers' market.

Transnational banks also provided the channels through which South Africa sold its Krugerrands, one-ounce gold pieces, abroad. This enabled South Africa to sell gold outside of traditional markets, thus avoiding depressing the world gold price. In 1975, Intergold, the marketing arm of South Africa's Chamber of Mines, reported about 21 percent of the nation's total gold production had been sold in this form, most of it to British buyers before the British government banned gold investments.* In 1976, Intergold hired the U.S. advertising firm, Doyle Dane Bernbach, to increase sales in the U.S. The goal was to sell a third of South Africa's annual output. A number of U.S. transnational banks handled the actual sales through their local branches.[61]

---

*A number of British were convicted of smuggling Krugerrands into Britain in violation of import restrictions imposed in 1976.

In 1977 Krugerrand sales brought R4365 million in foreign exchange to South Africa. The U.S. had become the largest market, followed by the F.R.G. U.S. citizens doubled their purchases of South African gold in 1978, with Krugerrands the most popular form of purchase.[62] Krugerrands sold to the United States in 1978 provided South Africa with $650.3 million in foreign exchange, and in the first six months of 1979, another $276.3 million. In 1979, The Republic Bank of New York sold two-thirds of its equity to Trade Development Bank Holdings, a Swiss intermediary for "private investors."[63] It became an "aggressive innovative retailer," one of the few selling gold in the U.S. It seemed likely that the bank had become a front for South African interests eager to expand the sale of gold still further in the U.S. market.

The Role of the Banks in Perspective

The transnational banks played a crucial role in funnelling capital accumulated around the world into the South African military-industrial complex. In the 1960s, as growing numbers of African states attained independence north of the Zambezi, the banks provided information and financial assistance to their closely related transnational industrial clients to facilitate their investment in strategic sectors of the South African economy. Throughout the rest of the continent, the banks engaged primarily in siphoning out investable surpluses produced through the extraction and export of crude raw materials and the sale of surplus manufactured goods. In South Africa, they helped mobilize domestic capital and brought in additional foreign funds to finance the minority regime's much vaunted "growth miracle."

Two big British banks, Barclays and Standard, closely interwoven with the mining finance houses as well as British mining, agricultural, and manufacturing interests, remained the backbone of the South African banking community. But the three biggest United States banks, operating directly through branches as well as indirectly through their penetration of British banking circles, had begun to muscle into the lucrative South African business, advising and consolidating the growing U.S. industrial interests there. By the late '60s, the Grossbanken of the Federal Republic of Germany, tied directly to the largest of their home-based industrial corporations with investments in South Africa, had also established an entering wedge through their "wholesale" banking links with domestic South African banks.

In the 1970s, stagnation coupled with inflation in their home economies spurred the transnational banks to compete more vigorously for profitable overseas business, especially in regional subcenters like South Africa. But the pattern of bank participation changed, for South Africa itself was caught in the grip of political-economic crisis. Its own economy was depressed, its vital manufacturing sector operated at low levels of capacity, and unemployment mounted. At the same time, the liberation of Mozambique and Angola, guerrilla warfare in Namibia and Zimbabwe (Southern Rhodesia), and the spread of open black resistance following the Soweto uprising threatened its very existence.

The transnational banks helped to channel domestic savings to transnational affiliates, domestic firms and parastatals, enabling them to continue to build up strategic sectors of the South African military-industrial complex. They loaned huge sums to the South African regime itself for direct expenditures on the growing military machine, both to provide economic stimulation and to adequately protect their clients' expanded industrial investments. Independent African states, their economies gripped in the spreading crisis, also borrowed heavily; but the transnational banks loaned about a fifth of all the funds they loaned throughout the entire continent to South Africa's minority regime. Even the International Monetary Fund advanced huge sums to South Africa, apparently convinced that the regime's systematic impoverization of the black population was commensurate with austerity it sought to impose on African-ruled countries forced to borrow from it.

In the late '70s, as world gold prices soared, the South African regime's immediate financial difficulties seemed temporarily resolved. The banks provided the essential conduit for gold sales abroad. At the same time, attracted by the profits to be gained, they continued to lend funds—now less visibly to avoid anti-apartheid objections—to finance the rising costs of oil, technology and military weapons, as well as to ensure repayment of the past South African debt with its high interest rates. The banks continued vital role symbolized, perhaps more than any other single feature, the dependent nature of development in South Africa's regional subcenter.

More significantly, the transnational banks' part in funnelling their nations' accumulated surplus capital into the repressive South African political economy illuminated their broader contribution to the shifting international division of labor initiated by transnational corporations seeking to maximize their profits at the expense of working people everywhere. On the one hand, they insisted, as a price for further loans, that communities at home reduce unemployment benefits and social services for which workers had fought for many decades. On the other, they demanded that Third World states, forced by the spreading international crises to borrow heavily from them, adopt International Monetary Fund-type "austerity" measures which would inevitably further reduce living standards of populations already at the hunger line. Meanwhile, the transnational bankers continued to reap profits by lending billions of dollars to prop up the South African minority regime's systematic exploitation of the great majority of the black population.

References

1. A number of organizations, ranging from the United Church of Christ Commission for Racial Justice to the United Electrical, Radio and Machine Workers of America and the International Union of United Automobile and Aerospace Workers, joined in support of the campaign to end U.S. bank loans to South Africa (Committee to Oppose Bank Loans to South Africa, 305 East 46th Street, New York, NY, Nov. 22, 1977); The World Council of Churches has taken a similar stand. Anti-apartheid activities are being focused on banks in England through the Anti-Apartheid Movement, and Eltsa (End Loans to South Africa). By 1973, Barclays had lost an estimated £10 million in accounts due to boycotts. In the F.R.G., and the Netherlands, the Anti-Apartheid Movement has also mounted a campaign against bank loans.

2. *South African Financial Mail*, Jan. 30, 1976, Barclays Bank Supplement. This and company annual reports are the source of information re Barclays Bank unless otherwise cited.

3. The information relating to Standard and Chartered Banking Group, unless otherwise cited, is from the parent company's annual reports and those of its South African affiliate.

4. The sources of information relating to Hill Samuel and its South African affiliate are the company reports of those two banks unless otherwise cited.

5. World Council of Churches, *Business as Usual: International Banking in South Africa* (Switzerland: World Council of Churches, 1974).

6. The information relating to U.S. banks' activities in South Africa is from relevant company reports of the parent bank unless otherwise cited.

7. D. Anyiwo, Appendix to Part III of A. and N. Seidman, *South Africa and U.S. Multinational Corporations* (Westport: Lawrence Hill & Co. and Dar es Salaam: Tanzania Publishing House, 1977).

8. *The Banker* (London) Aug. 1977.

9. Anyiwo, Appendix to Part III, *op. cit.*

10. *South African Financial Mail*, Apr. 15, 1977.

11. Calculated from "The Biggest Banks," *South African Financial Mail*, Apr. 23, 1976.

12. *South Africa Digest*, Nov. 3, 1978.

13. *South Africa News*, Jan. 30, 1976.

14. *Rand Daily Mail*, Jan. 14, 1977.

15. For discussion of merchant banks in South Africa, see World Council of Churches, *Business as Usual*, op. cit; and *South African Financial Mail*, Apr. 23, Jan. 30, and Oct. 29, 1976.

16. *South African Financial Mail*, "Ranking the Life Assurers," Apr. 23, 1976.

17. *South African Financial Mail*, Mar. 16, 1979.

18. *Ibid.*, Feb. 2, 1979.

19. *The Banker* (London) Sept. 1973, p. 117.

20. *The Banker* (London) "South Africa, A Survey", Sept., 1975.

21. *Rand Daily Mail*, Sept. 3, 1977.

22. *South African Financial Mail*, Barclays Bank Supplement, Jan. 30, 1976.

23. Commerzbank, Wem gehort zu Wem (Köln) 1976. Unless otherwise cited, the information re F.R.G. banks comes from their company reports.

24. *Newsweek*, Nov. 3, 1974.

25. Y. Kitizawa, *From Tokyo to Johannesburg* (New York: Interfaith Center for Corporate Responsibility, 1975).

26. *South African Financial Mail*, Nov. 12, 1976.

27. *Ibid.*

28. *South African Financial Mail*, Nov. 24, 1972.

29. The information re publicly issued bonds and credits has been collected and published in "U.S. Corporate Interests in South Africa," Subcommittee on African Affairs, Committee on Foreign Relations, United States Senate (Washington D.C.: Government Printing Office, 1977).

30. *South African Financial Mail*, May 21, 1976.

31. *Ibid.*, Aug. 27, 1976.

32. South African Reserve Bank, Quarterly Bulletin, Dec. 1976, pp. 364-5.

33. Letter from Mark C. Hennessey, Research Officer-International Bank of America, San Francisco Headquarters (Social Policy #3761) to Tim Smith, Interfaith Center of Corporate Responsibility, New York, Aug. 8, 1977.

34. *South African Financial Mail*, Apr. 7, 1978.

35. *Ibid.* June 23, 1978.

36. *Ibid.* Mar 17, 1978.

37. John Bell, Senior Vice President, Bank Communications, Bank America at Consultation on Banking and Investment Policies Sponsored by the General Council on Finance and Administration, The United Methodist Church, Indianapolis, Indiana, May 18-19, 1978.

38. *South African Financial Mail*, Oct. 7, 1977.

39. *Ibid.*, Mar. 31, 1978

40. *South African Financial Mail*, May 31, 1978.

41. *Ibid.*, Feb 3, 1978.

42. *Ibid.*, Mar. 31, 1978.

43. *Ibid.*, Feb. 3, 1978.

44. *South Africa Digest*, Jan. 24, 1978.

45. *Ibid.*, Nov. 3, 1978.

46. William Raiford, *Foundation for Foreign Policy Studies*, 1979.

47. *Star* (Johannesburg) April 20, 1979.

48. *Financial Times* (London) July 6, 1978.

49. *South African Digest*, June 22, 1979.

50. *Handelsblatt* (Düsseldorf) June 10, 1978.

51. *Ibid.*, Jan. 19, 1978.

52. U.S. Congress, House of Representative, Committee on International Relations, Resource Development in South Africa, Hearings, 94th Congress, 2nd Session (Washington, D.C.: U.S. Government Printing Office, 1976) p. 383, Table 11.

53. Business International Corp., Financing Foreign Operations, 1976.

54. Informationstelle Sudliches Afrika, e.V., Press Release, June 26, 1977.

55. Bundesminister für Wirtschaft LP, "Ausfuhrgarantien und Ausfuhrbürgschaften der BRD," 1976 BMWI Dokumentation (Bonn, '77); other BMWI, unpublished, documents; and *Informationstelles Südliches Afrika* Bonn, July-Aug. 77 (78/77).

56. *South African Financial Mail*, Dec. 2, 1977.

57. *Ibid.*, Nov. 11, 1977.

58. Business International Corporation, Financing Foreign Operations, 1976, summarizes these programs.

59. International Monetary Fund, *International Statistics*, 1977. See also the International Monetary Fund *Annual Reports* for relevant years.

60. *South African Financial Mail*, Mar. 26, 1976, May 8, 1977; see also *The Banker* (London) April, 1976: The details are "a closely guarded secret."

61. *South African Financial Mail*, Feb. 27, Oct. 22, 1977.

62. *African News* (Durham, North Carolina) Feb. 9, 1979.

63. *The New York Times*, July 8, 1979.

PART III
Towards the Transformation of Southern Africa

Deepening Underdevelopment   10

Impoverished Neighbors

The transnational corporations' competition to invest in strategic sectors of South Africa's military industrial complex contributed to the spread of underdevelopment throughout the neighboring countries of the region. It aggravated the contradictory forces that rendered the region a focal point of international concern by the 1970s. South Africa's state capitalist regime and the transnational firms investing there perceived South Africa as the vital subcenter, the regional core, for their expanding activities throughout the regional periphery. They viewed the surrounding countries as little more than vast labor reserves, additional sources of inexpensive raw materials and markets for South African industries.

Decades of colonial rule imposed institutional structures on all South Africa's neighbors' that were typified by disarticulated economies which became critically dependent on links with South Africa and western finance capital. The boundaries of the separate southern African states had initially been carved out by the colonial powers in their 19th Century scramble without regard to economic, ethnic, or geographic realities. Avaricious colonial adventurers and African efforts to retain some semblance of self-rule initially divided the vast land areas of the region into mini-economies: the extensive semi-deserts of Botswana and Namibia and the mountainous outcroppings of Lesotho and Swaziland peopled by half a million to little more than a million inhabitants each; the land-locked Rhodesias (later to become Zambia and Zimbabwe) and Nyasaland (Malawi) with populations of barely more than five million in more fertile land with more easily apparent valuable agricultural and mineral resources; and the much larger, oddly-shaped coastal regions of Mozambique and Angola, each with less than ten million inhabitants. (See Table 10.1)

Table 10.1.
Population, Life Expectancy and National Product of Southern African States, 1970s

	Area 000' km²	Population Mill. as at[2] Mid 1976	Population Growth rate 1970-75	Density People/ sq.km/	Life expectancy at birth 1970-75 (no. of years)	GDP 1975 U.S. $mill	GDP growth rate percent 1960/70	GDP growth rate percent 1970/76	GNP per capita 1976 U.S.$
Angola	1246.7	5.5	0.1	4.4	39	3476.1	5.1	1.0	330
Botswana	570.0	0.7	3.0[3]	1.2	44	342.0	5.4	24.9	410
Lesotho	30.4	1.2	2.2	39.5	46	110.3	3.0	4.0	170
Malawi	118.5	5.2	2.3	43.9	41	758.4	5.2	8.9	140
Mozambique	783.0	9.5	2.4	12.1	44	2687.9	4.8	–2.0	170
Namibia	824.3[1]	1.3	3.0	1.5	49	891.3	5.2	5.2	470[4]
Rhodesia (Zimbabwe)	390.6	6.5	3.5	16.6	52	2620.0	4.7	5.1	550
Swaziland	17.4	0.5	3.2	28.7	44	273.3	8.2	9.5	470
Tanzania	945.1	15.1	2.7	15.9	45	2553.2	5.4	4.2	180
Zambia	752.6	5.1	2.9	6.6	45	2231.4	4.0	3.1	440
Total/Average	5678.6	50.6	2.5[5]	8.9	45[5]	15943.9	4.93[6]	3.3[6]	280[5]
Republic of South Africa	1221.0	26.0	2.6	21.3	52	35294.2	6.2	5.6	1340

[1] Includes the area of Walvis Bay.

[2] Migrant workers are included under their home countries.

[3] 1971-1976.

[4] Only figures in this column are based on World Bank sources. For Namibia the following procedure had been used: The country profile 1977 ratio GNP/GDP has been used on the 1975 GDP figure increased by 10% for inflation 1975-76. This figure has been divided with the population figure given in the table.

[5] Weighted average, using mid-76 population as weights.

[6] Weighted average, using 1975 GDP as weights.

Source: Southern African coordinating conference, "Economic Dependence," Table 2 [Arusha: July, 1974] Demographic Yearbook 1976, (U.N.), World Bank Development Report 1978 Statistical and Economic Information Bulletin for Africa No. 10 (ECA).

It was not that these countries were small in land area. On the contrary, combined, they spread over a land almost as big as the continental United States and considerably larger than Europe. Nor was over-population a problem; all of them, even the most densely populated, Malawi, had far fewer people per kilometer than say, a typical European nation.

The basic problem confronting these countries was the poverty of the majority of the populations, reflected in part by relatively low per capita incomes. A third of the countries were among the world's "least developed," with per capita incomes below $200 in 1976. In the others, the income per capita appeared high, but cursory analysis showed that unequal distribution left most of their citizens' living standards no higher than their superficially more disadvantaged neighbors.

The causes of this pervasive poverty lay, not in the lack of natural resources, but the pattern of institutions imposed during the colonial and post colonial era. In all but mountainous Lesotho,* white settlers had appropriated the most fertile lands adjacent to the transportation network that radiated out from the South African hub. (See table 10.2)

Table 10-2.
Land Holdings of Settlers/Estate Farms as Percentage of Total Farm Area in Southern Africa, 1974

Country	Corporate Farms	Settler farms	%of farm land
Angola		8000	
Malawi	560	4000	50%
Mozambique			
Namibia		6500	50% of national land 98% of farmed land
Swaziland		790	46%
Rhodesia (Zimbabwe)		6682	47%
Botswana			15[1]
Zambia		700	20 miles both sides of railroad from Copperbelt to Rhodesia

Note: [1]Botswana's arable farm land constitutes 7 percent of the total national land area, due to lack of water supplies.

Source: U.S. AID, Development Needs and Opportunities for Cooperation in South Africa (Washington, D.C.: U.S. Aid, 1979).

*Overcrowding by Africans fleeing the better armed European invaders, continued use of outmoded technologies, and serious erosion of steep mountainsides sharply limited the agricultural potential of Lesotho.

Colonial taxation, credit and marketing structures geared to settler agriculture thwarted African efforts to develop modern farms. The importation of mass-produced manufactured goods undermined local handicraft industries. Colonial taxation forced Africans to obtain cash, pushing more and more adult men and some women out of rural hinterlands in search of paid jobs. In the Portugese colonies, forced labor hastened their exit. The assymetrical economies, dominated by settler-ruled export enclaves, provided only a few with cash employment.

Some found jobs on settler farms and estates in their home countries at wages even below those in South Africa. Only a relatively small number obtained manufacturing employment; colonial policies fostered the sale of imported manufactured goods, rather than construction of local factories. (See Table 10.3) Increasing numbers had no choice but to migrate as contract laborers to work on South African farms and mines.

Table 10-3.

Output of Manufacturing Industry as Percent of Gross Domestic Product and Exports, and Employment in Manufacturing as a Percent of Total Labor Force in Southern African States in the 1970s

State	Output		Employment	
	As % of GDP	As % of exports	numbers	percent of economically active population[3]
Angola (1973)	18-20	7	81,900	7.3
Mozambique (1973)	14	n.a.	99,500	2.6
Malawi (1977)	12	1.5	33,379	1.4
Lesotho (1978)	2.2	n.a.	6,582	1.0
Zimbabwe (1976)	24.5	n.a.	302,346	8.8
Botswana (1977)	n.a.	n.a.	4,150	1.2
Namibia (1977)	7.4	50[1]	13,000	4.3
Zambia (1972)	13.0	—	48,000	2.4
Swaziland (1971)	16.0	75[2]	6,500	3.2

Notes: [1]About half is in the form of processed meat, fish and vegetables for export.
[2]Mostly processed agricultural and forestry products (sugar, wood pulp, canned fruits, etc.) produced by transnationals and South African firms.
[3]Obviously, this percentage is greatly influenced by the definition of "economically active population," at best an estimate, taken from same source.

Sources: Statistics from U.S. AID, Development Needs and Opportunities for Cooperation in Southern Africa (Washington, D.C.: U.S. AID, 1979); Re Namibia, R. H. Green, "Namibia in Transition: Toward a Political Economy of Liberation?" T. Shaw, ed., The Future(s) of Africa (Boulder: Westview Press, 1980); Re Zimbabwe, Southern African Development Coordination Conference, Employment and Skills, Table 1.

The situation changed little—if anything it was further aggravated—during the years after South Africa's nearest English speaking neighbors raised flags proclaiming their independence: Zambia and Malawi in 1964, Botswana and Lesotho in 1966, and Swaziland in 1968.

South Africa's racist regime took advantage of the balkanization* of its neighbors to enhance its attractiveness to transnational corporate investors as the industrial core of the region. It even sought to replicate the balkanization on a smaller scale by imposing apartheid on its domestic African population: artificially separating so-called "tribes" into tiny Bantustans, and restricting their truncated political "rights" to separate voices in a white-ruled federation. By the late '70s, the South African regime once again proposed to include the neighboring mini-economies, with suitable acquiescent puppet regimes, in a "constellation of southern African states" under its political/military umbrella.[1]

The expansion of transnational corporate invesments in increasingly capital-intensive projects in South Africa, fueling that nation's rapid expansion, at the same time contributed to the further underdevelopment of South Africa's neighbors. In partnership with South African interests, the transnationals retained full control of the "commanding heights" of the neighbors' disarticulated peripheral economies. (See Table 10.4) Barclays' and Standard's branch banks, usually alone, but sometimes in collaboration with other transnational banks and/or local partners, controlled their commercial banking system, determining how much and who would receive credit. Transnational or South African trading companies shipped in high priced manufactured goods for those who could afford to buy them; and purchased the raw materials exports not directly handled by mining or agribusiness concerns. Transnational companies, frequently in partnership with South African mining finance houses, shipped away their rich mineral wealth for processing, either to their plants in South Africa or in their own distant homelands.

Limited Markets and Capital

Even if the government gained control of the commanding heights, none of the small individual states of southern Africa, alone, could fully develop its extensive known resources to build modern factories and spread productive employment opportunities throughout its economy.

*The term "balkanization" refers to the division of the Eastern European states which prevented them from uniting to resist the domination by the major European capitalist powers until they reached a significant degree of political-economic cooperation after they all adopted a socialist perspective following World War II.

Table 10-4.
Transnational Corporate Domination of "Commanding Heights" of Economics of South Africa's Neighbors in 1974
(prior to liberation of Portuguese colonies)

"Commanding Heights"	Neighboring Countries								
	Namibia	*Botswana*	*Lesotho*	*Swaziland*	*Zimbabwe*	*Malawi*	*Zambia*	*Angola*	*Mozambique*
Banks	Barclays, Standard, French bank	Barclays, Standard,	Barclays, Standard,	Barclays, Standard,	Barclays, Standard, National Grindlays Nedsual	Barclays and Standard own 49% and manage Commercial Bank; government owns 51%	Barclays, Standard, National Grindlays, conduct 80-90% of bank business	Barclays, Standard and Anglo-American held shares in Banco Standard-Totta Alliance (a Portuguese bank)	Barclays, Standard and Anglo-American hold shares in Banco Standard-Totta Mozambique (a Portuguese bank)
Basic industries	*uranium* Rio Tinto Zinc	*diamonds* DeBeers		*iron ore* Anglo-American	*iron & Steel* British Steel (32%)	none	*copper* Anglo-AMAX (in partnership with government, 51%)	*oil* Gulf oil Texaco *diamonds* DeBeers & Portuguese *iron ore*	none
Major Mines	*copper* Anglo-American AMAX,	*copper-nickel* Anglo-American AMAMX		*asbestos* Turner, Babcock, Newell	*chrome* Union Carbide Rio Tinto				

Major estates/ Agro-industry	Newmont, Falconbridge *diamonds*	DeBeers (primarily settler farms)	(government 15% share)	Lonrho Tate & Lyle Del Monte Nestles	Lonrho Tate & lyle Anglo-American BrookBond-Leibig	Lonrho	Bat, Tate Lyle (in partnership with government)	Zinc *Phosphates* AECI	Krupf	Anglo-American
Foreign and internal wholesale trade	All imports and exports handled by South African and transnational firms with South African Customs union.				All imports, exports go through Mozambique	36% of imports from South Africa, unknown % from Rhodesia — handled in close collaboration with South African and transnational firms within South African Customs Union	CBC (U.K. 49% Zambia government 51%) ZOK (formerly South African, taken by government 100%		Portuguese interests handled imports; Transnational mining, agri-business handled most exports	Portuguese interests handled trade, with growing South African and transnational involvement

Sources: Government reports and annual reports of companies.

Construction of basic industries to fully utilize their mineral resources required capital and markets far exceeding those of any one of them, alone. Their populations were small: None were as large as major cities of core industrialized nations: New York, Tokyo, or London. The mass of their people simply could not afford to buy sophisticated industrial outputs on a scale large enough to make factories of optimal size viable. Their per capita incomes were low, less than a tenth of that of advanced industrialized states, and separately even if they ended the drain of investable surpluses to South Africa and beyond, they could not accumulate the capital required to finance large scale basic industries.

Table 10-5 summarizes estimates of the gross domestic product and the potential available investable surpluses in southern African states in 1976, compared to South Africa's. As a result of the many decades of underdevelopment, the ten southern African states' gross domestic products combined, totalled little more than a third that of South Africa's. Separately, with a few exceptions, their potential investable surpluses were scarcely sufficient to finance more than one or two modern basic industrial projects.

Table 10-5.
Estimated Gross Domestic Production, Potential Investable Surpluses of Independent Southern African States Compared to South Africa, 1975

State	Gross Domestic Product (U.S. $millions	Estimated potential investable surpluses[1] (U.S. $millions)
Angola	3476.1	869.0
Botswana	342.0	85.5
Lesotho	111.3	27.8
Malawi	758.4	189.6
Mozambique	2687.9	671.9
Namibia	891.3	222.8
Swaziland	273.3	68.3
Tanzania	2553.2	638.3
Zambia	2231.4	557.8
Zimbabwe	2620.0	655.0
Total	15943.9	3985.9
South Africa	35294.2	8823.5

Note: [1]Estimated as 25 percent of Gross Domestic Product.

Source: See table 10.2 above (p. 237)

The difficulty of accumulating sufficient capital to build modern industries in any single state was aggravated in 1970s by the spread of inflation from core industrial capitalist nations throughout the Third World. The overall cost of construction of plant and equipment for modern factories in the United States almost doubled from 1970 to 1979, rising 19 percent in 1978, alone. (See Table 10-6)

Table 10.6.

CE PLANT COST INDEX	JAN '79 prelim.	DEC '78 rev.	NOV '78 final	JAN '78 final
(1957-59 = 100)	229.0	226.0	224.7	210.6
Equipment, machinery, supports	254.3	249.0	247.6	229.6
Construction labor	191.7	190.8	190.3	182.8
Buildings	220.5	218.0	217.8	207.0
Engineering & supervision	171.1	168.2	165.4	159.2
Fabricated equipment	251.1	245.2	244.1	226.6
Process machinery	240.4	237.8	235.8	219.1
Pipe, valves & fittings	288.8	279.8	278.1	256.0
Process instruments	225.0	223.5	221.7	20918
Pumps & compressors	269.6	268.1	266.6	248.4
Electrical equipment	175.5	174.1	173.5	162.5
Structural supports & misc.	265.2	258.7	258.0	235.5

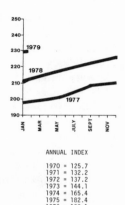

ANNUAL INDEX

1970 = 125.7
1971 = 132.2
1972 = 137.2
1973 = 144.1
1974 = 165.4
1975 = 182.4
1976 = 192.1
1977 = 204.1

New technological advances which rendered smaller sized plants viable for some industries partly offset the rise in capital costs. Brazil; for example, spent only $42 million in 1978 to build a 1,060 metric ton steel plant, using an oil gasification process for locally mined iron ore. [2] But even $42 million would have consumed a major share of the total estimated investable surplus of the smaller southern African countries. Zambia, in the early '70s, had planned to build a $100 million steel plant using gasification to process its known ore deposits, [3] but when world copper prices plummetted these plans had to be shelved.

Other, more technologically complex plants for producing petro-chemicals or continuously cast metal rods, for example, were prohibitively expensive. No individual southern African state, alone, had either the capital or markets to build one. Argentina constructed a relatively small petrochemcial plant for $800 million, a vast sum compared to the roughly $3 billion available for all investments in all the southern African countries outside South Africa. Even Argentina encountered difficulties with marketing and finance. [4]

Clearly, the individual countries of southern Africa would have to forego development of these kinds of projects for many years unless they could entice foreign governments or firms to invest to meet needs of their own or foreign markets. But transnationals had, in the past, been willing to finance large integrated manufacturing projects outside their own homelands solely in oppressive regional subcenters like South Africa.*

The mining finance houses and transnatioinal firms with regional offices in South Africa took advantage of and contributed to the neighboring countries' weaknesses to extract their mineral wealth in crude form, along with the investable surpluses created in the process. They entirely neglected the potential for building up regional industrial capacity outside South Africa's minority ruled economy. They mined some minerals for shipment in crude form to South African factories or for sale overseas. They simply ignored other deposits when they did not wish to open new mines that might compete with their own existing investments.

The consequences of the transnationals' centering investments on South Africa, despite the independent southern African states' efforts to build up their own industrial capacity, may be illustrated by a cursory survey of the uneven pattern of development of some of the region's major resources that persisted in the 1970s.

Take oil. Oil is absolutely essential, not only for fuel, but for lubrication of machinery and equipment. No industrial economy today can survive without oil. Although South Africa had no known oil deposits, Angola had reserves considered among some of the largest in the world. The U.S. firm, Gulf Oil, began drilling for oil in Angola late in the 1960s, during the last days of Portuguese rule. By the 1970s, despite Angola's attainment of independence, Gulf was pumping millions of barrels of oil from its Cabinda wells each year. But the oil majors built their main African refineries in South Africa. The Portuguese had constructed a small refinery in Luanda to process a little oil for local consumption, not more than 10 percent of its total crude production in the mid-'70s. They built another refinery in Mozambique at Lourenco Marques (now Maputo) to process imported crude. Lonrho had undertaken to construct a pipeline to ship oil to the minority regime in

---

*By the 1970s, they were selling their advanced technologies to large socialist countries like the Soviet Union and China, which had the necessary large internal markets and assumed responsibility for repaying the loans needed to buy them. This option was certainly not open to the smaller individual southern African states, and to date not to the larger ones either.

Southern Rhodesia from Mozambique, but it was never put into operation; so Southern Rhodesia, like the smaller neighboring countries,
remained dependent on South Africa for oil.

A few of the larger independent southern African states built small
refineries to reduce their dependence on the transnational oil majors.
The Tanzanian and Zambian governments invested state funds in small
projects built by the Italian firm, AGIP. Zambia shipped crude oil over
a thousand miles by pipeline to the copper belt from the Tanzanian coast
in order to end its dependence on oil imports from South Africa.

All the refineries outside South Africa in southern Africa were small.
Combined, their refined capacity was barely a fifth of South Africa's.
(See Table 10-7) Except for Angola's, they remained dependent on
crude oil imported at high prices through transnational corporate marketing networks. These extracted high rates of profit, raising delivered
prices well above those set by OPEC. None of the host countries
alone—not even Angola possessed the capital or markets required to
build a basic petrochemicals industry in association with its existing
refinery capacity.

Table 10-7.

Capacity for Refining Petroleum Products in Southern Africa, 1976

Petroleum Products	Angola	Mozambique	Tanzania	Zambia	South Africa
			in thousand metric tons		
Liquified petroleum gas	7	7	6	9	59
Motor Spirit	51	80	117	180	3,504
Kerosene	18	20	26	20	403
Met Fuel	56	7	44	40	283
Distillate Fuel oils	190	100	193	350	4,326
Residual fuel oil	342	200	358	200	3,187
Bitumen	5	25		5	319
Parafin wax					290
Total	664	439	744	799	12,371
% of regional total	4.4%	2.9%	4.9%	5.3%	82.3%
Crude petroleum known reserves	179,000	none	none	none	none
production	4,494				

Source: United Nations *Statistical Yearbook*, 1979

Several of South Africa's neighbors had extensive known deposits of iron ore. Some, like those of Angola and Swaziland, had been mined for export for years by transnational corporate interests. Krupp, of the F.R.G., shipped iron ore from southern Angola to its home plants. Anglo-American negotiated a profitable contract to ship away a whole mountain of Swazi iron ore to Japanese steel firms.[5] Known ore deposits in Tanzania, Zambia and Mozambique continued to lie fallow.

Only under the minority-ruled regimes of South Africa and Southern Rhodesia (See p. 264 below) had powerful state corporations, working with transnational corporate assistance, built industries to produce steel using local raw materials. Planners in Tanzania and Zambia proposed plants to process their countries' ores, but neither government could muster enough funds to construct them. Tanzania built a small plant to process imported scrap.[6]

The potential of using local iron ores to construct an integrated iron and steel complex to meet southern Africa's demands, outside of minority ruled South Africa, remained unrealized. All of South Africa's neighbors, with the exception of Southern Rhodesia, continued to import machinery and equipment embodying steel for their truncated industrial, argicultural, construction and transport sectors. A number still bought steel from South Africa's ISCOR. (See Table 10-8)

Copper, mostly produced in southern and central Africa, had for decades been one of Africa's leading exports.[6] Zambia's four vast mines, half owned by the government, half by Anglo-American and American Metal Climax (AMAX) still produced about 90 percent of that country's exports a decade after independence.[8] Although Zaire claimed 100 percent ownership of the mines developed under colonialism, the former owner, Union Miniere de Haute Katanga, still managed them and marketed the output, reaping a considerable share of the profits. The Zairois government had also welcomed the Anglo American Corporation along with U.S. and Japanese interests to open rich new ore deposits. In Namibia, the Tsumeb copper mine, predominantly owned by the U.S. firms AMAX and Newmont, remained the country's largest single employer. Botswana's Selebi-Pikwe nickel and copper mine, 85 percent owned by Anglo-American and AMAX, began to produce copper in the 1970s. The transnationals mostly ignored known copper deposits in northeastern Angola.

The transnational and South African copper firms built copper fabricating factories in South Africa, or shipped partially-processed crude materials back to their home plants. Only in Zambia, years before independence when—as Northern Rhodesia—it appeared firmly an-

Table 10-8.
Iron and Steel Production and Consumption in Southern Africa, 1976 (in thousand metric tons)

Production	South Africa[1]	Rhodesia (Zimbabwe)	Angola	Swaziland	Botswana	Lesotho	Malawi	Mozambique	Tanzania	Zambia
Steel	3,751	141	—	—	—	—	—	—	—	—
Pig Iron	3,750	260	—	—	—	—	—	—	—	—
Iron ore	9,800	384	1,644[3]	1,229	—	—	—	—	—	—
Consumption	16,066[2]	n.a.	172[3]	2	2	2	18	25	101	43
per capita (kilograms)	212	n.a.	29[3]	2	2	2	3	3	6	8

Notes: [1]including Namibia
[2]South Africa includes Botswana, Lesotho and Swaziland
[3]Angolan production for 1975, consumption for 1974

Source: United Nations *Statistical Yearbook,* 1977

chored within the South Africa's sphere of dominance, did the copper firms construct smelting and refining facilities to reduce the costs of shipping copper from that landlocked nation to their overseas buyers. In neighboring Zaire, Union Miniere spokesmen continued to argue in the early '70s that copper could not easily be refined in Central Africa for "technological reasons."[9] The Zairois government finally succeeded in pressuring Union Miniere into agreeing to build a refinery to process most Zairois copper on Zairois soil by the 1980s.[10] When Anglo-American and AMAX opened their mine in Botswana, they rejected the Botswana government's request to build on-site processing facilities or to ship their output to Zambia's smelting-refining complex. Instead, the companies planned to ship the crude minerals to AMAX's refinery in Louisiana, after which it was to be reshipped to Metalgesselschafte's fabricating plant in the F.R.G.[11] Newmont and AMAX contrived to ship much of Namibia's Tsumeb copper to the U.S. for processing, although at one stage they announced plans to build their own refinery in South Africa.

The only plants built for more advanced copper fabrication in the independent states were two tiny, less-than-optimal sized projects in Zambia and Zaire for producing copper wire. Zambia's plant was built with government funds and technological and managerial inputs provided by the U.S. firm, Phelps Dodge. It fabricated a tiny fraction of Zambia's copper almost entirely for local consumption. Once the plant was built, it closed the previously existing Zambian market for the already-established Zairois wire plant.[12] This constituted one more of a series of cases in which uncoordinated national planning efforts actually reduced interAfrican cooperation. (See Table 10-9)

Table 10-9.
Copper Production of Ores, Smelting and Refining in Southern Africa, 1976 (in thousand metric tons)

	South Africa[1]	Rhodesia (Zimbabwe)	Zambia	Zaire	Angola (1969)	Botswana
Copper ore	196.9	50.0	849.6	443.9	0.1	12.5
Smelted	198.0	23.5	712.9	408.2	none	none
Refined	95.6	23.5	694.6	274.0	none	none

Note: [1]includes Namibia

Source: United Nations Statistical Yearbook, 1977.

Southern Africa enjoyed abundant possibilities for producing hydro-electric power. These became increasingly significant as the costs of mineral fuel rose. Most of the potential, furthermore, lay outside the flat

Table 10-9.
Energy Production in Southern Africa, 1976
(million kilowatts per hour)

Type	Angola	Botswana	Lesotho	Malawi	Mozambique	Swaziland	Tanzania	Zambia	Zimbabwe	South Africa[2]
Total	1,300	332(th)	5(th)[1]	318	1,915	244	685	7,034	5,653	79,087
Hydro	950			283	1,510	101	500	6,784	5,853	1,876
Total	2,250	332	5	601	3,425	345	1,185	13,818	10,506	80,963
% of regional total	2.3%	0.3%	—	0.6%	3.5%	0.3%	1.2%	14.3%	10.8%	83.4%

Notes: [1]1967 data; none shown after, probably because Lesotho was included in South African grid
[2]includes Namibia

Source: United Nations *Statistical Yearbook,* 1977

249

plains that comprised much of South Africa. The South African regime therefore took measures to develop its neighbors' power to reduce its own dependence on imported mineral fuels. The biggest hydro-electric projects in southern Africa were those built by the South African government in collaboration with Portuguese and transnational corporate interests: The Cabora Basa Dam in Mozambique and Kunene project in Angola, both of which South Africa planned to integrate into a regional hydro-electrical grid to power its continuing industrial growth with the expansion of mining activities. The Kariba hydro-electric project was constructed in the years of the Federation of Rhodesia and Nyasaland on the Southern Rhodesian side of the border, primarily to provide electricity for the northern Rhodesian (now Zambian) copper mines, but also for new industries being built in Bulawayo and Salisbury. Once they attained political independence, the larger southern African states sought to build their own hydro-electrical capacity. The Zambian government built the Kafue hydro-electric project to reduce its dependence on the illegal Southern Rhodesian regime. The Kafue project provided additional electric power for new industries being built in the Kafue Valley. [13] Tanzania, after independence, invested scarce funds in expanding small scale hydro-electric projects to facilitate the spread of industry and modern agriculture. The much more extensive plans for a larger project at Stigler Gorge, [14] to electrify the entire Tanzanian countryside, proved too expensive to undertake until much later.

Truncated Manufacturing Sectors

The rapid expansion of South African industries tended to undermine and hinder the growth of the neghboring countries' manufacturing sectors. (See Table 10-2 above) It remained true, however, that even without South African competition, none of the southern African countries would for many years be able to mobilize the capital or markets needed to render basic industries viable. They appeared likely to remain dependent for a long time on importing basic equipment and machinery—much of it from South Africa—to implement their truncated industrialization programs. To a considerable extent, a number of them appeared likely to have to import even consumer goods and foodstuffs from transnational firms with factories in South Africa itself. Namibia was to all intents and purposes, treated as a province of South Africa. Botswana, Lesotho and Swaziland remained closely integrated within the South African Customs Union. They could not build factories capable of competing with those in South Africa. Furthermore, they had to purchase most of their imports directly from South Africa. The illegal Rhodesian regime was almost entirely dependent on South African machinery, supplies and equipment for its industrial growth, especially after Mozambique cut off its outlets to the sea through Beira and Maputo. Malawi, under Banda, remained closely linked with South Africa, economically as well as politically, buying large amounts of manufactured goods transshipped through Southern Rhodesia.

A decade after independence, even Zambia was still highly dependent on South Africa for the import of manufactured consumer goods, as well as equipment and machinery. When it reduced imports from Southern Rhodesia after UDI in compliance with the U.N. boycott initially it expanded its purchases of South African goods to about a fourth of its total imports. After the 1968-69 economic reforms, it was able to reduce South African imports to about 15 percent of the total, and still further to less than 10 percent when it closed the border with Southern Rhodesia in 1973.[15] At great cost, the Zambian mining companies actually flew in machinery from South Africa by air freight. In 1978, as South Africa's manufacturing economy stagnated under the prolonged impact of the economic crisis, Zambia was forced to reopen the railroad line through Southern Rhodesia allegedly to obtain essential materials and supplies.* Once the rail line was reopened to the south, South Africa's share of total Zambian imports increased, although data as to the actual amount was not yet available as this book went to press.

As a result of South Africa's domination of manufacturing production throughout the region, South Africa's neighbors, especially the smaller countries, found it difficult to build the industries which might have increased productivity and provided more employment opportunities throughout their economies. Expanding sale of goods produced in South African factories tended to squeeze out the remaining domestically-owned handicrafts, though government efforts preserved a few to attract tourists. Imported processed food stuffs undermined vestiges of self-reliant food output and marketing. The capital intensive processing facilities constructed by transnationals to lower shipping costs of mineral and/or agricultural produce provided relatively few jobs.

Only the larger number of higher income white settlers in Southern Rhodesia and the Portuguese in Mozambique and Angola and vigorous post-independence state participation in Zambia and Malawi succeeded in attracting Anglo-American and a few transnational manufac-

---

*It was speculated widely that the International Monetary Fund insisted on reopening the rail line before it would provide Zambia with additional much-needed funds.[16]

turing firms—most of which had regional headquarters in South Africa —to invest in factories to produce goods for local consumption. These produced primarily luxury goods for the high income groups, using imported parts and materials; and reinforced the geographically lopsided focus of growth around existing export-oriented urban enclaves.

Malawi's attempt to develop industry exemplified a typically increasing capital-intensity and diminishing contribution to local creation of employment. Two-thirds of the K18 million invested in new manufacturing plants in the 1970s was generated from locally produced investable surpluses; nevertheless, the new employment created annually dwindled from almost 900 in 1970 to barely 200 in 1976; the amount spent for each new job rose from about K4,000 to K10,234. [17]

The Drain of Investable Surpluses

The transnationals and South African interests continued to drain away a major share of the limited investable surpluses produced in the neighboring peripheral economies of the region, leaving them with relatively little funds to finance a more balanced, integrated pattern of development. The direct drain took the form of the outflow of profits, interest, dividends, and high salaries of expatriate personnel. Foreign firms shipped out additional funds indirectly through manipulation of terms of trade. While exact data as to the outflows from each country remained concealed as a result of transnational corporate control of the countries' commanding heights, estimates range from about 25 percent of the gross domestic product in the case of Zambia[18] to almost 40 percent in the case of Namibia. [19]

It was difficult to distinguish what portion of these surpluses went to South African-based enterprises to finance the continued strengthening of the South African regime; and what portion transnationals shipped to their overseas head offices. The consequences for the region's peripheral economies remained the same in terms of the loss of capital which might have helped them to build new industries to increase productivity and raise living standards of their peoples. As a result, whatever projects the countries' governments undertook, even those to provide infrastructure to enable South African-based transnational firms to exploit their mineral reosurces, required them to borrow heavily abroad. By 1976, many of them had borrowed sums totalling a major share of their gross domestic product. (See Table 10-11)

The increasingly funnel-shaped externally dependent economies of South Africa's neighbors remained incapable of providing enough jobs for the growing numbers of their citizens who were under- or un-

Table 10-11.
External Public Debt and International Reserves of Selected Southern African States, 1970 and 1976

	External Public Debt Outstanding and Disbursed				Gross International Reserves		
	(million U.S. dollars)		As Percentage of GNP		(million U.S. dollars)		In Months of Import Coverage
	1970	1976	1970	1976	1970	1976	1976
Malawi	121	258	37.7	37.5	29	26	2.4
Lesotho	8	15	8.1	8.5	—	—	—
Zambia	548	1,184	32.0	53.7	514	100	1.3
Rhodesia (Zimbabwe)	227	156	15.4	4.5	—	—	—
Botswana	—	161	—	55.3	—	—	—
Swaziland	—	39		20.1[1]	—	—	—

Source: U.S. AID, Development Needs and Opportunities, op. cit.

employed. Hundreds of thousands of workers, mainly men, were forced by the circumstances generated by systematic underdevelopment of their home lands, to migrate annually to work for cash as contract laborers. A very high percentage of these took jobs on South Africa's mines. As unemployment spread throughout South Africa's economy in the mid-'70s, spurred by growing mechanization introduced by trans-national corporate investments, these migrant workers were the first to be displaced. As unemployed South Africans took jobs in the mines, about a third of the mine labor force, formerly immigrants from neighboring countries, was displaced.* (See Table 5-3 in Ch. 5)

The neighboring governments, particularly those of Malawi, Mozambique and Angola, then confronted the immediate problem of reabsorbing tens of thousands of men who, over the years, had lost their skills and interest in agriculture.

The Struggle for Change

Botswana, Lesotho and Swaziland remained tightly knit into the South African orbit with little opportunity to more than marginally shape their own political economic destinies. Only Botswana sought to pursue a more independent course in cooperation with Zambia, but South

---

*South African estimates tend to ignore African women workers, but for the most part South African labor policies explicitly excluded female migrants from neighboring supplier states.

African and transnational control of its banks, trade and key extractive industries sharply curtailed this potential. Tiny Swaziland and Lesotho, remined little more than glorified "Bantustans," touted by South African minority rulers as examples for emulation by South African blacks once they, too, attained "independence" in a proposed South African "federation."

In Malawi (formerly Nyasaland), an agressive self-serving black president and his friends openly welcomed the support of South African and transnational corporate interests. Jailing their opponents, they leaned heavily on a close alliance with the South African regime to strengthen their personally advantageous rule.

Some of the larger states, in contrast, sought to attain a greater degree of self-reliant development. On attaining independence, Tanzania and Zambia halted any further migration of workers to South Africa. In 1967, Tanzania's political leaders published the Arusha Declaration, beginning to assert national control of the economy's commanding heights. At the same time, they proclaimed a perspective of gradual transformation towards their own brand of *ujamaa* socialism. (Discussed below, Ch. 12) In 1969, at Mulungushi, the government of neighboring Zambia, too, announced its goal of wresting the commanding heights from the far more entrenched transnational and South African corporate domination. Unfortunately, behind vague slogans of "humanism," an increasingly powerful bureaucratic bourgeoisie emerged to manipulate Zambia's expanded state power in a sometimes conflicting, sometimes collaborative relationship with the transnational corporate interests which remained a dominant feature of its landlocked national economy.

Nevertheless, as the transnational corporations multiplied their investments in South Africa in the 1960s and early '70s, the conflicts among fundamentally contradictory forces deepened throughout the region. In country after country, people organized increasingly effectively to demand an end to their growing dependence on and exploitation by minority regimes and their transnational corporate allies. Their struggles were not simply an extension of the nationalist movements that had freed almost fifty nations north of the Zambezi. They were rooted in southern African history; South Africans had founded the African National Congress in 1912, making it the oldest modern political organization of Africans on the continent. No longer could South Africa and its transnational corporate allies depend on supportive minority regimes in neighboring states to provide a buffer against infiltration or armed cadres to participate in the spreading armed struggle for freedom. The South African regime sought to implement a strategy of detente, seeking to convince friendly African states that, despite political differences, they could pursue a path of economic cooperation. When that failed, it sought to convince the western powers that they could serve the interests of peace in the region by entering into negotiations for gradual change—while it accelerated its efforts to attract transnational aid to build up its economic and military capacity.

Easily convinced, the transnationals' home governments—led by U.S. statesmen—first Secretary of State Kissenger (who retired and joined Chase Manhattan Bank's International Advisory Board) and then Secretary of State Vance—called for installation of so-called "moderate" black governments, elected by some form of majority vote. Voicing abhorrence of white racism, they sought to encompass the people's demands for freedom without altering the underlying, funnel-shaped political economic structures which had, over the years, made transnational corporate investments in the region so profitable. They urged implementation of a southern African version of the Kenyan model. Its advantages had been spelled out over a decade earlier by the then Kenyan colonial minister of agriculture, Sir Michael Blundell. Pressing to convince reluctant European settlers in Kenya of the necessity of granting Kenya political independence, he had argued:[20]

the only possible policy was a liberal one which attracted the best of the new African thought which was now coming to the fore, allied with measures which created a wider economic sphere for the African generally.

Blundel had explained,

As African political thought becomes more experienced in the actual practice of government, there will be a re-grouping on economic lines if democracy continues . . .; one party will be socialist and revolutionary in concept, looking to the landless and lower paid workers for support, while the other will increasingly be a progressive evolutionary alliance of the haves against the have-nots.

The southern African liberation forces, still battling the white minority regimes, on the other hand, had learned from the experiences of Kenya and other African states which had earlier gained independence in the north, as well as from their own struggles. The South West African People Organization (SWAPO) in Namibia, the Patriotic Front in Zimbabwa, and the African National Congress (ANC) of South Africa voiced their steadfast determination not only to oust the white minority governments but also to reorganize the distorted structures and institutions imposed by decades of colonial and post colonial rule. They emphasized that the issue was not one of the race of the ruling minority. Rather, it was the exploitative nature of the system itself which— despite the demonstrated value of the region's vast natural resources— condemned the majority of the population to poverty. They proclaimed their intent to prohibit a tiny minority of the population of any color from collaborating with transnational corporate interests to monopolize control over their farms, mines, and factories. They proposed to implement a fundamental socio-economic transformation to enable all the inhabitants to their nations to enjoy the full benefits of the rich mineral and agricultural wealth of their land. The "frontline states"—Botswana, Zambia, Tanzania, Mozambique and Angola—despite their own urgent problems, gave leadership to the Organization of African Unity in pledging support for their struggle.

References

1. *South African Digest*, April 27, 1979.
2. *Chemical Engineering*, Mar. 26, 1979.
3. R. Weiss, *Strategic Highways of Africa*, 1978.
4. *Chemical Engineering*, Mar. 26, 1979.
5. See Anglo American Corporation, *Annual Reports*.
6. *Tanzania's Second Five-Year Plan*, Vol. I, p. 86. United Republic of Tanzania (Dar es Salaam, 1969).
7. A. Seidman, *Planning for development in Sub-Saharan Africa* (Dar es Salaam: Tanzania Publishing House and New York: Praeger, 1974) Chap. 2.
8. Republic of Zambia, *Monthly Digest of Statistics*, (Lusaka: Central Statistical Office) Jan. 1977, p. 16.
9. A representative of Union Miniere repeated this assertion at a meeting of representatives of copper companies with Zarois government and academic personnel, Lubumbaski, 1973. Attended by one of the authors, A.S.
10. A. Seidman, ed., Natural Resources and National Welfare: The Case of Copper, (New York: Praeger, 1976) P. 290-91.
11. See R. Silitshena, "Mining and Development Strategy in Botswana" in *Natural Resources and National Welfare: The Case of Copper*, A. Seidman, ed. (New York: Praeger, 1976).
12. Seidman, ed., Natural Resources and National Welfare, *op. cit.*, p. 30.
13. For the amount of electricity produced by Kafue and other projects in Zambia, see *Republic of Zambia, Second National Development Plan*, Jan. 1972-December 1976 (Lusaka: Ministry of Development Planning and National Guidance, 1971) pp. 101-2.
14. Interview with L. Berry, former Director of Bureau of Resource Allocation and Land Use Planning, University of Dar es Salaam.
15. For details, see A. Seidman, "Distorted Import Substitution Industry: The Zambian Case" in *Journal of Modern African Studies*, 12, 4 (1974) pp. 601-631.
16. *South African Financial Mail*, Mar. 24, 1978.

17. U.S. Assistance for International Development and Opportunities for Cooperation in Southern Africa, "Malawi" (Washington, D.C.: U.S. AID, 1979).

18. A. Seidman, "The Have-Have Not' Gap in Zambia", (Lusaka, University of Zambia, mimeographed, 1979).

19. R. H. Green, "Namibia in Transition: Toward a Political Economy of Liberation?" to appear in T. Shaw, ed., *The Future(s) of Africa* (Boulder, Westview Press, 1980) table 5.

20. M. Blundell, *So Rough a Wind, The Kenya Memoirs of Sir Michael Blundell* (London: Weidenfeld and Nicolson, 1964).

The Seeming Paradox
of Southern Rhodesia*   11

In the late '70s, South Africa's rulers engaged in pressuring the tiny minority ruling Southern Rhodesia to open the doors of government to a few carefully selected blacks. The western powers urged South Africa to persuade the white Southern Rhodesians to accept a "moderate" black regime in preference to continuing the losing battle against guerrillas increasingly determined to carry through a more thorough-going political-economic reconstruction. The South Africans apparently realized they could only hope to stem the tide of fundamental revolutionary change in the region by installing a compromise regime capable of winning the support of the western powers.

These maneuvers underscored a more basic, though seemingly paradoxical, political-economic reality: The transnational corporations had elected to build South Africa up as the dominant regional subcenter, contributing to the systematic underdevelopment of the surrounding states. Yet they simultaneously assisted the minority regime of Southern Rhodesia to achieve a significant, albeit dependent, degree of industrial growth. This seeming paradox rested on several underlying and sometimes contradictory features of the relationships between the two minority ruled states:

1. South African and transnational corporate agro-business and mining companies sought to profit from rich Zimbabwean (the African name for Southern Rhodesia) mineral and agricultural resources and low wages—even lower than those prevailing in South Africa itself.

2. The Southern Rhodesian regime constituted a buffer between the newly independent black nations to the north and South Africa, which the South Africans were eager to retain.

*The United Nations continued to call the white Rhodesian regime "Southern Rhodesia" after UDI to emphasize that it remained illegally constituted. This term is used throughout this chapter for the same reason.

3. The South African whites were linked by ideology and even family ties to the white minority that illegally ruled Zimbabwe.*

4. South African manufacturing firms and transnationals' subsidiaries based in South Africa viewed Southern Rhodesia as an important market for their manufactured output, including military equipment. In response to the state capitalist measures introduced by the Rhodesian regime, they invested in last stage processing and assembly industries, contributing to a lop-sided pattern of dependent industrial growth.

Examination of the seeming Southern Rhodesian paradox provides further insight into the nature of transnational corporate activities in building South Africa up as an oppressive regional sub-center. At the same time, analysis of the characteristics of the Southern Rhodesian political economy may help to explain the role a liberated Zimbabwe may play in achieving the transformation of southern Africa.

This chapter will briefly survey, first, the colonial roots of the labor system which rendered South African and transnational corporate investment in Southern Rhodesia exceptionally profitable; secondly, the important role that South African and transnational corporations, operating from their regional headquarters in South Africa itself, played in fostering the spurt of economic growth that followed UDI, despite U.N. sanctions; and, thirdly, the sharpened military-economic crisis of the mid-'70s as a feature of the impact of the deepening general world crisis on southern Africa.

I. Before UDI: The Foundations of White-Minority Rule

The European invasion and colonization of the area known under colonialism as Southern Rhodesia (the country of Zimbabwe) took place around the turn of the Century. Foreign investors, backed by the colonial regime, aimed primarily to develop a source of cheap raw materials. Three major export sectors emerged by the 1920s—the foreign-owned, relatively large mines, and the mainly settler-controlled agriculture and small-scale mining. The settler producers depended on the British and South African companies that ran wholesale trade and finance. Much of the profit they reaped from Southern Rhodesia went to build up the South African economy, which was based on a similar racist system.

*For example, the wife of South Africa's Minister of Finance, Horwood, was the sister of the wife of the President of the Rhodesian regime, Ian Smith.

And what made it all profitable was cheap African labor. As one observer declared:

The very existence as well as the profitability of the small-scale mining and commercial enterprises depended on a guaranteed and continuous supply of *cheap* labor from the surrounding peasant communities. [emphasis in original.][1]

The colonial state intervened to ensure the low wages needed to guarantee the profits of foreign investors and settlers. It aimed deliberately to break down the traditional economy, forcing Africans to work for whites at wages below the level of subsistence for a family.[2] It restricted the land available to African cultivators, marking out the first reserves around the turn of the Century. The Land Apportionment Act of 1930 reserved two-thirds of the country for the 50,000 white settlers, allocating the remainder to the 1.1 million African inhabitants. In the following years, the African share increased to about half, but acreage per capita shrank steadily (see Table 11.3), while more and more Africans were pushed off "white" land. As early as the 1920s, observers reported serious overcrowding in the reserves.[3] The colonial regime used additional methods to force Africans into the wage-labor force, notably taxes (which had to be paid in cash) and discriminatory marketing and subsidy practices, designed to undermine African agriculture. (These policies resembled those introduced, with similar aims, throughout Britain's African colonies.[4])

The destruction of the traditional economy forced Africans to look for work on the white-owned mines and farms. By 1948, the success of the colonial policies was clear: in that year, 60 percent of all men had left Matabeleland to seek work as migrants; 40 percent had left Mashonaland South.[5] Usually, their families were not allowed to live with them. Wives and children were expected to continue subsistence farming in the reserves, lowering the pressure on employers to pay a living wage.

The white settlers and mining firms also received colonial government assistance to recruit workers from Nyasaland (now Malawi), Mozambique, Bechuanaland (Botswana) and Northern Rhodesia (Zambia). By 1941, foreign migrant workers constituted half the paid work force.[6]

Colonial legislation restricted Africans' attempts to resist employers. The Masters and Servants Act, passed in 1901 and in force in the 1970s, prevented black workers in agriculture, mining and domestic service from joining trade unions or striking. The Industrial Conciliation Act (first passed in 1934 and later amended) restricted the trade union rights of workers in other sectors.

World War II stimulated economic expansion in Southern Rhodesia by increasing the demand for raw materials, especially asbestos, chrome and coal. The gross national product rose from 27 million in 1939 to 35 million in 1944. Over the next seven years, it almost tripled, in current prices, reaching 100 million in 1951. [7]

During the Federation of the Rhodesias and Nyasaland, Southern Rhodesia's settler population further expanded industry at the expense of its northern partners. [8] Federation channeled about 70 million in taxes from the Northern Rhodesian copper mines to finance industrial growth in Southern Rhodesia. The two largest infrastructural projects built during Federation, the Kariba hydroelectric power project and the railway to Lourenco Marques were placed under Southern Rhodesian control. Nyasaland continued to provide cheap labor. Tariff barriers forced Northern Rhodesia and Nyasaland to buy Southern Rhodesian manufactures at prices frequently above international levels. Largely as a result of these policies, Southern Rhodesia's national product almost doubled, from 173 million in 1954 to 296 million in 1961. The share of manufacturing grew from 13 to 15 percent.

Federation broke up in 1963, largely as a result of African protest. A year later, Zambia and Malawi received independence. But Southern Rhodesia, which remained under white-minority rule, already had the most advanced manufacturing sector in sub-Saharan Africa outside South Africa. When not directly foreign-owned, however, industry depended on inputs provided by South African companies or the South African subsidiaries of transnational corporations. The continued existence of the migrant labor system, established before World War II, ensured their profits by holding wages at or below subsistence for the vast majority of African workers.

II. UDI 1966-1974

The Southern Rhodesian whites declared UDI (Unilateral Declaration of Independence) in 1965. Following an initial panic (reflected in a capital outflow, a sinking GDP and net white emigration) industry continued to expand. Between 1965 and 1974, the GDP rose, officially, from Rh$700 million to Rh$1300 million, at 1965 prices.* GDP per capita rose by 36 percent, to Rh$223, remaining well above that of Southern Rhodeisa's neighbors, except South Africa and Zambia. (The per capita figures, of course, concealed vast and growing inequalities in

*The minority regime may, however, have exaggerated the figures for propaganda reasons.

personal income.) Manufacturing rose from a fifth to a quarter of GDP. Agriculture and mining, together, also contributed about a quarter, but exported more than manufacturing. The share of agriculture stagnated mostly because sanctions cut tobacco sales. (See table 11.1).

Several factors contributed to this spurt in output. First, having declared UDI, the tiny white minority exercised its control of state power to duplicate the attractive climate for private investment found in its larger neighbor to the South. It systematized and expanded the exploitative, racist labor system. Simultaneously, it intervened directly to encourage domestic and transnational corporate investors, particularly to build up manufacturing.

Largely drawn by the lower labor costs that resulted, the transnational corporations invested heavily, often through South African regional headquarters and in cooperation with South African capital. They drained off surpluses from mining and agriculture through direct investment and, increasingly, expanded control of finance and trade. But they also found manufacturing more alluring than in independent Africa, even seeking to use Southern Rhodesia as an export base for some products, despite U.N. sanctions. Apparently, they were attracted to manufacturing by the abysmally low wages for blacks, even below those in South Africa; the regime's incentives to invest in industry; and the fact that a white government appeared, to them, inherently "stable"[9]—until the revolutionary armed struggle forced upon them the hollowness of this conclusion.

The factors that influenced transnational investors will now be considered in more detail. First, the effect of sanctions is described. The following sections deal with state intervention, both to provide direct incentives to investors and to hold down wages. The structure of transnational corporate collaboration is then reviewed.

Table 11-1.
Southern Rhodesian GDP, and Population, 1965-76

	1965	1970	1975	1976
GDP—at market prices ($ mn.)	733	1,073	1,994	2,108
in 1965 prices ($ mn.)	733	979	1,345	1,284
Population (thousands)	4,490	5,310	6,310	6,530
GDP per capita, in 1965 prices	163	184	210	197

Source: Central Statistical Office, *National Accounts of Rhodesia, 1976* (Salisbury: Government Printer, August 1977), Table 2.

Inadequate Enforcement of Sanctions

The majority of U.N. member-states sought to implement economic sanctions on the illegal regime in Southern Rhodesia. But the transnational corporations, in collaboration with the South African and fascist Portuguese regimes undermined them from the outset.

The secret U.S. government document, NSSM 39, explained in 1969 that the core capitalist nations called for sanctions because Britain wanted an excuse for its failure to take effective action against the illegal regime. The U.S., Britain and France vetoed sanctions on transport and communications links, making enforcement of the economic boycott difficult. Moreover, the British did not insist on full withdrawal, but merely prohibited the movement of goods and capital directly to or from Southern Rhodesia. This policy contradicted the interpretation most other U.N. members placed on sanctions. It made monitoring practically impossible, especially since transnational corporations continued to maintain ties with Southern Rhodesia through their South African subsidiaries, and South Africa refused to enforce sanctions at all.

At first, U.N. sanctions sharply reduced the import of consumer goods and the export of tobacco. The import of some capital equipment and the export of minerals continued through South Africa and Portuguese-ruled Mozambique. By the 1970s, markets had apparently been found for tobacco exports as well. By 1977, the regime claimed to have exported almost half of all estate production. [10]

The regime's military buildup provided a market for the manufactures that transnational corporations produced in their South African factories. By 1976, it was "an open secret that all Rhodesia's military equipment comes either from or through South Africa."[11] The regime imported airplanes, trucks and communications equipment, mostly produced by U.S. and other transnational firms, to offset its growing manpower shortage. [12]

Sanctions weakened the regime, nonetheless. Imports of capital equipment continued to be small, and in many industries plant had become obsolete by the early '70s. Manufacturing industries increasingly felt the lack of export markets, as low African wages restricted local consumption. And, unlike in South Africa, the regime could not develop its own arms industry.*

---

*It has been argued by the regime itself, as well as several articles,[13] that industrial growth in Southern Rhodesia after UDI resulted from sanctions themselves. Following the arguments of Andre Gundar Frank, it was claimed that the enforced isolation must have stimulated manufacturing. But growth was only possible because of the historically advanced levels of industrialization and high degree of state intervention. It seems probable that, had sanctions not been imposed, manufacturing industry would have expanded anyway—at greater cost to Zambia, Mozambique and the people of Zimbabwe. Moreover, greater transnational investment would have tied the core capitalist countries yet more tightly to the Smith regime.

State Intervention

The white-minority state, building on the industrial base founded before UDI, intervened to encourage investment by white settlers and foreign corporations. The most important form of state involvement was the rigidification and expansion of the migrant labor system, which further reduced real wages for Africans.

The state also channeled surpluses directly to producers, providing financial and technical aid, cheap credits, and assistance with internal and external marketing. Although agriculture earned the largest share of foreign exchange by the 1970s, subsidies were the main source of profits for most white farmers.[14] The state directed scarce foreign exchange to the manufacturing sector, allocating hard currency to industry to pay for inputs and equipment, and reducing less productive imports. By denying the normal city services, medical care, education and welfare to the African majority, the regime could hold taxes to a minimum. Infrastructure had been relatively well developed even before UDI.

The state invested directly in industry, working closely with transnational banks and corporations. The country's largest iron-and-steel producer, Risco, was owned jointly by the state and British Steel. The Industrial Development Corporation of Rhodesia (IDC) was controlled by the government, in association with all the transnational banks active in Southern Rhodesia (Barclays, Standard and Grindlays), Rhobank and the South African mining finance house, Anglo-American. The IDC reported that it maintained "close liaison" with the Association of Rhodesian Industries. It promoted industrial development through direct investment and loans, participating in projects that "left to itself, private enterprise might find of too long a term."[15] The IDC resembled the development corporations established throughout Anglophonic Africa (it was based on an Industrial Development Board founded in 1959), but was rather more vigorous. Before UDI, it provided a fundamental stimulus for the textiles industry, and invested heavily in metals production and financial services. After UDI, it greatly expanded its support for heavy industry, shifting two-thirds of its holdings to motor assembly, mining and metal products. The regime used the IDC to meet strategic needs, supporting industries of military significance and investigating oil-from-coal processes.[16] The IDC encouraged affiliates to export, where possible, and, with Standard, owned shares in the Export Credit Insurance Corporation of Rhodesia.

In general, direct state intervention in the economy followed the pattern typical for non-socialist developing countries, in Africa as

Table 11-2.

The Industrial Development Corporation, Distribution of Investments, 1967-1978 (percentages)

| | book value | | | | Market value |
Sector	1967	1973	1975	1978	1978
Clothing and footwear	4.5	1.4	0.2	0.4	2.0
Film (a)	—	*	1.1	0.1	1.8
Financial services	13.7	11.6	12.0	11.6	4.8
Metal products (b)	13.4	13.5	18.0	20.6	9.9
Mining (b)	4.8	37.3	18.6	22.2	48.0
Motor assembly (c)	—	17.8	36.9	18.1	19.4
Spinning, weaving, etc. (d)	48.1	9.7	6.4	10.7	5.6
Other**	14.5	8.5	6.3	11.6	8.5
TOTAL	100.0	100.0	100.0	100.0	100.0
Value (mn.)	2,1	R8,3	R$12,0	R$6,6	R$17,4

*less than 0.05 percent.

**Including, among other; chemicals, engineering, hotels, non-metallic mineral products, transport equipment, paper and printing.

—not listed.

a. Affiliate (IDC owned c. 50%) exported substantial share of its products in 1975, with 70% local content.

b. IDC owned shares in several mines, producing asbestos, tin, nickel, aluminum and, in cooperation with Falconbridge, gold. In 1978, it aimed to establish "an integrated aluminum industry" in Southern Rhodesia, in cooperation with an unnamed South African partner, through Aluminum Industries Ltd.

c. In 1973, the IDC was affiliated to Willowvale Motor Industries.

d. Mostly through Berkshire International (Rhodesia), which had two plants. The IDC owned 37%.

Source: Industrial Development Corporation of Rhodesia, Ltd., (Salisbury), Annual reports, 1973, 1975, 1978; Rhodesia; *Public Sector Investment, 1968-1971,* presented to parliament, April 1968 (Salisbury: Government Printers, 1968).

elsewhere. It aimed to reduce taxes and ensure the subsidized provision of infrastructure and basic inputs. The difference was that a white-minority regime ruled Southern Rhodesia. It reassured investors that their holdings were safe from expropriation as long as it remained in power, and expended great effort to maintain a cheap labor force.

Intensified Exploitation

The white-minority regime sought to establish a migrant labor system parallel to apartheid in South Africa. By 1976, 4.5 million people, seven-tenths of the total population, were crowded into the infertile lands of the reserves, renamed Tribal Trust Lands (TTLs). As Table

Table 11-3.
Rural Population Densities in Southern Rhodesia, 1969 and 1976

Land Category	Acres per Person 1969	1976
African land—TTL plus APL	14.3	9.9
European farming—all residents	40.2	34.4
Euopeans only	1272.8	1208.9
Total, rural land	20,4	14,7

Distribution of Land in Southern Rhodesia, by Quality*

Natural farming regions**	Total acerage (000s)	% in Af. areas	% in Eur. areas
I Rainfall=42 in.; specialized and diversified farming	1,515	13	71
II Rainfall=28-42 in.; intensive crop production and subsidiary livestock	18,145	25	69
III Rainfall=22-28 in.; semi-intensive cropping, more livestock	16,938	43	45
IV Rainfall=18-22 in.; semi-extensive livestock, limited cropping; tendency to drought, dry-spells	32,148	54	28
V Rainfall=under 20; only extensive farming base on natural grazing (veldt)	25,423	51	26
X Totally unsuitable—swamps, etc.	3,015	54	2
Total	97,184	45	38

*Where European and African lands together do not make up 100 percent, the remainder is in the National Land area.

**Only regions I-III are suitable for cropping. The quality ranges from I, the best, to X, the worst.

Distance from infrastructure of European and African areas, 1970

Distance Distance (miles)	Railroad station or siding European areas	African areas	Regional urban center European areas	African areas
within 10 mi.	35%	5%	10%	5%
11-50 mi.	60	55	70	35
51-100 mi.	5	40	20	50
over 100 mi.			0	10

Source: Roger C. Riddell, *The Land Problem in Rhodesia* (Gwelo: mambo Press, 1978), Table 6, p. 35, Table 1, p. 27; Table 7, p. 36.

11.3 illustrates, the amount of land allocated per African declined to less than ten acres by the mid-'70s; only a third of the land area of the TTLs was naturally suited for farming. Most African lands were over ten miles from railroad sidings, rendering shipment of crops for sale difficult if not impossible. Inequalities in land and cattle ownership made conditions in the TTLs even harsher. By the late '60s, 30 percent of the Africans living in Karangaland owned no cattle; 23 percent had over six head. In early 1977, an estimated 500,000 adults living in the TTLs had no land; there were 657,000 farmers. The size of plots also varied greatly. [17]

Huge inequalities in government aid ensured that African farmers could not compete with white settlers. In 1973-75, the regime spent R$8000 per white farmer in subsidies and assistance. It spent R$0.60 per African farmer. [18]

These deliberate policies generated a crisis in the TTLs. In 1962, the TTLs produced 160 kilos of maize per capita, 90 percent of the minimum needed for subsistence. Fifteen years later, they produced only 105 kilos per capita—around 60 percent of their needs. [19] In the early '60s, over half the TTL population relied on remittances from migrant workers merely to subsist. This dependence grew steadily after UDI. [20]

Simultaneously, the white-minority regime encouraged a tiny segment of the black population as a potential ally. It allowed Africans to buy farms in the African Purchase Lands (APLs), which made up 9 percent of all African land. Barely 1 percent of the African population managed to buy farms there. It has been argued[21] that the APLs were designed to promote an African petty-bourgeoisie, which would collaborate in maintaining the status quo. They offered a limited opportunity to a handful of successful African farmers and tradesmen, fostering the illusion of upward mobility.

But most Africans faced poverty in the TTLs, as the unequal distribution of land forced them to eke out a living on overcrowded, infertile lands or migrate to look for jobs at any wage offered in foreign- and settler-owned industry and agriculture. The result was high unemployment in the urban areas. The distorted character of post-UDI expansion further aggravated unemployment among the black population. Transnational corporations introduced increasingly capital-intensive technologies. Output per worker rose particularly rapidly in the sectors with the greatest direct foreign participation: manufacturing, finance and mining.

Between 1965 and 1975, the number of African formal-sector employees rose 57 percent, to 934,000 (although the number dropped in 1966-67 and again after 1975). Most of the increase in employment occured in the urban-industrial sectors. But growth in employment failed to keep pace with the expanding labor force. In the mid-'70s, the labor force grew by 100,000 a year, while the annual rise in black employment averaged only 24,000 a year. [22] A high proportion of the unemployed were young.

In all countries, unemployment spells hardship. In Southern Rhodesia, it meant: reduced consumption; sale of consumer durables; and reduced education for children. [23] But transnational corporations and settler-owned industry and agriculture benefited:

> The existence of a localized urban labor reserve—evident on the streets of the central business district, in the townships and the suburbs of white society—also produces a threatening impact on workers already in employment . . . It enables more-or-less instant replacement . . . and allows the "market enforcement" of a high level of labor discipline and subordination. [24]

Despite the pressures put on Africans to take any available job, mine owners and settler farmers complained constantly of a "labor shortage," because workers refused to accept the intolerable conditions they offered. They tended to employ indentured foreign labor, promoting lower wages throughout the economy. Nevertheless, the number of foreign workers dropped steadily, falling from 229,000, or 34 percent of the total labor force in 1969, to 214,000 (23 percent) in 1975. In the earlier year, although foreign-born workers were, officially, only "temporary migrants," two-thirds had resided in Southern Rhodesia over ten years. [25] They were nonetheless subject to deportation, giving employers a major weapon in depressing wages and conditions.

An effective color bar kept blacks out of better-paying jobs. Four out of five African workers were unskilled. About 50,000 were semi-skilled, and only 10,000 ranked as artisans, administrators or professionals. A survey in the mid-'70s showed half of all Africans with four to six years of secondary educations had not found jobs six months after leaving school. [26] Thousands more Africans with higher education left the country after UDI.

As a result of the migrant labor system, soaring unemployment and the color bar, most African wages stagnated at or below the subsistence level, as shown by comparison with the Poverty Datum Line (PDL). The PDL represented the absolute minimum needed for subsistence. It made no allowance for "saving, for emergencies, for necessary social services, for all forms of recreation and entertainment, for tobacco and drink, for trade union and church subscriptions, for burial societies, for newspapers, stationery, radios, odd bus rides, sweets, hobbies, gifts or comforts and luxuries of any kinds." [27] At the end of 1978, when the urban PDL for a family of six in Southern Rhodesia was about US$160 a month, half of all black workers received less than US$80. The wages of four-fifths of all employed Africans lay under the PDL. [28]

Unskilled workers, mostly migrants, earned well below the PDL in all sectors. A 1973 survey [29] covering 24,000 migrant workers living in Harari Township indicated their conditions. The workers lived in the bleak, crowded hostels the regime provided for nominally single workers, although 54 percent were in fact married with, on average, three children. Their families were forced to stay in the rural areas. At that time, the PDL for a family of five was Rh$53 a month. Two percent of workers surveyed earned over $54 a month; 89 percent earned less than $40. The average worker had resided over ten years in a hostel, visiting his family at weekly or monthly intervals, and sending money home regularly. Yet the rationale for paying below-subsistence-level wages was that they were really peasants looking for a little extra cash as temporary migrants.

High rates of unemployment and restriction of trade unionism among blacks created conditions in which, over the first decade of UDI, the real wages of blacks declined. The gap between black and white wages rose in most sectors of the economy (see Table 11.4). Whites—less than 4 percent of the population—received by far the greatest share of the growing national product. In 1974, the African majority received 37 percent of total disposable income, slightly less than in 1965. The gap between African and non-African per capita income had grown by about Rh$600 in 1965 prices, to reach $2175. [30] A survey pointed up the difference in living standards: in 1970, over 90 percent of white urban families had a car; 44 percent of African urban households had a bicycle. [31] At birth, life expectancy for Africans was 50 years; for non-Africans, it was 67. [32] Only a handful of blacks were better off—a few professionals, a tiny number of entrepreneurs with interests in hotels in the TTLs, trading, transport and real estate.

Between 1965 and 1972, wages paid to Africans equalled only 9 percent of the gross operating profits of all companies in Southern Rhodesia outside agriculture. [33] Profits for transnational banks and corporations and an easy life for the white settlers rested on misery for the vast majority of African workers and peasants.

...for those at the bottom of the pile, "the figures" represent poverty, unemployment, insecurity, malnutrition, disease, illiteracy, low life expectancy and even starvation. [34]*

*There were some inequalities among whites, although these "should not be taken to infer real material deprivation in any significant number of households." [35] During and after Federation it decreased as the political power and economic status of white workers grew. In 1959, 49 percent of all non-Africans were wage earners; by 1974, the number dropped to 39 percent; and in 1968, almost half of the heads of white urban households held professional, technical, administrative or management posts.

Table 11-4.
Average African Earnings in Southern Rhodesia for Selected Sectors, 1965-1975, in Current Rhodesian Dollars and Compared to Non-African[1] Earnings

Sector	1965 Dollars	1965 Non-Af.[1] African	1975 Dollars	1975 Non-Af.[1] African	1977 Dollars	1977 Non-Af.[1] African
Agriculture and Forestry	123	22:1	180	27:1	232	25:1
Mining and Quarrying	298	11:1	507	14:1	659	13:1
Manufacturing	419	7:1	724	8:1	918	7:1
Construction	372	7:1	404	8:1	739	9:1
Finance	524	5:1	1176	4:1	1725	3:1
Public Administration	340	8:1	852	7:1	1099	6:1
Private Domestic Service	240	4:1	356	2	424	2
Average, All Sectors	250	10.3:1	464	11.0:1	588	10.5:1

Source: Rhodesian "Ministry of Finance," *An Economic Survey of Rhodesia, 1977* (Salisbury: Government Printers, 1978)

Notes: [1]Southern Rhodesian statistics distinguish between Africans and "Europeans;" the latter category includes Asians and Coloureds, who as a rule earn rather less than whites.
[2]No non-Africans were employed in this sector.

African Employment by Sector

Sector	1965	1970	1977
Agriculture and Forestry	44.0	38.3	38.0
Mining and Quarrying	6.6	6.3	6.4
Sub-Total	50.7	44.6	44.4
Manufacturing	10.5	14.5	14.1
Electricity and Water	0.6	0.5	0.5
Construction	4.4	5.8	4.6
Finance, Insurance and Real Estate	0.3	0.4	0.4
Distribution, Restaurants and Hotels	6.2	5.9	5.8
Transport and Communications	2.4	3.3	3.5
Public Administration	3.1	3.8	4.8
Education	3.6	3.1	3.3
Health	1.0	1.0	1.1
Private Domestic Service	14.4	13.5	13.6
Other Services	2.6	1.0	3.8
Total—Percent	100.0	100.0	100.0
Thousands	656,000	934,00	901,000

Source: Rhodesian "Ministry of Finance," op. cit.

Transnational Corporate Collaboration

In 1978, the local manager of a major F. R. G. chemicals company declared:[36]

Without the political trouble, Rhodesia would be an optimal country for investment: low wages, low taxes, outstanding infrastructure, raw materials in excess, highly developed agriculture—a situation that exists nowhere else in Africa.

In fact, until 1974, "the political trouble" barely disturbed the transnationals, which apparently expected the regime to remain in power indefinitely. They invested in Southern Rhodesia primarily through their South African subsidiaries, hoping to penetrate independent African countries as they had during the years of Federation. Transnational corporate involvement varied from sector to sector, however. They dominated finance and trade, which enabled them to extract profits from mining, agriculture and other sectors without outright ownership. But they invested directly in the larger mines, estates and manufacturing, alongside and in collaboration with local state and private capital, maintaining their control of rich Southern Rhodesian resources and markets and benefiting directly from low-cost labor. By 1975, foreign capital controlled an estimated 70 percent of mining and manufacturng activity.[37]

Transnational corporations shipped more capital into Southern Rhodesia, officially, than they took out every year between UDI and 1976, except in 1966 and 1972. Capital imports totalled about Rh$400 million, with Rh$102 million in 1975 and Rh$26 million in 1976. Investment income leaving the country officially totalled Rh$300 million.[38] Real profits of foreign firms were greater, but much of their income remained in the country or was shipped out in concealed form.

South Africa constituted the primary source of capital and international trade links for Southern Rhodesia. South African capital grew more important after UDI. By the mid-'70s, it was estimated that South African investment there totalled £200 million (roughly double the 1963 figure), out of total foreign investments of £500-£600 million.[39] South African companies controlled at least five of the top ten industrial companies in Southern Rhodesia.

Trade between South Africa and Southern Rhodesia reflected the essentially neo-colonial relationship that persisted between the two countries. Southern Rhodesia exported to South Africa mostly crude agricultural and mineral products, and a few light manufactures, mostly apparel and radios, assembled by low-cost labor from imported parts. It imported manufactured goods, particularly machinery and petroleum. South Africa re-exported about half the crude products it imported from Southern Rhodesia, processing some of them first.

The mining finance houses were the largest South African investors in Southern Rhodesia. As elsewhere in the region, these companies typically invested in cooperation with each other, South African para-statals, and/or foreign transnational corporations. The Southern Rhodesian subsidiary of Anglo-American, Amrho, held listed investments worth Rh$26.4 million at market value in 1977, and unlisted shares worth Rh$31.8 million at book value. Anglo had invested extensively in both mining and agriculture, as well as holding major financial and manufacturing interests. Its chairman, Oppenheimer, sat on the board of Barclays Bank International; Barclays' Southern Rhodesian subsidiary was one of the two largest banks in the country. Anglo was probably the largest single foreign investor in Southern Rhodesia.

Virtually all significant investments not made by or in cooperation with South African interests were controlled by British and U.S. firms, usually through South African subsidiaries. Officially, the book value of British investments[40] in 1974 (the latest official figures) totalled £114 million, more than double the 1965 figure of £62 million, and almost 15 percent of total British investment in Africa outside South Africa. Figures for British holdings in agriculture and finance were not given, but the major investors in both sectors were British transnational corporations and banks. About £17 million was invested in trade; and about £10 million in mining and quarrying. The largest share of reported investments—£66 million—was in manufacturing: £9 million each in food, drink and tobacco, chemicals, and metal manufacturing. Thus manufacturing made up almost 60 percent of reported British investments in Southern Rhodesia, compared to about 35 percent in the rest of Africa, outside South Africa. British investment in Southern Rhodesian manufacturing was exceeded in absolute terms only by that in Nigeria, a country with a populaton over ten times as large, and South Africa.

The U.S. did not publish data on investments in Southern Rhodesia, although these apparently grew rapidly after 1960. Despite occasional rhetorical statements, the U.S. government did not enforce sanctions very carefully. Between 1971 and '77, the Byrd Amendment permitted the import of chrome from Southern Rhodesia. In 1977-78, it was reported that U.S. oil companies were supplying the Southern Rhodesian regime and that a number of U.S.-made aircraft had found their way to the regime's military. It is difficult, however, to trace exactly the roles of many U.S. transnationals, as they invested in Southern Rhodesia through South African subsidiaries, often held in turn through Canadian and British affiliates. Two of Southern Rhodesia's four largest banks were subsidiaries of British transnational banks with strong U.S. associations.

F.R.G. investments in southern Africa mushroomed in the late '60s and early '70s. Virtually all investments by F.R.G. transnationals in Southern Rhodesia were made via subsidiaries in South Africa, by far the largest area of F.R.G. investment on the continent. Throughout southern Africa, F.R.G. firms concentrated on manufacturing, especially machinery and chemicals, as they apparently could not compete with the more established British, U.S. and South African interests in mining, trade and agriculture. Almost every F.R.G. transnational involved in chemicals, electronic equipment and auto production maintained representation in Salisbury. Reportedly, they supplied primarily fertilizers, pharmaceuticals, capital equipment, autos and tractors—products with important military applications. The most important F.R.G. purchases from Southern Rhodesia were tobacco, asbestos, chrome, graphite and tea. [41] The F.R.G. government refused to prosecute sanctions breaking very vigorously, particularly when perpetrated by the South African subsidiaries of F.R.G. firms. [42]

In contrast to Britain, the U.S. and the F.R.G., the Japanese government dealt most circumspectly with the white-minority regimes in southern Africa. It barred Japanese firms from investing in South Africa, limiting their opportunities for involvement in Southern Rhodesia. U.N. reports indicated, however, that some of the raw materials obtained by Japanese companies from South Africa under long-term contracts might have originated in Southern Rhodesia. [43]

Transnational Corporate Finance

The full extent of transnational banks' domination of finance remained difficult to discover, in Southern Rhodesia as elsewhere. It was clearly the key link in transnational corporate expropriation of the country's wealth. Black wages were relatively higher in this field, but this was unimportant: profits depended on extracting surpluses from other sectors, and black finance workers constituted less than one half of 1 percent of all black employees. Far more significant, virtually every commercial bank in Southern Rhodesia, as in all southern Africa (with the partial exception of South Africa), was controlled by transnational corporate interests. They made possible the expansion of other sectors by local entrepreneurs and foreign investors, profiting indirectly from interest, commissions and fees. In agriculture, for instance, most white farmers depended on banks for credit and access to export markets. Transnational banks control of finance facilitated transnational domination of trade and the mining industry, and opened the doors for transnational corporate investment in agro-business and manufacturing industries. Simultaneously, the banks provided critical external linkages and pipelines for hard currency for the beleaguered minority regime.

The dominant banks in Southern Rhodesia were the imperial British banks, mostly established there since long before UDI. In the 1960s and '70s, the largest U.S. banks established linkages to the British parent banks, giving them entree to their networks in Southern Rhodesia and throughout the Commonwealth.

The British bank, Barclays, had 37 branches and 50 fixed and mobile agencies in Southern Rhodesia in 1974. Barclays' Rhodesian affiliate advertized[44] that—sanctions or no sanctions—

Barclays today has more than 5000 offices throughout the world and stresses as part of its services its strong internationalism. It operates from the Salisbury office a business and trade promotion division . . .

The parent bank was linked to the Bank of America, the largest U.S. bank, through the Societe Financiere Europeene, a consortium bank.

The Standard Bank of Rhodesia, the second largest bank there, reported assets at the end of 1973 of over Rh$200 million, up 130 percent from 1965. It owned 44 branches and a network of static and mobile agencies throughout the country. A member of the Standard group, the Rhodesian Insurance Bankers, provided general, life and export and domestic credit insurance. Another group member, Standard Financial, offered long-term finance, hire-purchase credit and leasing facilities for industry. By 1975, the bank had acquired 12.6 percent in the Export Credit Corporation of Rhodesia, an affiliate of the parastatal, the IDC of Rhodesia. Standard built 11 new branches and increased its staff by 20 percent between UDI and 1974.[45]

The National Grindlays Bank, the newest and smallest bank in Southern Rhodesia, owned assets at the end of 1973 of Rh$35.5 million. Grindlays, the parent bank, is owned 49 percent by the second largest U.S. bank, Citicorp, and 41 percent by the U.K. bank, Lloyds. A subsidiary took over the Ottoman Bank in Southern Rhodesia three years after UDI, and opened a finance house two years later.

The third largest bank in Southern Rhodesia, Rhobank, had assets at the end of 1973 of Rh$74 million. It was the only bank with significant local involvement—Southern Rhodesian interests owned 30 percent. The South African bank, Nedsual, which is associated with Anglo-American, owned the remaining two-thirds of equity. Rhobank was particularly involved in financing the tobacco trade. Neficrho, Rhobank's merchant bank, assisted Southern Rhodesian firms to obtain export and import finance and foreign exchange, presumably through the parent company's South African links.

The British bank, Hill Samuel, in which the U.S. bank Citicorp also owned shares, had five subsidiaries in Southern Rhodesia, held through its South African subsidiary, Hilsam. The United Dominions Trust, a major British trading finance firm, retained its interest in the financial institution, UDC Ltd., through its South African affiliate of that name.

Transnational banks based in the F.R.G., U.S. and Switzerland entered into wholesale operations in South Africa, but it remained impossible to gather information on the extent to which they helped arrange international credits for Southern Rhodesia. On June 30, 1976 the Southern Rhodesian regime reported external debts of Rh$77 million, about 85 percent of which were raised through "registered stock issues in London." There is virtually no data on the individual banks involved in these transactions, however.

Agribusiness

At the time of UDI, despite the growth of manufacturing during Federation, agricultural production remained Southern Rhodesia's main source of exports, its economic backbone. As elsewhere in Africa, the transnational corporations owned some plantations and processing facilities, but established a virtual monopoly over the trade in agricultural produce and inputs. After UDI, they were able to funnel this trade through their regional headquarters in South Africa. As elsewhere in Africa, they reinforced the colonial pattern of development. They provided credit and markets primarily for the large settler estates, and encouraged the production of tobacco, most of which had to be sold and processed overseas. They profited largely because of the amazingly low labor costs in Southern Rhodesian agriculture. Then, while inflation and low pay put a balanced diet out of reach for many Africans, the country exported maize and beef to South Africa and even overseas. Where the transnational corporations invested in local processing of foodstuffs, they manufactured mostly luxuries for the white population (often based on imports), beer and cigarettes.

Tobacco continued to be Southern Rhodesia's most important agricultural export after UDI, although sanctions initially cut into sales. By 1973, the Southern Rhodesian regime was able to end the payment of subsidies to white tobacco farmers that had made up for lost export markets. In 1975, exports reached 200 million pounds, mostly sold to Holland, Belgium and the F.R.G.[46] These exports had to be handled by the seven transnational corporations that, in the 1970s, controlled 90 percent of tobacco manufacturing in the western world through direct ownership and licensing. They constituted the world's "most nearly perfect oligopoly."[47]

As in so many industries, the greatest share of profit in tobacco production comes from processing. The British American Tobacco Company (BAT), which had important holdings in both Southern Rhodesia and South Africa, reportedly paid local farmers elsewhere a fourth of the price it received for the finished products (such as cigarettes) in 1978.[48] In Southern Rhodesia, the transnationals made superprofits as a result of low labor costs, paying low (secret) prices—reportedly two thirds the world tobacco price.[49] Rhobank played an especially important role in handling tobacco exports: its general manager was director of five tobacco storage and sale companies.

BAT and Rupert/Rembrandt, a South African company that owned L&M in the United States, processed tobacco for the domestic Southern Rhodesian and South African markets. Rothmans of Pall Mall, a Rembrandt subsidiary, owned a Southern Rhodesian firm that was the 15th largest manufacturing company in the country in 1974, with reported profits of Rh$1 million.

Sugar, mostly produced on large foreign-owned estates, was the largest export crop after tobacco. The three biggest estates were controlled through South Africa. The Huletts Corporation of South Africa owned five estates and derived a third of its profits from Southern Rhodesia. The Anglo-American Corporation had shares in several of these estates. The British company, Tate and Lyle, also owned an estate.

Estates also produced beef, maize and some cotton, both for local consumption and export to neighboring estates. Two British companies, Lonrho and Brook Bond Liebig, both with extensive South African interests, owned ranches of over 400,000 hectares. Liebig owned 77,000 head of cattle in 1977, as well as "thousands of hectares of orchards and vegetable farms" and related canning and distribution activities.[50]

The transnationals engaged in trade and production of agricultural products profited primarily from low labor costs. Over a third of all black wage earners in Southern Rhodesia still worked in agriculture in the late '70s. They earned wages below those in any other sector save domestic service. Permanent workers received an average of under Rh$20 a month, less in real terms than in 1948; their real take-home pay had dropped steadily in the ten years following 1963. The 28,000 contract and 93,000 casual workers—respectively about 8 and 22 percent of the agricultural labor force—earned even less than permanent workers. Apparently wives and even children of farm workers were more or less openly forced to work at peak seasons, for considerably lower pay than full-time workers.[51] A farm workers' union existed after 1964, but government and employers, including the large foreign-owned estates, fought it bitterly. It had less than a thousand paid-up members in the mid-'70s.

Agricultural workers were also stratified, but with only a tiny handful at the upper levels. In 1975, 46 percent of permanent farm workers and virtually all migrant and casual laborers earned less than Rh$10 a month. Just 0.6 percent of permanent workers were paid over Rh$70 a month. *Ten* African workers in agriculture earned over Rh$300 a month.[52]

Such wages hardly assured subsistence. Malnutrition and tuberculosis rates on the estates were probably even higher than in the TTLs. On one farm, a study[53] found that among the 57 workers' families, a total of 60 children—more than one out of five of all children born to the families—had died. Of the remaining children, over half lived with relatives in the TTLs, foreign countries or elsewhere, as their parents did not earn enough to support them on the farm. The survey showed how unemployment forced workers to accept farm employment. Only three of them had always had a job in the ten years to 1975; 54 had been unemployed for six months or less; five, for over two years.

Increasing output per employee and per dollar of wages accompanied low agricultural pay. Between 1963 and 1974, output per dollar of wages rose by 44 percent in real terms, to Rh$5.60. Profit per worker rose from about Rh$0.90 in 1966 to Rh$1.75 in 1974.[54] Nonetheless, many settler farmers were heavily in debt.

But the large foreign-owned plantations faced no obvious economic problems in the mid-'70s. A number made no bones about paying low wages. Triangle Ltd., owned by Hulletts, reported that "malnutrition will be a permanent feature of both Triangle Estates and the [nearby] Tribal Trust areas."[55] The manager of a major South African-owned tea estate said that, "What we are really aiming at in the long run is *family* participation—the wife, husband and children all working on the plantation."[56] (Anglo-American owned a small share in the estate.) In some cases, however, transnationals created a small, more stable strata of better-paid African employees in semi-skilled and skilled jobs, while using extremely poorly paid migrant labor for unskilled work. Triangle, with over 6000 employees, aimed to restrict permanent workers to "the most productive and valuable labor." It expected migrant workers to support themselves partially through ties to the local TTLs.[57]

The Mines

Cecil Rhodes and his invading gang did not discover the vast gold mines they had hoped would rival South Africa's. But Southern Rhodesia was endowed with a number of smaller mineral deposits. With agriculture, mining provided the nation's primary source of foreign exchange earnings. Historically, Southern Rhodesia boasted a higher degree of exploration than most of independent Africa, however, suggesting that the white-minority regime's claim to control a very large share of the world's mineral resources might be exaggerated. Aided by transnational corporations, mining output expanded greatly after UDI. Nickel production, for instance, climbed from 780 tons in 1965 to over 15,000 tons a year in the mid-'70s.

As usual in southern Africa, a partnership between South Africa mining finance houses and British and U.S. capital, with frequent South African or Southern Rhodesian state participation, employed low-paid African miners to dig out copper, lead, chrome, asbestos, gold and other metals and precious stones. Besides holding down wages to guarantee profits, the regime gave direct financial and technical support to mining companies, as a primary source of foreign exchange.

Some 57,000 Africans worked on the mines in Southern Rhodesia in 1977, earning an average of Rh$55 a month. Their real wages had dropped 16 percent between 1959 and 1974. In 1975, the average real wage rose slightly, from Rh$20 to Rh$27 in 1965 dollars, but part of this increase reflected the promotion of a tiny group of black workers to "white" jobs. About 60 percent still earned less than Rh$30 a month; about a third of these were employed by the smaller, locally owned mines.[58] African miners earned even less in Southern Rhodesia than in South Africa.

The Anglo-American Corporation operated the most extensive mining and refining properties in Southern Rhodesia, including a ferro-chrome smelter (one of three in the country) and the largest coal and nickel producers. An affiliate, Messina (Transvaal) Development, owned seven copper mines and a refinery.

Table 11-5.

Anglo-American Mining Operations in Southern Rhodesia

Southern Rhodesian Company	Activities
Wankie	Coal mining—largest producer in Southern Rhodesia; a plant produces coke and gas. Spent Rh$40 million on modernization and to double output of coke in 1971-76. 1978 profits—Rh$2.6 million.
Rhodesian Nickel	Operates a mine in Bindura, Filabusi and Shamva Districts. Together with Johannesburg Consolidated Investments, a mining finance house in which Anglo owns 41% opened Shangani mine in 1976.
Bindura Smelting & Refining	Smelted and refined ores from Rhodesian Nickel/JCI mines. Annual output in mid-'70s—c. 5000 tons of 99.95% nickel cathodes. Produced copper as a by-product.
Messina (Tvl.) Dev. Corp. Rhodesian Alloys	Controlled by Anglo with another mining finance house, Anglovaal. Owned seven mines in Southern Rhodesia, with combined output of C. 30,000 tonnes a year. Processed output at Alaska smelter, near Sinoia. Operates a ferroshrome smelter at Gwelo.
Iron Duke	Produces pyrites at an iron mine near Mazoe, which are used to make sulphuric acids for smelters and in fertilizers.
Dorowa (affiliate)	Owned by AECI, in which De Beers, a member of the Anglo-American Group, owned 42½ percent; ICI (U.K.) owned 42½ percent. Mined apetite for phosphates, which were processed into super-phosphates for fertilizers.

Transnational mining companies from the U.S. and Britain were also deeply involved in exploiting Southern Rhodesia's mineral wealth. Most had extensive interests in South Africa, Namibia and other southern African countries. The U.S. company, Union Carbide, mined and smelted chrome in Southern Rhodesia; it had extensive refining facilities in South Africa. It had strongly lobbied the U.S. Congress to pass the Byrd Amendment (1971-77), permitting the shipment of chrome to the U.S. in violation of U.N. sanctions. The narrow veins in Union Carbide's Southern Rhodesian mines could only be mined profitably with low labor costs. In 1977, the mines were reported closed when exports to the U.S. were cut off. Falconbridge, a Canadian subsidiary of the U.S. firm, Superior Oil, owned shares in a nickel mine and operated a gold mine, in cooperation with the parastatal, IDC. It produced about half a ton of bullion annually in the mid-'70s.

Rio Tinto Zinc, one of the largest U.K. mining transnationals, with major interests throughout southern Africa, operated two nickel mines and a smelter, refinery and cobalt recovery plant in southern Rhodesia. It produced about 3500 tons of refined nickel a year in the mid-'70s.

Another British firm, Lonrho, which originated in Southern Rhodesia, was the country's largest gold producer (2.3 tons a year). A subsidiary ran two mines and a refinery producing about 6000 tons of copper a year, as well as some gold and silver, in the mid-'70s.

Oil

Southern Rhodesia had no known petroleum deposits, although it possessed extensive coal reserves. Effective sanctions on oil could have brought down the white-minority regime. Lack of oil would have crippled the Rhodesian military, which required high mobility to make up for the lack of manpower. The transnational oil majors had established extensive refining capacity in South Africa,* enabling them to evade the OPEC boycott and ship the needed supplies to the Rhodesian regime. Even after Iran stopped oil sales to South Africa in 1979, supplies merely became more problematic and expensive; they were not stopped.[59] See Chapter 8 above.

Until 1976-77, at least, Mobil, Caltex and Shell-B.P. sold oil through a series of bogus intermediary companies to avoid direct shipment to Southern Rhodesia. Mobil documents referred to a "carefully planned 'paper-chase'. . .to disguise the final destination of these products . . .primarily to hide the fact that Mobil South Africa is in fact supplying Mobil Southern Rhodesia with products in contravention of U.S. sanctions regulations."[60]* The South African subsidiaries of British Petroleum, owned by the U.K. government, and Shell had a similar arrangement. They swapped oil with the French parastatal, Total in South Africa, which shipped it direct to Southern Rhodesia.

After 1978, the South African parastatal, SASOL, apparently supplied all the petroleum needs of the Rhodesian regime. It purchased oil from the refineries established by the oil majors in South Africa. As in other industries, the U.S. and British oil firms aimed merely to conceal sales across Southern Rhodesia's borders. All retained ties to subsidiaries, openly distributing their products throughout the country, with their home governments' tacit approval.

In the last week of 1978, freedom fighters fired rockets into the major petroleum storage area in Salisbury, burning 22 of the 28 major tanks, or about 17 million gallons of gas and aviation fuel. The area was owned by B.P. and Shell; Caltex and Mobil also stored oil there. Smith called it "one of our biggest setbacks since the terrorist [sic] war began."[62]

---

*In 1979, it was also reported that Mobil was selling oil via the Ivory Coast to Southern Rhodesia. Mobil denied the report.

The Manufacturing Boom

Southern Rhodesia's manufacturing output more than doubled in the ten years to 1974. It grew most after 1968, expanding at a faster pace than the rest of the economy. Extensive state support and transnational corporate involvement enabled manufacturing firms to circumvent sanctions. Nevertheless, they remained, for the most part, "backyard companies producing import substitutes."[63] The rapid growth in manufacturing both reflected and contributed to the contradictions inherent in the country's political economy. The illegal regime attracted investments, oppressing the population so as to guarantee a cheap, "disciplined" labor force—which made it dependent on South Africa and the transnational corporations for its continued survival.

As output expanded between 1965 and 1974, employment in manufacturing rose from 10.5 to 14.5 percent of the wage labor force. But output per worker grew even faster, jumping 70 percent in the same period. The transnationals introduced the capital-intensive tech nologies needed to profit from production of luxuries for high-income whites, potential exports and military equipment. Although wages in manufacturing were higher than in mining and agriculture, they remained lower than in South Africa. They averaged Rh$78.50 a month in 1977, below the Poverty Datum Line and a bare seventh of the average wage for white workers.

Use of advanced technologies in Southern Rhodesia's narrow market led to a high degree of concentration, which strengthened the hold of the transnational corporations. In 1968, only one company, often affiliated to a transnational, produced almost 70 percent of each industrial product. The result was apparently "high entrepreneurial returns, high prices and poor quality."[64]

In these conditions, manufacturing remained critically dependent on transnational corporate involvement. Most intermediate and invest ment goods were still imported, primarily through the South African affiliates of transnational corporations. Although a third of manufacturing output consisted of metal products and machinery, about half this figure represented production of crude metals, largely for export, rather than capital equipment or inputs for domestic manufacturing. Instead of spreading to the countryside to provide employment throughout the nation, manufacturing remained concentrated in Salisbury and Bulawayo, where three quarters of all industry was located.

British firms, which remained predominant, set the typical pattern.* They invested heavily in production of food, drink and tobacco; chemi-

---

*Britain is almost unique in publishing figures on its investments in Southern Rhodesia, presumably because of its historic ties with that country.

cals; and electrical and non-electrical machinery (about 9 million in each industry). These investments were significantly greater than in most independent African states, where all British investment in manufacturing, combined, came to only about 300 million. (On the other hand, they were insignificant compared to the capital poured into South African manufacturing in the same period.)

A brief industry-by-industry summary reveals some of the structural problems that plagued Southern Rhodesian manufacturing. Although more advanced than in most independent African countries, it remained reliant on the basic industries transnational corporate investments had built up in South Africa; and it was hardly oriented towards filling the needs of the majority of the population.

In Southern Rhodesia, unlike South Africa, foreign capital played an important role in light industry. To a large extent, this reflected the continuing importance of transnationals in agro-business. In Southern Rhodesia, they produced primarily for the luxury market. They clearly did not go out of their way to make available inexpensive staple foods needed by low-income Africans. Reflecting this orientation, the food industry appeared to be one of the most capital-intensive in the country.[65]

Rhodesian Breweries, an affiliate of South African Breweries (linked to Anglo), produced beer and food. It was one of the ten largest Southern Rhodesian firms. Coca-Cola and Schweppes were bottled and distributed throughout the country. Lever Brothers, associated with the transnational trading corporation, Unilever, manufactured and sold detergents, soaps and cheeses. A Nestles affiliate sold tinned milk, baby foods and instant drinks. Other companies with agricultural estates—including Liebig, Rothmans, Tate & Lyle and BAT—processed and sold locally a tiny fraction of their output, and imported related consumer goods.

The Southern Rhodesian state intensified its intervention after UDI to stimulate greater development of more basic industry. Inevitably, however, it remained heavily dependent on transnational corporations, especially those based in South Africa which collaborated extensively with mining finance houses and parastatals there.

In 1977-78, 250,000 tons of raw iron and 150,000 tons of raw steel were produced in Southern Rhodesia.[66] Output of metals stood at much more than twice 1964 levels, although it had dropped after 1975. The largest producer, by far, was Risco, a parastatal in which the British public corporation, British Steel, owned about a third. Risco's iron-and-steel complex, near QueQue, used about a million tons of iron ore annually. The huge South African iron-and-steel parastatal, ISCOR, established a subsidiary to distribute its own products and those of several other firms, and collaborated extensively with RISCO.

In the early 1970s, RISCO greatly expanded its production. It had to import machinery and equipment, requiring a large amount of foreign exchange. In 1974, reports smuggled out of Southern Rhodesia revealed a plan to arrange the necessary capital and export markets through several transnational corporations and banks. Two international consortium banks, the European Banking International Company (EBIC) and the associated European-American Banking Corporation (EABC) planned to organize a multi-million loan, guaranteed by a group of Rhodesian banks, including the local subsidiaries of Barclays and Standard. EBIC was formed by the Deutsche Bank (F.R.G.); Midlands (U.K.); the Societe General de Banque (Belgium); and the Societe Generale (France), among others. It was to participate through its representative office in South Africa, its only one on the continent, which specialized in wholesale banking. The loan was to be funnelled through Switzerland, which is not a U.N. member and did not enforce sanctions. Voest, the Austrian parastatal, agreed to supply 8 million, help design the plant, and supply patented oxygen-blast furnaces. (Voest had similarly helped ISCOR to expand its South African facilities.) Klöckner and Neunkirchner of the F.R.G. agreed to buy 100,000 tons of Southern Rhodesian steel in 1973-74, and 400,000 tons annually thereafter. The steel would be routed through Switzerland.[67] Although international publicity disrupted the plans, capital investment in steel production in Southern Rhodesia reportedly climbed dramatically in the early '70s, suggesting partial implementation.

By 1976, Southern Rhodesia production of chemicals and petrochemicals had risen 90 percent about 1964 levels. Although it stagnated over the next two years, it reportedly rose again, slightly, in 1978.[68] But the tiny Southern Rhodesian market could not support the huge economies of scale required for profitable production of most basic chemicals. The industry remained dominated by transnational corporations operating through their South African subsidiaries. For local consumption they produced only fertilizers and explosives for the white-owned estates and mines. Most African farms were too small and poor to purchase sufficient chemical fertilizers or insecticides; nor, unlike the white estates, could they normally obtain credits from private banks or the state.

The largest chemicals group in Southern Rhodesia was owned by AECI, the South African affiliate of the British Imperial Chemicals Industries (ICI) in collaboration with De Beers. One AECI subsidiary met almost the entire Southern Rhodesian demand for superphosphate

fertilizers, utilizing phosphates mined by a subsidiary. It also manufactured crop chemicals. Other subsidiaries sold explosives and blast-
ing accessories, industrial chemicals, acrylic sheet, polyethylene,
PVC and vinyl products, apparently mostly produced in South Africa.

Although fertilizers were needed throughout the southern African
region, and despite its network of subsidiaries and affiliates there, ICI
did not set up major fertilizer production outside Southern Rhodesia
and South Africa. As a result, Zambia had to partially open its border to
Southern Rhodesia (which had been closed in 1973) primarily to obtain
fertilizers in 1978.*

Virtually all the other transnational chemical corporations operated
from a base in South Africa. Most were involved primarily in distribution of products manufactured either in South Africa or overseas.

The Southern Rhodesian affiliates of Dunlop (U.K.) and Goodyear
(U.S.) both sold tires and other rubber products, manufactured in their
South African plants and overseas. Goodyear manufactured tires in
Southern Rhodesia, using imported rubber. Tire production directly
assisted the regime's military in its attempt to maintain the greatest
possible mobility.

British data on investment suggests a high degree of transnational
corporate investment in Southern Rhodesia's electrical industry. Most
was limited to assembly and distribution of imported parts and equipment. Many electrical appliances have military applications, and
helped the regime to reduce its labor needs.

The U.S. company, International Telephone and Telegraph (ITT) got
involved in Southern Rhodesia through its South African subsidiary. It
retained ties to the Supersonic Radio Manufacturing Company of
Rhodesia, which produced radios, record players and television sets at
Bulawayo for sale in Southern Rhodesia, South Africa and Namibia.[69]
An affiliate of the Dutch transnational, Philips (which owned several
plants in South Africa) assembled radios and televisions for domestic
sale from imported parts.

Other transnational subsidiaries merely distributed imported products, mostly through their South African subsidiaries. An official of
AEG, one of the largest F.R.G. electrical firms, pointed out that, "We,
too, cannot ship directly to Salisbury, but we can supply Johannesburg.
And then the people in Johannesburg do what they think best."[70]
Another of the largest F.R.G. electronics firms, Siemens, had an office
in Salisbury and reportedly shipped telephone equipment to the tele-

---

*It is noteworthy that most fertilizer demand came from the huge "line-of-rail" maize
estates in Zambia, owned with few exceptions by British, South African and Southern
Rhodesian settlers—who presumably lobbied for this solution.

Table 11-6.
Transnational Corporate Investments in Southern Rhodesian
Chemicals Industry

Home country	Parent firm	Activities in Southern Rhodesia
U.K.	ICI	Owned 42½% of AECI, one of the two largest South African chemicals firms (De Beers also owns 42½%). AECI has a plant and widespread distribution network in S.R. Owned ICI South Africa, which distributed plastics, industrial and mining chemicals, medical and veterinary products and dyes in S.R.
	Shell Chemicals	Sales in S.R. (Shell has a major refinery in South Africa, and was implicated in illegal sales of petroleum to S.R.)
	British Oxyegn	Sales of chemicals in S.R. A major subsidiary in South Africa, Afrox, holds its subsidiaries throughout southern Africa.
F.R.G.	Hoechst	One of the three largest chemicals firms in the F.R.G. Distributes chemical dyes, plastics, mining and agricultural chemicals and pharmeceuticals, apparently produced in part by its South African subsidiary (its largest in Africa).
	Bayer	One of the three largest chemical firms in the F.R.G.; had a distribution office in Salisbury, and an affiliate, Bayer Agro-Chem. (In South Africa, produced insecticides, some of which could be used as nerve gases.)
	BASF	One of the three largest chemicals firms in the F.R.G.; had a distribution office in Salisbury. (Its largest African subsidiary was in South Africa.)
U.S.	Johnson & Johnson Cheeseborough Ponds Colgate Palmolive	Distribution agencies in S.R. All have larger South African subsidiaries.

phone office in Bulawayo from Munich, via Johannesburg. AEG and Siemens number among the largest investors in South Africa, where they produced basic electrical equipment, much of it used by the military.[71]

The British General Electric Company's South African subsidiary owned a Southern Rhodesian agency (the General Electric Company Rhodesia), which sold industrial and mining fans, washing machines, switch boards, motor control gear, electrical distribution equipment and light fittings. A number of other electrical transnationals, including Bosch (F.R.G.) and Sharp (Japan) also maintained distribution agencies.

Almost all the largest automobile companies had major facilities in South Africa. They evidently traded extensively with Southern Rhodesia, but details were hard to come by. They concentrated on assembly and sale of private autos, a luxury in the African context. The regime's army also relied on motor vehicles to offset manpower problems created by its minority position.

Datsun-Nissan reportedly sent unassembled auto kits to Southern Rhodesia via Mozambique before 1974. The deal was camouflaged in normal shipments through Mozambique of unassembled Datsuns for sale in South Africa. In Southern Rhodesia, the kits were put together at the Ford and BMC plants in Salisbury and Umtali. It is not clear if Ford and BMC autos were also assembled, although Ford could have produced knock-down kits in its large South African plant. Toyota and Peugeot, both with South African operations, reportedly assembled their models in Southern Rhodesia[72] (a procedure presumably simplified after Anglo took over Peugeot's South African operations, continuing to produce its models). Furthermore, British Leyland, controlled by the British government and with a large South African plant, distributed trucks in Southern Rhodesia through an affiliate. V.W., associated with the F.R.G. government and also with large South African investments, had an office in Salisbury.

The Consequences

The spurt of economic growth in peripheral Southern Rhodesia after UDI was severely limited by fundamental contradictions. Only the handful of white settlers and transnational corporate investors benefited significantly. Transnationals operating from their South African headquarters continued to reap profits from their control of finance and trade. Mining and agriculture remained dependent on export markets and foreign inputs, both subject to sanctions. Manufacturing aimed at the luxury white market, the military and export—although the hoped-for foreign markets never opened up. This orientation, and the dependence on transnational corporations, led to growing capital-intensity despite high unemployment.

By the mid-'70s, the contradictions inherent in this pattern of growth could no longer be glossed over. They were aggravated by and contributed to the general crisis, that spread from the developed capitalist countries to settle on southern Africa. For most blacks, excluded from political power, conditions steadily worsened. Wages, in real terms, stagnated or even fell. Overcrowding, hunger and disease spread through the TTLs.

Manufacturing displayed the greatest problems. The domestic market was small, particularly given abysmal wages for the African majority and relatively capital-intensive techniques with large economies of scale. As a result, import-substitution potential was exhausted by 1975.[73] But abhorrence for white-minority rule closed most foreign markets. Moreover, in the late '70s South Africa insisted on a new trade agreement to protect its own manufactures as international markets stagnated. Deteriorating equipment further reduced competitiveness, as lack of foreign exchange and sanctions blocked the import of machinery and spare parts. When available, these were often of poor quality. After 1975, only the textile industry found substantial export markets (mostly in Europe), because "Rhodesia [counted] in the internatonal textile industry as a cheap-labor country, right behind South Korea and Taiwan."[74] In 1978, textiles also succumbed: production fell 4 percent that year.

Between 1975 and '77, the GDP dropped 6 percent; but manufacturing output decreased yet more rapidly. Military demand became ever more important. Most of the surviving manufacturers were "related to the arms industry."[75] The regime predicted a further drop of 7 percent in the GDP in 1979.

As the crisis spread, African employment fell by 33,000, almost 4 percent in the years 1974-77. A further decline was officially predicted for 1978. Thousands of Southern Rhodesian workers migrated to South African mines to escape unemployment. In 1976, the South African mines recruited 30,000, but new laws and lower South African demand reduced the number the following year. A 1974 survey of 100 contractees found 93 were unemployed when recruited; 22 had been jobless for two years or more. Almost all would have preferred manufacturing jobs in Southern Rhodesia, but only six would accept agricultural work and less than half mining jobs there, because of low wages. The South African mining companies paid the migrants Rh$1.63 a shift, "well in excess of rates on most Rhodesian mines"[76]—although the same South African companies, Anglo, JCI, and so on—ran the largest mines in both countries.

The greatest weakness in the "development" fostered by trans national corporate investment in Southern Rhodesia was precisely its foundation: the exclusion of the majority of the population, the Africans, from participation except as low-cost labor. They never accepted minority rule without resisting. After the first armed struggle against colonialism was defeated, other forms of organization—primarily political parties and trade unions—developed. The draconian measures introduced to try to destroy them indicated the resistance movement's strength. The modern armed struggle began in the 1960s. Cooperation with Pretoria and transnational corporations guaranteed the illegal regime the arms and war material it needed to oppose, in the short run, the popular revolution. But the weakness of white-minority rule became more and more obvious. After Mozambique won independence, even the most ardent backers of white-minority rule could recognize the end.

The spreading war for liberation had far-reaching economic consequences for the white-minority regime. In early 1979, it spent about R1 million a day on the war,[77] although the South African regime apparently met most of the bill. Military-related expenditures rose from 31 percent of the budget in 1973-74 to 45 percent in 1977-78, while gross fixed capital formation dropped from 24 to 18 percent of GDP in 1974-76.[78] Net white emigration climbed steadily to 14,000 in 1978; that is, in that year alone, one in 15 whites left the country. This outflow had major political implications, as well as reducing the supply of white skilled workers for the army and industry.

The black population suffered the minority regime's vengeance. Hundreds were detained, jailed or executed. By 1978, martial law ruled more than nine-tenths of the country. The regime's collective punishments for Africans in the rural areas, affecting over a million people by 1978, included: confiscation of all property, including cash; confiscation of cattle; and destruction of villages, including food reserves, wells and fields. The result in some areas was starvation.[79] Between 1974 and 1978, almost a million Africans were forced into "protected" villages that resembled concentration camps. They were overcrowded and lacked adequate housing, sanitary arrangements and food. Frequently residents were prevented from caring for fields and cattle.[80] By 1979, the regime had closed 949 schools and 124 clinics in the rural areas.[81] Its forces wantonly tortured and killed hundreds of black civilians and a few progressive whites.

Not surprisingly, many Africans fled the country. The total number of Zimbabwean refugees in Botswana, Mozambique and Zambia reached about 150,000 in 1979; Botswana alone reported that 100 arrived daily.[82] Many planned to join the freedom fighters and return to liberate their country.

Transnational corporate investors finally began to get nervous; "Ever more enterprises try to transfer their business to neighboring South Africa, or, through dangerous transactions, to get invested capital overseas."[83] Groups of industrialists began to pressure the regime for reforms, hoping to limit their losses from the war while avoiding the fundamental political-economic change promised by the liberation forces.[84] The political charade led to a so-called "internal settlement," replacing outright white-minority rule by a government in which a tiny group of favored blacks cooperated with the white landowners and industrialists in a desperate attempt to stave off real change.

The transnational corporations and their white allies attempted to impose a parallel economic model, similar to that introduced in many other British colonies at independence. They sought to build on existing inequalities in order to entrench a tiny black elite as allies. As early as 1977, "reforms" nominally allowed Africans to buy land in white rural areas. But white estates were prohibitively expensive; between March 1977, when the new law was passed, and October 1977, Africans had purchased exactly two white farms. *

As in Kenya, several transnationals sought to establish agricultural programs directly involving a few black farmers. In 1979, Dunlop, a British rubber company with extensive South African holdings, reportedly began to collaborate with Tilcor, a Southern Rhodesian parastatal, to establish rubber plantations in the TTLs. The scheme aimed to assist black farmers to grow rubber, with state participation to create the necessary infrastructure and marketing arrangements. Analogously, transnational corporations in other sectors hired a few black managers and skilled workers. They apparently hoped to convince local and foreign critics their hiring policies were no longer racist, as well as to strengthen the black middle class to defend the status quo. In addition, the emigration and drafting of whites after 1974 had drained off skilled workers, making promotion of blacks a necessity.

Behind the facade of non-racialism, many firms found it possible to cut their wage bills. In 1975, 613 jobs that blacks had taken over from whites since 1974 were surveyed: wages had fallen in 49 percent of them. [85] Transnationals could pay skilled black workers less than white Rhodesians—and a tiny fraction of wages in the U.S., Europe or Japan. They still employed most blacks in unskilled, poorly paid jobs, with only a handful being promoted to executive posts. The overwhelming majority of managers remained white.

A few black faces in government, without fundamental political-economic change, would lead to only minor wage increases and ensure that long-term control was maintained. The migrant labor system would survive, and wages would remain a fraction of those transnationals had to pay in the core capitalist countries. The corporations hoped sanctions would be lifted and markets opened up in the neighboring countries. The U.S., Britain and the F.R.G. espoused this view, demanding the

---

*The decision on desegregating land in the urban areas was left up to the (all-white) city councils.

abolition of (most) legal racism while protecting the interests of foreign investors.* Even South Africa's white-minority regime began to take this position, at least part of the time. But many white settlers resisted it, apparently fearing increased African competition, above all, and greater labor costs.

Summary and Conclusions

The short-lived economic spurt enjoyed by the white minority in Southern Rhodesia contained fundamental contradictions, rooted in the very factors that led to increased transnational corporate investment. A tiny number of whites grew immensely wealthy, while the living conditions of the vast majority of Africans degenerated to starvation levels. Transnational corporate investments aggravated these problems. To maximize their profits, the companies maintained low wages for blacks and directed production to the white luxury, export and military markets. On the one hand, this orientation resulted in increased capital intensity and still greater unemployment and regional disparities within the country. On the other hand, it meant growing overproduction and falling output.

But the main threat to the system was popular resistance: the liberation movement fought for real independence, with the basic political-economic changes needed to ensure that economic growth would raise living standards and employment levels, benefiting the people, not just of Zimbabwe itself, but of the entire southern African region. These factors culminated in the military-economic crisis which confronted the white-minority regime in the late '70s, a crisis that reflected the growing insecurity of foreign domination and white-minority rule throughout the African continent.

***

This book was already in press when the ZANU-PF forces—much to the surprise of western commentators (blinded by their own bounded rationality!)—won an overwhelming victory in the British-sponsored elections. The Patriotic Front, ZANU and ZAPU, together controlled 77 of the 80 black seats in the new government, led by Robert Mugabe.

*In 1977, for instance, Anthony Crosland, then British foreign secretary, remarked that Smith's rejection of the Anglo-American proposals would lead to "chaos and Marxist rule."[86]

This chapter has exposed the extent to which in Zimbabwe, as in South Africa itself, the (white) minority in collaboration with transnational corporations, employed racism to mask its use of state power to shape a political economic structure to squeeze the last penny of profit out of the vast majority of the (black) population. Simply to incorporate a few blacks into the ruling circles would not alter the fundamental conditions impoverishing the people. As both wings of the Patriotic Front had emphasized throughout the years of their armed struggle, full liberation required the complete reconstruction of the national political economy to enable the peasants and wage earners—employed and unemployed—to share in the ownership and development of the means of production for the benefit of all. The experience of Zimbabwe's neighbors illustrates that numerous obstacles, political and economic, strew the path to attainment of this goal. Nevertheless, the new Patriotic Front government, for the first time, confronted the opportunity of achieving it.

More than that: The Patriotic Front victory, consolidated through years of guerilla struggle supported by the Front Line States, created an exciting potential for a new realignment in southern Africa: the possibility that the independent states might join together to end their political economic dependence on South Africa's minority regime and its transnational corporate allies. Together, they could sieze the opportunity to create the necessary new regional, as well as national, institutional structures to carry through an industrial transformation to provide productive employment opportunities and higher living standards for all the inhabitants of the southern third of the continent.

The remaining chapters of this book, drawing on the experiences of Zimbabwe's neighbors as well as those of the rest of independent Africa, seeks to address the problems and possibilities of realizing this perspective.

References

1. Duncan Clarke, *Contract Workers and Underdevelopment in Rhodesia* (Gwelo: Mambo Press, 1974), p. 7.

2. See Robin Palmer and Q. Neil Parsons, *The Roots of Rural Poverty in Southern Africa* (London: Heinemann, 1972), and Robin Palmer, *Land and Racial Domination in Rhodesia* (Berkeley: University of California, 1977).

3. Roger C. Riddell, *The Land Problem in Rhodesia* (Gwelo: Mambo Press, 1978); see also, Palmer, *op. cit.*

4. See Robert Seidman, *The State, Law and Development* (New York: St. Martins Press, 1978), 83ff.

5. Clarke, *op. cit.*, p. 5. fn.

6. *Ibid.*, p. 13.

7. Zdenek Cervenka, "Rhodesia (Zimbabwe)," in Dieter Nohlen and Franz Nascheler (eds.), *Handbuch der dritten Welt*, Vol. II, Pt. II (Hamburg: Hoffman und Campe Verlag, 1976), pp. 650-60.

8. Richard Sklar, *Corporate Power in an African State* (Berkeley: University of California, 1975), p. 16.

9. This sort of mentality was illustrated by an article in *The New York Times* on September 22, 1979, by John Burns. He reported that whites in Southern Rhodesia felt they could defeat the liberation movement for no reason save that the guerrillas were black—and apparently Burns considered this plausible.

10. Rhodesian Ministry of Finance, *An Economic Survey of Rhodesia, 1977* (Salisbury: Government Printers, July 1978), p. 8.

11. *The New York Times*, November 20, 1976.

12. *Tagesspiegel* (West Berlin), December 15, 1978.

13. A.M.M. Hoogvelt and D. Child, "Economic Blockade and Development," *Monthly Review*, Vol. 25, No. 5, Oct. 1973.

14. *Frankfurter Rundschau*, December 15, 1978.

15. IDC of Rhodesia (Salisbury), Annual Report and Accounts for 1974, p. 3.

16. IDC of Rhodesia (Salisbury), Annual Report and Accounts for 1978.

17. Riddell, *op. cit.*, pp. 48-50; see also Clarke, *op. cit.*, p. 26.

18. Riddell, *op. cit.*, p. 18. See also Center of African Studies, Universidade Eduardo Mondlane, "Zimbabwe: Notes and Reflections on the Rhodesian Question" (Maputo: mimeo, July 1977), p. 17.

19. *Frankfurter Rundshau*, December 15, 1978.

20. Duncan Clarke, *The Distribution of Income and Wealth in Rhodesia* (Gwelo: Mambo Press, 1977), pp. 43-4.

21. See e.g. Riddell, *op. cit.*, p. 8; Clarke, *The Land Problem, op. cit.* p. 26; and Centre of African Studies, Universidade Eduardo Mondlane, *op. cit.*

22. Colin Stoneaan, *Skilled Labour and Future Needs* (London: CIIR, 1978), p. 22.

23. Duncan Clarke, *Unemployment and Economic Structure in Rhodesia* (Gwelo: Mambo Press, 1977), pp. 41-2.

24. *Ibid.*, p. 38.

25. B. Mothobi, "Cheap Labour Policy: Migrant Labour," in *Zimbabwe Review* (Lusaka), VII.7/8 (1978), Table 3.

26. Riddell, *Skilled Labour, op. cit.*, p. 27.

27. Roger C. Riddell and Peter S. Harris, *The PDL as a Wage-Fixing Standard* (Gwelo; Mambo Press, 1975), p. 18.

28. *Frankfurter Rundschau*, 15 December 1978.

29. Clarke, *Unemployment and Economic Structure, op. cit.*, pp. 36 ff and Table 27.

30. *Ibid.*, Tables 4 and 8.

31. *Ibid.*, p. 57.

32. Duncan Clarke, *The Economics of Old Age Subsistence in Rhodesia* (Gwelo: Mambo Press, 1977), pp. 35-36.

33. Peter S. Harris, "Industrial Workers in Rhodesia, 1946-'72: Working Class Elite or Lumpenproletariat?" in *J. Southern African Studies* (Maryland), April 1977.

34. Clarke, *The Distribution of Income, op. cit.*, p. 9.

35. *Ibid.*, p. 17.

36. Quoted in, *Deutsche Zeitung/Christ und Welt* (Bonn) October 20, 1978.

37. Franz von der Rop and Peter Waller, "Die Entwicklungsperspective fuer Zimbabwe," in *Aussenpolitik* (Hamburg) 4th Quarter, 1978, p. 471.

38. Rhodesian Ministry of Finance, *op. cit.*

39. John Sprack, *Rhodesia: South Africa's Sixth Province* (London: International Defense and Aid, 1974).

40. Data on U.K. investment from U.K. Board of Trade, *Trade and Industry*, Feb. 21, 1977.

41. *Deutsche Zeitung/Christ u. Welt* (Bonn), October 20, 1978.

42. See *Der Spiegel* (Hamburg), 29/73, "Rhodesian-Boycott: Was Sie Wollen". *Officially*, F.R.G. exports to Southern Rhodesia sank from DM7 mn. in 1974-77, and its imports, from DM1.2 mn. to DM 1.1 mn. See Statistisches Bundesamt, *Statistisches Jahrbuch 1978 fuer die BRD* (Stuttgart: W. Kohlhammer GmbH, 1978).

43. See reports of the special committee of the U.N. Security Council on sanctions.

44. Thom's Commercial Publications, *Industry and Commerce of Rhodesia, 1974* (Salisbury: Mardon Printers, 1974).

45. *Ibid.*; see also Standard, Annual Report, 1975 (London).

46. Centre for African Studies, Universidade Eduardo Mondlane, *op. cit.*, p. 17.

47. *In These Times* (Chicago), 24/30, January 1979.

48. *Ibid.*; the reference is to Brazil.

49. *The International Herald Tribune* (Paris), November 18/19, 1978.

50. See Liebigs' advertisement in *The Rhodesia Science News* (Bulawayo), J. The Rhodesia Science Association, XI.8 (August 1977).

51. Duncan Clarke, *Agricultural Plantation Workers in Rhodesia* (Gwelo: Mambo Press, 1977), pp. 208ff.

52. Clarke, *The Distribution of Income, op. cit.*, pp. 32-3, 39.

53. Clarke, *Agricultural Plantation Workers, op. cit.*, pp. 208 ff.

54. Richard Robbins, *The Agricultural Sector of Zimbabwe* (Washington, D.C.: U.S. AID, mimeo, August 1978), Table 12; Centre for African Studies, Universidade Eduardo Mondlane, *op. cit.*, p. 38.

55. Quoted in Clarke, *Agricultural Plantation Workers, op. cit.*, p. 237.

56. Quoted in Clarke, *ibid.*, p. 50.

57. *Ibid.*

58. Clarke, *The Distribution of Income*, p. 37-8.

59. *Frankfurter Allgemeine Zeitung*, February 5, 1979; *The Economist* (London), February 24, 1979.

60. Cited in Interfaith Center for Corporate Responsibility *The Oil Conspiracy* (New York: ICCR, 1977).

61. *Africa News* (North Carolina), March 9, 1979.

62. See *Newsweek* January 1, 1979; *Nuernburger Nachrichten*, December 14, 1978; *Tagesspiegel* (West Berlin), December 15, 1978; *Financial Times* (London), December 14, 1978.

63. *Financial Mail* (Johannesburg), Apr. 22, 1970.

64. Quoted in *Der Spiegel, op. cit.*

65. Capital-output ration calculated from Central Statistical Office, *National Accounts* (Salisbury: Government Printing Office, 1978), Tables 6 and 31.

66. *Deutsche Zeitung/Christ u. Welt* (Bonn), October 20, 1978.

67. *The Sunday Times* (London), April 14, 1974.

68. Frankfurter Allgemeine Zeitung, February 5, 1979.

69. U.N. Center on Transnational Corporations, *Activities of Transnational Corporations in Southern Africa* (New York: United Nations, 1977.).

70. Quoted in *Der Spiegel, op. cit.*

71. *Der Spiegel, op. cit.* See Ch. 7 above for details of South African holdings.

72. *Sunday Times* (London), July 14, 1974; *Deutsche Zeitung/Christ u. Welt* (Bonn), October 20, 1978.

73. Ropp and Waller, *op. cit.*; *Weser-Kurier* (Bremen), February 27, 1979.

74. *Blick durch die Wirtschaft* (Frankfurt/M), November 8, 1978.

75. *Ibid.*

76. Clarke, *The Distribution of Income*, pp. 39-41.

77. *Frankfurter Allgemeine Zeitung*, February 5, 1979.

78. Duncan Clarke, *The Unemployment Crisis* (London: CIIR 1978), Tables 3 and 4.

79. See, e.g., *Neue Zuerchner Zeitung*, March 22, 1974.

80. International Defence and Aid, *Zimbabwe: The Facts About Rhodesia* (London: IDA, November 1977).

81. *Frankfurter Rundschau*, January 30, 1979.

82. *Suddeutsche Zeitung*, March 22, 1979; *Neue Zuerchner Zeitung*, March 22, 1979.

83. *Frankfurter Allgemeine Zeitung*, February 5, 1979.

84. See the "Minister of Finance," quoted in Clarke, *The Unemployment Criris*, *op. cit.* The F.R.G. paper, the *Frankfurter Allgemeine Zeitung* (March 9, 1977) reported that, "Above all, in the business world, which had considerable influence [sic] there is pressure for a concrete and visible transition to majority rule, as every delay makes a peaceful solution with the moderate black nationalists more difficult." The trans nationals have, of course, propagated their own definition of "majority rule" and "moderate." Similarly, a spokesman for Liebig, which just a few years earlier had advertised itself as "The Rhodesian Food People," remarked hopefully that "if a settlement was reached in Rhodesia, [Liebig's] interests could play quite a considerable part in the food production of the region." (*African Development*, May 1976). By implication, the company expected there to be no real land reform.

85. Roger Riddell, *The Land Question* (London: CIIR, 1978); *Neue Zuerchner Zeitung*, Feburary 25, 1977 and March 12, 1977.

86. Clarke, *The Distribution of Income*, *op. cit.*, p. 21.

87. *Financial Times* (London), January 26, 1977; see also *Der Spiegel*, 21/77.

88. *Financial Times* (London), January 29, 1979; *The Times* (London), November 29, 1978.

The Struggle
to Build Socialism   12

Two decades of political independence in Africa north of the Zambezi sharply exposed the pitfalls besetting the path down which the western powers, backed by the South African regime, sought to force the people of Zimbabwe. Clearly, only fundamentally restructuring inherited political-economic institutions could enable the new states of southern Africa to meet the pressing needs of their impoverished populations. Absent this transformation, expanded transnational corporate investment merely reinforced external dependence and impoverishment. Domestic investments, too, when not directed to changing inherited, distorted resource and institutional patterns, essentially only deepened disproportions in the national economies, binding them tighter into relations of unequal exchange in the world capitalist commercial system. Experience in independent Africa, as well as in the rest of the Third World, convinced the southern African liberation movements that transition to some form of social ownership of the region's mines, factories and farms was crucial.

But even after winning state power, the liberation movements could not expect to build socialism overnight. They inherited dualistic political economies. The transnationals and their local associates profited from narrow, export-oriented sectors using relatively modern tech nologies. Through these enclaves, they indirectly exploited the more technologically backward peasant hinterlands. Restructuring the dominant institutions in order to construct more balanced, integrated economies inevitably required a prolonged transitional period.

Experience throughout the developing world suggested that, after gaining state power, the liberation movements of southern Africa would first have to implement two interrelated sets of institutional changes. On the one hand, they would need to reinforce their political base, strengthening the alliance of workers, peasants and "committed petty bourgeois" elements[1] and involving them in decision-making relating to the transformation process. These classes—which, in peripheral economies, were far from clearly defined[2]—would have to realize that they would be the primary beneficiaries of the proposed transition towards socialism. Party cadre would have to help these groups acquire an adequate political understanding. New institutional structures were needed to give them an increasingly determinant voice at all levels of the new admininstration.

This task would be far from easy. In Africa, tiny urban working classes often lacked strong political consciousness, sophistication or organization. Frequently, they failed to understand the causes and consequences of inherited external dependence and the underlying structures of power.[3] Communication and political work with the peasantry was hampered by illiteracy and dispersion throughout remote rural hinterlands. Colonial policies and institutions systematically isolated intellectuals. They had played on ethnic conflicts in an attempt to break up political unity. The cadre of the liberations movements in southern Africa needed to discover how to mobilize the population to overcome these obstacles. Major steps had been made in the struggle for freedom; but experience in independent Africa showed that the complexity of problems encountered in building socialism could shatter the people's initial impetus and cohesion. As a result, in many African countries, a "bureaucratic bourgeoisie"—civil servants, managers of state corporations, the politicians themselves—had been able to increase their control of the state machinery and subvert the process of change to their own ends.[4] A qualitatively different level of organization and political awareness emerged from the southern African liberation struggles; but real, democratic participation in and control of national administration by the mass of workers and peasants had to be continuously expanded and deepened.

Experience elsewhere[5] suggested, furthermore, that the liberation movements would simultaneously have to ensure effective state control over the commanding heights of the national political economy: basic industries, banks and financial institutions, and foreign and domestic wholesale trade. The requisite institutions and policy changes could only be forced through from a position of political strength based on growing popular backing, participation and direction. Democratic state control over the commanding sectors is a minimum requirement for carrying out the long-term development strategy needed to build socialism: restructuring the inherited, disproportional and externally dependent political economy to shape integrated, balanced structures which could provide productive employment and higher living standards for the mass of the population. Examination of the causes of poverty in southern Africa, as in the rest of Africa, showed why.

—In southern Africa, and everywhere else on the continent, uncontrolled transnational corporate investment in *industry*, designed to maximize short-run profits, led to production of the wrong goods for the wrong consumers in the wrong places. They drained out the resulting investable surpluses, reinforced external dependence, and further impoverished the workers and peasants. If a democratic state controlled basic industry, it could begin to reorient the output of existing plants. It could spread new projects throughout the countryside, to employ a growing numbers of rural workers in processing local agricultural and mineral resources to meet the nation's basic needs.

—In southern Africa, and throughout the continent, transnational trading corporations controlled *foreign and internal wholesale trade*. They fostered the export of crude materials to associated factories in "traditional markets" back home, or in regional bases in South Africa. They squandered hard-earned foreign exchange to import luxuries and semi-luxuries, or materials for local assembly for the wealthy few who could afford them. State control could facilitate the marketing of more processed exports. It could aim to raise foreign exchange earnings by seeking alternative markets, for instance in socialist or other developing countries. Limiting imports to essential capital and equipment could spur the development of production by local workers using local resources to meet the working population's needs. State control of internal wholesale trade, together with the spread of cooperative or state retail stores, could facilitate the distribution of consumer necessities at fixed, low prices.

—Transnational corporate control of the *banks and financial institutions* formed a key link in foreign control of African political economies. It fostered monetary and credit policies enhancing the profitability of production of crude materials for export, and of luxury and semi-luxury items using imported parts and materials for the narrow high-income groups. The banks granted credit primarily for the big mining firms and agribusiness, the settler estates and trading firms. They typically turned down requests by African peasants, and made few loans to develop the truncated manufacturing sector. Democratic state control of these institutions, in contrast, could ensure them support for the reorientation of industry and agriculture to meet the needs of the people. In addition, the banking and credit system could be used to supervise plan fulfillment. They could ensure that projects were realistic, plans adhered to, and import restrictions respected.

Control of these commanding heights by a democratic state could facilitate the development of a long-range (say, 20 years) strategy to restructure the national economy. This would provide the general direction and continuity for democratically formulated and implemented intermediate plans, lasting five to seven years. This kind of long term approach is required because development of political, economic and labor power processes involved in creating a balanced, integrated and socialized economy requires decades. Over time, planning in this context could achieve the following goals: First, it could reduce transnational corporate and financial influence, ensuring national control over the accumulation and allocation of investable surpluses, which could then be directed to balanced, integrated national development. Second, it could direct available material resources to the construction of appropriate industries, specifically related to increasing agricultural productivity. Over time, this would increase productive employment opportunities in both agriculture and industry, producing an increasing range of goods to meet the needs of the population. Third, enforcement of an equitable incomes policy could direct investable surpluses to critical productive sectors in accord with an overall financial plan. Fourth, plans could expand and improve the form and content of educational and training programs, systematically linking them to the provision of the growing numbers of qualified men and women needed to staff new industrial and agricultural projects.

If, and only if, backed by the united participation of working people and peasants, the creation of appropriate new institutions to ensure state control could, in other words, make it possible to draw up the long-term political-economic strategies needed to develop an integrated economy. Such strategies would form a framework for establishing necessary linkages: new industries to provide essential tools and inputs to increase farm productivity throughout the rural areas; and to process and distribute farm produce, so as to provide more food, better housing and adequate clothing for the mass of the peasantry. Only a long-term perspective would make possible the direction of investable surpluses—previously drained from the region's economies to South Africa and beyond—to finance plans for balanced industrial and agricultural development.

A range of complex and contradictory processes are involved in the transformation to socialism. This chapter will briefly review the problems and opportunities encountered by three of the larger southern African states, Tanzania, Mozambique and Angola. All three announced changes in political and economic institutions aimed at initiating the transition to socialism. It should be emphasized that the past development of underdevelopment in these countries means the process of building socialism must be expected to take a long time. President Julius K. Nyerere of Tanzania declared:[6]

In 1967, a group of youth who were marching in support of the Arusha Declaration asked me how long it would take Tanzania to become socialist. I thought 30 years. I was wrong...I am now sure that it will take us much longer.

By 1980, Tanzania had enjoyed less than two decades of political independence. Mozambique and Angola had been free for just five years.

Tanzania After the Arusha Declaration

Tanzania remained the only former British colony whose government was still explicitly dedicated, after almost two decades of independence, to the attainment of socialism. For the first five years of that period, its government sought to pursue policies generally recommended by conventional western wisdom, embodied in proposals made by World Bank experts: Expand export crops and provide education and social services. Over time, they said, a multiplier effect would spread development throughout the nation. During that period, President Nyerere and the political party, the Tanganyikan African National Union (TANU), sought to consolidate their links with the people. President Nyerere himself devoted the first year after independence to organizing TANU to build a mass base. Over the years, a large proportion of the population was brought together into ten-house cells, purportedly designed as a channel for two-way communication between the leaders and the people. The extent to which party members become imbued with a clear socialist perspective was less clear.[7] President Nyerere himself was an avowed pragmatist. It has been claimed that the leadership of TANU was never really devoted to the cause of building socialism. This argument asserts that "petty bourgeois" elements sought to advance their own interests, rather than to implement the transition to a fully socialized political economy.[8] The effect of uniting TANU with the Zanzibar ruling party to build the CCM in 1977, did not seem to fundamentally eliminate that danger.

Tanzania's early efforts to expand export crops succeeded: Output of coffee, cotton, and tea multiplied. But world prices fluctuated, their declines sharply reducing returns to the nation. The promised multiplier effects failed to materialize. In 1966, other events led to a reevaluation and fundamental revision of national policy. First, the Ghana coup, following a precipitous drop in world cocoa prices, ousted

President Nkrumah, who for years pursued a similar development policy.[9] Secondly, the British and their western allies officially deplored the Unilateral Declaration of Independence by a white minority in Southern Rhodesia, but refused to take definitive action which could have insured an early peaceful transition to majority rule in nearby Zimbabwe.

In 1967, Tanzania's leadership pronounced the Arusha Declaration.[10] They introduced measures designed to exert direct control over the "commanding heights." They nationalized the banks, including the domestic branches of the powerful Barclays and Standard banks which dominated the economy. They nationalized and began to integrate the business of the major importing and internal wholesale companies. They acquired 51 percent of the shares of a handful of the local affiliates of transnational firms, including the British American Tobacco Company, Portland Cement, and Metal Box,—all firms with much larger holdings in South Africa. The list, as President Nyerere quipped, was very small because "You can't nationalize nothing."[11] They tackled the massive reorganization of the institutions governing these key sectors in an effort to ensure that they would play a more constructive role in directing surpluses to a preferable development pattern.

These measures have been evaluated elsewhere.[12] Serious problems were encountered in reshaping the old institutions and creating new ones to ensure that state participation in these critical sectors really enhanced the welfare of the masses of the population.

One serious weakness was the failure to devise a long-term industrial strategy to restructure the national economy.[13] As a result, the guidelines for state intervention remained vague. No carefully formulated physical plans were designed to create industrial poles of growth to stimulate agricultural and smaller scale industrial activities throughout the national economy. Not enough attention was directed to producing critical tools and equipment at appropriate levels of technology, as well as low cost consumer goods to raise the living standards of the lower income groups.

A few attempts were made to move in this direction. The second five-year plan sought to formulate specific social criteria for eventual incorporation into a long term industrial strategy. Efforts were made to decentralize development planning, but for the most part these focused on construction of social facilities and infrastructure. Specific plans for industries to spur productive activities in every region lagged. Government ministry personnel had been trained to provide social services, leaving productive activities to the private sector. The National Development Corporation which handled government investment in industry was guided more by short-term profit-maximizing perspectives within existing constraints and resources, rather than by identifying and developing new projects that could reshape those constraints and resources over time.

A Harvard team, invited to produce an industrial strategy, came up with a range of options mostly focusing on import substitution possibilities utilizing local raw materials. But little was done to work out concrete physical plans for industries to produce the essential tools and consumer necessities to transform the quality of life in the countryside. Nor was adequate attention directed to developing long term plan perspectives or involving the people themselves in the formulation and implementation of proposals to link new industries to expansion of agricultural output. [14]

Implementation of the Arusha Declaration did, however, foster the rapid growth of the parastatal sector with the concomitant emergence of a group of corporate managers with significant power. Over time, their interests appeared to diverge from those of the working people and peasantry. In Tanzania, as elsewhere, this danger appeared likely to be aggravated by the fact that, especially in the industrial sector, the government had to rely on foreign "partners"—the transnationals retaining the minority shareholdings—for capital, technology and technical expertise. Corruption* at parastatal levels was not identified as the major problem in Tanzania, but it seemed probable that foreign partners exerted various pressures to persuade parastatal personnel to adopt policies consonant with company interests which varied from Tanzania's.

The Tanzanian government introduced a number of measures in an attempt to ensure that the parastatal and top civil service personnel made development decisions directed to attainment of national goals. [16] A leadership code prohibited government and party personnel from participating in private business. The nationalization of rental housing restricted opportunities for speculative real estate investment. Nationalization and reorganization of the banks permitted, not only redirection of credit to key agricultural and industrial projects, but also a systematic checkup on the use of investable funds by parastatal firms and organizations. TANU published guidelines designed to facilitate worker participation in industrial projects.

*Transnational firms, seeking to maximize their global profits, have—as recent evidence in the U.S. indicates—systematically engaged in making deviation from national goals financially attractive to government officials. [15]

The dilemma confronted by Tanzania faced every African country seeking to restructure its inherited, externally dependent economy. Inevitably, they had to deal with large agglomerations of capital and capital-intensive technologies introduced by transnational corporations into their narrow export sectors. The deliberate colonial policy of excluding Africans from educational facilities undoubtedly rendered it more difficult to implement policies to ensure worker participation in decision-making relating to these activities. Tanzania's efforts to deal with these issues were significant. By the mid-'70s, however, they were also being criticized as inadequate.[17] There seems little question that Tanzania's leadership needed to intensify its efforts to create the appropriate institutions, along with educational programs, to enable workers to play an increasingly politically conscious role in shaping the long term strategy of transformation as well as defending their immediate day-to-day interests.

Tanzania's political leadership insisted that taking over control of the commanding heights was necessary but not sufficient to initiate the transition to socialism. They argued that it was essential, simultaneously, to achieve a form of social ownership and production in the rural areas in what they termed *ujamaa villages*. Meaning "familyhood", the term ujamaa was adopted because it was said to imply community sharing in what was assumed to be a traditional mode. Ujamaa villages were to be created by bringing scattered Tanzanian families together to form villages where they could work collectively to expand production as well as build improved clinics, schools and other social services in the rural areas.

The World Bank, in an early pre-independence study, had urged the construction of villages, rather than persistence of the traditional pattern of isolated homesteads, to make community services viable. The government had initially attempted expensive village schemes along the lines recommended, but they had foundered due to bureaucratic administrations and impossibly heavy expenditures.[18]

The post Arusha Declaration *ujamaaization* program was to be different. It was to emphasize expansion of agricultural output by development of cooperative efforts. These villages could then use the resulting increased incomes to finance expanded social services. At the same time, President Nyerere had argued, creation of *ujamaa* villages would help to avoid the rural stratification characteristic of cash crop areas in Africa.[19]

Evidence indicated, however, that stratification had already emerged in Tanzania's coffee and cotton regions. Class divisions already hampered efforts to realize *ujamaa* ideals. In Sukumaland, for example, studies in the early '50s showed significant differences between farmers in size, capital equipment and access to markets and credit. In Bukoba, traditional semi-feudal relationships had rigidified with the growth of coffee production, developing into openly antagonistic class differences.

In the early '70s, government and party leaders began to raise the pressure for accelerated movement into villages purportedly organized along *ujamaa* lines. Reports of coercion began to surface. Many families had reluctantly entered this first stage of the *ujamaaization* process, having been simply forced to leave their separate homesteads to live on village sites. (See Table 12.1). Not infrequently, pre-existing patterns of stratification were imposed on new village administrative structures, enabling wealthier farmers to manipulate them in their own interests. To the extent that the costs of villagization and administrative structures were financed out of what little cooperative production was undertaken, the returns of peasants were substantially reduced, their future participation discouraged. Little attempt appeared to have been made to involve poorer peasants together with those better off in increasingly productive cooperative activities to reduce inequality and raise overall living standards. Yet the increased collective ownership of tools and land to raise productivity and simultaneously reduce and eventually eliminate stratification was to have been the crucial phase of *ujamaaization*.

Table 12-1.
The Struggle for Rural Socialism in Tanzania (Percent of rural population in Tanzania estimated to be in Ujamma villages: 1969-1976)

Year	Percent
1967	0.0%
1968	0.7
1969	1.7
1970	4.4
1971	12.5
1972	15.6
1973	15.5
1974	19.1
1975	66.6
1976	91.3

Note: The term "Ujamaa village" is used in the popular rather than legal sense.

Source: D. J. McHenry, "The Struggle for Rural Socialism in Tanzania," in C.G. Rosberg and T. M. Callaghy, Socialism in Sub-Saharan Africa—A New Assessment, (Berkeley: Institute of International Studies, Univerity of California, 1979) p. 43.

It should be borne in mind that reallocation and development of agricultural resources is a slow, time consuming process: It takes six months to a year simply to plow, sow and harvest even a single crop, whether for sale or home consumption. While expanding cash crop output, peasant families must continued to produce their own food-stuffs—often, in East Africa, produced primarily by women—if they are to remain self-sufficient at least during the transition to greater (planned) participation in an expanding national division of labor. The integration of these activities in the context of increasingly productive collective activities using improved tools and equipment could be expected to take years. Nevertheless, the government apparently re-quired the new villages to sell their collectively produced crops through marketing boards at lower prices than those for which they were ulti-mately sold. Subsistence crops, on the other hand, remained untaxed. This probably contributed to discouraging further collective efforts.

Unfortunately, Tanzania's accelerated *ujamaaization* program co-incided with the drought of the early '70s. Crop output fell drastically in large areas of the Tanzanian countryside, as well as throughout much of the rest of the continent. As a result, Tanzania was forced to import thousands of tons of grain to avoid famine. This, combined with the rising costs of oil and import of finished manufactured goods on which the economy still relied, as well as parts and materials for new in-dustries, contributed to worsening balance of payments deficits. To cover these, Tanzania, like many other third world countries, had to borrow heavily abroad. For the first time, it became heavily indebted to the International Monetary Fund.

Tanzania's heavy foreign borrowing appeared likely to endanger its efforts to implement a self-reliant transition to socialism, especially as the government began to adopt typical International Monetary Fund-type remedies.[20] As elsewhere, these tended to throw the burden of the financial crisis on the working people. The government reduced public employment, adding to the growing numbers of workers in search of productive employment opportunities. It devalued the currency, auto-matically raising the prices of imported spare parts and materials, as well as oil, thus pushing up prices throughout the national economy.

These policies appeared likely to jeopardize Tanzania's state goal of transforming the economy to build socialism. The actions of the Tan-zanian Parliament in 1978—raising the salaries of top government personnel and introducing strong measures to prevent domestic criti-cism (including closing the university and detaining student leaders)—did not auger well. The government began to call for increased private investment, but it did not, despite Monetary Fund pressure, sell off its state shares of industries or other critical sectors of the economy.

In late 1978, Tanzania's economic problems were aggravated when the Ugandan dictator, Idi Amin, sent troops across the border in blatant aggression.* Tanzania mobilized tens of thousands of troops and finally, in close cooperation with Ugandan organizations and individuals, ousted Amin. But the social and economic disruption in Uganda left the authorities there heavily dependent on Tanzania for assistance, which the latter, pushed still further into debt by war costs, could ill afford.

Despite these difficulties, Tanzania, as a Front Line State, continued to aid the southern African liberation movements in their struggle to end white minority rule. It provided them with facilities for training cadres and took a leading role, along with Mozambique and Angola, in mobilizing broader African and international support.

At the end of 1979, President Nyerere publicly denounced the Monetary Fund for requiring further "austerity" measures in return for additional funds, and the Tanzanian government sent the team of Fund advisors home. Western governments and financial institutions withheld additional assistance previously promised.

Whether Tanzania could successfully surmount this new difficulty appeared likely to depend in part on whether it could obtain assistance from other socialist or OPEC countries. But the critical factor still appeared to be the degree to which working people in the cities and rural areas mobilized and united to carry through further necessary changes to build a more self-reliant industrially and agriculturally integrated economy.

The Tanzanian people's experience in this effort to transform the national political economy along socialist lines suggested some of the difficulties likely to be encountered as liberation movements undertook to build socialism elsewhere in southern Africa. Contradictory factors operated at every level, from the difficulty of organizing peasants into collective productive units to avoiding the emergence of a bureaucratic elite allied with transnational corporate interests. Foreigners found it easy to "armchair" theorize. It seemed more useful, however, to attempt to explain the concrete causes of the problems confronted, based on a

---

*Amin's motives were unclear. Some said he sought to turn aside internal Ugandan discontent. It was reported[21] that his regime had trained troops for the black puppet leaders who acquiesced to Ian Smith's proposals for an "internal" settlement in Southern Rhodesia. Perhaps he was convinced that some kind of election, followed by international recognition of the Rhodesian regime, would ensure him support in defeating Tanzania.

realistic assessment of existing constraints and resources as the foundation of efforts to search for more effective future policies. Tanzania's experience underlined the difficulties likely to confront any country with small investable surpluses which sought through increased socialization of the means of production to attain self-reliant, integrated, balanced development. The education and involvement of the masses of the people in the complex process of restructuring critical local and national institutions was an imposing task. Disengaging those institutions from domination by transnational corporate interests to facilitate that socialization process was by no means simple. While dealing with these difficulties, Tanzania'a political leaders had to focus their attention on formulating and implementing physical and financial plans allocating resources in directions most likely to lead to self-reliant, integrated national development.

Tanzania's party and government went further along these lines than did most of their neighbors to the north. But social change takes time. Mistakes were inevitably made. The real test, in Tanzania as elsewhere was whether new channels were being institutionalized through which mistakes, once made, could be corrected, and, over time, further essential changes could be carried out.

Mozambique and Angola

The historical experience of Mozambique and Angola differed fundamentally from that of Tanzania. The latter, a somewhat neglected British protectorate, was granted independence in 1962 with relatively little struggle. The British colonialists had concluded, after years of expensive warfare against the forest fighters in Kenya, that settler/company influence and wealth could best be maintained "by other means."[22]

The peoples of Angola and Mozambique, in contrast, waged more than a decade of guerrilla war against one of the most economically backward, and politically repressive powers of Europe before they finally won independence in 1975. The Portuguese fascists clung to their colonies as the foundation of their own retarded industrialization program. They systematically shipped to Africa their surplus rural population in Portugal, making them settler farmers, and coercing African peasants to work for them to expand export crops in the colonies. They welcomed transnational and South African corporate investment, primarily to mine their colonies mineral deposits, especially in Angola, one of the richest pieces of real estate on the continent.

Their aim was the ruthless extraction of crude agricultural and mineral produce to build up their own home industries: Some they shipped at below world prices to provide essential raw materials for their own emerging industrial sector; the rest they sold to earn foreign exchange to pay for the economic and military costs of financing their home industries and perpetuating their colonial rule.

In the course of the years of liberation struggle, the leadership of the guerrilla fighters in Mozambique and Angola began to forge sound political institutional and ideological foundations for transforming their national political economies. They studied the experience of the African states which had attained only "a formal independence, an independence of the anthem and the flag."[23] Frelimo, for example, created new state structures in the northern areas of Mozambique as it liberated them. Frelimo cadres helped the Mozambiquan peasants learn that not only the Portuguese rulers, but also the traditional authorities, blocked creation of participatory democratic structures. In Mozambique, as in Angola, years of struggle taught the necessity of adopting rational, scientific approaches, rejecting superstitious beliefs that attributed causal powers to supernatural beings and their associated traditional "representatives" on earth. Women, who grew much of the foodstuffs, joined the guerrilla cadre and became integrated into the decision-making structures of newly liberated villages.

The late Agostinho Neto, first President of liberated Angola, declared that it was necessary to "free and modernize our peoples by a dual revolution: against their traditional structures which can no longer serve them, and against colonial rule.[24]

Samora Machel, President of Mozambique asserted,[25]

When we took up arms to defeat the old order, we felt the obscure need to create a new society . . . in which all men free from exploitation would cooperate for the progress of all. In the course of our struggle, in the tough fight we have had to wage against reactionary elements, we came to understand our objective more clearly. We felt especially that the struggle to create new structures would fall within the creation of a new mentality . . .

This, Machel argued, called for overcoming individualism, for the liberation of women, for building attitudes of collective responsibility. The liberation movement had to break with the pre-colonial as well as the colonial heritage, for "in order to lay the foundations of a prosperous and advanced economy, science has to overcome superstition."

To ensure adequate food production and provide school and medical facilities during the armed struggle, the liberation forces encouraged the peasants to organize communal productive activities: collective use of the land and of their simple tools to maintain an adequate level of production to feed the liberated zone populations. Frelimo even managed to export small amounts of agricultural produce through Tanzania to earn foreign exchange to pay for essential manufactured equipment and materials. At the same time, men and women worked together to set up small scale industries for artisans to produce and repair tools and equipment, clothing and simple household articles. These activities involved the creation of new, participatory institutions. By the time independence was formally achieved in June, 1975, the liberation movements in both countries had already built some of the new productive and state institutions required to institute a fundamental political economic reconstruction.

Portuguese soldiers, disillusioned and embittered by prolonged military service against the increasingly militant liberation armies, toppled the Portuguese dictatorship in 1974. The new Portuguese government eventually ceded complete political independence to the African liberation forces. Most of the settler populations, frightened by false rumors of black reprisals, fled, often smashing the machinery and equipment they could not take with them. The past Portuguese policy of restricting African education left the two new nations with less than 10 percent of the population who could read and write. Even fewer could manage the sophisticated machines and complex institutions introduced by the colonialists in the export enclaves. In Angola, the invasion by U.S.-supported forces of Holden Roberto's FNLA from the north, and the South African army from the south* forced the new MPLA government to call upon Cuban assistance.

The liberation movement's ties to the Cubans went back to the early '60s when their cadres first went to Cuba to study. The fact that the Spanish language is close enough to Portuguese to facilitate communication, and shared ideals of liberation, fostered liaison between them. The Cuban's conventional weapons and troops reinforced the MPLA guerilla fighters, enabling them to defeat the invading forces in the north and the south. In the years that followed, Cuban aid was gradually transformed to provide increasing amounts of technical assistance: teachers, medical assistants, doctors, engineers, agronomists, to replace the hundreds of thousands of skilled Portuguese who had fled, as well as to provide new services to help the peasantry raise productivity and improve their living standards.

*The South Africans insisted they had been promised U.S. military support for their invasion, assistance which was only thwarted by the reluctance of the U.S. Congress to engage in another Vietnam-type involvement.[26]

Independence confronted the Angolan and Mozambiquan peoples with new problems: How to restore the productive facilities in industry and agriculture destroyed by departing Portuguese, and raise the levels of productivity as the foundation for improving living standards throughout the countryside? How to reorganize the inherited national state structure, established by the Portuguese in collaboration with the transnational corporate interests that dominated the so-called "modern" export sectors: the harbor, transport facilities and estates near Maputo (formerly Lourenco Marques) and Beira, as well as the giant hydroelectric project at Cabora Basa in Mozambique; the oil wells (Gulf Oil of U.S.), the iron mines (the F.R.G. firm, Krupf), the diamonds (DeBeers, an affiliate of the South African Anglo-American Corporation) and the spreading settler estates of Angola? How to reincorporate and employ the many tens of thousands of workers, primarily from Mozambique but also Angola who previously had migrated to South African and Namibian mines and farms to earn cash? On top of all this, the independent governments faced constant threats of invasion and massive destruction by the southern minority regimes. For Mozambique this threat became a reality after it cut off the Rhodesian transport routes to the sea in conformance with the U.N. boycott, a move which cost it almost $200 million a year in foreign exchange earnings alone. As the Rhodesian minority government became increasingly desparate, its planes flew bombing missions deeper and deeper into Mozambique, claiming to attack only Patriotic Front camps. but actually also bombing Mozambique villages and infrastructure and killing Mozambique citizens.

Angola, likewise, confronted continuing open and covert South African hostility. The South Africans provided acknowledged military and logistical support for Savimbi's UNITA. South African armed forces repeatedly invaded Angola and bombed southern Angolan villages. Allegedly, they directed their attacks against guerrilla base camps of SWAPO, the Namibian liberation movement recognized by the U.N. in reality, they killed many Angolans as well as Namibian refugees.

The new governments of Angola and Mozambique devoted the first few years after independence primarily to restoring and maintaining basic services and the production of necessities, recuperating from years of warfare and the disruption by departing Portuguese. Simultaneously, they tackled the process of taking over and reorganizing the inherited bureaucratic government structures. Industries and estates

*The Angolan-Namibian border, imposed by the 19th Century Scramble for Africa, cut across the territory of the Ovimbundu who continued to live and maintain community ties in both countries.

abandoned by the Portuguese had to be brought back into production. Committees of workers, long excluded from decision-making, managed as best they could to solve production problems. They had to rebuild transport links and repair vehicles sabotaged by departing owners. In major cities, tens of thousands of former squatter compound dwellers were assigned to live in suburban type houses, left by fleeing Portuguese tenants. Many enjoyed running water, electricity and clean, airy rooms for the first time in their lives. Nevertheless, city administrations, especially in Angola, encountered added problems as refugees continued to crowd into the cities. Urban populations were encouraged to participate in voluntary city cleaning campaigns. Maputo in Mozambique—formerly a city of crime and corruption—was transformed into one of the cleanest cities on the continent. Citizens waiting in queues for goods in inevitably short supply felt safe in leaving their bags to hold their place in line while they went off to chat in the shade of nearby trees.

Both in Mozambique and Angola, the liberation movements began the long process of reorganizing national institutional structures to implement the longer term transformation process. They declared their determination to restore the productive levels of 1973 by 1980, focusing on restructuring existing productive capacity to meet the basic needs of their populations. At the same time, both announced their intention of building Marxist-Leninist vanguard-type parties to carry through the transition to socialism. As Basil Davidson, an astute longtime observer of the African scene, emphasized.[27]

(T)hese movements may be said to have been the first in Africa to have fully indigenized a marxist analysis; and they were certainly bent on finding an alternative to the capitalist nation-state. But what their evolution really displayed was an African politics of mass participation in a mature phase. Their search for an alternative derived from the nature and application of that politics.

Frelimo's Third Party Congress* presented a program similar to that advanced in Angola. It declared that its political base was to be the working class as the leading class, in alliance with the peasants—the great majority of the population—as the "principal force." It sought to "free the peasants from the narrowness of traditional production and encourage them to engage voluntarily in higher forms of productive and collective life." It proposed to win intellectuals, small property owners,

*The two previous ones were held during the war itself.

and artisans over to this basic alliance. In this context, it aimed to carry through a People's Democratic Revolution moving towards state and cooperatively held property as its economic base.

The Congress outlined its objectives in this early stage[28] as: an end to foreign dominaton and the consequences of traditional-feudal and capitalist-colonial rule;

extension of democratic people's structures throughout the country to involve the "broad laboring masses" in decision-making as the foundation for a new form of state power;

a "struggle on the production front" to satisfy people's basic needs for food, clothes;

strengthening the nation's defense capacity.

Attainment of these objectives, the Congress held, would build the political, scientific and material bases for the passage to the next stage, that of the socialist revolution. At the same time, Frelimo embarked on the process of reinforcing its links to the population, while ensuring its membership included only the best cadre, as a vanguard party. There would be no place for those who engaged in politics merely for personal advancement.

The Central Committee of Angola's MPLA—Partidade do Trabalho* explained that during the phase of national reconstruction, 1978-80, it aimed to formulate a guide for the process of national reconstruction. Although lack of personnel, data and economic control hindered detailed, comprehensive planning, a general strategy to guide development had to be worked out:[29]

Concrete circumstances . . .have still not allowed formulation of a unified plan, setting out times and specific institutions for the period until 1980. A great shortage of experienced cadres and a serious lack of meaningful statistical information persisted . . . .Nevertheless, the Central Comittee (sought to set goals) as guides for action, as general directions of the Party for practical activity in the area of socio-economic development of the country.

The new governments moved deliberately to take over the commanding heights of the national economies.

They gradually placed the entire banking and financial institutional structure under national control in both countries. Initially, the post-revolutionary Portuguese government nationalized the leading banks and turned their local branches over to the newly formed African governments. By the end of 1978, both states had fully nationalized the

*Like Frelimo, the MPLA transformed itself into a democratic-centralist party, the MPLA—Partidade do Trabalho, Party of Labor.

last of the smaller banks. This facilitated government efforts to control expenditure of scarce foreign exchange and direct credit to critical sectors of the economy.

Beginning with the trading firms abandoned by the Portuguese, the governments extended their control over export-import and internal wholesale trade. At first, their primary aim was simply to provide adequate food and necessities for the people. Immediately after independence in Luanda, for example, only 119 stores—government and private—remained open to feed Luanda's remaining population of over 100,000. Gradually, a system of people's stores and cooperatives, together with some small private stores, spread throughout the countryside.

Government wholesale trading firms sought to ensure adequate distribution of basic necessities at fixed prices in all regions. Over time, they aimed to rebuild trading networks, not to meet the luxury consumption demands of the rich, as in the past, but to ensure the increasing availability of low priced necessities for low income groups throughout the rural and urban areas.

In the case of basic industries, the governments' decisions were, in many instances, hastened by the flight of the Portuguese. As Lobo de Nascimento, Angola's First Vice President, explained:[30]

In fact, we have no choice but to build socialism. Over 90% of the Portuguese fled the country after abandoning their plantations and enterprises ; they forced our hand. Some sectors—foreign trade for instance—we had not intended to nationalize, but the Portuguese who ran it pulled out. If the State does not handle it, who will? So we find ourselves taking it over along with many sectors that were not in our original plans.

The MPLA—PdT had initially called for state control of only the largest industrial and agricultural units in Angola, but to revitalize various sectors of the shattered economy, the government had no choice but to embark on an extensive program of nationalization of hundreds of farms, small as well as large. By 1977, it had begun to introduce guidelines for joint state-worker management, seeking to guarantee worker participation at all levels of enterprise.

In the case of large transnational corporations whose managers were willing to try to work out a modus vivendi, the new governments, both in Mozambique and Angola, introduced increased state participation, but did not attempt to take over entirely until they could adequately train their own cadres. Angola, for example, acquired a majority of the shares of Gulf Oil,[31] and Diamang, leaving the foreign partners (the U.S. firm,

Table 12-2.
Industrial Branches in Angola, 1973 (as percentages of total production by value)

Branch	% of the total production value
Food	36
of which	
Milling	5.4
Fodder production	2.0
Sugar refining	2.4
Fishery products	4.6
Bakeries	4.3
Animal oils and fats	6.0
Textiles and ready-made clothing	12
Breweries	10.8
Tobacco	5.4
Cement, concrete, glass, tiles	5.3
Chemical industry; paints, soap, industrial alcohol, explosives, matches	5.0
SUBTOTAL	74.5
Oil derivatives: petrol, asphalt, butane	3.8
Cellulose and paper mills	3.0
Metallurgical industry	3.7
Vehicles: assembly of motor vehicles, production and assembly of bicycles, motor-cycles	2.8
Plastic industry: pipe, fabrics, bags, domestic articles, Shoes, packing industry	2.3
Iron and steel industry: reinforcing bars, steel pipes	2.4
Rubber industry: tiles, shoe soles, industrial rubber	2.3
Other industries: tanning, leather and leather goods, manufacture of machines (not included), timber industry, furniture industry, shoe industry, electrical machines and electrical articles	5.2
TOTAL	100.0

Source: Backlund, Biureborgh, Hellstrom, IUED, *The Angolan Economy*, March 1977

Gulf, and Anglo-American affiliate, DeBeers, respectively) to manage them and market their products abroad. The more than half a billion dollars Angola's government received in annual revenues from Gulf played a critical role in enabling the government to get back on its feet during the phase of national reconstruction. Likewise, Mozambique left its basic transport industry in Maputo in the hands of South African experts, and acquiesced to continued South African management of Cabora Bassa.

These measures required fundamental re-examination of the inherited sets of state and private institutional structures controlling these critical sectors. The new state structures for directing them could

Table 12-3.
Production of Selected Industrial Products in Mozambique, 1973, 1976 ('000 tons)

	1973	1976
Flours	166	200
Fats and Oils	54	50
Beverages and drinks (including packaging)	201	143
Animal feedstuffs	40	33
Crude Oil	794	374
Timber	155	119
Cement	611	210
Fertilizer	62	33
Chemicals	43	20
Cotton textiles and yarn	7	n. a.
Pulp and papper	33	17
Metal products	64	36

Sources: Noticias 2/18/79 and government sources.

not simply replicate those created to involve peasants in governing rural liberated zones during the phase of guerrilla war. The new governments had to deal with the sophisticated complex institutions governing the capital-intensive machinery and equipment characteristic of the "modern" sector. To ensure that these projects contributed to restructuring the lopsided inherited political economy, they had to re-examine and revise old laws, institutions and administrative regulations introduced by the Portuguese colonists. This required new skills and approaches at all levels, from involving workers on the shop floor in decisions to dealing with complex transnational corporate managerial issues, technologies and marketing structures.

While embarking on these programs, the governments and parties of Mozambique and Angola began to formulate a long-term development strategy, to be introduced in 1980, to attain balanced integrated economies capable of spreading productive employment opportunities into all sectors of the national economy.[32] They proposed to develop heavy industry, utilizing their existing resources as the driving force for all other industries. In the countryside, they emphasized the voluntary formation of cooperatives. In Mozambique, these were to be developed along the lines of communal villages earlier established in liberated zones. An emphasis on increased regional balance within each country, overcoming the sharply dualistic patterns imposed during the colonial era, was an integral feature of the long term strategy proposed.

Both parties proposed a new fiscal regime to accompany the physical plans formulated to implement their long term strategies. The state sector was expected to play an increasing role in mobilizing and reinvesting nationally produced investable surpluses. Progressive taxation was to contribute to increasingly equitable distribution of incomes. State banking and financial institutions were to direct credit primarily to state firms and cooperatives. State projects' returns were to become an increasingly important source of investment funds.

Both Frelimo and MPLA—PdT announced as their explicit underlying labor and social policy the creation of conditions necessary to dignify work as the motive force of social development. Work was to become the criterion for distribution of the results of production. As the MPLA—PdT declared, it sought to build a society:[33]

in which work is the right of all citizens, and its alienated character will be lost, in which work as a means for subsistence becomes an honorable task.

The parties aimed to eliminate unemployment, create and dynamize workers' organizations, and encourage socialist emulation to achieve increased productivity while paying each according to work done.

Both parties stressed arming the working class with essential political, technical and scientific knowledge through rapid training and specialized courses in all industrial firms and cooperatives. They emphasized the importance of emancipating women in this process. In the area of health, they proposed to spread preventative medicine across the countryside, rather than build expensive hospitals and specialized curative facilities in a few urban centers. As Frelimo declared, education and culture lie at the "heart of the formulation of the New Man, free from obscurantism and capable of assimilating critically the political, scientific, technical and cultural knowledge transmitted to him."

Implications For The Future

The liberation movements of southern Africa argued for a planned development far different from the illusory "trickle down" promised by the economic soothsayers of transnational corporate power. They pledged to enable the African populations themselves to shape their own destinies: to examine the potentials of their land's vast mineral and agricultural wealth, to devise the appropriate technologies and institutions to ensure its development, not to enrich a minority or far-off transnational interests, but to meet their own basic needs.

But the liberation movements offered no easy path to the future. As almost two decades of Tanzanian experience, and the few short years in Mozambique and Angola, suggest, achievement of the kinds of institutional changes required to transform the inherited distorted political economies of southern Africa was immensely complex and difficult. On the one hand, the movements had to exercise their newly-acquired state power to control the commanding heights to implement long-term strategies for socio-economic transformation. On the other hand, creation of new institutions to ensure growing popular participation at all levels of the new state structures remained crucial to avoid the emergence of a new political-managerial elite which could manipulate state machinery to benefit themselves and the transnational corporations. Only the full participation of an increasingly educated and politically-conscious working population could ensure the realization of plans taking advantage of every potential opportunity for self-reliant nationwide development. The old adage, "two steps forward, one step back," seemed more than a little relevant. As the slogan adopted by Frelimo and MPLA—PdT reiterated, "A luta continua"—the struggle continues.

References

1. Cf. A. Cabral, *Revolution in Guinea, An African People's Struggle* (London: Stage 1, 1969).

2. B. Davidson, *Let Freedom Come*, (New York: Little Brown & Co., 1978).

3. R. Sandbrook and R. Cohen, *The Development of an African Working Class - Studies in Class Formation and Action* (Toronto: University of Toronto Press, 1975).

4. This danger has been discussed from various perspectives by various authors, including I. Shivji, *The Silent Class Struggle in Tanzania* (Dar es Salaam: Tanzania Publishing House, 1973); R. B. Seidman, *State, Law and Development* (London: Croom-Helm, 1978); R. Sklar, *Corporate Power in An African State - The Political Impact of Multinational Mining Companies in Zambia* (Los Angeles: University of California Press, 1975).

5. See A. Seidman, *Planning for Development in SubSaharan Africa* (Dar es Salaam: Tanzania Publishing House and New York, Praeger, 1974).

6. The Arusha Declaration, Ten Years After (Dar es Salaam: Government Printer, 1977) p. 1.

7. K. Levine, "The TANU Ten-House Cell System," in L. Cliffe and J. S. Saul, *Socialism in Tanzania, an Interdisciplinary Reader*, Vol. 1, *Politics* (Nairobi: East African Publishing House, 1972). The problems of ten-cell leaders are also discussed in K. K. S. Musoke, "The Establishment of Ujamaa Villages in Bukoba Rigazi (Nyerere) Village: A Case Study" (Mar. 1970); "A Collection of Essays on Ujamaa Villages" Dar es Salaam: University of Dar es Salaam, Political Science Department, Mar. 1971; A Nimtz, "Ten-House Cell Leaders as an Index of Political Change: The Case of Bagamoyo," J. F. O'Barr, TANU Cells and Their Leaders; The Pare Case," and J. Samoff, "Agents of Change-Cell Leaders in an Urban Setting," papers presented to African Studies Association, 14th Annual Meeting, Nov. 3-6, 1971, Denver, Colo.

8. Cf. I. G. Shivji , *The Silent Class Struggle, op. cit.*

9. Described in A. Seidman, *Ghana's Development Experience 1951-66* (Nairohi· East African Publishing House, 1978) passim.

10. J. K. Nyerere, "The Arusha Declaration: January 29, 1967" A Selection from *Writings and Speeches*, 1965-1967 (Dar es Salaam: Tanzania Publishing House, 1968) pp. 231-250.

11. *Jenga*, No. 1, 1968, p. 2-3.

12. Eg. L. Cliffe and J. Saul, *Socialism in Tanzania, op. cit.*

13. One was proposed in the Second National Development Plan (Dar es Salaam: Government Printer, 1970), but no concrete overall industrial strategy has since been made public or implemented.

14. Nyerere, "The Arusha Declaration" *op. cit.*

15. E.g. see *The New York Times*, re Sudan, Sept. 2, 1978; re Honduras, July, 1978; re Indonesia, July 10, 17, 21, 1978.

16. These are outlined in R. B. Seidman, *State, Law and Development, op. cit.*, Ch. 21.

17. Shivji, *The Silent Class Struggle, op. cit.*

18. L. Cliffe and G. Cunningham, "Ideology, Organization and the Settlement Experience in Tanzania," Rural Development Research Committee, Paper No. 3, University College, Dar es Salaam, 1968.

19. J. K. Nyerere, *Socialism and Rural Development* (Dar es Salaam, 1967).

20. The International Monetary Fund when it provides credit to a given country may also require that it pursue policies considered essential to restore its balance of payments equilibrium. See C. Payer, *The Debt Trap: The IMF and the Third World* (Penguin, 1974).

21. *The New York Times*, Mar. 11, 1979.

22. M. Blundell, *So Rough a Wind, The Kenya Memoirs of Sir Michael Blundell* (London, Widenfled and Nelson, 1964).

23. "Frelimo, The African Lesson," in C. G. Rosberg and T. M. Callaghy, *Socialism in Africa, A New Assessment* (Berkeley: Institute of International Studies, University of California, 1979).

24. B. Davidson, *In the Eye of the Storm: Angola's People* (Garden City, New York: Doubleday, 1972).

25. B. Davidson, *Let Freedom Come, op.cit.*, p. 350.

26. *Quarterly Economic Review* (Economist Intelligence Unit) 1st quarter, 1979, "Angola-Guinea-Bissau".

27. B. Davidson, *Let Freedom Come, op. cit.*, p. 353.

28. Mozambique Information Agencies, Bulletins No. 9 and 10 (Special Congress Issue) (Maputo: 1977).

29. *Angola's Plan Prospects*, translated from German by N.S.M.

30. *Guardian*, London, Mar. 24, 1977.

31. PTL—Petroleum Taxation—Petroleum Legislation, Report Africa, Oct-Nov. 1978.

32. Mozambique Information Agencies, Special Congress Issue, op.cit. spells out these perspectives for Mozambique; and indicates the Angolan view.

33. *Angola's Plan Prospects, op. cit.*

Towards Integrated
Regional Development 13

Introduction

Harsh economic realities urged the newly politically independent nations of southern Africa to press for economic integration in the 1980s. Even Tanzania, Mozambique and Angola, though much larger in terms of geographical space and population size than their neighbors, confronted severly limited growth potentials as long as they sought to achieve the transition to socialism on their own. Yet if the newly independent nations of the region could unite, together, they could transform the regional political economy into a powerful modern industrialized unit. Even excluding South Africa, they possessed the essential resources to build complex basic modern industries required to provide productive employment and raise the living standards of the entire regional population. Their parties and governments knew these facts. The problem was primarily institutional: How to unite their divided political economies, shaped by decades of colonial rule to depend on South Africa and the transnational corporations? South Africa itself remained dominated by a well-armed minority regime which, together with the transnationals, aimed to exploit regional markets, resources, and labor, rather than facilitate development to meet the needs of the people.

Efforts to hasten transformation through regional cooperation would have to start, then, with growing coordination between the independent states. The first stage would be directed to attaining self-reliant regional industrial and agricultural development which simultaneously reduced and finally terminated dependence on minority-ruled South Africa. It would require that the participating states attain an adequate degree of control over the commanding heights of their economies—the banks, trade and basic industries—to formulate and begin implementation of national plans to restructure their own economies. In the process, their governments could seek ways to integrate their political economies with each other, while progressively reducing the institutionalized ties binding them to South Africa. To the extent that they succeeded over time, they would simultaneously help weaken the minority regime's oppressive rule over the people of South Africa itself.

Once the people of South Africa won their liberation, the states of southern Africa could all join together in a second stage of regional integration. In this second stage a liberated South Africa could join its neighbors to create a new pattern of relations, one built on the foundation of mutual benefits through planned regional development designed to meet the needs of all the region's inhabitants.

This second stage lay some place in the future. But the intensification of armed struggle within South Africa in the late '70s suggested that it might well be introduced before the end of the century. Once the necessary political conditions had been created, integration in this second stage would multiply the potential for rapid regional transformation by building on the extensive industrial base in South Africa itself.

The following sections of this chapter will deal primarily with the potential advantages of regional integration during the first stage, in which countries bordering on South Africa could build their own industries and agricultural development while reducing their dependence on the minority-ruled, military industrial complex of South Africa.

Initiating the First Stage: The Arusha Coordinating Conference[1]

In July, 1979, the Front Line States held a conference in Arusha, Tanzania, to initiate coordinated regional development. They declared as their objectives:

1. the reduction of economic dependence, particularly on the Republic of South Africa;
2. the forging of links to create a genuine and equitable regional integration;
3. the mobilization of resources to promote national, interstate and regional policies;
4. concerted action to secure international cooperation within the framework of our strategy for economic liberation.

In pursuit of these objectives, the Front Line States' spokespersons proclaimed their intention of formulating joint strategies and priorities:

The Front Line States will identify areas in which, working in harmony, we can gear national development to provide goods and services presently coming from the Republic of South Africa and weave a fabric of regional cooperation and development.

The Front Line States agreed to hold annual Southern African Development Coordination meetings as a "mechanism for surveying results, evaluating performance, identifying strengths and weaknesses and agreeing on future plans . . .(through) sustained cooperation over two decades." They declared their conviction that the time had come to establish a "new economic initiative for Southern Africa," and invited the international community to help within a framework of "known and accepted objectives:"

—"Equitable development within the Southern Africa region; unbalanced development within or among States is divisive and ultimately weakening."
—"Development must avoid the creation of new and excessive dependent relationships."
—"External aid must be directed to the real needs of the people and countries as identified by their government.
—"In the interests of reducing external dependencies regional, development strategies should be given special attention."

The participants added:

"It is hoped that this Conference will mark the beginning of a new approach to coordinated development of a region comprising countries of different resources, histories and philosophies bound together by their geography, poverty and aspirations. It is an ideal which the international community is invited to share."

The initial advantages of regional integration envisaged by the Coordinating Conference in this first stage, those that already existed despite the uneven levels of development characteristics of the region in the 1970s, appeared significantly greater than those available to the individual states taken separately. Given the known mineral and agricultural resources, the per capita incomes and estimated populations of South Africa's neighbors, integration would vastly expand their available market and collective resource base. The participating states could undertake large industrial projects that they could not otherwise even consider.

The total population of the region, excluding South Africa, was over 50 million (See table 10.1 above). The available regional market, even given the low per capita income, would be over $15 billion, permitting domestic consumption of a significant share of new industries output. The annual investable surpluses available for investment in new industries at about 25 percent of the regional product would be about $3.75 billion. This would provide sufficient capital to ensure that significant steps could be taken to begin to build key new integrated industries over a 20-year period.

Viewed in a dynamic perspective, over time, the possibilities arising from regional integration in this first stage, (despite the exclusion of South Africa) would be far greater. As the governments cooperated to invest available surpluses in a coordinated way to build infrastructure and industries throughout the region, both the market and the surpluses would expand at a rapid rate. Over a 20-year period, say from 1980 to 2000, assuming a plausible annual growth rate of the regional product of about 6 percent a year, the annual market could expand to $48 billion. The investable surplus over these 20 years could be expected to total $150 billion. Of course, this sum represents the total of all surpluses for the entire 20-year period, generated in increasing annual amounts. About a tenth—$12 billion—would be generated in the 20th year. This growth of the regional investable surplus would permit financing of an expanding range of new industries, linked to and stimulating the use of the region's resources, to increase productive employment opportunities and raise living standards in every participating state.

Realization of these perspectives would require careful physical and financial planning. The region's national planners would, as a first priority, need to formulate a long-term regional development strategy within which each participating nation could implement its own national plans for balanced industrial and agricultural growth. A brief ouline of a possible coordinated regional plan strategy suggests the kinds of modifications needed to achieve maximum potential regional growth, and illustrates some of the problems as well as the possibilities which might be encountered.

Coordinated Planning of Regional Infrastructure

The Arusha Coordinating Conference proposed, as a first step, the creation of a Southern African Regional Transport and Communications Commission to coordinate the use of existing systems and the planning and financing of additional regional facilities. Located in Maputo and serviced by a small technical unit, it would coordinate transport and communications among participating states and other "genuinely independent states in the Southern African region." The Conference viewed improved transport and communications as criticial to achievement of development coordination in the region for the following reasons:

1. without it the landlocked states, and especially Zambia, will be unable to sustain their present levels of support for the liberation struggle much less to increase them and to set in motion a steady reduction of links with the Republic of South Africa (RSA);

2. however future structural changes affect extraregional trade, today such trade is vital to every economy in the region and so, therefore, are improvements in service and reduction of costs;

3. clear possibilities exist for reduction of dependence on RSA and building of regional interaction, and many could be utilized fairly soon with economic as well as political gains;

4. mutual interests in cost reduction, revenue generation for coastal states and making possible development of isolated areas are clearly perceived by Southern Africans and therefore one major precondition for coordination program is met more clearly than in some other sectors.

The new Commission could start immediately to decide questions about what kinds and where transport networks should be constructed to facilitate the spread of productive activities throughout the region.

Southern Africa was better served by rail than most of the rest of the continent. But the colonial regimes built railroads primarily to ship heavy mineral products from the mines to the coast for South African factories or export to foreign markets. (See map) Nevertheless, partly as a result of efforts of already independent African states, cross continental rail lines already existed. One ran from Luanda in Angola through southern Zaire into Zambia's copper belt. From there, the new Tazara Railroad ran down to Dar es Salaam on the Tanzanian coast. Another ran through Zimbabwe to Beira in Mozambique.

Realization of the existing railroads' full potential contribution to self-reliant regional integration outside South Africa's sphere of control required political agreement among the liberated states of the region, including Namibia and Zimbabwe. Beyond that, it would necessitate the coordinated utilization of the equipment and rolling stock. These had been haphazardly purchased by different administrations from different sources and were far from interchangeable. Not even the tracks of the different lines were of the same gauge.

The participating states would need to plan new railroads to link all the liberated states and facilitate the transport of heavy bulk produce

SOUTHERN AFRICA

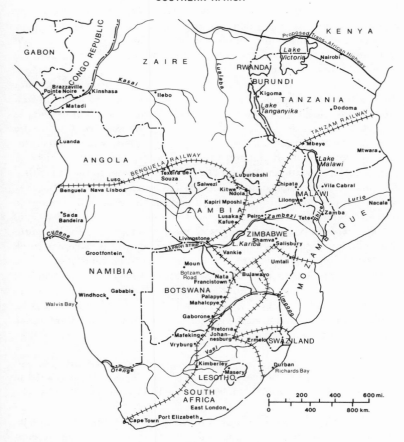

within the region. Namibia, for example, had no rail ties with any of its neighbors except South Africa. New tracks might be laid to Botswana and/or Angola. Likewise, the railroad initially built in Southern Angola to ship iron to the sea might be extended to tie into the line to Zaire and Zambia to the north.

But railroads were expensive to build. In the late '70s, they cost an estimated $1 million per kilometer when built by conventional western techniques. Even the Tazara railway, built by more labor intensive methods with Chinese assistance, probably cost about $400,000 per kilometer. [2]

Once built, furthermore, railroad transport capacity is inflexible. Railroads can only carry goods where tracks have been laid. On the other hand, they can carry heavy bulk produce relatively cheaply. They are easier to maintain and repair than trucks and roads, an important consideration in early stages of development when skilled workers are in severely scarce supply.

Roads for truck transport are cheaper to build and provide greater flexibility than railroads. Feeder roads may be built to open up new areas, some adjacent to railroads, others from remote hinterlands to major consuming areas. Men and women can be mobilized in the dry season to work on roads, their efforts supplemented by imported earth-moving equipment. Estimates indicated a two-lane tarmac road in tropical Africa would cost about $43,000 a kilometer in the late '70s.[3] All-weather dirt roads could be constructed at still lower costs, but they would require constant maintenance and repair, especially under the impact of torrential tropical rains. The maintenance and repair of trucks, especially in early stages of road development, furthermore, would be a constant problem. The life expectancy of the average truck in Africa is typically measured in months rather than years.

The Arusha Coordinating Conference also focused on the problems of energy supply for the region. Expanded regional industry, linked to stimulating agricultural productivity and raising rural living standards, would require continually growing power supplies. As the Conference report on energy pointed out:

Data . . . in Southern Africa are meager, contradictory, unreliable and out-dated. There is neither a statistical nor even a solid judgmental base on which to build policy options with any confidence except in the most general terms.

It emphasized, therefore, as a first priority the collection of a real data base "compromised of surveys and feasibility studies done by consultants for international agencies, national governments and, in minerals, private firms."

Outside of South Africa, southern Africa'a primary source of energy for the general population remained the traditional ones of wood and charcoal. But these were becoming increasingly scarce. In Tanzania alone, it was estimated that per capita consumption of wood fuel totalled between 1½ and 2 kilograms per person per day, or about 27 million tons of fuel wood for the entire nation in 1975.[4] In the Usambara Mountains, the 173 inhabitants of Kwemetzu Village alone, utilized 1360 trees a year. Multiplying this times the 270,000 people in the mountains, experts forecast a "critical shortage" of fuel wood in a few generations. Already, women spent one out of every two days scouring the countryside for wood to keep the family warm and provide cooking fuel. In Lesotho, extensive burning of trees by rural families had already denuded wide areas of trees, thus contributing to serious erosion. Furthermore, neither wood nor charcoal provide adequate power for more than tiny, artisan-type industries. While these would undoubtedly be encouraged in early stages of a long-term development strategy, over time their productivity would be enhanced by conversion to the use of electrically-driven equipment and machinery.

Coal is widely available throughout the southern African region, but it is too difficult to obtain and too expensive for the ordinary inhabitant. Most coal is consumed by industrial, primarily mining, projects. Yet about 14 percent of the world's known coal reserves are located in Africa, about 80 percent of them in southern Africa. Coal was extensively mined in Zimbabwe, Zambia and Swaziland for local use. It could be developed far more widely for both consumer and industrial purposes on a regional scale.

The Arusha Conference report on energy suggested that its future use should be integrated with planning for regional electricity development. Some types of coal, further, are suitable for coking, and could be utilized for a regional iron and steel industry. Finally, since coal is not homogeneous, and its deposits differ immensely in quality, the export and import of coal *within* the region could be planned to maximize their utility.

Hydroelectric power, however, once installed, is cheaper than coal or oil. * Hydro-electric power engenders few of the pollution problems caused by the use of other fuels. The Kariba, Kafue, Cabora Bassa and Kunene dams (see above, p. 248) already probably produce sufficient power for the initial stages of regional industrial and agricultural expansion. The more widespread use of this extensive existing power, as well as its future expansion, would, however, require two kinds of developments over the next twenty years. A region-wide grid would need to be planned to ensure that all parts of the region had access to the power produced. Construction of substations would be needed to transform the high voltage produced at the plant sites to levels permitting its use in smaller scale industries and agricultural projects throughout the

*It is also cheaper than nuclear power, although southern Africa, in particular Namibia and perhaps Tanzania, have uranium in economically viable quantities. There are many questions about the utilization of nuclear energy for production of power, including potentially serious pollution charges. The cost of producing nuclear power would probably far exceed that of hydroelectricity, given the extensive potential for producing the latter in southern Africa.

region. Over time, new hydro-electric projects might be built, like that proposed in Stigler's gorge in Tanzania, to provide additional sources of power. The spread of the use of electric power should provide a constantly expanding market for wire and electrical machinery and equipment, providing a continual stimulant for the region's rich copper mines.

Southern Africa abounds, as well, in oil, natural gas and uranium deposits. Angola's oil constituted its primary source of revenues in the late '70s, almost all of it exported. Botswana, Lesotho and Namibia also had hopeful signs of oil, and Mozambique certainly had oil. Yet all the independent Southern African countries suffered from the rising prices of imported oil. Attention to utilization of regional oil to meet regional needs within the framework of regionally integrated plans for development could considerably reduce costs.

As for uranium, in additon to Namibia's Rossing Mines, developed by South African interests in collaboration with the British transnational, Rio Tinto Zinc, evidence existed of deposits in Zambia, Tanzania and Angola. F.R.G. interests were engaged in exploring Tanzania's uranium potential. The Italian firm, AGIP, was studying Zambia's deposits which had actually been partially developed in the late '50s before independence.

These potential energy sources all needed to be coordinated within the framework of a regional energy development plan.

But roads, railways and power sources should not be constructed without simultaneously planning the location of new agricultural and industrial projects designed to spread increasingly productive employment opportunities to all states throughout the region. It cannot be assumed—as orthodox western theory so often does—that "market forces" will somehow automatically lead to the establishment of factories and farms in new areas opened up by new infrastructure. On the contrary, experience throughout Africa suggests that existing "market forces" typically reinforce and aggravate patterns of uneven regional development. To ensure an increasingly even and mutually beneficial spread of the regional division of labor, the regional planners will need to relate their proposals for infrastructural links to plans for new industries in the context of a long term regional industrial strategy.

The Ingredients of a Regional Industrial Strategy in Stage I

National and regional planners would, first, need to examine in depth the existing distorted structure of inherited industries in each country, and how it contributed to the disarticulation of the regional economy.

Second, they would need to consider the potential of each country's known resources for creating basic regional pole-of-growth industries which might help to achieve more rapid growth of an increasingly integrated and balanced regional industrial structure. On this basis, they would need to coordinate their national plans to change existing industries and create new ones to ensure the spread of productivity and rising living standards in all sectors of the regional economy.

The inherited industrial structure was dominated by transnational corporate factories designed to meet the demand of a narrow high-income elite as an extension of their more basic industrial plant in South Africa and/or in their home countries. This bequeathed on southern African industries a highly dualistic pattern. Regional planners would need to identify the appropriate sequence for the reorientation of existing industries, and which new industries should be built.

In the early years, regional planners would probably concentrate on surveying and coordinating the expansion of industries to facilitate increased agricultural productivity, spread specialization and exchange throughout national and regional economies, and raise the standards of living of the mass of the region's inhabitants.

Few southern African countries boasted any sort of industry producing simple agricultural tools and equipment which the majority of rural peasants could afford to buy and had the skills to use. The big estates and plantations imported most agricultural machinery largely from transnational corporate factories based in South Africa. Most peasants, on the other hand, used little more than hoes and cutlasses for their tiny semi-subsistence farms. Relatively small scale factories could be constructed first to produce simple, inexpensive tools which peasants could afford and would know how to use: animal-drawn ploughs, wheelbarrows, scotch-carts,* cutlasses, hoes, shovels, and axes. Over time, as workers acquired the skills and peasants learned to use more complex tools and cooperated to accumulate the funds necessary to buy their output, larger regionally based factories could be built to produce more complicated machinery and equipment like tractors and electrically-driven water pumps for irrigation.

A similar dualism characterizes the transport industry. Already, in several southern African countries, last-stage assembly plants produced several models of automobiles and trucks from parts and materials imported from transnational manufacturing corporations. Meanwhile, the great majority of southern Africans must walk, carrying their goods on their heads. Only a few can afford even bicycles.

*Simple, two wheel carts made out of the axle and wheels of discarded cars.

Planners need to develop a transport industry designed to contribute more effectively to the spread of specialization and exchange to meet the needs of the majority of the region's inhabitants. The proliferation of assembly plants, producing new types of cars and trucks for which most parts would need to be imported, would need to be halted. The assembly of private automobiles, already well-advanced in several countries, would be discouraged; these consume capital and resources for private use that could better be devoted to producing public transport and trucking industries. Only a limited range of public transport vehicles and sturdy trucks, capable of carrying goods and people to remote rural areas, should be introduced. This would facilitate the local manufacture, over time, of standard spare parts and equipment, as well as the training of workers to operate them.

Fairly early, probably in the first years, a regional plant should be constructed to manufacture sturdy bicycles for short-distance, small scale transport. For a number of years, many of the parts for the trucking and transport industries, even for bicycle assembly, would probably continue to be imported. As soon as possible, however, plans should be implemented to produce increasing numbers of the parts in local factories. Repair shops should be established throughout the region, stocking these standard parts and supplies. Workers would need to be trained to install them. This would help to overcome the chronic wastage of vehicles which break down or encounter accidents in remote areas. Eventually fully integrated factories should be built to produce complete vehicles, including the engines, in the region.

The consumer goods industries—typically the most developed in southern Africa as in most third world countries—are likewise characterized by dualism. At one extreme, big modern capital-intensive factories employ a hundred or more workers, using imported machinery and equipment to produce high-quality, high priced items for those wealthy enough to buy them. The drinks industry, producing beer and commercial soft drinks like Coca Cola, was a leading sector in terms of local value added in many countries. Large scale, centralized plants also baked bread and produced cigarettes, tobacco, textiles and more complex consumer items like transistor radios. Typically, constructed by transnational firms seeking to gain a foothold in the locally protected market, these plants imported parts and materials from the parent corporation for local processing in order to add the necessary "made in Africa" label: flour was imported for bread; polyester and nylon yarns were imported for textiles; cloth was imported for clothing; the electrical, plastic and metal parts were imported for the radios.

At the other extreme, small local enterprises, little more than artisan shops, produced low cost items consumed by the majority of people who barely earned subsistence incomes: tailor and seamstress shops; "home-made" bakeries, usually run by women; shoe-makers; home-brewing. These employed men and women, using simple hand tools, in what had come to be termed the "informal sector."

Planners should encourage small-scale handicraft workers to form cooperatives to purchase improved tools and equipment to expand their output. Eventually, they could accumulate sufficient capital to buy power driven machines and build small factories. Some of the large, capital-intensive plants producing luxury and semi-luxury items for the high income market, on the other hand, could be reconverted to process local materials and produce a lower cost range of goods designed more specifically to meet the needs of the great numbers of lower income people. Workers participating in these large plants should be encour-aged to participate in this redesigning process to ensure that their talents and skills are maximized and expanded to facilitate augmented productivity.

Transformation of both the small-scale artisan and large scale capital intensive plants would necessitate, over time, the construction of local industries to manufacture appropriate new machines and equipment. Gradually, the development of new engineering skills and construction of local machine shops would lay the foundation for the growth of basic industries producing increasingly complex machinery and equipment for both agriculture and industry.

While focusing initially on industries to augment agricultural pro-ductivity, facilitate transport and manufacture consumer necessities, regional planners would need simultaneously to take stock of the pos-sibility of building regionally-oriented pole-of-growth industries utiliz-ing regional resources to stimulate a more rapid regional transformation to self-reliant, balanced growth.

A pole-of-growth industry is one which is sufficiently large to stimu-late a chain of growth throughout an entire geographical area. It may be defined[5] as an economic complex which, through its linkages with many sectors of the economy, may stimulate extensive and rapid growth rates. The total size of the original focal point industry and those growing in connection with it must be large enough, and the rate of growth for their products rapid enough, to furnish a substantial impact on the entire economy.

Several industries may form a single growth pole. Several such poles may exist in one economy. A growth pole industry might, for example, be a large sugar mill, like the ones built in Zambia and Tanzania. Its initial establishment might presuppose an export market for sugar in Africa or abroad, as did the project constructed by Lonrho in Swaziland in the late '70s.

By itself such a factory cannot fundamentally alter the economic structure, or even provide many new jobs or skills. If adequate capital was available and markets could be found for its output, however, proper planning might ensure that it contributed to growth of an extensive industrial complex. Sugar refining could contribute through *planned* forward links to the growth of a number of industries.

Sugar itself is technically no less satisfactory than coal, soft wood and maize derivatives as a base for synthetics. Molasses, a by-product of sugar refining, may be used as a base for several chemical and synthetic products. Alcohol, for industrial uses as well as beverages, is another potential sugar by-product. Bagasse, crushed sugar cane, may be used to produce several types of paper and hardboard, and for furfural, an important base for plastics.

Turning to backward linkages, a sugar mill could create an enlarged market for cash crop farmers, providing incentives for them to expand their output and apply improved techniques. The growth of industries around the mill would, at the same time, increase the non-farm working force, creating an additional demand for domestic food supplies, further augmenting local farmers' markets and incomes. The additional rural incomes generated could create increased demand for fertilizers, cloth, refined sugar, and construction materials which could be produced by the expanding industrial complex. The growth of skilled cadres of workers and organization capacity generated by the construction, maintenance and repair industries could stimulate further growth in other sectors of the economy.

The scheme would be practical, however, only if markets existed for sugar, plastics, fibers, hardboard, and related products, and if the funds earned could be used to buy fuel, fertilizers, machinery and intermediate inputs for the plastics and fiber industry, and consumer goods to meet increased urban and commercial farmer demand. Smaller southern African states like Swaziland and, to date, even larger countries like Zambia and Tanzania, have been unable to take advantage of these possibilities. They typically have neither the internal markets for the outputs, nor the capital to buy the necessary inputs of machinery and equipment and complementary consumer goods.

A regional development strategy could help possibilities for developing poles of growth designed to hasten the industrial transformation of the region. More basic industrial complexes, like iron and steel, petrochemical industries, and fertilizers projects undoubtedly would have greater potential than sugar as poles of growth to stimulate regional transformation. A steel industry, based on southern Africa's rich iron deposits, might, over time, be expanded to produce steel for construction of new factories, and the necessary materials for production of parts and equipment for increasingly complex tools and machinery for the agricultural and transport industries. A petrochemicals industry, as envisaged at the Arusha Coordinating Conference, might produce fertilizers and explosives for the mining industry, and, in the long run, materials for a growing range of modern consumer goods industries.

Divided, the countries of southern Africa are less likely to realize the potentials of these kinds of basic industries than those of a sugar industry, for the size of markets and amounts of capital required would be far larger. Analysis of the available material resources, markets and capital of southern Africa taken as a whole suggests, however, that it might be possible, in the context of a coordinated regional plan, to ensure that each participating state could, over a 20-year period, benefit from the construction of pole of growth industries and associated linkages. The issue of which industry should ultimately be built in which country would obviously require major engineering and feasibility studies which have yet to be undertaken. Only after these have been made and compared for relative advantages and disadvantages as between alternative sites for particular projects could participating states determine the actual locational pattern. The underlying goal would be to construct at least one pole of growth industry in every country to stimulate and contribute to realization of more advanced national and regional plans. The suggestions made below are merely illustrative of some of the possibilities.

A regional iron and steel industry could be built on the foundations that already exist in a liberated Zimbabwe. During the first five-year plan period, the Zimbabwe industry could be analyzed and developed along lines that would link it most effectively to steel-using activities throughout the region: factory and bridge construction, production of simple tools and machines, railroad tracks, and so forth. Over time, the Zimbabwean industry could be expanded in a way complementary to the development of existing ore resources in Angola, Mozambique, Zambia and Tanzania. A second iron and steel project might, after some years, be established in southwestern Angola on the other side of the continent to meet the needs for steel there.

Zambia's copper smelting and refining industry, as a result of the peculiarities of its historical ties to South Africa, was among the most advanced in any independent third world country. In the first five-year plan period, it would be advisable to explore the possibility of expanding it to process some of the output of neighboring countries. Over time, a second processing complex might be established in association with another of the large regional copper deposits, perhaps near Namibia's Tsumeb mine. As the regional plan for expanding energy output became implemented, the market for products using copper-based inputs—especially electrical equipment and appliances—would expand. Fabricating plants could be built to produce wire and other copper-using equipment to facilitate increased productive activities in other spheres. Since fabricating plants tend to be relatively small and footloose, several might be built closer to the major markets in two or three countries throughout the region.

A large oil refinery might be constructed in Angola, sufficient to produce refined oil products for all the southern African states which still relied on South Africa. This project could be designed so that, over time, it could be expanded to create an advanced petrochemicals industry.

Given Angola's already existing industrial base, it could in the course of a twenty-year perspective plan produce a significant number of petro-chemical based materials for use throughout the region. Some of these could be further processed in Angolan factories. Others could be shipped to smaller fabricating plants elsewhere in neighboring states.

Tanzania might build a pole of growth industry to produce fertilizers to augment agricultural output throughout the region. It possesses phosphate deposits which it has not yet been able to exploit adequately because of the heavy capital cost and lack of a large enough internal market to consume the output of a project designed to take advantage of the economies of scale.

Yet the southern African states, outside of South Africa, together consume enough imported phosphatic fertilizers to provide a market large enough to make the project viable. (See table 13.1) Over time, as their incomes grow and their agricultural sectors are developed, they may be expected to increase their consumption of fertilizers to levels commensurate with those enjoyed in South Africa. The growth of the market would, over time, make it possible to establish additional fertilizer projects in other parts of the region.

Botswana's meatpacking industry could be expanded to sell tinned and frozen meat to areas which do not yet produce enough for their local needs. At the same time, hides might be processed to provide materials for a shoe and leather products industry. Over time, this could be

Table 13-1.

The Consumption of Phosphatic Fertilizers in Southern Africa, 1976 (in thousand metric tons)

Fertilizer	Angola	Botswana	Lesotho	Malawi	Mozambique	Swaziland	Tanzania	Zambia	Rhodesia (Zimbabwe)	South Africa
Phosphatic	3.5[2]	1.0	1.0	3.2	2.9[3]	1.5	10.9	17.9	43.0	362
Nitrogenous	11.2[4]	1.0		18.9	6.7[5]	6.0	14.5	39.8	80.0	304.7
Potash	6.9[6]			3.0	1.6[7]	2.4	4.3	6.1	33.0	130.7
Total consumption	21.6	2.0	1.0	25.1	11.2	9.9	29.7	63.8	156.0	953.4
$ of regional consumption	1.7%	0.1%	0.1%	1.9%	0.9%	0.7%	2.3%	5.0%	12.3%	74.9%

Notes: [1]includes Namibia;
[2]1974;
[3]4.1 in 1972;
[4]1972;
[5]9.0 in 1973;
[6]1973;
[7]2.7 in 1972.

Source: United Nations *Statistical Yearbook,* 1977.

integrated with shoe and leather products industries created in neighboring states.

All of these and other possible industries would require careful feasibility studies. Each would need to be examined in terms of specific linkages that could be constructed within the home-base country, and those extended to neighboring states. The raw materials bases exist for more: Botswana, Zambia, Zimbabwe and Tanzania have coal resources. Namibia has uranium deposits that are among the largest known in the world. What is essential is that a regional planning agency begin as soon as possible to gather and process the necessary data to formulate a long term regional industrial strategy which ensures that each participating state benefits from the establishment of an appropriate pole of growth using its basic resources.

The Inadequacies of a Common Market Approach

Implementation of a regional industrial strategy would require regional cooperation involving major changes in the inherited political-economic institutions which currently enable South African and allied transnational corporations to shape the economic development perspectives of most of the separate states.

As the Arusha Conference reports suggest, and experience in Africa and elsewhere proves, the common market pattern of integration, widely advocated by conventional western wisdom, would be incapable of achieving the desired coordinated, balanced regional development. The theory implicitly underlying common market proposals is that participating nations may more effectively attract transnational corporations to invest in new industries by building joint infrastructure and introducing common tariffs to protect the resulting combined and enlarged market. Experience proves, however, that the transnational corporations, seeking to take advantage of these features, tend to invest in ways which further aggravate uneven and externally dependent development throughout the resulting region.

The consequences of over half a century of the South African Customs Union (1910 to the present) illustrate the world-wide experience of common markets. As this book has sought to show, transnational corporations, especially in the last two decades, have been attracted to invest in southern Africa. But their investments have been concentrated in South African industrial centers: the Transvaal, Cape Town and Durban. They have not even been spread evenly throughout South Africa itself. Far less have transnationals invested significant amounts in manufacturing industries in the other member states of the Customs Union. On the contrary, basing themselves in the South African regional subcenter, they have viewed the neighboring countries primarily as additional markets and potential sources of mineral and agricultural wealth. Efforts to build competing industries in any country within the Union other than South Africa have been thwarted by the clear competitive advantage of the large scale firms located in South African industrial centers. Transnational corporate investments attracted by the South African Common market have contributed significantly to the underdevelopment process which has drained the neighboring countries of raw materials, manpower and investable surpluses.

Some may argue that the South African Customs Union experience is not typical because of the peculiar characteristics of the dominant racist regime. Examples elsewhere in Africa expose that argument as false. The short-lived Federation of Rhodesia and Nyasaland (1953-1963) showed similar tendencies. [6] In that case, the settler-dominated regime of Southern Rhodesia was able to use the Federation structure to impose taxes to capture a share of the investable surpluses produced by the copper mines of Northern Rhodesia (now Zambia). The revenue was used for expansion of infrastructure to attract transnational corporate investment around Salisbury and Bulawayo. Labor migrated from Nyasaland (now Malawi) to provide the necessary manpower. The higher-than-world-prices of goods produced in the Southern Rhodesian factories raised the cost of living in neighboring countries, and added to the drain of potential investment funds. The growing African protests against these as well as racist features of the Federation led to its breakup as a prelude to the ultimately successful attainment of political independence for Zambia and Malawi.

Common market proponents may still object: The Federation of Rhodesia and Nyasaland, like the South African Customs Union, was dominated by white settlers. Absent this feature, they may claim, a common market could provide equitable benefits to all concerned. But this myth should have been finally shattered, once and for all, by the consequences of the decade and a half of post-independence experience of the East African Common Market. Next to the South African Customs Union, the longest lived common market on the continent (it was initiated in the 1920s), the East African Common Market, exhibited all the same tendencies, not only before, but also after the participating members won political independence. [7] Over the years, Uganda, Tanzania and Kenya had created an extensive joint infrastructure, including a common postal and telecommunications system, a joint harbors, railways, and airlines operation, and an agreement to work towards greater monetary and fiscal coordination. It had received world-wide acclaim as a model of common market integration.

Analysis of the factors that finally led to the collapse of the East African Common Market showed once again that the underlying cause lay in the way common market institutions inevitably tended to attract private investors to locate industry in the more developed areas of the region, especially in Nairobi and Mombasa in Kenya. This hindered efforts to build projects to attain more balanced integrated regional growth for the benefit of *all* the regional inhabitants. The danger was actually forecast by consultants from the World Bank and Arthur D. Little, who advised Tanganyika, upon attainment of independence, to concentrate on expanding agricultural exports. The experts explained that Tanganyika could not hope to attract foreign investments in industry in competition with Kenya. They warned there was "little reason to believe that Tanganyika can become a manufacturing center" for exports to neighboring countries "will probably be exceeded by imports from these areas, particularly Kenya, because of the substantially greater impetus Nairobi already has as a processing center."[8]

During the several years that it sought to follow these experts' advice by expanding agricultural exports, the Tanzanian Government joined forces with Uganda to attempt to alter the Common Market's inherent tendencies to concentrate development in Nairobi and Mombasa. The fruit of this joint effort was the Kampala Agreement, which included a somewhat *ad hoc* proposal for planned allocation of new industries to achieve a more balanced regional growth pattern.* The Kenyan Parliament, early reflecting the entrenchment of a bureaucratic bourgeoisie along the lines forecast by Sir Michael Blundell,[9] rejected the Kampala Agreement. Instead, the common market members agreed that member states could impose a "transfer tax" on the sale of goods from one member state to any other if the latter attempted to establish an industry to produce the same item. The "transfer tax" was, in effect, another name for an internal tariff. Its imposition was clearly the beginning of the end for the common market. Tanzania established a rubber tire plant in accord with the proposals set forth in the Kampala Agreement, investing government funds in cooperation with a U.S. transnational firm, in hopes of selling tires throughout the regional market. Kenya shortly afterwards attracted another U.S. firm to invest in a still larger tire plant. The only role the transfer tax could play in this context was to

---

*The Kampala Agreement was not designed within the framework of an adequate regional industrial strategy capable of transforming the regional economy, but it is possible that, over time and with experience, it might have been improved.

limit the market of both plants to the individual member country. Neither could expand its output to the point where it would pay to process locally grown (as opposed to imported) rubber.* Both plants, therefore, remained dependent on imports of partially processed crude rubber from the U.S. firms' plantations elsewhere.

Similar decisions thwarted the establishment of other pole of growth industries which might have stimulated wider changes throughout the region. Neither Tanzania nor Uganda, alone, could afford to build an optimum-scale industry using their own iron-ore unless they could sell steel to the entire East African market. Instead, Tanzania and Kenya both built small-scale steel plants using imported scrap. Neither Tanzania nor Uganda could build an optimally-sized plant to produce fertilizers from their known phosphate deposits without guarantees that they could sell them to farmers throughout the region. Instead, all three countries constructed less than optimally-sized plants using imported raw materials and producing fertilizers for sale in their own countries at higher-than-world prices. Predictably, all three countries competitively constructed new textile factories since these required only relatively small amounts of capital and small markets. By the 1970s, as a result, the combined textile capacity of their plants exceeded the effective regional demand.

Anyone examining these trends could have predicted the ultimate break-up of the East African Common Market. Its final demise did not occur because of the brutal eccentricities of Uganda's Idi Amin or the publicized failure of member countries to contribute to financing joint infrastructural projects—although these aggravated the underlying differences. Rather its ultimate break-up was almost inevitable because the so-called market forces, insofar as they operated, stimulated private firms to invest in ways tending to accelerate growth in Nairobi and Mombasa at the expense of the neighboring countries.

These African common market experiences are not unique. They have been replicated in Latin America and Asia. The underlying explanation lies in the fact that private investors, seeking to maximize short term profits, inevitably tend to invest in patterns which aggravate external dependence and uneven development in third world countries. Common market institutions are typically designed to do no more than extend the field of operation of transnational manufacturing corporations from the confines of one nation to the broader arena of the region. They are inherently incapable of altering this basic tendency.

*Rubber had been one of Tanganyika's primary exports in the days of German rule prior to World War I.

The Arusha Conference documents spelled out the inadequacy of the common market approach to integration:

The first main problem with common markets or customs unions is the growth of regional inequalities i.e. regional distribution of benefits and costs of cooperation. Unless mechanisms can be developed to offset differential gains and losses, there will, inevitably, be pressures created in the less well off countries to opt out of the agreement and to seek an alternative status that will improve their position. A basic requirement, therefore, for this degree of cooperation is political, that the participating states be prepared to forego a degree of autonomy in decision taking for the common good of all partner states, and that the political will exists on the part of the states who benefit most from the union to develop mechanisms to transfer part of their benefits to the not-so-fortunate countries.

Joint State Control of the Commanding Heights

Attainment of balanced regional agricultural and industrial development would require creation of new institutions capable of capturing the investable surpluses produced within the region and reinvesting them according to plan to implement the desired long term development strategy to transform the regional political economy. These new institutions would have to ensure close coordination of the state controlled commanding heights of the participating states. In particular, they would need to coordinate their policies relating to regional pole of growth industries; regional export-import and internal wholesale trade; and regional banking and financial institutions. [10]

This would require a willingness to bargain out differences and work out mutually beneficial, long-term, bilateral and multilateral agreements. Such institutions would make possible growing regional integration in the coming decades, so that the independent states of southern Africa could take advantage of economies of scale well out of reach for the individual countries by themselves. But none of the participating states could commit their resources, financial or material, to regional projects, unless each could be guaranteed that the other states would meet their commitments. Moreover, each would need to know that all projects would contribute to improved utilization of their own resources.

Blueprints of institutional arrangements to achieve an adequate degree of coordination among member states could only be drawn up on the spot. In developing the needed institutions, experiences elsewhere, for instance in the Adean Pact in Latin America or the Council for Mutual Economic Assistance (CMEA) among the socialist states of eastern Europe, should be studied. Even in the short run, simply expanding the exchange of information would help improve coordination among the countries. This is particularly true in the case of trade and infrastructure, as well as tax and other financial policies. Even in the case of industry, knowledge of developments in neighboring countries would facilitate national planning.

Within this context, projects could be devised and carried out on a bi- or multilateral level. Such projects would contribute most to the economy if they formed part of a national plan—or, given the optimal political conditions, a regional development strategy. The type of arrangement used, in any case, would clearly have to be both binding and flexible, shaped to maximize inter-state cooperation on each project, given political and economic constraints. Helpful signs suggested that the necessary agreement might be in the process of being forged as the decade of the '80s opened. The Arusha Coordinating Conference, itself, was one. More than that: the largest states in the region—Tanzania, Mozambique, and Angola—were committed to a socialist transformation of their national economies. The five Front Line States had achieved a significant degree of political agreement in support of the liberation movements. The liberation movements of Namibia and Zimbabwe participated in the Arusha discussion and one would hope their governments, once established, would join in the formulation of the long term strategy and plans to implement it.

Attainment of a planned regional industrial transformation over the next 20 years would necessitate going further to achieve formal, if flexible, institutional arrangements to ensure joint state control of the commanding heights of the region. The primary purpose of regional integration would be the planned allocation of resources to facilitate creation of pole of growth industries taking advantage of economies of scale which the individual, balkanized states of southern Africa, alone, could not realize: large sized modern iron and steel projects, petrochemicals complexes, copper refineries and fabricating plants. None of the participating states could commit their resources—financial or physical—to these regional projects unless each in some way could be guaranteed that the other states would fulfill their commitments. Each would need to know that all the projects would contribute to further development of their local resources, producing the kinds and amounts of outputs needed to spread increasingly productive employment opportunities in other sectors of their own economies as well as throughout the rest of the region. Some illustrations may, however, suggest the range of possible approaches that could be employed in the three key areas. They might include long term contractual relations, joint control mechanisms and/or joint investments:

Coordination Relating to Pole of Growth Industries

The state managers of an iron and steel industry established in a liberated Zimbabwe, for example, might make long term contracts to buy agreed-upon quantities of ore and coal, say, from Mozambique and/or Tanzania at agreed upon prices. This would enable these countries to plan expansion of their mines and the necessary infrastructure, as well as the associated agricultural and industrial inputs. The Zimbabwean project likewise would be contracted to produce particular kinds of steel of appropriate standard specifications at fixed prices which could be used in construction of projects to stimulate productivity in industry and agriculture throughout the region; and the neighbors would contract to buy increasing amounts of its steel output to ensure the whole project's viability. In the same way, inputs and outputs and their prices would need to be guaranteed by some form of contractual relationship to develop pole-of-growth projects in other countries: an enlarged oil refinery and petrochemicals industry in Angola; a copper refining and fabricating industry drawing on outputs from Zambia, Botswana and Namibia; etc.

Foreign firms—socialist or capitalist—might help to provide management personnel and technolgical expertise, as well as imported machinery and equipment until regional cadres could be trained to take over. But basically, each project would need from the outset to be sufficiently controlled by member state agencies which could be held responsible for the fulfilment of its contracted role.

Coordinaton of Foreign and Regional Wholesale Trade

To facilitate the expansion of overall regional trade, as well as planned exchange of particular commodities required to ensure the viability of new pole of growth projects, long term institutional coordination would be essential. Already, the larger independent southern African states have created various forms of state trading corporations and marketing boards. These would need to coordinate their activities to create the framework for expanding interstate trade as well as to maximize the benefits of developing foreign trade outside the orbit of South African domination.

Joint state trading company policies would not aim to achieve regional autarky, ending trade with the rest of the world. Rather, they would seek to reduce dependence on uncertain outside sources of supply, as well as to end domination by South African-based trading firms; and contributed to the creation of new projects to spread productive employment opportunities through expanded trade within a more balanced, integrated regional economy. At the same time, they would be able, through their coordinated efforts, to bargain more effectively for more equitable and mutually beneficial trading relations with foreign partners. [1]

a. State trading companies could coordinate their region-wide wholesale trading activities to ensure that goods produced in one country would be distributed and consumed in accord with the regional plan of neighboring states, facilitating the increase of regional specialization and exchange for all commodities. Initially, they could coordinate their activities to reduce imports of processed agricultural products from outside the region, ensuring greater sales between neighbors as their output expanded. Over time, as basic pole of growth industries were constructed, joint state trading company activities could implement long term contracts to ensure that their output was sold throughout the region to replace imported items.

b. State trading agencies could share personnel and information to broaden their knowledge and contacts as to domestic markets and sources of supplies, as well as those of old trading partners outside South Africa and new ones in other third world states, socialist countries and competing capitalist nations. This would enable them to sell their produce at better long-term, stable prices, and in exchange, improve their purchases of essential machinery and equipment for the region's planned industrial growth.

c. By acting in concert, state trading companies could enhance their bargaining power for purchasing machinery and equipment and arriving at better contracts for the sale of the region's exported produce. As a region, they would enjoy a more diversified bill of exports, giving them more leeway to demand better terms of trade for specific items. If necessary, they would be able to withhold part or all of particular exports from the world market until prices became better. Their greater combined strength would enable them, too, to play a more effective role in producer-country associations, like OPEC (for oil) or CIPEC (for copper).

d. As a regional trading group, it should be possible, over time, for the southern African states to purchase their own shipping facilities. This would enable them to make significant savings in foreign exchange costs of importing and exporting commodities, and to sell their produce in markets which otherwise might not be available to them. As the Arusha Coordinating Conference documents point out, Tanzania, Zambia, Uganda and Kenya already jointly own a shipping fleet. This could be expanded to meet the regional needs.

e. As pole of growth industries increased the processing of regional raw materials, the state trading firms could combine their bargaining leverage to sell a greater share of the region's exports in processed form, thus augmenting the value added: selling steel instead of iron ore; refined copper ingots, copper cables and wiring, instead of crude smelted copper; refined petroleum products instead of crude oil.

Coordination of Money and Banking Institutions and Policies

A primary argument for regional integration is the necessity to accumulate and reinvest regional surpluses to finance planned pole of growth industries. At the same time, the production and sale of goods throughout the region in accord with the physical plans for expanding industry and agriculture requires long term price stability. These requirements necessitate close coordination of money and banking institutions and policies to implement the critical aspects of a regional financial plan parallel to and complementing the physical regional plans.

Financial planning at a regional level would require coordination of national financial plans in relation to taxation; incomes policies affecting wages, salaries and profits; and money and credit. In southern Africa, new state institutions dealing with these issues would need to coordinate their activities to end their past dependence on South African and transnational financial institutions. State ministries of finance would need to meet to discuss guidelines for coordinating tax and incomes policies.

The difficulties of achieving coordination here was illustrated by the differences existing in these policies which Tanzania and Zambia sought to reconcile in order to establish a pay scale for the workers and managers of the Tazara Railroad.[11] Tanzania, following the Arusha Declaration in 1967, had reduced the gap between the highest and lowest incomes in the public sector (including parastatals) to a ratio of 1:18. In addition, it had imposed heavy taxes on luxury and semi-luxury items to discourage their import and to capture a share of profits to be made by their sale. Zambia, in contrast, inherited a ratio of 1:27 between the highest and lowest government salaries, and 1:50 in the mineral-rich parastatal sectors.

Zambian government officials argued that higher salaries in the latter sector attracted capable civil servants out of state employment. They urged widening the government ratio—including that of railroad workers—to one closer to that prevailing in the parastatal sector. They objected to the imposition of higher income taxes on the wealthy elite or higher indirect taxes on luxury items they might wish to purchase. Clearly, if these two and other countries sought to participate in a more integrated regional financial as well as physical planning exercise, they would need to agree to tax and incomes policies. These would need to be designed, not to directing potential investable surpluses to the private pockets of a bureaucratic/managerial elite, but to finance the expansion of productive employment opportunities in regional industry and agriculture to raise the living standards of the majority of the regional population.

Equally important, participating states' banks and financial institutions would need to coordinate their policies to mobilize and direct investable surpluses to planned industrial and agricultural projects within a framework of stable regional prices. Over time, as growing specialization and trade increased between the participating states, it would be important to move towards a common currency.

Initially, prices for the planned outputs could be set in terms of each country's currency for sale in that country. The higher costs of production of countries with overvalued currencies could be offset by charging higher prices for goods shipped in from countries with lower values. Over time, the differences in cost structures and currencies could be reduced. As trade between the countries became common, prices for all commodities would be the same throughout the region. This gradual approach could only be implemented, however, if the commodity exchange was handled entirely by state trading firms and financed by state banks seeking to maximize interstate trade and long term regional growth. Private trading firms and banks, seeking to maximize short term profits, would undoubtedly seek to encourage production in lower cost areas and sales in higher priced areas, distorting the regional plan.

Joint state-owned banks and financial institutions would need to extend credit to planned industry and agriculture within the framework of national and regional financial plans to ensure balanced budgets and stable prices, adjusting the regional price structure to absorb the import of inflation characteristic of the capitalist world with the least possible disruption. State banks' control over deposits and coordinated state bank policies would provide important information to joint financial state planners as each industrial and agricultural project utilized funds to implement physical plans. Their new investable surpluses would be pooled and invested according to the requirements of regional as well as national plans. Interest could be charged at rates designed to stimulate desired patterns of production.

The Arusha Coordinating Conference documents recommended several steps to enable the participating states to benefit from some of the advantages of a common currency without initially giving up the national autonomy embodied in national central banks and separate currencies. The member banks could peg the value of their individual exchange rates to each other in a fairly rigid, semipermanent way. Domestic monetary and fiscal policies could be harmonized by quarterly meetings of the finance ministers. A clearing arrangement could be established to settle net indebtedness among participating states to facilitate trade between them. It might be located in one of the existing central banks or in a proposed Southern African Development Bank (see below). Credit might be extended by allowing debtor states to delay settlement over a period of time, either on a regular short term or a seasonal basis.

Over time, the participating states might pool their reserves for foreign trade purposes. This would require coordinated exchange control regulations and policies, necessitating a considerably greater agreement on long term development perspectives.

Immediately, the participating states might establish a Southern African Development Bank to facilitate regional cooperation. Its role and operating principles would need to be laid out clearly, and would need to be consistent with the maximum degree of economic cooperation envisaged as initially feasible. The authorized capital of the Bank might be contributed on a per capita income or per capita exports basis. Outside aid donors, banks, etc., could be encouraged to invest funds in Bank projects as long as control remained vested in the member states. Over time, the Bank might need to invest in projects in each country in accord with its capital contributon, but it might also encourage foreign investors to invest funds to reduce regional inequities.

As these arrangementes were being worked out, the participating countries should simultaneously develop coordinating facilities to train staff for monetary institutions. Existing facilities could be reviewed, and new ones created as necessary, perhaps in coordination with the Development Bank. A planning unit for formulation of further plans along the lines suggested could also be housed in the Development Bank.

The above list is merely suggestive of some of the kinds of problems and possibilities which member states would confront in seeking to achieve adequate control over the commanding heights of the regional economy to implement a regional industrial strategy.

The Second Stage of Southern African regional integration

Efforts to attain effective regional integration among the already independent African states will not take place in a vacuum. Their attempts to achieve self-reliant regional development, ending the domination by South Africa's state capitalist regime, will be part of the external features of an on-going struggle for liberation of South Africa itself. By the late '70s, the organization and armed struggle of the South African liberation movement was becoming more openly effective. How long it would take for the increasingly conscious black liberation movement to attain full rights remained unknown; but that they would ultimately win that goal was never in doubt.

It should be emphasized that once the participating states can introduce the necessary institutional changes to begin to implement self-reliant regional development plans, they will contribute to weakening the South African subcenter, aiding the liberation struggle of the people of that country. On the one hand, as they build up their own economies, they will find it more possible to strike better bargains with transnational corporations, as well as other third world and socialist firms, to acquire needed capital, manpower training and technology. On the other hand, as they begin to cut off the source of low cost labor and raw materials, limit the markets for South African-based manufacturing industries, and end the drain of investable surpluses to South Africa, they will undermine the features which transnational corporations found so attractive there. In this context, the South African liberation forces will be able to accelerate the pace of their efforts to free their own people.

Once South Africa was liberated, its restructured economy could be integrated into a second stage of southern African regional development. Given South Africa's already extensive industrial growth, it undoubtedly would contribute significantly to accelerating regional industrial transformation.

There is little point in trying to draw a blueprint of this second stage of regionally integrated development. Its potentials, however, need to be kept in mind by regional planners seeking full political and economic freedom for their peoples over the next decades.

Summary and Conclusions

The potential for the industrial transformation of southern Africa was great at the beginning of the 1980s. The region contained vast mineral deposits and rich agricultural resources capable of sustaining pole of growth industries designed to stimulate development in every participating country.

This potential appeared unlikely to be attained, however, unless essential institutional changes could be made to ensure joint state action to control the basic regional industries, foreign and international wholesale trading, and the banking and financial institutions. Some states had initiated action to attain national control over these sectors. The first tentative steps had been directed to formulating regional links and joint development perspectives as the foundation for long term regional development strategy.

Regional integration would clearly have to be accomplished in two stages: First, to break the domination of South Africa's minority regime and associated transnationals, the already independent states would have to reshape their physical and institutional structures together, excluding South Africa. Once the people of South Africa had won their liberation, South Africa's industrial might could be integrated into the second stage of regional development, accelerating the more rapid transformation of the entire region.

References

1. Declaration by the Front Line States made at Arusha, July 3, 1979 "Southern Africa: Toward Economic Liberation" (Arusha: Southern Africa Development Coordination Conference, July, 1979); this and the accompanying papers prepared for that conference are the sources of all materials referred to from that conference in this chapter.

2. Conventional railroad estimate cited by a spokesperson for Alcan Company, based on experience in tropics, in interview with author, A. S. Tazara railroad cost calculated from overall cost of Tazara Railroad with an appropriate inflationary factor.

3. Survey of cost of building roads in southwest Guinea Bissau, 1977, Guinea Bissau Ministry of Natural Resources, 1978.

4. Eastern Africa Environmental Trends Projects Program for International Development, *Fuelwood and Energy in Eastern Africa*, Clark University, 1978.

5. R. H. Green and A. Seidman, *Unity or Poverty? The Economics of Pan Africanism* (Harmond, Worth: Penguin African Library, 1968) pp. 63.

6. W. J. Barber, *Federation and Distribution of Economic Benefits A New Deal in Central Africa* (ed. C. Leys and C. Pratt) (London: Heinman, 1960).

7. For some of problems, see A. Seidman, *Comparative Development Strategies in East Africa* (Nairobi: East African Publishing House, 1970), especially re manufacturing industries.

8. Arthur D. Little, Inc., *Tanganyika Industrial Development, A Preliminary Study of the Basis for the Expansion of Industrial Processing Activities*, on behalf of the Ministry of Commerce and Industries, Government of Tanzania, under contract with the U.S. Agency for International Development, 1961.

9. M. Blundell, *So Rough A Wind* (London: Widenfeld and Nelson, 1964).

10. In the context of the possibilities of continental unification, these issues are considered in R. H. Green and A. Seidman in *Unity or Poverty? The Economics of Pan Africanism* (Harmondsworth: African Penguin, 1968). The discussion there incorrectly rejects the potential for regional integration of the kind here suggested, but nevertheless does raise the critical issues in concrete terms.

11. Data from documents available in Ministries of Finance in Zambia and Tanzania.

Epilogue

In the quarter of a century following the WWII, as the British and French colonial empires crumbled, transnational corporations intensified their competitive efforts to invest in a handful of the more oppressively-ruled countries in the third world. They poured advanced technologies, along with their capital, into strengthening these as regional subcenters to facilitate their access to the raw material wealth and markets of the surrounding nominally independent nations.

But the transnationals' investments fostered a contradictory pattern of political economic expansion that thwarted the regional inhabitants' demands for the spread of productive employment opportunities and better living standards. On the one hand, they fostered interlinked industrial and military growth that aggravated the oppression and impoverishment of the vast majority of the subcenters' populations, propping up repressive regimes which sought to hold back change. On the other, the resulting lop-sided growth of the regional core, as illustrated in the South African case, intensified the process of underdevelopment in the neighboring countries.

Nor did transnational corporate investments to strengthen oppressive regional subcenters benefit the working people of the core capitalist countries: the United States, Western Europe or Japan. On the contrary, it became increasingly apparent over time that the corporate managers viewed their investments in these new areas as a means of reducing production costs, forcing workers in their home-base countries—who had over previous decades won better wages, working conditions, and improved social services—into competing for jobs with the most oppressed peoples of the third world.

Transnational corporate spokesmen claimed that, by investing in South Africa, they shaped the optimal market for their export of machinery and intermediate goods. They argued this provided new employment possibilities for workers in their home countries. For at least the largest transnationals, expanded investments and sales in South Africa certainly seemed a very profitable short-term alternative. Companies like the U.S. Ford Motor Company planned to expand their South African production despite the economic stagnation that gripped that nation in the 1970s. Their promises of improved conditions for their South African workers proved false; Ford itself dismissed 700 workers, practically the entire black labor force, from its Port Elizabeth assembly plant in 1979 because they demanded the right to organize a union of their own choosing. The transnational spokesmen, nevertheless, persisted in offering a simple choice: continued investment in regional subcenters like South Africa, no matter how distasteful the ruling regimes; or further unemloyment for home-country workers producing the machinery and equipment they sold there.

But in reality, the on-going struggle for liberation in southern Africa posed far more complex issues for consideration by the working people and intellectuals of the core capitalist nations: those embodied in the ongoing process of the changing international division of labor and fundamental international social change. Spurred by the technological revolution created by their continued accumulation and reinvestment of capital, transnationals transferred entire factories to regional subcenters. There, in the context of the low levels of productivity prevailing in the third world, as exemplified by the South African experience, these relatively capital-intensive industries squeezed out small scale handicrafts and artisan's shops, and led to the layoff of redundant workers. But the same plants, in the technologically sophisticated industrial structures of core capitalist nations, had been relatively labor-intensive, employing thousands of workers. G.M., Ford, and Chrysler, for example, which by the 1970s each had subsidiaries or affiliates in South Africa, had laid off hundreds of thousands of workers in the U.S. by the end of the decade. U.S. Steel and the U.S. rubber companies, which also owned investments in South Africa, followed suit.

At the same time, the growth in the core capitalist states of distributive trades and financial sectors—hiring increasing numbers of women whose wages were less than two thirds those of men—reflected the shifting international division of labor manipulated by transnationals seeking to maximize their returns. Unemployment mounted in the core capitalist countries throughout the 1970s, reaching the highest levels since World War II. Even when production recovered from the mid-decade "recession," employment continued to stagnate.

The so-called "mature industrial areas," the "stagnant" northeast of the U.S. and England, the iron and steel centers of France and the F.R.G.—the birthplaces of the capitalist industrial revolution—suffered the most. As the transnationals sought to shift the burden of the multiple crises of the 1970s onto the shoulders of the working people in these areas, their material working and living conditions deteriorated. Banks and corporate leaders insisted that cuts in welfare and social services, as well as wages, were the prerequisite to industrial recovery. At the same time, the corporate managers called for increased govern ment assistance and reduced taxes on their own businesses. The lobby ing of the giant U.S. auto firm, Chrysler, for a billion-dollar government loan at the end of the '70s was only a recent and widely-publicized example. The F.R.G. and Japanese governments had long intervened directly to strengthen their nation's privately-owned industrial oligo-polies, first to withstand U.S. corporate penetration, and then to expand sales and investments abroad. Both the British and French governments had long participated directly in national petroleum industries to pre-vent the U.S. oil majors from swallowing them entirely. The British government had nationalized the ailing mining and steel industries and, as the crisis matured in the 1970s, completed its takeover of Leyland, the only sizeable remaining locally-owned auto company.

But the choice confronting the citizens of the core capitalist nations involved more than the loss of jobs and lowered living standards. By the late '70s, the real danger emerged that South Africa's determination to thwart the liberation movements' efforts to achieve fundamental politi-cal economic reconstruction might lead to a wider war. South Africa's military build-up had provided the transnationals with an at least temporary market for their mounting surpluses of capital and equip-ment; but it also furnished the minority regime with the arrogance that comes of possessing the most sophisticated weapons of war. South African Prime Minister Botha announced trivial cosmetic changes and maneuvered politically to coopt black middle class elements into his own state machinery as well as to install them in neighboring Zimbabwe and Namibia. But he clearly rejected more basic change. Instead, his troops invaded Angolan villages, and South African-assisted white Rhodesian airforce pilots systematically bombed Zambian bridges to cut off their access to neighboring states, and smashed Mozambican industrial sites as well as refugee camps. The ill-concealed 1979 nuclear explosion off the South African coast signalled the regime's preparedness to go the limit.

The transnational corporate managers lobbied their governments to adapt to the continued South African domination of the region, mas-querading behind marginal changes and common markets in the context of what South Africa's Prime Minister euphemistically termed a "con-stellation of states." But the working people and those concerned with human rights had another option. The liberation movements in southern

Africa were not merely fighting to oust hated regimes. They aimed, more basically, to restructure their national and regional political economies to spread productive employment and raise the incomes and living standards of their peoples.

Worldwide evidence (See Table E-1) shows that the countries characterized by balanced, expanding industrialized development provide far larger markets for the sale of goods produced in the factories of core industrial nations than does the distorted, minority-dominated regional economy of southern Africa. Trade in manufactured goods bulks far larger in quantitative terms between industrial capitalist nations than with impoverished underdeveloped third world lands. In recent years, socialist countries, relatively little affected by the deepening crises wracking western nations, have also purchased increasing amounts of goods manufactured in leading capitalist nations. It seems reasonable to suggest that, if the liberation movements achieve their proclaimed goals, their peoples will be able to purchase far greater quantities of machinery and equipment than is now possible.

To attain balanced, integrated development as shown in Part III above, however, the African peoples must win state power and exercise control over the commanding heights of their economies in order to plan and implement long-term industrial and agricultural growth. They will need to create democratic, participatory state structures capable of carrying out plans to achieve systematic improvement in the material conditions of life of the majority of their populations. This type of planning would differ dramatically from the extensive state intervention typified by the South African regime, designed to provide benefits to the transnationals while coercing the masses of the people into a low-paid, impoverished labor reserve. In short, growth controlled by and shaped in the interests of the African peoples could, over time, create a framework for the expansion of trade that would be far more beneficial, not only for themselves, but also for the working peoples of the mature industrial areas.

Those transnationals which had invested heavily to build up the military-industrial infrastructure of the oppressive South African regional subcenter would, of course, lose their seemingly guaranteed and highly profitable luxury and military markets. Those firms willing to adapt their investment and productive schedules to the independent African states' development plans, however, might still continue a profitable business. Gulf Oil, for instance, reports that the MPLA government in Angola, planning long term growth to meet its citizens' needs, provides an unusually stable, strong framework for a mutually beneficial relationship. Gulf has agreed to turn over a majority share of its local affiliate to the government, to train more Angolans, and to prepare for the eventual loss of managerial control. In return, it is able to pump increasing amounts of oil from Angolan wells for profitable world markets. A Gulf spokesman testified in Washington, D.C., in early 1979 that Angola provided an outstanding investment environment.

In the longer run, balanced integrated growth in southern Africa, as throughout the third world, could lead to increased trade on the basis of growing equal exchange which would clearly benefit the working people of the core industrial countries, as well as the new African states. As table E-1 shows, even industrialized South Africa, despite the truncation of its domestic market through the systematic impoverishment of the black majority, carries on twice as much trade per capita with the capitalist industrial states as do the rest of the African countries. In fact, South Africa's trade with the developed capitalist states—while vital to its minority regime—is marginal to the latter, even to its leading trade partners. South Africa's trade is a tiny fraction—less than one percent—of the developed capitalist countries' exports or imports. The U.K., South Africa's leading trading partner, sells less than 21 percent of its exports to South Africa. Only the U.K. and Japan buy more than one percent of their total imports there.

If over the next 20 years, the rest of the states of southern Africa could escape South African domination to achieve rates of growth comparable to those attained by South Africa over the last two decades, they would become far more valuable trading partners than South Africa to the core industrial nations than can South Africa, alone. The larger regional population, participating fully in the development process and taking advantage of their far more extensive natural resources, would, as table E-2 shows, provide markets almost three times South Africa's current market. Together with a liberated further industrialized South Africa, characterized by a more equitable distribution of income, their market could grow to almost six times that of South Africa's current market. Tens of thousands of workers could find jobs producing the machines and equipment for sale to facilitate industrial transformation throughout southern Africa in the interest of the people of the region. In return, southern African farms, mines and factories could ship them increasingly processed mineral- and agriculturally-based products. By the 21st Century, over a hundred million well-fed, well-clothed, and well-housed citizens of an increasingly productive and integrated industrially and agriculturally developed southern Africa could continue to buy the goods produced in the more mature industrial areas in the context of a pattern of exchange based on a newly created mutually beneficial comparative advantage.

The realization of this perspective would undoubtedly require that peoples of the older industrial regions re-examine and participate in reorganizing the institutional structures governing their own lives. Back in the 19th Century, when small farms and factories competed for local markets, it may have made sense for state legislatures to pass incorporation legislation authorizing private entrepreneurs through the exercise of property and contract rights to decide how to allocate local resources within the confines of state and national borders. As the 20th Century draws to a close, however, serious questions should be asked about the wisdom of permitting global corporate managers to make the crucial decisions shaping an increasingly distorted international division of labor to maximize their own short term profit expectations. Is this really the best way to make decisions as to what is produced? where it is produced? who should be employed? what wages they should receive? Is it reasonable or socially justifiable—given the vast economies of scale of modern technology—to leave such decisions to a few handfuls of men sequestered high in polished skyscraper board rooms overlooking New York, Bonn or Tokyo, Paris or London?

Whatever answers may be given to these questions, it is surely in the long run interests of the peoples living and working in the core nations to support the on-going struggle of the liberation movements for freedom and development in southern Africa. For only in that way can the peoples of that region plan and work to achieve peacefully the fundamental social and industrial transformation—taking advantage of the vast technological advances that have been created over the last 200 years—to broaden their own productive employment opportunities and raise their standards of living.

Table E-1.
Trade of Leading Developed Market Economies with Each Other, with South Africa, and with Other African States, as a Percentage of All Their Trade, and in Terms of Per Capita Trade with Their Trading Partners (1977)

Country trading partner	IMPORTS FROM			EXPORTS TO		
	$000	% of total imports	Per capita[2] imports from trading partner ($)	$000	% of total exports	Per capita[2] exports from trading partner ($)
Developed market economies[1]/						
Developed market economies	517,741,000	69.2	663	517,741,000	69.2	663
South Africa	5,383,000	0.7	217	5,643,000	0.7	225
Rest of Africa	38,010,000	5.0	95	42,262,000	5.8	105
United Kingdom/						
Developed market economies	47,269,805	74.3	61	41,069,682	71.5	53
South Africa	1,669,057	2.6	66	1,024,709	1.8	41
Rest of Africa	2,676,440	4.2	7	4,239,591	7.4	11
United States/						
Developed market economies	79,771,731	54.0	102	74,948,581	62.8	96
South Africa	1,337,958	0.9	53	1,078,949	0.9	43
Rest of Africa	15,628,154	10.6	39	4,378,911	3.6	11
Federal Republic of Germany/						
Developed market economies	75,068,211	74.5	96	89,636,247	76.0	115
South Africa	817,221	0.8	32	1,126,441	1.0	45
Rest of Africa	6,582,743	6.5	16	5,661,783	4.8	14
Japan/						
Developed market economies	27,416,045	38.9	35	38,212,206	46.4	49
South Africa	934,794	1.3	37	761,606	0.9	30
Rest of Africa	1,192,862	1.7	3	5,717,957	7.1	14
France/						
Developed market economies	49,070,498	69.8	63	44,969,929	71.0	58
South Africa	482,410	0.7	19	496,946	0.8	20
Rest of Africa	5,585,985	7.9	14	8,620,850	13.6	21

Notes: [1]Includes United States, Canada, South Africa, United Kingdom, Belgium, Denmark, France, Federal Republic of Germany, Ireland, Italy, Austria, Finland, Iceland, Norway, Portugal, Sweden, Switzerland, Greece, Malta, Spain, Yugoslavia, Israel, Japan.
[2]Dollar value of trade with trading partner divided by trading partner's population.

Source: Calculated from United Nations Yearbook of International Trade Statistics, 1977, Vol. I (New York: 1978); UN Statistical Yearbook, 1978.

Table E-2.

Estimated exports to industrialized southern African states in the Year 2000, assuming rates of growth similar to that of South Africa over the last 20 years (in 1977 prices)[1]

| Trading partner | Exports to southern Africa | |
	Excluding South Africa ($000)	Including South Africa ($000)
Developed market[2] economies	15,750,000	32,622,000
United Kingdom	2,870,000	5,910,000
United States	3,010,000	6,050,000
Federal Republic of Germany	3,150,000	6,304,000
Japan	2,100,000	4,304,000
France	1,400,000	2,084,000

Notes: [1]Estimates based on assumption that southern African states reach levels of industrialization comparable to that of South Africa's today; and that income is more equitably distributed among the regional population.

[2]For countries included , see note (1) of table E-1, p. 353

Source: Calculated from United Nations Yearbook of International Trade Statistics, 1977, Vol. I (New York: 1978); and United Nations Statistical Yearbook, 1978.

Index

Transnational Corporation Index

*This index includes, not only transnational corporations, but also the major South African parastatals and mining finance houses which are so intertwined with transnational finance capital that it is difficult to separate them.**

*The subsidiaries are typically to be found under the name of the parent or group holding company. The most commonly used name is listed; these may be the acronyms.

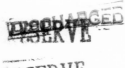